Physical Activity Sciences

Claude Bouchard, PhD
Université Laval, Sainte-Foy, Québec

Barry D. McPherson, PhD
Wilfrid Laurier University, Waterloo, Ontario

Albert W. Taylor, PhD, DSc
University of Western Ontario, London, Ontario

Editors

Human Kinetics Books
Champaign, Illinois

Library of Congress Cataloging-in-Publication Data

Physical activity sciences / editors, Claude Bouchard, Barry D.
  McPherson, Albert W. Taylor.
        p.   cm.
     Includes bibliographical references and index.
     ISBN 0-87322-334-9
     1. Physical education and training--Study and teaching--Canada.
  I. Bouchard, Claude.   II. McPherson, Barry D.   III. Taylor, Albert
W.
  GV365.5.C2P48   1991   72535
  796'.07'0971--dc20   91-2011
                                                          CIP

ISBN: 0-87322-334-9

Developmental Editors: June I. Decker, PhD, and Marie Roy
Managing Editor: Larret Galasyn-Wright
Assistant Editors: Valerie Hall, Dawn Levy, and Elizabeth Bridgett
Copyeditor: Bruce Bethell
Proofreader: Stefani Day
Indexer: Barbara Cohen
Production Director: Ernie Noa
Typesetters: Sandra Meier and Angela K. Snyder
Text Design: Keith Blomberg
Text Layout: Tara Welsch and Denise Peters
Cover Design: Jack Davis
Illustrations: Gretchen Walters
Printer: Braun-Brumfield

Printed in the United States of America

10 9 8 7 6 5 4 3 2 1

Human Kinetics Books
A Division of Human Kinetics Publishers, Inc.
Box 5076, Champaign, IL 61825-5076
1-800-747-4457

Canada Office:
Human Kinetics Publishers, Inc.
P.O. Box 2503, Windsor, ON N8Y 4S2
1-800-465-7301 (in Canada only)

UK Office:
Human Kinetics Publishers (UK) Ltd.
P.O. Box 18
Rawdon, Leeds LS19 6TG
England
(0532) 504211

Dedicated to the memory and contributions of
Barbara A. Brown
(1950 – 1990)
Teacher, Scholar, Friend

Contents

Preface

Since the late 1970s the physical activity sciences have grown both as a body of knowledge and as a source of employment opportunities. During this time, Canada has become an international leader in the physical activity sciences and professions. Many of our scientists are among the most creative and productive in the world, and many of our public- and private-sector agencies have initiated highly innovative policies or programs that are copied and implemented elsewhere in our ever-narrowing global society. Consequently, new and challenging opportunities for rewarding, satisfying careers have emerged in a variety of sport- and fitness-related occupations designed to meet Canada's needs as it becomes a more physically active and health conscious society.

The physical activity sciences at the university level have seen constant progress, both in research and in professional preparation. There is now a network of academic units in all sorts of institutions, whether private or public; Anglophone or Francophone; large or small; or undergraduate, graduate, or research-oriented. These academic units encompass more human and material resources than ever before; as a result, they are producing more graduates for the various areas of professional service and research than in the past.

There have also been changes for the more numerous practitioners in the field, whose positions now require activities and the delivery of programs that were not contemplated even 10 years ago. New opportunities are emerging constantly for those who are well trained and willing to accept new challenges and assume added responsibilities. Traditional professional organizations have grown, and new, and perhaps better-focused, societies have been created to meet the particular needs of practitioners in specific areas.

To better prepare for these new career possibilities today's student must acquire a broad and thorough understanding of the entire field, even though some of the subfields may seem less important and less well understood. The aspiring physical activity sciences practitioner must also learn that we do not as yet have all the answers or even know all the questions we must ask to obtain as complete an understanding as possible of this complex, multidisciplinary field. This text, therefore, introduces emerging and unifying concepts from all the various subdisciplines and areas of professional practice. Furthermore, we include sections about the major scientific and professional organizations and the principal sources of scholarly and professional information (e.g., journals, books, and government documents and policies) to help the reader become an active learner and participant in this exciting field.

This book is written to provide Canadian university undergraduates with an introductory text that describes and integrates the scientific and professional components of the physical activity sciences from a Canadian perspective. Previous textbooks were often designed for students in programs that prepared them for professional practice as teachers of physical education or community recreation personnel. These textbooks presented a fragmented view of the field and did not meet the expectations of students who sought a broad and comprehensive understanding of the human physical activity sciences and professions. This text, however, provides just such a comprehensive overview, presenting the major concepts and theories unique to the field as well as the most pressing issues facing it. To this end, leading Canadian scholars and practitioners of national or international reputation were invited to describe their own subfields.

This textbook's four parts and 29 chapters introduce the reader to the essential components of the physical activity sciences and professions. The first part includes a brief historical and contemporary overview of the physical activity sciences as a field of study and as professional activity. The second describes the search for knowledge from the perspectives of the physical, biological, and social sciences. The third part describes the various domains of professional practice in which policymakers and practitioners apply the knowledge and deliver services. The final section considers possible future scenarios in the areas of research, policy, and program development.

We were fortunate to obtain contributions from most of the leading physical activity professionals and scientists in Canada. On behalf of the readers, who constitute the next generation of scientists and practitioners, we thank these authors for their willingness to share their knowledge and expertise with their successors. We also thank our colleagues in our respective universities and the staff at Human Kinetics who helped us publish this book.

We hope this publication will stimulate the thought and action of both faculty and students, who together are the major stakeholders in the future development of the physical activity sciences and professions in Canada.

C. Bouchard
Université Laval

B.D. McPherson
Wilfrid Laurier University

A.W. Taylor
University of Western Ontario

Acknowledgments

The editors would like to thank all the authors who so graciously contributed to this introductory text. We also express our gratitude to Jean-Yves Dallaire, Lyse Jobin, Louise Lussier, Marc Landry, and Martine Marcotte from Laval University, who were very helpful in the preparation of the final document. Thanks are also conveyed to Dr. Rainer Martens for his interest in this Canadian venture and to the people at Human Kinetics Publishers for their professional support in the production of the book.

About the Authors

Editors

Claude Bouchard is a professor of exercise physiology in the Département d'éducation physique, Université Laval, Sainte-Foy, Québec. He holds a BPéd (Laval) and an MSc (University of Oregon, Eugene) in physical education and a PhD (University of Texas, Austin) in anthropological genetics. He founded
the Laboratoire des sciences de l'activité physique in 1974 and chaired the department of Laval from 1981 to 1983. His research, which deals with the role of genes in adaptation to exercise, training, and various nutritional stresses, has been supported by the main Canadian granting agencies and, more recently, by the U.S. National Institutes of Health. He has authored or coauthored several books and more than 300 professional and scientific papers. He was the recipient of the Honor Award from the Canadian Association of Sport Sciences/Association Canadienne des Sciences du Sport (CASS-ACSS) in 1988.

Barry D. McPherson, dean of graduate studies and director of research at Wilfrid Laurier University, Waterloo, Ontario, has a BA and an MA from the University of Western Ontario and a PhD from the University of Wisconsin. He has been active in the sociology of sport for over 15 years, having served as
president of both the North American Society for the Sociology of Sport and the Canadian Association of Sport Sciences, as well as serving on the editorial boards of many leading journals in the sport sciences. His recent research focuses on aging. He is the author or coauthor of six books, including *Aging as a Social Process* (Butterworths) and *The Social Significance of Sport* (Human Kinetics), and has presented over 65 papers at professional meetings, including many on the child in sport.

Albert W. Taylor is dean of the Faculty of Kinesiology and professor of physiology in the Faculty of Medicine at the University of Western Ontario, London, Ontario. He has degrees from Western Ontario (BA, HBA), the University of British Columbia (MSc), Washington State (PhD), and London
Institute of Technology (DSc Hon). He has held appointments at Alberta, Montreal, McGill, Queensland, and Western Ontario in physical education, medicine, physical and occupational therapy, and physiology. Dr. Taylor's research and more than 100 publications deal with the adaptive response of skeletal muscle substrates and enzymes to exercise and training. His studies have been supported by granting agencies in Canada, Great Britain, Australia, and Belgium. In 1987 he was the recipient of the Honor Award from the Canadian Association of Sport Sciences/Association Canadienne des Sciences du Sport (CASS-ACSS).

Contributors

Gilles Bérubé is the director of the undergraduate studies and is involved in the administration and management areas of the curriculum in the Département d'éducation physique, Université Laval, Sainte-Foy, Québec. He has a BEd in physical education and an MSc in pedagogy (Laval) and is associ-  ate director of the department at Laval, where he has been involved in all the major changes in the undergraduate physical activity sciences curriculum that have taken place over the years.

Barbara A. Brown died on August 11, 1990, after a courageous battle with cancer. As an associate professor of kinesiology at the University of Western Ontario, London, Ontario, her teaching and research interests were in the area of sociology of sport and leisure. She earned a BPHE (Toronto) in  physical education, an MA (Waterloo) in recreation studies, and a PhD (Waterloo) in kinesiology, focusing on the sociology of sport. Her major research interests centered on the study of women and sport, children's sport, and aging. Her research was funded by the Social Sciences and Humanities Research Council, Fitness Canada, and the Ontario Ministry of Tourism and Recreation.

Jean Brunelle is a professor of teacher education in the Département d'éducation physique, Université Laval, Sainte-Foy, Québec. He has a BA and a BPéd (Laval), an MSc (Université de Louvain), and a doctoral degree in physical education (Université de Liège). He founded the Laboratoire de re-  cherche en enseignement de l'activité physique and chaired the Department of Physical Education at Laval from 1969 to 1971. His teaching and research interests include teaching analysis and strategies of supervision to improve teaching effectiveness.

Albert V. Carron is a professor in the Faculty of Kinesiology at the University of Western Ontario in London, Ontario. He received a BPE degree and an MA degree in physical education from the University of Alberta in Edmonton and an EdD degree in educational psychology and physical education  from the University of California at Berkeley. His research has been in group dynamics, with a special focus on coach-athlete interaction, leadership, and group cohesion.

P. Chelladurai is a professor of kinesiology at the University of Western Ontario, London, Ontario. He holds a BCom and DPE (University of Madras, India), an MA in physical education (University of Western Ontario), and an MASc and a PhD in management science  (University of Waterloo). He teaches both undergraduate and graduate students at Western Ontario and has extensive experience as a national volleyball team member and coach in India. Dr. Chelladurai served on the board of the North American Society for Sport Management and is the author of sport management chapters, a textbook, monographs, and numerous research articles. His research has been supported by Canadian granting agencies.

Laurie D. Clifford is a research associate at the Rick Hansen Center, Department of Physical Education & Sport Studies, University of Alberta, Edmonton, Alberta, where she is responsible for the Adult Fitness & Lifestyle program. She has a BPE (Brock) and an MA (University of Alberta) in physical education.

David A. Cunningham is a professor in the Faculty of Kinesiology and the Department of Physiology at the University of Western Ontario, London, Ontario. He holds a BA (University of Western Ontario), an MSc (Alberta), and a PhD (University of Michigan). His general research activity has been in the

function of the cardiorespiratory systems. From 1966 to 1969 he worked on the Tecumseh Community Health Study at the University of Michigan; in 1969 he joined the faculty at the University of Western Ontario and became involved in a multicenter study of exercise and coronary heart disease rehabilitation. During this period, he started a study on the relationship of activity and growth of children. He is now the research director of the Centre for Activity and Ageing at the University of Western Ontario.

Martine Epoque is a dance and eurhythmics teacher in the Département de danse, Université du Québec à Montréal, where she is chairperson. She has a CAPEPS (ENSEP, Paris) and a Certificat de rythmique (Institut Jaques-Dalcroze, Genève). She won the Clifford E. Lee choreography award in 1983 and was honored by Le Salon de la danse and l'UQAM (1984). Founder, artistic director, and choreographer (Le Groupe Nouvelle Aire from 1968 to 1980 and Danse Actuelle Martine Epoque since 1982), her choreographies have been presented throughout the world. She has created new techniques for dance and eurhythmics trainings and conducted research dealing with choreographic relation between music and dance.

Ian M. Franks is an associate professor of motor learning in the School of Physical Education and Recreation, University of British Columbia, Vancouver, British Columbia. He has a Teaching Diploma (St. Luke's College, Exeter University), a BEd (McGill University), and an MSc and a PhD in physical education (University of Alberta). His research focuses on the learning of skilled actions and has been funded by NSERC. He is also director of the Centre for Sport Analysis at UBC, which he founded in 1983 and which has been responsible for developing several computer-aided sport analysis systems that are currently in use throughout Canada and the U.S.A.

Phillip F. Gardiner is professor of exercise physiology and director of laboratories at the Département d'éducation physique, Université de Montréal, Montréal, Québec, as well as associate member of the School of Physical and Occupational Therapy, McGill University. He holds degrees in physical education (BPHE, MPE, Windsor; PhD, Alberta) and received 2 years of postdoctoral experience at UCLA's Neuromuscular Research Laboratory with R.V. Edgerton; he recently spent a sabbatical year studying with Dr. D. Kernell, Department of Neurophysiology, University of Amsterdam. He has published many research articles on the adaptation in nerve and muscle tissue resulting from various interventions, including exercise.

R. Gerald Glassford was the dean of the Faculty of Physical Education and Recreation at the University of Alberta, Edmonton, Alberta. He is a former high school teacher who was appointed to the Faculty of Physical Education in 1965 after receiving his BPE (UBC) and MA (U of A) degrees. He subsequently completed his PhD at the University of Illinois and was appointed as chairman of the Department of Physical Education in 1972. Dr. Glassford is an associate fellow of the American Academy of Physical Education, a local and national CAHPER honor award recipient, and a widely known researcher in his field. His most recent projects have been cochairing the Canada Fitness Survey and serving as Canada's representative to CESU of the World Universiade Federation (FISU). He is currently a member of the Board of Directors and the Technical Committee of the Alberta Sport Council, a member of the Senate of the University of Alberta, and a member of the Executive Committee of the Alberta Universities Co-ordinating Council. He has served on a wide range of university committees and has held executive posts for a number of provincial, national, and international professional associations.

Norman Gledhill is a professor in the graduate program in exercise and sports science, Department of Physical Education, York University, Downsview, Ontario. He received his bachelor's and master's degrees in physical education (exercise physiology) from the University of Western Ontario  and his PhD in physiology from the University of Wisconsin. He has been president of the Sport Medicine Council of Canada and the Canadian Association of Sport Sciences (CASS) and was a founder of Sport Canada's antidoping program, the CASS Fitness Appraisal Certification and Accreditation Program, and the CASS High Performance Athlete Testing Centre Accreditation Program. Dr. Gledhill currently chairs the Medical/Scientific Committee of the Canadian Figure Skating Association and the International Squash Racquets Federation.

Paul Godbout is a professor of measurement and evaluation in the Département d'éducation physique, Université Laval, Sainte-Foy, Québec. He has a BPéd (Laval) and an MSc (University of Illinois, Urbana-Champaign) in physical education, and PhD (Florida State University, Tallahassee) in edu-  cational research. He was secretary of the College of Education (1967-1970) and chairman of the Physical Education Department (1977-1980) at Laval. He has also presided over many professional preparation program committees in the last 15 years. His research deals with measurement and evaluation in physical education, athletics, and physical fitness.

David Goodman is an associate professor of motor control in the School of Kinesiology, Simon Fraser University, Burnaby, British Columbia. He has a BPE and an MPE from the University of British Columbia and a Teaching Certificate from Simon Fraser University; he completed his PhD at the Uni-  versity of Iowa. Dr. Goodman's research has focused on the coordination of interlimb control in ecological settings and the problems of human-computer interaction. In addition, Dr. Goodman developed the first computer interactive video

analysis system for ice hockey. The majority of his research funding comes from NSERC and Microtel Pacific Research.

Joyce Gordon is the director of community services for the Donwood Institute in Toronto, Ontario. From 1982 to 1988 she was the employee fitness coordinator for the Ontario Ministry of Tourism and Recreation. She has a BS in kinesiology from the University of Waterloo and a Teaching Certificate. A found-  ing member of the Ontario Fitness Council and the Ontario Corporate Fitness and Lifestyle Council, she has provided leadership in the corporate fitness field to professionals and the public through consultation, development of resources, research projects, and promotion. She has also served on advisory boards to colleges, universities, and the national task force on employee fitness.

Terry R. Haggerty is currently an associate professor of exercise and sport science at Pennsylvania State University, University Park, PA. He holds a BA in biology and a BPHE (Queen's University); an MA in physical education and a Diploma in education (the Uni-  versity of Western Ontario); and a PhD in educational administration (State University of New York at Buffalo). His sports experience includes playing intercollegiate football and basketball at Queen's and high school and university coaching, as well as serving as business manager of Intercollegiate Athletics, a Special Olympics volunteer administrator, and a university professor in both Canada and the United States. He has served on the board of the North American Society for Sport Management and is the author or coauthor of several monographs, chapters, and research articles.

Fernand Landry is currently professor at Université Laval, Sainte-Foy, Québec. He holds degrees in physical education (BSc, Ottawa) and exercise physiology (MSc and PhD, Illinois) and has done postdoctoral work in circulation research and cardiovascular rehabilita-  tion at the University of Freiburg, Germany. He has acted as department head at both Ottawa (1964-67) and Laval (1969-76). Landry is both a founding member and past president of CASS-ACSS (1971-1972) and a past president of the Canadian Fitness and Lifestyle Research Institute, as well as a member of the Canadian Olympic Association, vice president for North America of Conseil International pour l'Education Physique et les Sciences du Sport/International Council on Sport Sciences and Physical Education (CIEPSS-ICSSPE), and a permanent collaborator on the International Olympic Academy.

Madeleine Lord is a dance professor in the Département de danse, Université du Québec à Montréal. She has a BPéd (Laval) in physical education, an MSc (Laval) in education, and an EdD (University of North Carolina at Greensboro) in physical education with emphasis in dance. She was the coordinator of the Certificat en danse at the Université de Montréal (1982-1986). Her research interests are in dance teaching effectiveness and dance semiotics.

David Magee is a professor in the Department of Physical Therapy at the University of Alberta, Edmonton, Alberta. He has a BA (Lakehead), a Diploma in physical therapy (Alberta), a degree in physical therapy (Alberta), an MSc in sport sciences (Alberta), and a PhD in sport sciences (Alberta). He was one of the founding members of the Sport Medicine Council of Canada and president of that organization for two terms. Prior to that, he was chairperson of the Sports Physiotherapy Division of the Canadian Physiotherapy Association for 4 years. His research is in isokinetic exercise, and he is currently the national team physical therapist for synchronized swimming and a consultant for the Edmonton Oilers hockey team and the Edmonton Eskimos football team.

Klaus V. Meier is a professor of philosophy and sociology of sport and play in the Faculty of Kinesiology at the University of Western Ontario, London, Ontario. He holds a BA (Western Ontario) and an MA (University of Illinois, Urbana-Champaign) in the field of philosophy, as well as a BPE

(McMaster), an MA (Western Ontario), and a PhD (Illinois, Urbana-Champaign) in physical education. For the past 15 years he has been editor-in-chief of the *Journal of the Philosophy of Sport*. He has also served as president of the Philosophic Society for the Study of Sport.

Michelle F. Mottola is an assistant professor with a joint position in the Department of Anatomy, Faculty of Medicine, and the Faculty of Kinesiology, at the University of Western Ontario, London, Ontario. She is also an affiliate of the Pregnancy/Perinatology Division of St. Joseph's Hospital, the Lawson Research Institute, in London, Ontario. She has an Hons. BA in physical education (University of Western Ontario), an MSc in exercise physiology (University of Alberta), and a PhD in anatomy (University of Alberta). Her research interest includes the effects of pregnancy and exercise on the maternal system and fetal development. She has received funding from Natural Science and Engineering Research Council, Canadian Fitness and Lifestyle Research Institute, and internal grants from the University of Western Ontario.

Georges-André Nadeau is a professor of outdoor education in the Département d'éducation physique, Université Laval, Sainte-Foy, Québec. He has a Brevet A (ENL); a BPéd and a Licence EP (Laval); an MA, and an EdS in curriculum development–outdoor education; and a PhD (Michigan State University, East Lansing) in outdoor education. Nadeau is the coordinator of the outdoor education program at Laval, which he began. He has been involved with conservation agencies, first with provincial organizations but more recently with international groups such as NASCO, where he served as Canadian commissioner and chairman of the North American Commission (1984-1988). His professional and scientific activities deal with the analysis and the evaluation of the effectiveness of "teaching in the out-of-doors." He has been supported by the Gouvernement du Québec and by Université Laval grants.

Earl G. Noble is an associate professor of exercise physiology in the Department of Kinesiology at the University of Western Ontario, London, Ontario.  He has a BSc and MSc (University of Waterloo) in kinesiology and a PhD (Washington State University) in physical education. Director of the Exercise Biochemistry Laboratory at the University of Western Ontario, his research deals primarily with the adaptive capacity of skeletal muscle and its response to a variety of stressors.

Donald H. Paterson is an associate professor in the Faculty of Kinesiology, the University of Western Ontario, London, Ontario. He has a BSc (York University), an MA (University of Western Ontario), and a PhD (University of Toronto, preventive medicine and biostatistics).  His research specialization encompasses cardiorespiratory responses to exercise and adaptations with physical training. In addition to publishing on cardiac rehabilitation, pediatric work physiology, and the physiology of aging, he has contributed to sport by creating Level III coaching theory, applying sport science in rowing and squash, and serving as president of the Canadian Association of Sport Sciences. He is currently associate director of the Centre for Activity and Ageing.

François Péronnet is professor of exercise physiology and director of the Département d'éducation physique, Université de Montréal, Montréal, Québec. He received his undergraduate training in physical education at the Ecole Normale Supérieure d'Education Physique et Sportive in Paris and  his MSc (exercise physiology) and PhD (physiology) at the Université de Montréal. His research, which is supported by the main Canadian granting agencies, deals with the role of the sympathetic system in the adjustments to exercise and the bioenergetic determinants of endurance. In 1981, he was awarded the New Investigator Award of the American College of Sports Medicine for experimental work on the control of heart rate during exercise in sympathectomized dogs.

Susan K. Pfeiffer is an associate professor in the School of Human Biology, University of Guelph, Guelph, Ontario. She holds BA, MA, and PhD degrees, the latter two in anthropology from the University of Toronto. Former president of the Canadian Association for Physical Anthropology, Dr. Pfeiffer  has published research in many areas of biological anthropology, including environmental adaptation and reconstruction of prehistoric lifestyles.

H. Arthur Quinney is a professor and chairperson in the Department of Physical Education and Sport Studies at the University of Alberta, Edmonton, Alberta. His primary area of research interest is exercise testing and exercise prescription for fitness and elite sport performance. He is the founder  and director of the University of Alberta Fitness Unit and is active in a number of fitness-, sport-, and sports-medicine-related agencies and associations provincially and nationally.

Gerald Redmond is a professor in the Faculty of Physical Education and Recreation at the University of Alberta, Edmonton, Alberta. He has a DPE (Loughborough), an MSc (Massachusetts), and a PhD (Alberta). He served as president of the International Association of the History of Sport and  Physical Education (HISPA) from 1981 to 1984 and was appointed Fellow of the British Society for Sports History (1985) and Corresponding Fellow of the American Academy of Physical Education (1986). Dr. Redmond has published widely and presented at many international conferences. In 1989 he was an Alberta Visiting Fellow at the University of Edinburgh, Scotland, and for the 1989-90 academic year he was awarded a McCalla Research Professorship at the University of Alberta.

Greg Reid is a professor in the Department of Physical Education at McGill University, Montréal, Québec. He has a BEd (PE) from McGill, an MS from UCLA, and a PhD from Pennsylvania State University. His research deals primarily with motor performance and learning of children who are physi-cally awkward and of persons with disabilities such as mental impairments, learning disabilities, and autism. His research has been funded by Fitness Canada and the Canadian Fitness and Lifestyle Research Institute.

Benoît Roy is a professor of biomechanics in the Département d'éducation physique, Université Laval, Sainte-Foy, Québec, where he teaches anatomy and biomechanics. He has a BPéd (Laval), an MSc (University of Oregon, Eugene), and a PhD (University of Wisconsin) in physical education. Dr. Roy has been a consultant with sport governing bodies and the Coaching Association of Canada, and his research deals with sport biomechanics: running, cross-country skiing, and lower back evaluation.

Art Salmon manages the Fitness Section in the Sports and Fitness Branch of the Ontario Ministry of Tourism and Recreation, Toronto, Ontario. He holds a BPE and an MSc from the University of Ottawa and is currently a PhD student at York University with a research emphasis on employee fitness. Prior to joining the Ontario government he was a member of the physical education staff at the Ottawa YM-YWCA for 10 years and was the coordinator of employee fitness programs for the federal government's Department of Public Works. He is a past chair of the Canadian Association of Sport Science's Fitness Appraisal Certification and Accreditation Program and was a member of the board of directors of the 1988 International Conference on Exercise, Fitness and Health. He is currently on the Board of Directors of the Canadian Fitness and Lifestyle Research Institute.

Jacques Samson is a professor in biomechanics in the Département d'éducation physique, Université Laval, Sainte-Foy, Québec. He has a BPE (Ottawa), and an MSc and a PhD (University of Illinois). He chaired the department at Laval from 1976 to 1977 and from 1983 to 1987. He is currently assistant to the vice-rector for human resources at Laval. He has served on numerous sport organizations at the provincial, national, and international level. His main professional and scientific activities are currently in the area of sport development, the training of high-performance athletes, and coaching development.

Judy M. Sefton, who holds a BSPE, a BEd, and an MSc from Saskatchewan and a PhD from Alberta, is the director of the Alberta Center for Well-Being, Edmonton, Alberta. Her research interests pertain to personal and situational factors influencing youth sport involvement and attrition and psychological aspects of health and well-being.

Roy J. Shephard is the director of the School of Physical and Health Education and professor of applied physiology within the Department of Preventive Medicine and Biostatistics, Faculty of Medicine, University of Toronto, Toronto, Ontario. Prior to coming to Toronto, he held appointments in the De-partment of Cardiology at Guy's Hospital, the RAF Institute of Aviation Medicine, the Department of Preventive Medicine (University of Cincinnati), and the UK Chemical Defence Experimental Establishment. He holds BSc, MBBS, PhD, and MD degrees from London University and a DPE (*Honoris Causa*) from the University of Gent. He is a former president of the Canadian Association of Sport Sciences and the American College of Sports Medicine.

Robert D. Steadward is the chair of the Department of Athletics and professor in the Department of Physical Education and Sport Studies, University of Alberta, Edmonton, Alberta. He has both a BPE (Distinction) and an MSc from the University of Alberta and a PhD from the University of  Oregon. Steadward founded the Rick Hansen Center at the University of Alberta in 1978 and has been its director since its inception. He has been involved with sport and recreation programs for the physically disabled at the national and international level for over 20 years. His research deals with the assessment and prescription of health, fitness, lifestyle, and sport-training programs for physically disabled people. The Rick Hansen Center, unique in the world, has been supported by major grants and donations from Canadian agencies and the Province of Alberta.

Marielle Tousignant is a professor of pedagogy in the Département d'éducation physique, Université Laval, Sainte-Foy, Québec. She has a bachelor's and a master's degree from Laval and a PhD from the Ohio State University. She has been an active member of the Groupe de recherche en enseig-  nement de l'activité physique since 1973. In addition to teaching, she is involved in correlational and qualitative research on teaching effectiveness.

A.E. (Ted) Wall is a professor of adapted physical education in the Department of Physical Education, McGill University, Montréal, Québec. He has a BEd in physical education and an MA in education from McGill and a PhD from the University of Alberta. Wall chaired the Department of Physical

Education and Sport Studies at the University of Alberta for 3 years prior to returning to McGill as chair in September 1986. His research on physically awkward and mentally handicapped children from a knowledge-based perspective has been funded by Max Bell Foundation; IBM Canada and Fitness Canada; and the Alberta Recreation, Parks and Wildlife Foundation.

Leonard M. Wankel, who holds a BA in physical education and a BEd from Saskatchewan, and an MA and PhD from Alberta, is a professor in the recreation and leisure studies department at the University of Alberta, Edmonton, Alberta. He previously taught at the University of Waterloo and 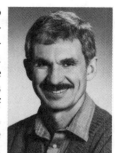 McMaster University. His current research interests include motivational interventions for facilitating exercise involvement and factors influencing motivation and satisfaction in youth sport.

Magdeleine Yerlès is a professor of sociology of sport in the Département d'éducation physique, Université Laval, Sainte-Foy, Québec. She has a CAPEPS (ENSEP, Paris) and an MSc and a PhD in physical education (University of Illinois, Urbana-Champaign). Currently chair-  person of graduate studies, her research bears on volunteering in sport and sport as a cultural phenomenon.

Part I

Introduction to the Physical Activity Sciences

Part I includes two foundational chapters that set the stage for the study of the science and service components of our field, which are examined in detail in the remainder of the volume.

Chapter 1 introduces the physical activity sciences by providing a definition of the field and identifying some of the problems currently confronting its scientists and practitioners. This chapter also indicates the relative status of the physical activity sciences with respect to other disciplines and fields of human inquiry. Chapter 2 presents a brief historical account of the events that have led to the development of the physical activity sciences. Although the emphasis in this chapter is on the Canadian context, it also identifies important events that have taken place elsewhere in the world.

Chapter 1

The Field of the Physical Activity Sciences

Claude Bouchard

For the physical activity sciences, providing a coherent account of the field is not as straightforward as we might wish. The field has changed so rapidly in the last decade or so that conceptual and organizational structures have not always kept pace. Unlike well-established disciplines such as biology or physiology, physical activity sciences is not a simple, fully conceptualized field of study but a dynamic one with major achievements and potentials that are only now being recognized. Scholars and practitioners still debate about the field's identity, arguing about the main unifying concepts and about professional and scientific boundaries. These debates are likely to continue for many years, and you, as a new student in the field, will play a role in them as your career unfolds.

What began as programs designed to train physical education teachers evolved into programs aimed at producing valid research and knowledge about all facets of physical activity. This journey from an emphasis on teacher training to an emphasis on research has not followed a simple path. The field first evolved from *physical culture* to *physical education*, with no appeal to research to determine the method or rationale of what was taught. Teaching and coaching methods were based on what others had found to work through unsystematic trial and error. In the 1960s, however, *physical education* was redefined to include professional activities outside the educational system, such as coaching, fitness leadership, and exercise management. People working in these areas began to demand more, and more valid, information to better serve their clients. At first, individuals

trained in physical education departments provided the increased research to fill this need. Since the 1970s, however, scholars in other disciplines (from molecular biology to sociology) have initiated research on problems related to sport and other physical activities. In addition, practitioners have initiated applied research to address practical issues they encounter in their professions. The conceptual difficulty of organizing such a wide range of approaches and concerns into a single entity has resulted in increasing discomfort for a growing number of physical activity sciences professionals and students. In particular, we need to define more clearly our mission, our responsibilities, and our research agenda. This chapter offers a brief description of the current malaise and presents an approach that may serve as a remedy.

The Debate Over Identity

In the U.S.A. alone, there are more than 1,000 bachelor's degree programs in the areas of health, physical education, and recreation combined, and about 500 master's programs, and 125 doctoral programs. Efforts made by the Canadian taxpayer in higher education in our field are proportionately less than these investments of the American society, but they are not drastically different. With only about 35 Canadian universities offering academic programs in the field, and just a handful of professional and scientific societies, reaching a new consensus on changes needed to improve our position for the future should not be an insurmountable task.

The history of physical education, like so many other areas of human endeavor, is characterized by debates and tensions that have generally resulted in positive changes and growth. The label *physical education* (the usual term for the field) is a remnant of the period when those who studied it planned either to teach and direct programs of physical activity within the curriculum or to coach an extracurricular activity. The term has survived as a label to represent the whole field, yet merely considering the evolution of the names of related professional organizations shows the obvious need to expand its scope. The current, expanded concept of physical education includes elements from health, recreation, safety, outdoor education, dance, and more recently, fitness and wellness.

Numerous scholars have addressed the issue of "identity" since the early 1960s, and a number of major conferences have been held on the subject. Many individuals have argued that a designation such as physical education is conceptually and semantically unsound for either a field of study or a spectrum of varying professional practices. During the decade from the mid-'60s to the mid-'70s, the work completed by individual scholars, by institutions of higher learning, and by professional and learned societies in the United States, Canada, and elsewhere, recognized the identity problem and proposed various solutions. The consequent attempts to create a label satisfactory to both the disciplinarians and the professionals in the field have yielded more than 20 distinct labels in the literature (see Table 1.1 for a list of the most popular proposals). The physical activity sciences label is a rather recent one.

Basic Concepts and Definitions

The notion of the physical activity sciences and its relative position in the structure of knowledge and human activities cannot be understood without first defining a few other concepts. Among these, the following four are the most important:

1. a discipline,
2. a field of study,
3. a subfield of study, and
4. an area of professional practice (or service area).

A **discipline** can be defined as one of the major or primary scientific areas of human knowledge

Table 1.1 A Short List of Distinct Proposals Concerning the Identity of Our Field

Author	Year	Proposed name
Larson, L.A.	1965	Activity sciences
Kenyon, G.S.	1969	Sport sciences
Sage, G.H.	1969	Kinesiology
University of Illinois	1969	Exercise sciences
Powell, J.T.	1971	Human kinetics
Bouchard, C.	1974	Physical activity sciences

Note. Adapted from Bouchard (1974). See Bouchard (1974, 1976) for details and a more complete listing.

(e.g., mathematics or physics). In theory, a discipline can develop without associated areas of professional practice. A **field of study** results from the integration of knowledge derived from several disciplines and applied in one or more professional practices (e.g., medicine, pharmacology, nutrition, genetic engineering). A **subfield** is much the same as a field but is rooted more specifically in one of the related disciplines (e.g., psychological pharmacology, social medicine, exercise physiology). An **area of professional practice** or a **service area** can be defined as a domain in which society has a specific need for competent services requiring proper vocational training, knowledge, and skills (e.g., technician, nurse, general medical practitioner, physical educator).

The Field of the Physical Activity Sciences

Initially, scholars argued that because the focus of those involved in the field is sport, sport sciences appropriately characterizes the entire profession. This is an attractive solution, but it proved inadequate because of its inherent conceptual limitation. The notion of sport, although a broad and useful one, cannot represent the entire realm of interest, which includes other types of physical activity such as dance and exercise. Indeed, the term *sport* could become as limiting as the term *physical education* has already become.

The object of interest common to the scientists and professionals in question is physical activity—perhaps more precisely human physical activity. Although there are no universally accepted rules for such matters, from the previously given definitions physical activity sciences appears to be a field of study rather than a discipline.

The physical activity sciences may be defined as the field of study devoted to

- *the understanding of all aspects of human physical activity (biological, physical, behavioral, and social), and*
- *the application of this understanding to meet the needs of the entire population (male or female; disabled or gifted; child, adult, or senior).*

The expression *physical activity sciences* has a clear and easily recognizable focus, namely, human physical activity in all its forms and types. The subfields stem naturally from the various disciplines or other fields of study that touch on human physical activity or provide concepts and methods capable of describing and explaining it from a particular perspective (see Table 1.2). Some individuals, particularly scientists active in the biological sciences component of the field, may elect to pursue their studies using animals; in fact, this may be their only choice, given the nature of their research or practical considerations. Even so, their ultimate goal is to increase the body of knowledge on human physical activity.

Table 1.2   The Field of Study and Some of Its Essential Dimensions

Field of study:	Physical activity sciences
Object of study:	Human physical activity
Subfields of study:	Social, behavioral, physical, and biological sciences applied to the study of physical activity
Areas of professional involvement:	Professional services offered to both genders across the spectrum of age in healthy, disabled, and gifted individuals.

The concept of the physical activity sciences brings a real coherence to the current spectrum of scientific and professional activities. It conveys a sense of unity and brings together individuals who, in spite of different backgrounds, training, and interests, feel that they are colleagues. Human physical activity is an indisputable reality that is and will continue to be studied by researchers with a variety of interests and backgrounds. It already enjoys a vital existence, even though as a field of study largely nurtured in faculties, schools, or departments of physical education across North America it remains ill-defined and conceptually ambiguous.

The growing popularity of physical activities of all kinds, the increasing sophistication of organizations offering physical activity programs, and the proliferation in services to support individuals and their organizations have resulted in considerable functional differentiation for physical activity specialists. These professionals, who are increasingly less likely to work in a school setting, constantly urge the profession as a whole to adapt in terms of the field's body of knowledge, theoretical framework, organizational structure, and professional concerns. They continue to press for changes in the perceived mission of the field, calling for increased coherence that will produce a clear field of human activity with related areas of scientific research and professional practice.

It is important to recognize that all the components of the field of study are, to a certain extent, interdependent (see Figure 1.1). Full development of the field depends on the status of both the service components and the research and science components. Poor development or atrophy of one component will retard progress of the others and weaken the whole.

This field of study already exists as such in some Canadian academic settings and is blossoming into a vital component in the larger university community. The development of the scientific areas is examined in detail in chapters 4 to 15 with reference to a dozen subfields. Although there are considerable differences among these subfields, they are growing rapidly in stature, prestige, and recognition, both within the field and in related disciplines.

The professional components also participate in this vitality. The contexts in which people engage in physical activity and the reasons for which they do so have become extremely diversified. Several areas of professional practice have enjoyed sustained growth, and others are clearly emerging. Contemporary professional practice in the field is described in terms of 11 different areas in chapters 17 to 27. Here also, the general picture is rather impressive. The professional components do not act in isolation, however, and must continuously acquire new knowledge from research in the various subfields and from policy analysis if they are to remain useful and viable. Clearly, there must be increased interaction between individuals engaged in research and practitioners in an area, particularly

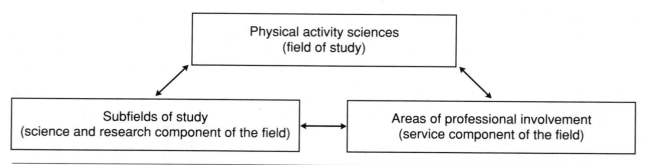

Figure 1.1   The interaction between the physical activity sciences and the field's research and service components.

given the rapidly changing scientific data base and the diversified needs of the consumers.

No matter what role a person plays—in this field or any other—the surest road to success is to strive for excellence and to increase professional interaction. If the field is to remain academically and professionally viable, the leadership of both professional societies and academic units must make concrete decisions and take firm collective measures in a concerted effort to describe the field of study in a clear, logical manner and to precisely identify the related areas of professional practice. Excessive rigidity in favor of saving the label *physical education* for a parent discipline would be unwise. Physical education remains a perfectly adequate term for the activities of professionals who provide instruction and activity programs in the context of the school system, but it is time to move and build a modern, flexible, and appropriate field of study that will accommodate *all* who are trained in and contribute to the physical activity sciences. We encourage you to play a part in this movement in the years ahead.

Summary

The concepts and structures used in this field, in Canada and elsewhere, are changing rapidly. Because the focus is on human physical activity, the term *physical activity sciences* is more appropriate for both scientists and practitioners than the older, more common term, *physical education*. The newer term will encourage individuals with different backgrounds and interests to communicate and interact by establishing a common sense of purpose and collegiality for all involved, both scholars and professionals, across the range of contexts.

References and Further Readings

Bouchard, C. (1974). Les sciences de l'activité physique: Un concept fondamental dans notre organisation disciplinaire et professionnelle. *Mouvement*, **9**(2), 117-129.

Bouchard, C. (1976). The physical activity sciences: A basic concept for the organization of the discipline and the profession. *International Journal of Physical Education*, **13**, 9-15, and **14**, 10-15.

Brooks, G.A. (1981). *Perspectives on the academic discipline of physical education*. Champaign, IL: Human Kinetics.

Cassidy, R. (1972). Should we drop the designation physical education in favor of a different name? [Monograph]. *The Academy Papers, The American Academy of Physical Education*, No. 6, 1-4.

Corbin, C., & Eckert, H. (Eds.) (1990). *The evolving undergraduate major*. Champaign, IL: Human Kinetics.

Hayden, F.J. (Ed.) (1980). *Body and mind in the 90's / Le corps et l'esprit—prospective pour 1990*. Hamilton, ON: The Canadian Council of University Physical Education Administrators.

Henry, F.M. (1964). Physical education: An academic discipline. *Journal of Health, Physical Education and Recreation*, **35**, 32-33.

Kenyon, G.S. (1969). A sociology of sport: On becoming a subdiscipline. In R.C. Brown & B.J. Cratty (Eds.), *New perspectives of man in action* (pp. 163-180). Englewood Cliffs, NJ: Prentice Hall.

Kroll, W.P. (1982). *Graduate study research in physical education*. Champaign, IL: Human Kinetics.

Larson, L.A. (1965). Professional preparation for the activity sciences. *Journal of Sports Medicine and Physical Fitness*, **5**(1), 15-22.

Massengale, D. (Ed.) (1987). *Trends toward the future in physical education*. Champaign, IL: Human Kinetics.

Powell, J.T. (1971). Physical education: Discipline or profession? *CAHPER Journal*, **37**(4), 18.

Rarick, G.L. (1967). The domain of physical education as a discipline. *Quest*, **9**, 49-52.

Sage, G.H. (1969). Is the term ''physical education'' obsolete? *Gymnasion*, **6**(1), 10-12.

Chapter 2

History of the Physical Activity Sciences

R. Gerald Glassford

According to the Leakeys, a family of eminent anthropologists and geologists who have made important finds in the fossil record of early humans, the species *Homo sapiens* arose in the vast savannah lands along the forest fringe of Africa. The species was a brilliant design for survival and physical activity: a biped short on speed but capable of great feats of endurance, with a superbly articulated opposable thumb; excellent binocular vision; and a three-layered brain composed of a core similar in structure and function to a reptile's, a cortex, and a large neocortex vital for reasoning power. These human anatomical features accompany a range of highly adaptable physiological mechanisms and rather sophisticated abilities to respond readily to mental, spiritual, emotional, and social changes. Ultimately these responses result from complexes of enzymes, chemicals, acids, bases, and salts; a system of neurons, dendrites, axons, and nerve ganglia; a finely tuned musculoskeletal system; and an elaborate community of cells and nutrient fluids that helps the body systems maintain homeostasis (a dynamic balance in and among body systems). For many of these mechanisms, physical activity is the tuning force. We understand this today because of the physical activity sciences but in the past it was not common knowledge.

Prehistoric Beginnings

The upper Stone Age, or Neolithic, natives who inhabited North America before the arrival of Eu-

ropeans were well aware of the importance of physical activity to their well-being. Within their cultural patterns they stressed all fundamental forms of physical skills, and young males faced a stringent array of tests in endurance, strength, and power to become warriors. These people intuitively knew the law of effort—the more a muscle works the more it develops; they also knew that adaptation to physical stress involves multiple processes and that adaptation never localizes in one region or organ but rather mobilizes the entire body. Theirs was a wisdom of the body that few Europeans possessed in the 15th to 16th centuries, when they came to North America as adventurers, explorers, and settlers.

A World Transformed

The arrival of the European settlers altered many of the ways of Indian life, including religion, livelihood, perspectives of time, and ultimately patterns of physical activity. Garrisoned officers and soldiers introduced new forms of games (Lindsay, 1970); farmers and traders brought new dances, jigs, and reels; and priests brought taboos that resulted in the loss of traditional native social behavior patterns. Physical activity remained a part of the natural pattern of life, but it became less important than it had been before the Europeans came.

No social group is free from the impact of change and Europeans experienced their share, too. During the 18th and 19th centuries, Europe experienced at least five different revolutions (scientific, agrarian, commercial or economic, transportation, and democratic) that together swept the world in a blitz known generally as the Industrial Revolution (Glassford & Redmond, 1988). Nothing was sacred before its onslaught.

New Systems of Education and Physical Activity

The industrial revolution completely transformed the system of education along with other systems. Previously, most people simply learned by doing and working closely with their own families, but the need within the emerging industries for a supply of educated workers forced a new system of education, resulting in the creation of schools as we know them today. The people responsible for schools' curricula recognized the importance of physical activity and devised systems of physical education. Per Henrik Ling developed a system of gymnastics in Sweden, Jahn devised the German *turnverein*, Nachtegall emerged as the father of military gymnastics in Denmark, and Archibald MacLaren played a similar role in England. These systems, and many others, were imported to North America and became, in whole or in part, the physical activity programs of the early North American schools.

Developments in Canada

Leadership is a fundamental requisite to change, and both Upper and Lower Canada provided dynamic leaders during the mid to latter 1800s. In 1847 Egerton Ryerson, the chief superintendent of education from 1844 to 1876, toured Europe, where he visited programs based on the philosophies and curricula of Pestalozzi, Jahn, Ling, Guts Muths, and MacLaren. These visits made a lasting impact on Ryerson, who returned to Upper Canada to create the Toronto Normal School and new syllabi for the physical training of teachers and school-aged students. These school programs blended military drill, gymnastics, and games (Morrow, 1975); typical of them was a program in the Montreal area, where an immigrant Englishman named Frederick Barnjum created a joint physical activity program for students of Montreal High School and McGill University (Cosentino & Howell, 1971). Barnjum, a disciple of MacLaren, built his curriculum around military gymnastics, drill, calisthenics, and games. Of greater significance than the curricular content was the fact that, counter to the values of the mid-19th century, he encouraged girls to participate in these programs. Two of Barnjum's students, Robert Tait McKenzie and James Nais-

mith, were later to become legends in physical education. McKenzie taught first at McGill and later, from 1890 until 1938, at Pennsylvania University, but arguably his greatest legacy to physical activity was his brilliant sculpting. Naismith was appointed to Springfield YMCA College, a pioneer physical education institution, where he created the game of basketball.

Emerging Patterns in the U.S.A.

Physical activity programs developed along similar lines in the United States, but the thrust toward change was even more dynamic. The U.S.A. had an even greater need for schools and curricula because of an accelerated growth in population spurred by rapid changes in technology and the development of new political ideologies based on principles of personal freedom. The pattern of change in the United States—"discovery, application, impact, discovery" (Toffler, 1970)—affected many parts of life, including sport, games, and physical education. These were swept into the stream of change that eventually led to the physical activity sciences. It was a change brought about by people who were prepared to take risks and to speak out on important issues. In 1749 Benjamin Franklin, a known risk taker, spoke strongly of the importance of physical activity in maintaining overall good health. His words were heeded, and in the explosive development of schools in the early 1800s the curricula often highlighted physical activity (Barney, 1979). Disciples of the European physical education pioneers reshaped the programs of educational institutions such as the Round Hill School, Harvard, Yale, Amherst, and the Boston Normal School of Physical Education. Leaders such as Beck, Follen, Dio Lewis, Beecher, Hitchcock, and Sargent created standards of program excellence that raised the understanding of physical activity to new levels across the nation. Hitchcock's curriculum at Amherst, for example, was based on physiological principles and scientific methods, and from 1860 onward it was emulated and improved on by other universities and colleges. In many important ways, the Amherst curriculum provided the base for our modern programs in the physical activity sciences.

Sport and Its Impact

While education shifted to a systematized structure the games/sport phenomenon grew in popularity throughout North America in a less organized way. The British officers who came to North

America were predominantly from the wealthier upper classes and had been educated in the public schools of Great Britain. These schools supported strong sporting traditions, and their graduates understandably carried their sports with them wherever they journeyed. Cricket, rugby, horse racing, fox hunting, the regattas—all were popular and were introduced into North America. By the early part of the 19th century the first of many sports clubs were already forming (Lindsay, 1970). Not to be outdone by the militia, the traders of the Hudson's Bay Company, many Scots by birth, brought with them their traditional highland games, the sport of curling, and early forms of golf (Redmond, 1982). French Canadians, on the other hand, adopted as popular pastimes the Indian activities of canoeing, snowshoeing, activities that demanded physical strength, and games such as lacrosse.

The shift from a rural to an urban lifestyle increased the importance of sport throughout North America. "The city environment lent itself to the sporting movement in America" (Barney, 1988, p. 182), and by the mid-1800s the sport entrepreneurs and promoters were already commercializing the rapidly growing spectator activities. Popular targets for their attention were horse racing and boxing (the latter fueled by the excitement of a "world boxing championship" match between Tom Hyer and James "Yankee" Sullivan in 1849) (Barney, 1988). International rowing and sculling matches between Canadian and American athletes and their European counterparts captured the imagination and attention of people on both sides of the Atlantic, as did the America's Cup, games of lacrosse, and a bat-and-ball game that evolved from English rounders into North American baseball.

The growing importance of sport resulted in a major change within the physical activity structure of higher education: From an obscure place on campuses, sport became a dominant element. Interuniversity play required standardized rules, and the newly evolved forms of sport—American and Canadian football, ice hockey, basketball, and athletics (formerly the principal domain of the Scottish Caledonian Society)—were fused into campus life (Barney, 1988; Redmond, 1971). The stage was set for the emergence of the physical activity sciences.

Education and Its Control

Although the physical education focus of the powerful philosophies of education imported from Europe resulted in curricula that required adolescent students be taught drill, calisthenics, and gymnas-

tics each week, there was additional impetus for this development. The new political policies of democracy ended the era of the professional, mercenary armies, a change in the value structure of nations that signaled the need for a physically fit citizen army able to protect its country. A range of military drill-oriented programs developed across Canada stimulated, in part, by the need for young men fit to bear arms. The distribution of powers to the federal and provincial governments established by the British North America (BNA) Act placed the control of education under the jurisdiction of the provinces. This fragmentation of authority was the principal cause of an uneven development of physical activity programs in schools, colleges, and universities across Canada and today remains the primary cause of differing approaches to curricula in our schools.

a

b

Handheld dumbbells (a) of the 1890s era were used as a form of resistance exercise in physical activity programs (each weighs 2.7 kg). Today's technology gives us machines such as this Nautilus resistance exercise equipment (b), which is designed with eccentric cams to provide maximum resistance over a full range of movement.

New Structures and Functions

During times of rapid change new functions are matched with appropriate changes in structures. From the latter part of the 19th century through the early decades of the 20th century was a period of great changes that produced new structures.

Wars and threats of war plagued many nations during this time, and Canada's need for a physically fit population was the primary reason that Lord Strathcona (christened Donald Smith and the principal force behind the building of the Canadian Pacific Railway—CPR) created the Strathcona Trust Fund in 1908. The trust supported the preparation of teachers of military drill and physical training and the formation and instruction of cadet corps. Its impact was felt in every province. Despite the fact that military drill was the primary component of the syllabus, prospective teachers were instructed in the fundamentals of physiology, health, and anatomy; it was a scant overview, but it was a start.

The holocaust of World War I (1914-1918), however, signaled the downturn in the popular acceptance of military drill in schools. Spurred by the efforts of Cartwright and Lamb, who were highly critical of military personnel teaching in schools, institutions began to move away from programs based on military drill and physical training. Physical education in general thrived, however, primarily because of a new group of leaders.

Teacher Preparation

Although the Hamilton School of Physical Culture (originally the Barton School for Scientific Physical Training) was operating by 1889 (Cosentino & Howell, 1971) and preparing Canada's first physical educators, the recognized need to prepare teachers with a deeper understanding of the importance of physical activity to health and well-being led in 1910 to the creation of Toronto's Margaret Eaton School of Literature and Expression (which quickly evolved into the Margaret Eaton School of Physical Education for Women).

In addition, McGill University in Montreal continued to provide major national leadership in the development of physical activity sciences. McGill built on the foundation provided by Barnjum, McKenzie, and Naismith by appointing Ethyl Mary Cartwright to its staff in 1906 and Dr. A.S. "Dad" Lamb in 1912. A 4-week summer school for physical education professional preparation was offered in 1911, the curriculum of which included physiology, history, genetics, anatomy, hygiene, first aid, anthropometry, kinesiology, pedagogy, gymnastics, games, and aquatics (Meagher, 1965). The following year it was expanded to a full academic year program open to all students, but the format was altered in 1933, when a new curriculum was created that was restricted to students who already held an arts or science degree. Elsewhere, the program at the University of Toronto was addressing the importance of physical education as early as 1915, and by 1927 this university offered a physical education diploma. The development of similar programs at other universities followed the models established by McGill and Toronto.

Organization

In 1933, determined to solidify the ground gained over physical training, military drill, and calisthenics, Lamb and others created the first quasi-professional national organization, the Canadian Physical Education Association (in 1948 the link with health and recreation was recognized and the name was altered to the Canadian Association for Health, Physical Education and Recreation—CAHPER). This association provided a national forum for sharing the concepts that would shape the next half-century of development in physical education and the physical activity sciences (Gurney, 1983). The membership had a strong action orientation and provided the lobbying force necessary to generate changes in federal legislation, alterations in academic programs, and the creation of new national associations.

Legislation

Foremost in federal legislation was the National Physical Fitness Act, which was promulgated in October, 1943 (Sawula, 1977). The Act was formed on the basis of the Dominion Youth Training Program and the Unemployment and Agricultural Assistance Act; it was also shaped by the Provincial Recreation Movement, which originated in British Columbia during the late 1930s (Schrodt, 1979). The National Physical Fitness Act was designed to improve the health, nutritional understanding, and physical fitness (physical activity levels) of Canadians. In most senses the Act failed to accomplish its goals, but it achieved one important gain in that it helped change the concept of physical fitness throughout Canadian society. Physical fitness was no longer perceived as significant only in time of war but now recognized as a vital part of daily life. Consequently, physical education grew in diversity and complexity, which stimulated Canadian universities to develop new degree programs in the field.

Sport Participation

Concurrent with these changes were shifts in the physical activities generally known as sports. A pervasive force in the emerging image of sport was viceregal patronage. The support of the governor-general added to the acceptability of sport participation by all Canadians. (Table 2.1 contains a summary of viceregal involvement in Canadian sport.)

This sort of emphasis helped sport become an important part of physical education programs in schools and universities as well as activity-based clubs and organizations, notably the YMCAs and YWCAs. Major international sport festivals emerged (e.g., the Olympic and Commonwealth Games), gained in popularity, and by the mid-20th century became a social force that commanded the attention of politicians, communications media, economists, and educators.

The cultural ethos (including the seeds from which the science of physical activity would spring) of sport, health, physical education, and recreation assumed new functions and new structures through the first half of the century, and the stage was set for 4 decades (the 1950s through the 1980s) of accelerated development in the field.

Emergence of the Physical Activity Sciences

History is created by many variables that force changes in what often appear to be undesirable directions. To see an instance of this in the development of the physical activity sciences we need to return to 1943 and the National Physical Fitness Act.

National Physical Fitness Act

The intent of the Act was to encourage Canadians to become more involved in physical activities; this was a period of war and the government of Canada wanted a physically fit nation. The Act was poorly framed and administratively unwieldy, however, and consequently it was repealed in 1954. A backward step, some might suggest, but despite its short life it stimulated the formation of the Canadian Sports Advisory Council (CSAC) in 1951, which became the Amateur Sports Federation of Canada in 1972. These bodies helped provide a new model for sport in Canada. The loss of the Act also galvanized professionals, academicians, and concerned politicians to work together to produce replacement legislation. This effort gained momentum as a result of yet another undesirable event, the negative press coverage generated by the results of the Kraus-Weber tests of fitness levels for European youth and their North American counterparts. North American children, it was found,

Table 2.1 Viceregal Patronage of Sport in Canada

Governor-General	Symbol	Date	Sport
Lord Dufferin	Governor-General Medals	1874	Variety of sports
	Governor-General Prize	1880	National curling championships
Lord Lorne	Governor-General's Silver Cup	1881	National curling championships
	Governor-General's Silver Cup	1883	Dominion rifle championships
Marquis of Lansdowne	Lansdowne Cup	1888	Dominion rifle championships
Lord Stanley	Stanley Cup	1894	Dominion hockey championships
Marquis of Aberdeen	Governor-General's Prize	1894	Ontario curling championships
	Aberdeen Cup	1895	Canadian golf championship
Earl of Minto	Minto Cup	1901	Dominion lacrosse championship
	Countess of Minto Prize	1903	Dominion skating championship
Earl of Grey	Grey Cup	1909	Dominion rugby football championship
Duke of Connaught	Connaught Cup	1912	Dominion soccer football championship
	Connaught Cup	1912	Dominion figure skating championship

Note. Reprinted from McLaughlin (1981) by permission.

performed less well than European youngsters. Using these data in an address to the Canadian Medical Association in June of 1959, the Duke of Edinburgh challenged Canadian physicians to support the drive for new legislation that would emphasize the importance of fitness and sport.

"An Act to Encourage Fitness and Amateur Sport"

This legislation came in September, 1961, and was entitled Bill C-131, "An Act to Encourage Fitness and Amateur Sport." (The statute has been updated as part of the revised statutes of Canada, 1989, project; see Appendix B for the revised version.) The Act's impact continues to be felt in the growth of new programs, the establishment of research-funding institutions, and the heightened awareness among Canadians of the importance of physical activity and the physical activity sciences. Critical to the development of the physical activity sciences in Canada was the provision, through the Act, of a system of bursaries, or fellowships, designed to assist the academic preparation of professionals in the field. Hundreds of Canadians who won these awards gained master's and doctoral degrees; today they form a significant part of Canadian university staff in the field.

Degree Programs

The importance of these scholars themselves must be placed in perspective with another growth factor: the creation of the degree programs in physical education that subsequently evolved into programs of physical activity sciences. Early university programs were based on a teacher training model, and most graduates found employment in the nation's schools. In an effort to gain greater control over the curriculum and to reduce the limitations of scope produced by the narrower mandate of faculties of education, leaders in the field lobbied for independent degree programs and, subsequently, independent facilities. The first of these was created at the University of Toronto in 1940, and in less than 4 decades more than 30 others followed (see Table 2.2). Within a half-century a totally new field of undergraduate study had emerged—the field of physical activity sciences.

These programs were an essential beginning, but only that. Soon thereafter graduate programs were rapidly established at both the master's and doctoral level (see Table 2.2). The positivist model

of science and a strong discipline orientation provided the foundation for these programs. The sharpened focus on the disciplinary base seemed to be a clear response to the challenge issued by the American scientist Franklin Henry in his classic article "Physical Education: An Academic Discipline" (1964). Henry forced leaders to consider the vital distinction between the discipline of the field and its professional application.

Change of Curriculum Focus

Within many universities the preparation of physical education teachers maintained a position of importance in the degree programs, but others built curriculum on a disciplinary core: exercise physiology, biomechanics, ergonomics, kinesiology, anatomy, psychomotor learning, the sociology of activity, or growth and development, to name a few. The names of many of the faculties often changed to reflect this shift in direction as programs were baptized in human kinetics, kinanthropology, kinesiology, human movement studies, and physical activity sciences.

It is important to realize the motive behind this shift—a motive well framed by McPherson and Taylor (1980):

It is assumed that "the fundamental function of the universities . . . [is] to preserve, to transmit and to expand human knowledge" (Healy, et al., 1978:100). Thus, a major purpose, although not the sole purpose, of a university is to serve as a center for higher learning where the research enterprise is the mechanism for creating and applying new knowledge. This is what distinguishes a university from a college . . . , and if physical education is to continue as a viable profession or discipline within a university, then those in the field must engage in research to contribute to both the goals of their institute, and to the discipline. (p. 166)

The focus of this shift was to be the creation of a legitimate field of scientific inquiry designed to enhance our understanding of the broad phenomenon of physical activity and the development of researchers who would look for functional or causal relationships and be critical and rational in their analysis of the nature and value of physical activity. Programs in the physical activity sciences are taking form, but the road is long and the tasks far from complete. The appropriate balance between basic and applied research has yet to be

Table 2.2   Commencement Dates of University Physical Activity Sciences Related Degree Programs

University	Location	Date Bachelor's level	Date Master's level[a]	Date PhD level
University of Toronto	Toronto	1940	1962 (MSc)	
McGill University	Montréal	1945	1969 (MA)	
University of British Columbia	Vancouver	1946	1959 (MPE)	
Queen's University	Kingston	1946	1975 (MA, MSc)[b]	
University of Western Ontario	London	1947	1963 (MA)	1978[c]
University of Alberta	Edmonton	1949	1961 (MA, MSc)	1967
University of Ottawa	Ottawa	1949	1969 (MPE), 1967 (MSc)	
Université Laval	Québec	1954	1973 (MSc)[d]	1980
University of Saskatchewan	Saskatoon	1954	1965 (MSc)	1969
Université de Montréal	Montréal	1955	1969 (MSc)[e]	1977
McMaster University	Hamilton	1956	1976 (MSc)	
University of New Brunswick	Fredericton	1957	1975 (MPE)	
Memorial University	St. John's	1960	1973 (MPE)	
University of Calgary	Calgary	1964	1987 (MPE)	
University of Manitoba	Winnipeg	1964	1979 (MPE)	
University of Victoria	Victoria	1964	1975 (MEd)[f]	
University of Waterloo	Waterloo	1964	1974 (MSc)[g]	1976
Simon Fraser University	Burnaby	1965	1970 (MSc)[h]	1975
University of Windsor	Windsor	1965	1970 (MHK)	
Université de Sherbrooke	Sherbrooke	1965	1979 (MSc)	
Dalhousie University	Halifax	1966	1970 (MSc)[i]	
St. Francis Xavier	Antigonish	1966		
University of Lethbridge	Lethbridge	1967		
University of Regina	Regina	1967		
York University	Downsview	1967	1976 (MA, MSc)	
Lakehead University	Thunder Bay	1969	1976 (MA)	
Université de Moncton	Moncton	1969		
Université du Québec	Montréal	1969	1986 (MA, MSc)	
Université du Québec	Trois-Rivières	1969	1977 (MSc)	
Acadia University	Wolfville	1970		
Brock University	St. Catherines	1973		
Brandon University	Brandon	1977		
Université du Québec	Chicoutimi	1977		
University of Winnipeg	Winnipeg	1977		
Concordia University	Montréal	1978		
Laurentian University	Sudbury	1979	1979 (MA)	

Note. [a]Taken principally from Martens (1986). [b]MSc (nonthesis) added in 1983. [c]Offered in exercise physiology. [d]MSc (professional) offered in 1973 and MSc (research) added in 1978; PhD (physical activity sciences) in 1980. [e]MSc (physical activity sciences—research); MSc EP (physical education—professional); PhD (physical activity sciences). [f]MEd (physical education); MEd (curriculum studies); MA (physical education) added in 1978. [g]MSc (kinesiology); MSc (recreation and leisure studies) added in 1975; MSc (health behavior) added in 1976; PhD (kinesiology—psychomotor behavior, sociology of sport in 1976; biomechanics added in 1983; work physiology in 1986; health behavior in 1987). [h]MSc (kinesiology); PhD (kinesiology). [i]MSc (kinesiology) added in 1987; MA (health education) added in 1987; MA (leisure studies) added in 1987; original MSc terminated in 1986.

achieved, and one of the great challenges of the future will be to bring together the important scientific discoveries likely to emerge at the biochemical and molecular level with the human need to be involved with health-enhancing physical activity. The Canadian Association of Sport Sciences (CASS/ACSS) has accepted this as part of its mandate.

The Canadian Association of Sport Sciences/Association Canadienne des Sciences du Sport

Following the enactment of Bill C-131 it became apparent that some members of CAHPER and the Canadian Medical Association (CMA) shared an interest in the scientific study of physical activity, sport, and fitness. In 1967 at a landmark meeting in Saskatoon, Saskatchewan, 28 professionals from both fields collaborated to create CASS/ACSS, citing the following as their objectives:

- To establish an association of professional persons interested in the scientific aspects of sport and fitness in Canada
- To promote and advance medical and other scientific studies dealing with the effect of sports and other physical activities on the health of human beings at various stages of life
- To cooperate with other organizations and physicians, physical educators, physiologists, and other scientists who are concerned with various aspects of human fitness
- To organize scientific meetings, the purpose of which is to provide a forum for the exchange of views and scientific information related to sport and fitness
- To promote, encourage, and correlate research in these fields
- To encourage the collection and circulation of information and literature related to sport and fitness
- To offer advice to the public and members of the different disciplines involved in sport sciences in matters pertaining to sport sciences
- To represent members of this association in their relationship with government and with other national and international organizations
- To receive moneys through membership fees and other sources for the furtherance of the objectives and purposes of this association

CASS/ACSS has provided vital leadership in the physical activity sciences by hosting specialized national conferences, creating fitness appraisal certification and accreditation in Canada, and publishing the *Canadian Journal of Sport Sciences*. The membership has created the guidelines for professional conduct and standards of ethics essential to any professional association.

Current Trends

The rapid growth in the physical activity sciences over the last 3 decades has produced major changes in university curricula, discipline development, research methodologies, program philosophy, and terminology (Hayden, 1980). Concurrent and intimately linked with these changes has been the emergence of sport as a major cultural institution (possibly the most rapidly growing cultural institution in the world at this time). Used in connection with the notion of sports as they are now construed, the term *amateur* has lost any significant meaning and has fallen into disuse. The operating mode of sport has also changed. The *Report of the Task Force on Sport for Canadians* (1969) produced widespread restructuring, including the creation of Sport Canada, Recreation Canada (later Fitness Canada), Participation Canada (later ParticipAction), a Cabinet Minister status for the Fitness and Amateur Sport Branch (1976), and, in 1985, a government-supported but structurally independent corporation entitled the Canadian Fitness and Lifestyle Research Institute (CFLRI).

As Naisbitt (1984) has stated, this has been a period of great change, a time in parenthesis, a time of challenges, questions, and opportunities: "In the time in parenthesis we have extraordinary leverage and influence—individually, professionally, and institutionally—if only we can get a clear sense, a clear conception, a clear vision of the road ahead. My God, what a fantastic time to be alive" (p. 223).

Those who have been in the field of the physical activity sciences for some years are excited by what has happened and share a powerful sense of optimism about the future, but the future of this field, the development of its potential, really belongs to *you*, the beginning student! You will be among the pioneers who will develop the clear conception and vision Naisbitt identifies as the challenge. You will help create the new era of physical activity sciences. For those among you who are willing to take the risk and dedicate yourself to this important and growing field of study and research it *will* be a fantastic time to be alive.

Summary

For most of its existence the necessity for movement dominated the lifestyle of *Homo sapiens* and organized activity programs were not needed. But that changed in modern times. The Industrial Revolution produced a wide range of lifestyle shifts. Significant for the physical activity sciences were the proliferation of school systems and the resultant inactivity of students, and the spread of democracy that produced a need for a physically fit citizenry capable of defending their freedoms. These changes placed an emphasis on the importance of physical activity programs for children. Physical education and sport programs became an integral part of the school curricula. Many of the programs initially focused on military drills, but new philosophies of education and an expanded application of the methods of science quickly broadened the field's scope. The current status of the physical activity sciences is an outcome of decades of philosophical and scientific metamorphosis and years of commitment by scholars in the field of physical education, physical activity, and sport.

References and Further Readings

Barney, R.K. (1979). Physical education and sport in North America. In E.F. Zeigler (Ed.), *History of physical education and sport* (pp. 171-227). Englewood Cliffs, NJ: Prentice Hall.

Cosentino, F., & Howell, M.L. (1971). *A history of physical education in Canada.* Toronto: General.

Glassford, R.G., & Redmond, G. (1988). Physical education and sport in modern times. In E.F. Zeigler (Ed.), *History of physical education and sport* (pp. 103-171). Champaign, IL: Stipes.

Government of Canada. (1969). *Report of the task force on sports for Canadians.* Ottawa, ON: Author.

Gurney, H. (1983). *The CAHPER story: 1933-1983.* Vanier, ON: The Canadian Association for Health, Physical Education and Recreation.

Hayden, F.J. (Ed.) (1980). *Body and mind in the 90's.* Hamilton, ON: The Canadian Council of University Physical Education Administrators.

Henry, F.M. (1964). Physical education: An academic discipline. *Journal of Health, Physical Education and Recreation,* **35**, 32-33.

Lindsay, P. (1970). The impact of the military garrisons on the development of sport in British North America. *Canadian Journal of History of Sports and Physical Education,* **1**, 33-34.

Martens, F.L. (1986). *Basic concepts of physical education: The foundations in Canada.* Champaign, IL: Stipes.

McLaughlin, M. (1981). *Vice-regal patronage of Canadian sport: 1867-1916.* Unpublished master's thesis, University of Alberta, Edmonton.

McPherson, B.D., & Taylor, A.W. (1980). Physical activity scientists: Their present and future role. In F.J. Hayden (Ed.), *Body and mind in the 90's* (pp. 165-180). Hamilton, ON: The Canadian Council of University Physical Education Administrators.

Meagher, J.W. (1965). Professional preparation. In M.L. Van Vliet (Ed.), *Physical education in Canada* (pp. 64-81). Scarborough: Prentice Hall.

Morrow, L.D. (1975). *Selected topics in the history of physical education in Ontario: From Dr. Egerton Ryerson to the Strathcona Trust 1844-1939.* Unpublished doctoral dissertation, the University of Alberta, Edmonton.

Naisbitt, J. (1984). *Megatrends.* New York: Warner Books.

Redmond, G. (1971). *The Caledonian games in nineteenth-century America.* Teaneck, NJ: Fairleigh Dickinson University Press.

Redmond, G. (1982). *The sporting Scots of nineteenth-century Canada.* London and Toronto: Associated University Presses.

Sawula, L. (1977). *The National Physical Fitness Act of Canada, 1943-1954.* Unpublished doctoral dissertation, University of Alberta, Edmonton.

Schrodt, B. (1979). *A history of Pro-Rec: The British Columbia Provincial Recreation Programme, 1934-1953.* Unpublished doctoral dissertation, the University of Alberta, Edmonton.

Toffler, A. (1970). *Future shock.* New York: Random House.

Part II

The Search for Knowledge: Research Areas in the Physical Activity Sciences

Part II contains a discussion of research and scholarly inquiry in the physical activity sciences. Chapter 3 deals with growth of science in the Western world in general and in Canadian society in particular and points to the important role scientific method plays in the production of knowledge. The following chapters introduce the various subfields of scientific research contributing to the development of the physical activity sciences. Each subfield is described in terms of its content, concepts, recent research (highlight), research methods, career opportunities, organizations, publications, and other important current issues.

Chapter 3

Science and Physical Activity

Fernand Landry

The main objective of science is the pursuit of knowledge: understanding the nature of matter and the nature of humankind—its environment, origin, and destiny. In principle, science is universal and without frontier, yet to many of us, scientific activities appear to be restricted to a given society, to particular groups of professional people within that society, and to the evolution of their professional field and its practices.

Science is a significant force in our lives that searches for solutions to societal problems and explores factors that influence these problems. In most technologically advanced societies, science is seen as an instrument for personal, economic, social, cultural, and political development:

The development and vitality of scientific research appear as indices that increasingly reveal the dynamism of societies and cultures. Science contributes to human existence in so many ways . . . , it opens so many new horizons to one's imagination and intelligence . . . , and its applications transform daily lives to such an extent . . . that those who would fail to recognize and appreciate what is truly at stake in this area of human endeavour would quickly become marginal and would find themselves at the mercy of what is pursued elsewhere in the world. (Gouvernement du Québec, 1979, pp. 7-8)

Science is one of the indispensable elements of contemporary culture. Together with its associated technology it has had an irreversible impact on world economics and politics and, as a result, on lifestyle, education, and the health and well-being of a substantial proportion of the population, especially in Western societies.

There are many who see some results of scientific discovery and technological progress as dangerous or even harmful. Many of these phenomena, however, such as dehumanization, pollution, and the arms race, are more the fallout of economic or military-political influence and domination than of science per se. Indeed, most problems that cross national borders and social systems are multifaceted, involving not only technical and scientific considerations but also economic, moral, legal, ideological, and political ones.

Science, Knowledge, and Culture

Though science and philosophy are very different enterprises, they provide complementary ways of perceiving and coping with reality. Each brings its unique perspectives to any debate wherein a great number of disciplines and fields of study come together to form a body of knowledge (Landry, 1981). In particular, philosophy serves to clarify and categorize the activities of science. The part of epistemology, or the theory of knowledge, that deals with contemporary science has generated a literature on a range of topics, including history, comparative classifications, hierarchies, and values, as well as present-day problems and issues. The interested student should consult Blanché (1983), *Encyclopaedia Universalis* (1985), *Encyclopedia Britannica* (1980), Kuhn (1970), Popper (1965), or Toulmin (1977).

Science and the Physical Activity Sciences

A broad, objective, and coherent perspective describing human physical activity could not have emerged without the complementary contributions of the various subfields of study currently viewed as the *physical activity sciences*. As far back as 1911, on the occasion of the 25th anniversary of the American Physical Education Association (presently AAHPERD), President Meylan (1911) stood unequivocally in favor of an increasing reliance on quality scientific information:

> We have cleared up the bitter controversies that had been raging between exponents of various systems. . . . Broad minded and progressive men and women in the profession, after mature deliberation and experimentation of the various systems, gradually worked out principles and devised methods based upon the sciences of anatomy, education and hygiene, and adapted to American conditions. (p. 354)
>
> But the growth and extension of physical education have enlarged the horizon . . . and brought forth new and larger problems for solution. On the scientific side, we must ascertain many facts yet unknown concerning the effects of exercise. . . . On the educational side, we need a more complete correlation with the educational curriculum. . . . Finally, the increasing importance and complexity of physical education demand a higher type of teachers and directors. (p. 359)

In the course of their evolution, the physical activity sciences have created a fascinating body of knowledge containing a vast amount of scientific information on voluntary and observable bodily movement, in particular, on controlled exercises undertaken for development, education, training, conditioning, fitness, recreation, rehabilitation, improved performance, or enhanced health and well-being.

Physical activity sciences spans a cluster of subfields of study covering a range of topics from low-level exercise to athletic performance of the highest international caliber. Each subfield enriches the whole, providing a unique perspective with a specific approach and its own distinct issues. Together, the subfields have spurred extraordinary momentum for the development of the area. Chapter 1 already covered the background concepts, distinctions, and major issues; we can summarize the characteristics of the present dynamic state of knowledge with two observations:

1. Human physical activity (in terms of its present types, forms, requirements, and potential usefulness) covers an ever-increasing portion of human experience at the individual, social, national, and international levels. At the same time, it unequivocally has been defined as a particular field of scientific and scholarly inquiry. Furthermore, the resulting body of knowledge has become an area of scientific specialization for undergraduate, graduate, and postdoctoral work across Canada.

2. The body of knowledge is not merely useful but essential in the task of justifying exercise and sport, whether (a) in their own right, as widespread forms of human activity together with their implications, or (b) in their relationship to the very nature and finality of the human being as an individual and as a social being.

The field of physical activity sciences has now acquired its place in the sun. It has gained status within the vast domain of science and thus achieved strategic significance: It now has a life of its own. This identity is a consequence of the cumulative work of a multitude of men and women in two interrelated streams of activities. One force, which has tended toward unification, is the development and systematic interpretation of knowledge; the physical, biological, and social sciences are the main providers of this perspective (part II, chapters 4 through 15). The other force, which has tended toward specialization, is the systematic application of knowledge in a wide variety of sectors; such activity bears witness to the extent of the overall professional commitment and, in the end, to the true social significance of the various fields of study (part III, chapters 16 through 27). Nevertheless, such a multisectoral application of knowledge is intimately and irrevocably linked to the rapid evolution of science and technology.

The Exponential Growth of Scientific Activity

Currently, huge resources are devoted to scientific activities, particularly in the developed countries. UNESCO (1986) estimates that around 1980 the developed countries accounted for 88.8% of the world's scientific personnel (scientists, engineers, technicians, and auxiliary personnel). In addition, the developed countries accounted for as much as 93.8%, $207.8 billion in U.S. dollars, of the world's resources allocated to research and development (R&D). Although not adjusted to reflect inflation, the international investment in scientific activity increased 183% from 1975 to 1980 and as much as 334% from 1970 to 1980. On the side of worldwide manpower potential, UNESCO estimated an average of 848 scientists and engineers engaged in R&D activities for 1980 per million population; the average was 2,679 for North America, which was 3.2 times the world average and 1.5 times that of Europe. (The USSR is excluded from the European average because all categories of its scientific personnel are listed under one broad category, "scientific workers.") Expenditures for R&D, again around 1980, were highest in North America and Europe, both in terms of percentage of world investment (32.1% and 34.0%, respectively) and Gross National Product (2.33% and 1.79%, respectively).

Given these numbers, it is not surprising to learn that during the first three-quarters of this century scientific activity and its consequences in the technical and economic fields have more than doubled every 10 years. In contrast, activity not directly related to science has tended to double only every 30 to 40 years. The impact of R&D has thus been enormous, particularly in the developed countries, where it has markedly affected the quantity and quality of goods and services in such diverse areas as transportation, communications, housing, nutrition, education, health, wellness, and—our focus of interest—leisure and recreation, sport, and fitness.

Science in Canada

Canadian federal expenditures for research, development, and associated scientific activity were about $6.9 billion in 1986 (*Canada Yearbook*, 1988). Nonetheless, these large expenditures corresponded to only 1.3% of the Gross Interior Product ($509 billion); U.S. expenditures were 2.7% of its GIP. Furthermore, the Canadian percentage was by far the lowest among the six other major partners of the Organization for Economic Cooperation and Development: Japan, 2.6%; Federal Republic of Germany, 2.5%; Sweden, 2.4%; Switzerland, 2.2%; France, 2.1%; and Holland, 2.0%.

Another indicator of overall scientific activity is the proportion of federal funds and manpower

allocated to other sectors. In 1986 the federal government spent $3.33 billion on the natural sciences and $894 million for the social sciences. Federal employees involved in R&D numbered 16,441 person-years in the natural sciences around 1986 and 8,823 person-years in the social sciences. Thus, the natural sciences garnered 73% of the total expenditures and 64% of the scientific manpower.

A 1982 survey of scientific activity in the physical activity sciences (Kerr, personal communication, August, 1982) indicated that for the fiscal year 1981, 153 scientists in 22 Canadian institutions of higher learning were receiving grants from a number of sources, including the National Science and Engineering Research Council, the Social Sciences and Humanities Research Council, Health and Welfare Canada, Fitness Canada, and Sport Canada, as well as other federal, provincial, and philanthropic agencies.

The Information Society

Along with developments in information technology, the exponential growth of scientific activity has produced an explosion of scientific information. Each discipline and field of study, including the physical activity sciences, has contributed to and benefited from this explosion. Creating, processing, distributing, and assimilating huge amounts of scientific information has become one of today's most formidable tasks.

To get a feel for this growth, consider some of the following figures. Around 1800, 100 science-oriented periodicals were published; by 1900 the total had increased to around 10,000, and 50 years later the count reached 50,000. Nor has this prolif-

The information explosion—where will it lead? *Note.* Photo courtesy of the Institute for Scientific Information.

eration abated: *Ulrich's International Periodical Directory* (1987-88) catalogues 70,730 periodicals, and another 5,500 were added in 1988. In addition, Ulrich's companion volume on irregularly issued serials and annuals lists another 35,900 titles.

Indeed, the periodicals may constitute only the tip of the iceberg. Around 1982 it was estimated that between 6,000 and 7,000 scientific articles were written each day. By the mid-1980s the amount of scientific and technical information available was increasing about 13% annually—a 100% increase every 5.5 years. And that's just the beginning. The rate may soon jump to more than 40% annually if new and more powerful information-processing systems continue to be built, and there is little reason to think they will not. These systems have already revolutionized the storage and retrieval of data: In 1987 as many as 1,341 periodicals and abstracting and indexing services were available internationally as on-line data bases.

Information Pollution?

''We are drowning in information, but starved for knowledge'' (Naisbitt, 1982, p. 24).

The entire field of physical activity sciences is part of the current information upheaval. In fact, the information overload in the physical activity sciences may seem overwhelming. This phenomenon is not new, however, it is just more prevalent and apparent than it was in the past (Michael, 1984). The field has accumulated ever-increasing amounts of information not only because of increased activity in its constituent subfields but also because the field itself has broadened. The number of subfields continues to rise, both in the physical and biological perspectives (physiology, biochemistry, molecular biology, genetics, medicine, biomechanics, human factors, motor control, and motor learning) and in the social sciences perspective (social psychology, sociology, anthropology, and history, philosophy and pedagogy of sport and exercise).

There are inescapable dilemmas and paradoxes associated with the information revolution. Michael (1984) has pointed out that information has basically two broad, interrelated functions: the ''conservative'' function of producing reliable answers and the ''undermining'' function of asking unsettling questions. No one, whether student, professional, or scholar, can avoid the perpetual task of choosing the appropriate information. The essence of the challenge is to be well informed . . .

about quality information. Implicitly, there are reactive and proactive aspects to this endeavor. To deal with the reactive aspects you should follow Bunge's (cited in *ISI Press Digest*, 1985) advice about sorting out science from pseudoscience:

> Scientists and philosophers tend to treat superstition, pseudoscience and antiscience as harmless rubbish or even as proper for mass consumption. . . . This attitude is most unfortunate for (a number of) reasons. First, superstition, pseudoscience and antiscience are not rubbish that can be recycled into something useful; they are intellectual viruses that can attack anybody, layman or scientist, to the point of sickening an entire culture and turning it against scientific research. . . . Second, the emergence and diffusion of pseudoscience and antiscience are important psycho-social phenomena worth being investigated scientifically and perhaps used as indicators of the state of health of a culture (or a profession). Third, pseudoscience and antiscience are good test cases for any philosophy of science. (p. 12)

To deal with the proactive side, you should learn to plan and plan to learn. Essentially, this means actively choosing the information you use so that you are not overloaded by the enormous variety available. Ultimately, you must decide what to take in during your course of study as you define your own personal, professional, and social reality. Indeed, the very process of becoming a private or public individual within the profession, and of assuming your own social and personal reality, depends to a large extent on the system-creating power of knowledge and information.

Table 3.1 summarizes some of the dilemmas and paradoxes associated with the information explosion. The three-way collision of science and technology, entrepreneurialism, and social philosophy gives you considerable freedom in the choice and use of information. Beyond that, you must have a choice as to whether or not you wish to contribute to the creation of new knowledge by pursuing a graduate degree and a career in the physical activity sciences: You can place yourself anywhere between the extremes of driving the system or simply being driven by it. It is in this sense that Toffler (1983) refers to a profession as a cognitariat, that is, a group of people ''possessing organized information, imagination, and other cultural qualities essential for production. It owns the means for the production of more information. It owns what might be regarded as either an essential

Table 3.1   Some Dilemmas and Paradoxes Associated With the Knowledge (K) and Information (I) Explosion in Science/Physical Activity Sciences

Positive aspects/circumstances	Negative aspects/circumstances
Ever more K and I is created, processed, and disseminated.	Circumstances are created that reduce or defy the control of K and I: "running constantly just to keep in place".
Increased K and I tends to raise the understanding of a given phenomenon or situation.	Ironically more K or I may only partly reduce (or even deepen) feelings of uncertainty.
K and I help clarify issues and purpose and establish viable practice.	K and I often obscure choices and may not facilitate arriving at informed decisions and models for change.
Increased K and I gives some individuals ever-greater access to a more complex and turbulent world.	Increased K and I condemns some to deeper isolation and alienation.
K and I bring more ideas and facts to the "market place."	More K and I raises the "noise level" and brings more challenges to understanding, consensus making, governing, and networking; it renders difficult a "communality of interpretation."
Unprecedented amounts of K and I can be brought to bear on systemic issues of policies and actions.	People who must use the information to make decisions may become overloaded or frustrated.
K and I tend to make humans irreversible in their experiences, beliefs, and expectations.	Human situations (i.e., knowledgeable vs. unknowledgeable persons in a profession) unfortunately do not average out or balance; the interplay between polar circumstances may or may not be professionally or socially desirable.
K and I facilitate the coherence of a group, centralization or control of influence/power, voluntary specialization, and networking.	K and I may lead individuals and/or groups to splinter or isolate themselves, disrupting social responsibility or accountability.

Note. Adapted and expanded from Garfield (1985) and other sources.

raw material or, alternatively, a kit of mental tools" (p. 112).

Data Bases and Other Reference Tools in the Physical Activity Sciences

In your search for answers, you probably have already encountered the electronic formats that have irrevocably replaced traditional literature retrieval systems. In their place are networks of prodigious and comprehensive international data bases and information products and services that are available in a variety of formats and use a multitude of search methods. These formats are powerful, workable, and relatively inexpensive tools. Table 3.2 contains a sample of some of the most formidable access mechanisms, data bases, and other information products and services in the physical activity sciences that are currently available and indicates their extent, rate of growth, and the efficiency of their technology.

Data bases such as *Biosis Previews* (1987), *Medline* (1987), *Embase* (1987), and *Science Citation Index*

(1980-84) constitute a gold mine of quality information on physical activity from the perspective of the physical and biological sciences. *Social Scisearch* (1987), *Sociological Abstracts* (1987), *SIRLS* (1987), *Psycinfo* (1987), and *ERIC* (1987) provide quality information from the perspective of the social sciences. Other data bases, such as *Sport* (1987), *LC-MARC* (1987), and *Dissertation Abstracts International Online* (1987) provide extensive multidisciplinary coverage from both these perspectives (as does the AAHPERD publication *Completed Research in Health, Physical Education and Recreation,* 1985).

Fortunately, the trend toward specialization between and within fields has been counterbalanced by an equally significant movement. Information technologies "have brought back order to the chaos of information and data pollution" (Naisbitt, 1982, p. 24). The true enemy is not the sheer bulk of information but uncontrolled or disorganized information. Most new scientific information is found in periodicals, journals, and serials, which continue to be the primary sources of current, topical news in all fields of endeavor. Comprehensive, international data bases and information products can help direct and control individual searches through this material. *Current Contents* is

Table 3.2 Characteristics of Selected Data Bases Relevant to Physical Activity Sciences

Name of data base	Main orientation	Number of independent sources[a]	Started[b]	No. of records/date	Update frequency	On-line access[c] (X = yes)	Dominant perspective (X = yes) Biological	Social
MEDLINE (Medlars on line)	Biomedicine	3,000 70 countries	1966	> 5,300,000 Sep '87	Monthly	X	X	X
EXCERPTA MEDICA (Embase)	Human medicine and related disciplines	3,500 110 countries	1974	> 3,000,000 Oct '87	Monthly	X	X	X
BIOSIS PREVIEWS (Biological Abstracts)	Biological/life sciences	9,000	1969	> 5,340,000 May '87	Twice a month	X	X	
SCIENCE CITATION INDEX	Science in general	3,000,000 source articles	80-84	> 43,000,000 Dec '86	5-year periods	X	X	X
ERIC (Education Resources Information Center)	Educational resources and materials	~750	1966	> 632,000 Oct '87	Monthly	X		X
SOCIAL SCISEARCH (Social Science Citation Index)	Social, behavioral, and related sciences	3,900	1970	> 1,500,000 Jun '87	Every 2 weeks	X	X	X
SOCIOLOGICAL ABSTRACTS	Theoretical, methodological sociology	1,600 worldwide	1963	> 181,000 Jun '87	5 times a year	X		X
PSYCINFO (Psychological Abstracts)	Psychology and related behavioral/social sciences	1,050	1967	> 589,000 Sep '87	Monthly	X		X
DISSERTATION ABSTRACTS INTERNATIONAL	Doctoral dissertations, selected master's theses	University Microfilms International (UMI)	1861	> 940,000 Sep '87	Monthly	X	X	X
LC MARC (Library of Congress Machine Readable Cataloging)	Monographic works	Multilingual sources	1968	> 2,300,000 Sep '87	Monthly	X	X	X
SIRLS (Sociology of Leisure and Sport Abstracts)	Social science literature	International sources	1975	> 20,500 Aug '87	—	—		X
COMPLETED RESEARCH IN HEALTH, PHYSICAL EDUCATION AND RECREATION	Master's, doctoral theses	USA; Some CDN sources	1959	> 16,400 May '85	Yearly	—	X	X
SPORT (Sport Information Resource Center)	Sport bibliography	>2,000	1975	> 202,900 Oct '87	Monthly	X	X	X

[a]Journals, periodicals, monographs, books, theses, etc. in various combinations.

[b]Inclusive dates, within data bases, vary considerably between subject areas.

[c]Consult local library for access mechanisms, services, and costs.

a weekly offering that reproduces tables of contents from the world's leading journals and books; it is one of the most commonly used information products in the physical activity sciences. *Current Contents* is available in seven disciplinary editions, including "Life Sciences," "Social and Behavioral Sciences," and the "Arts and Humanities."

The print medium still makes a contribution, of course. In addition to these data bases there are excellent reviews of scientific documentation on a wide variety of areas related to physical activity. As a general rule, these reviews are written by experts with international reputations. *Exercise and Sport Sciences Reviews*, published annually under the sponsorship of the American College of Sports Medicine since 1973, are classic examples in the physical activity sciences. This series has issued 18 books to date (1990), providing 207 different written reviews by 316 authors and coauthors, 7,452 pages of text, and some 25,335 references.

These tools give you new and hitherto undreamed of possibilities. You can access, sort, select, and use the most recent information and data with relative ease and then synthesize what you have found, establishing a sense of unity, strength, and purpose in your individual and collective endeavors. Moreover, you can identify converging as well as diverging or even opposing values and viewpoints, particularly among the more applied sectors of the physical activity sciences such as physical education, fitness, health promotion, and high-performance sport.

Potentials, Implications, and Consequences in the Study of the Physical Activity Sciences

Mauviac (1968) calls the 20th century "this strange century of sport." Physical activity has taken hold everywhere, manifested not only in the ubiquity of competitive sport at all levels but also in international trends, Sport-for-All, Trimm, and fitness and wellness movements around the world. Leisure-time physical activity is increasingly practiced by citizens of all ages and both sexes, in a wide variety of forms and venues, and for many motives. Moreover, physical activity is now a matter of interest to a broad spectrum of organizations and agencies, whether educational, governmental, private, philanthropic, or commercial.

This growth has seen an increase in the number and complexity of associated problems. New questions continue to surface, many of which concern the fundamental mechanisms of biological adaptation or maladaptation to exercise and training. Others deal with learning, the use and enjoyment of movement patterns and skills, and the production of a capacity and readiness for athletic performance. In addition, there are questions concerning the patterns of physical activity that meet individual needs, interests, and requirements and that develop and maintain physical fitness levels satisfying well-being, risk reduction, and health promotion concerns.

These issues have obvious biological, social, psychological, educational, and technical aspects, yet on a broader scale they also involve administrative, economic, legal, political, and, therefore, ethical considerations (Grupe, 1986). In the last few decades, the physical activity sciences have spread through other areas of inquiry like the rays of the sun through the atmosphere. This has not been merely a luxury: The diffusion has contributed significantly to the physical activity or exercise phenomenon in all its forms; moreover, the resulting feedback has increased the coherence and identity of the various constituent subfields.

Even so, further activity and development within each subfield is necessary, yet this alone is insufficient for the development and diffusion of knowledge and information in the physical activity sciences. Broader social questions and issues, such as establishing values, norms, and priorities for service for the entire population, will require more linkages and increased cooperation within and between the various subfields.

The beginning student must realize that the choice of this profession as a career and subsequent level of personal involvement are matters of great importance to society as a whole. The professions in question are first and foremost service vocations. Chapters 4 through 15 of this book describe what is happening in 12 subfields of study. Practical considerations forced some restrictions on what was included; nonetheless, this section provides a substantive introduction to the focal concerns, efforts, and scientific activities in the profession.

Summary

Science is a significant factor affecting personal, economic, social, cultural, and political development in varying degrees. In Western societies, science has had an irreversible impact on the education, lifestyle, health, and well-being of the citizenry. The theory of knowledge that deals with contemporary science has generated an extensive literature that deals with complementary ways of perceiving and coping with reality. A broad, objective, and coherent body of knowledge pertaining to human physical activity has gradually emerged and evolved into a particular field of scientific and scholarly inquiry: the physical activity sciences.

Just as science in general has known an unprecedented and exponential growth in the 20th century, so has the entire field of physical activity sciences become part of the current information upheaval. This situation brings inescapable dilemmas to students and professionals alike: drowning in information, yet thirsty for knowledge. Fortunately, the trend toward specialization in knowledge and information is counterbalanced by a movement of equal significance: the availability of a vast array of information technologies and services.

An invitation is extended to students to try and keep in step with current developments and activities in their own areas of interest, to involve themselves personally in their profession, and to realize that contemporary issues and problems in their profession involve not only biological, social, psychological, and technical aspects, but also administrative, economic, legal, political, and thus philosophical and ethical considerations.

References and Further Readings

American Alliance for Health, Physical Education, Recreation and Dance. (1985). *Completed research in health, physical education and recreation* [Machine-readable data file]. Reston, VA: Author.

American College of Sports Medicine. (1973-1990). *Exercise and sports sciences reviews.* Vols. 1-3, New York: Academic; Vols. 4-5, Santa Barbara: Journal Publishing Affiliates; Vols. 6-11, Philadelphia: Franklin Institute; Vol. 12, Toronto, ON: Collamore; Vols. 13-16, Toronto, ON: Macmillan; Vols. 17-18, Baltimore: Williams and Wilkins.

Biosis Previews [Machine-readable data file]. (1987). Dialog Information Service, Files 5, 55.

Blanché, R. (1983). *L'Epistémologie* [Epistemology] (3rd ed.). Paris: Presses Universitaires de France.

Dissertation Abstracts International Online [Machine-readable data file]. (1987). Dialog Information Retrieval Service, File 35.

Encyclopaedia Universalis. (1985). "Epistémologie." Partie 3, Histoire et structure de la science; section 1: Qu'est-ce qu'un état de la science à un moment donné; section 3: La dialectique interne du progrès scientifique ["Epistemology." Part 3: History and structure of science; section 1: What is a status of science at a given time; section 3: The internal dialectic of scientific progress].

Encyclopedia Britannica. (1980). "Philosophy of Science." Part 3: Deeper issues and broader involvements of science.

ERIC (Educational Resources Information Center) [Machine-readable data file]. (1987). Dialog Information Retrieval Service, Files 1, 2.

Excerpta Medica [Machine-readable data file]. (1987). Dialog Information Retrieval Service, Files 72, 73, 172.

Frayssinet, P. (1988). *Le sport parmi les beaux-arts?* [Sport among the fine arts?]. Paris: DeMeyer.

Garfield, E. (1985). When information overload is too much of a good thing. *Current Contents, 3,* 3-5.

Gouvernement du Québec. (1979). *Pour une politique québécoise de la recherche scientifique.* Québec: Editeur Officiel du Québec.

Government of Canada. (1987). *The Canada Yearbook 1988, 120th Anniversary Edition.* Ottawa: Supplies and Services Department.

Grupe, O. (1986). Künftige Aufgaben und Probleme der Sportwissenschaft [Future tasks and problems in sport science]. In K. Heinemann & H. Becker (Eds.), *Die Zukunft des Sports* [The future of sports] (pp. 162-268). Schorndorf: Hofmann.

Institute for Scientific Information Press Digest. (1985). **3,** 12.

Institute for Scientific Information. (1990). *Current Contents* [Machine-readable data file]. Philadelphia, PA: Author.

Kuhn, T.S. (1970). *The structure of scientific revolutions* (2nd ed.). Chicago: University of Chicago Press.

Landry, F. (1981). Sciences, sport sciences, Olympism and international understanding. In O. Szymiczek (Ed.), *Official report of the 21st session of the International Olympic Academy* (pp. 184-197). Athens: Editions of the Hellenic Olympic Committee.

LC-MARC (Library of Congress Machine Readable Cataloging) [Machine-readable data file]. (1987). Dialog Information Retrieval Service, File 426.

Medline (Medlars on line) [Machine-readable data file]. (1987). Dialog Information Retrieval Service, Files 152, 153, 154.

Meylan, G.L. (1911). Presidential address. *American Physical Education Review,* **16,** 353-359.

Michael, D.N. (1984). Too much of a good thing? Dilemmas of an information society. *Technological Forecasting and Social Change, 25,* 347-354.

Naisbitt, J. (1982). *Megatrends: Ten new directions transforming our lives.* New York: Warner.

Popper, K.R. (1965). *Conjectures and refutations: The growth of scientific knowledge.* London: Routledge.

PSYCINFO (Psychological Abstracts Information Service) [Machine-readable data file]. (1987). Dialog Information Retrieval Service, File 11.

SIRLS (Sociology of Leisure and Sport Abstracts: A Review of Social Science Literature) [Machine-readable data file]. (1987). Waterloo, ON: University of Waterloo.

Social Scisearch [Machine-readable data file]. (1977). Dialog Information Retrieval Service, File 7.

Sociological Abstracts [Machine-readable data file]. (1987). Dialog Information Retrieval Service, File 37.

Sport [Machine-readable data file]. (1987). Dialog Information Retrieval Service, File 48.

Toffler, A. (1983). *Previews and premises.* New York: Morrow.

Toulmin, S. (1977). *From form to function: Philosophy and history of science in the 1950s and now.* Mequon, WI: Daedalus.

Ulrich's International Periodicals Directory 1987-88. New York: Bowker.

United Nations Educational, Scientific and Cultural Organization. (1986). *The statistical yearbook.* Paris: UNESCO Editions.

Section 1

Physical and Biological Perspectives

This section focuses on the various physical and biological subfields of the physical activity sciences. Chapters 4 through 9 discuss anatomy, physiology, biochemistry, medicine, biomechanics, and motor control and motor learning.

Chapter 4

Anatomy and Physical Activity

Michelle F. Mottola

Anatomy is the basis on which the science of the human body is built. As such, anatomy and physical activity is a subfield of the physical activity sciences. The term comes from a Greek word, *anatemnein*, which means to cut or dissect. Anatomy can be studied at different levels of specificity. It encompasses not only the description of the surface of the body and of the different parts of the body—gross, or large, anatomy—but also the study of small, individual cells under a microscope, or microanatomy (histology). Embryology, or the study of life before birth, is another part of anatomical science, as is neuroanatomy, which describes the interactions of the brain and spinal cord. In other words, anatomy involves taking the body apart, even down to individual cells, to understand how these parts relate to one another and function together during life.

• • •

Anatomy is the study of body structure, from cell (microanatomy) to parts and systems (gross anatomy).

• • •

The discipline of anatomy dates back to ancient times, as far back as the Egyptian dynasties. Nevertheless, the Greek scholars Hippocrates and Aristotle are usually considered to be the founders of scientific anatomy (O'Railey, 1985). Anatomy has a language of its own partly because the ancient scholars first described the parts of the body in Greek or Latin. Understanding Greek or Latin is not essential to the study of anatomy, but associating the derivation of the terms to their anatomical meaning will help in remembering them. For example, many anatomical terms indicate shape, size, location, or function as their foreign cognates indicate.

Anatomical language describes not only the structure or function of the parts of the body but also the positional relationships between various body structures. The standard position on which all descriptive relationships are based is called **anatomical position**. Anatomical position (see Figure 4.1) refers to a person standing erect, facing forward, with the feet together. The upper limbs are at the side of the body with the palms of the hand facing forward, the fingers stretched or extended, and the thumbs pointing away from the body. In describing anatomical relationships of a body in this position, one would say, for example, that the belly button is anterior (front), whereas the back is posterior.

Major Concepts

Before we can understand movement and relate it to performance, which is the goal of biomechanics, and before we can understand how biological systems work under repeated stress, which is the goal of the biochemistry and physiology of exercise, we need a working knowledge of anatomical structure and functions. In addition, understanding anatomical structure and relating structure to function is also necessary for developing rehabilitation programs for athletic injuries. Indeed, the discipline of anatomy is shared by many specialities in the biological sciences because it provides the basic understanding of how the body functions through its structure and how it adapts to various changes

Some Examples of Anatomical Terms

Attribute	Anatomical Term	Meaning
Shape	Quadratus	4-sided
Size	Major	Greater
	Minor	Lesser
Location	Carpi	Wrist
	Pollicis	Thumb
Function	Flexor pollicis longus	Flexes the thumb
Anatomical position	Anterior	Front
	Posterior	Back
	Superior	Above
	Inferior	Below
	Proximal	Closer to body
	Distal	Farther from body
	Medial	Near midline
	Lateral	Away from midline

Examples: One would say, "My eyebrows are superior to my eyes, my elbow is proximal to my hand, or my little finger is medial to my thumb, in anatomical position."

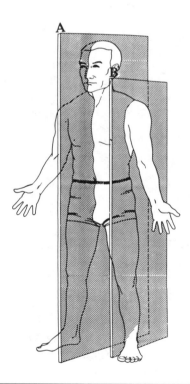

Figure 4.1 The anatomical position. Line A denotes the midline of the body; Line B denotes imaginary line through shoulder joint parallel to midline of the body, where flexion of the arm occurs. (Although in the anatomical position the legs should be together, the model's legs are shown apart to better illustrate the planes of the body.)

such as disease, injury, rehabilitation, training, pregnancy, and so on.

The human body comprises many functional systems that act in harmony to sustain life. Each system consists of associated organs (two or more specific tissues from specialized groups of cells) that usually have common or specialized functions. The extent to which each of these systems functions determines the quality of life. Tables 4.1, 4.2, and 4.3 list the systems of the body and a few of the major functions associated with each.

Coordinated performance requires that all the anatomical systems function in harmony. Five of these systems play major roles in movement, both directly and indirectly. Let's consider the biceps brachii muscle (found in the front of the arm) as an example of how each system must function together to produce coordinated movement. Two of the systems involved in movement and physical activity are the skeletal (bony) system, which provides the framework, and the articular (movable joints) system (refer to Table 4.1), where movement occurs between two or more bones. A third system, the muscular system (specifically, skeletal muscle; see Table 4.1), connects the bones so that movement occurs at the movable joints.

The biceps brachii muscle (which is a voluntary skeletal muscle) crosses two joints and therefore moves both of them. The term *biceps* comes from Latin roots meaning two heads; thus, there are two

Table 4.1   Anatomical Systems and Major Functions Relating Directly to Movement

Systems	Functions
Skeletal system (bones)	Supports the body; protects the organs; provides muscle attachment; blood cell production; stores minerals (calcium).
Articular system (joints) fibrous cartilagenous synovial	Provides a junction between two or more bones—joints may or may not be movable.
Muscular system skeletal	Contraction produces voluntary movement, usually of bones at joints; maintains posture and produces heat.
cardiac	Contraction produces involuntary movement of heart muscle (heart beat); heart pumps arterial (oxygenated) blood to body and receives venous (deoxygenated) blood from body to pump to lungs for oxygenation.
smooth	Contraction produces involuntary movement of hollow organs (stomach, intestines, uterus, and bladder) and constriction of arterial walls.

heads or sites of bony attachments, both of which cross the shoulder joint to form a large muscular belly in the front part of the upper arm. From this muscular belly the biceps brachii muscle sends a tendon to attach to or insert in the radius (a bone located on the lateral side of the forearm in anatomical position). When the biceps brachii muscle contracts (pulls) it can flex not only the elbow joint (bringing the forearm up to touch the upper arm) but also the shoulder joint (bringing the upper arm forward to touch the ear; see Figure 4.1, line B). A muscle will act on or move a joint only if it crosses that joint, and some muscles (e.g., the biceps brachii) cross more than one joint, therefore providing movement at all those joints they cross.

If the biceps brachii muscle is to function, the nervous system (Table 4.2) must coordinate movement at the joints by sending messages from the brain through the spinal cord to the nerves. Each nerve in the neuromuscular system has a specific target site that causes a certain part of the muscular system to function. For example, an electrical impulse must travel along a nerve to stimulate the biceps brachii muscle to pull on the forearm and flex the elbow joint.

Another important system necessary for movement (and for continued life!) is the circulatory system (Table 4.2). This system provides the oxygen and nutrients that movement requires. Oxygen and nutrients are transported via the blood through a network of tubes, or arteries, from the left side of the heart (the pump) to the working systems. Somewhat like a gasoline engine, a working biceps brachii muscle needs not only a "spark" from the nervous system but also "fuel"—oxygen and nutrients. Arteries supply these and other substances to every tissue they pass, and it is common for more than one artery to supply each tissue.

Another network of tubes, called veins, takes the waste products of work (e.g., carbon dioxide) via the blood back to the right side of the heart. From the right side of the heart this venous blood is pumped to the lungs, where the respiratory system (see Table 4.2) exchanges carbon dioxide for oxygen. The oxygenated blood is then brought back to the left side of the heart, and the cycle continues.

Without the circulatory system there is no life. If the arteries serving a tissue are crimped in some way, the tissue will die, hence the usefulness of having more than one source of blood for each tissue. Nerves, on the other hand, provide the "spark" for movement. If a nerve is cut, the tissue will still live (because the arteries are intact), but it will not function. This is often seen in victims of automobile accidents whose spinal cords have been cut. The connecting nerves will no longer be able to carry electrical impulses to the tissues below the cut, for example, the skeletal muscles, and this tissue will no longer function. The muscles involved atrophy, or waste away.

Atrophy of skeletal muscle may also occur if a limb is immobilized, for example by a cast used to set a fractured bone. Thus, if a fractured upper arm bone (humerus) is immobilized to allow it to heal, the skeletal muscles of the arm (e.g., the biceps brachii muscle) will reduce in size because they have not been allowed to function, even though all the nerves are intact. It is not enough for each system to be intact; each system must be

Table 4.2   Anatomical Systems and Major Functions Relating Indirectly to Movement

Systems	Functions
Circulatory system	
cardiovascular (heart, arteries, veins, and blood)	Heart pumps blood carrying nutrients and oxygen through arterial tree to tissues; venous network carries deoxygenated blood and waste products from tissues back to heart; prevents bleeding by forming clots (blood); regulates body temperature (blood).
lymphatic (lymph, lymph nodes, lymph vessels, and lymph glands—spleen, thymus, tonsils)	Provides alternate route for fluid to return from tissues to cardiovascular system; defends tissue against infection and is involved in immunity against disease-causing agents.
Respiratory system (nose, throat, voice box, bronchii, lungs)	Exchanges oxygen for carbon dioxide (lung); filters particles, controls temperature and moisture of inspired air (nose and respiratory tubes); aids in speech (voice box); and used in sense of smell (nose).
Nervous system	
central nervous system (CNS)	
brain (cerebrum, cerebellum, midbrain)	Controls behavior, intellect, memory, bodily functions, sensations, and special senses—vision, hearing, taste; coordinates movement, etc.
spinal cord	Connects the brain to peripheral nervous system via a series of ascending and descending tracts.
peripheral nervous system	Connects spinal cord (CNS) to body tissues and systems.
afferent (sensory)	Carries sensory information (touch, pressure, pain) to spinal cord (CNS).
efferent (motor)	
somatic	Carries motor impulses from spinal cord (CNS) to skeletal muscle.
autonomic (sympathetic and para-sympathetic)	Carries motor impulses from CNS to smooth muscle, cardiac muscle, and glands.

allowed to perform its specific function(s), or the tissue involved will react or adapt accordingly, such as atrophy of skeletal muscle when movement is prevented. If all systems are intact, however, when movement may once again occur the skeletal muscle involved may return (through rehabilitation and therapy) to normal size and performance.

Similarly, when a system is forced to perform or function repeatedly beyond its usual levels the system once again responds or adapts to the challenge placed on it. For example, if the biceps muscle is forced to function against resistance (e.g., a 5-pound weight placed in the hand), the work performed by this muscle increases. Repeating this performance until the biceps brachii muscle can no longer move the weight is one of the ways in which weight lifters and bodybuilders create hypertrophy (increase in size) of skeletal muscle. This challenge to the skeletal muscle must be re-

peated many times a week over an extended period of time, consistently increasing the work load little by little until the biceps brachii muscle becomes stronger and is capable of performing more work. This is a very simplified example, however, for the amount of hypertrophy of skeletal muscle depends not only on the amount of work done but also on hormones (see Table 4.3) and genetic differences.

Building muscle mass is one example of how training can produce anatomical alterations in a functioning system. Another example is forcing the heart and circulatory system to function more efficiently by moving greater quantities of blood to the large groups of skeletal muscles over an extended period of time. The heart must beat more quickly and pump more blood to strenuously working muscles to supply adequate oxygen and nutrients and eliminate waste products. This challenge to the heart muscle also must be repeated

Table 4.3   Other Anatomical Systems and Major Functions

Systems	Functions
Integumentary system	
skin	Protects body from bacteria and harmful light rays; controls body temperature; helps prevent water loss; synthesizes important compounds; receives stimuli from environment, etc.
hair and sebaceous glands	Protect skin; glands supply oil to keep skin waterproof and pliable.
nails	Protect fingers and toes.
sweat glands	Regulate heat.
connective and adipose tissue	Connects tissues; provides strength and support; can contain and store fat.
Digestive system (mouth, esophagus, stomach, small intestine, large intestine, rectum, anus, and associated organs—salivary glands, pancreas, liver, gall bladder)	Provides processes to break down food particles (mouth, salivary glands, stomach, liver, gall bladder, and pancreas); absorbs food particles (small intestine) and water (large intestine); stores glycogen and detoxifies blood (liver); and eliminates wastes.
Urinary system (kidneys, ureters, bladder, urethra)	Controls water elimination and mineral balance (kidneys); eliminates liquid waste.
Reproductive system	
female (ovaries, uterine tubes, uterus, vagina—birth canal)	Ovaries produce eggs (ova); uterine tubes transport eggs; uterus stores eggs temporarily (not fertilized) until menstruation, or for 9 months during pregnancy (fertilized).
male (testes, vas deferens, prostate, penis)	Testes produce sperm; vas deferens transports sperm; prostate secretes fluid to transport sperm; penis eliminates sperm.
Endocrine system (pituitary, pineal, thyroid, parathyroids, thymus, adrenals, pancreas, ovaries [female] and testes [male])	Produces hormones (transported by blood through the circulatory system) that regulate specific body activities.

many times a week over an extended period of time, consistently increasing the distance covered or the duration of the activity (as in jogging, swimming, and biking). Physiological adaptations eventually result from such training: The circulatory system becomes structurally stronger and requires less energy to perform at a given work load. Describing these physiological adaptations falls in large part to exercise physiologists and biochemists, but for any biological function to change or adapt, the underlying anatomical structure must also respond to change.

Demands are routinely placed on biological systems, and the underlying anatomical structures adapt functionally in response to the demands placed on them by normally functioning systems. When the demands overpower the ability of the system to respond, the result can be injury, illness, disease, and even death.

Methods and Technologies in Anatomy

Given the broad scope of the anatomical sciences—from the large structures of the body you can see and touch to the microscopic anatomy of the cells that make up those structures—it is not surprising that methodologies and technologies employed by other disciplines in the exercise sciences are also used by anatomists. For example, at a gross level, many individuals use size and weight changes to measure how anatomical systems adjust to structural and functional alterations, such as the increase in muscle mass with exercise training or the decrease in muscle mass with immobilization. At a more minute level, many people examine changes in cell structure and function by culturing isolated cells on glass plates, exposing these cells to different environments, and then monitoring the reactions—for example, exposing isolated heart cells to various hormones secreted during exercise.

Another way to examine alterations of specific tissues—for example, skeletal muscle—is to analyze the biochemical or histochemical properties of the muscle before and after training and then compare the results.

Major Research Questions

Anatomical research encompasses many fields, of which the physical activity sciences is only one small part: immunology, cellular and molecular biology, embryology, development and growth, histology and morphology, neuroanatomy, physiology, and reproductive biology, among others. Unfortunately, very few anatomy departments across the country participate in research specifically addressed to questions dealing with physical activity. Many scholars in the anatomical sciences, however, are involved in cancer research using isolated cells, in brain and spinal cord research, or in identification and rehabilitation of various disease states such as atherosclerosis or diabetes. In addition, many anatomists are involved in embryological or fetal research, exploring, for example, how embryological skeletal muscle forms and relating this to the problems seen in adult muscular diseases.

Learned Societies

There is no learned society devoted solely to anatomy and physical activity because, as mentioned previously, many anatomy departments do not participate in physical activity research. However, most anatomy departments and medical schools or faculties (or affiliates) are associated with an anatomical society. In Canada there is only one such society, the Canadian Association of Anatomists, which is a member of the Canadian Federation of Biological Societies. Every Canadian university with an anatomy department or equivalent

Guidelines for women who wish to exercise during pregnancy should be individualized for each person and substantiated by research.

part of a medical school belongs to this association. Membership requires approval based on scientific contribution to the field of anatomy.

The major anatomical society in the United States is the American Association of Anatomists. Its membership criteria are sponsorship by a member; affiliation with an anatomical school, department, or affiliate; and publication of at least one paper in an anatomical journal. There is also an International Congress of Anatomists, which promotes international scholarly anatomical research. In addition to these anatomical societies, individuals interested in anatomy and physical activity belong to the American College of Sports Medicine; this society has a membership for anatomists and combines physiology, biochemistry, biomechanics, and sports medicine with physical activity.

Journals and Other Publications

There is no Canadian journal associated only with anatomy. In the United States and abroad, however, there are many anatomical journals, such as the

- *Journal of Anatomy* (Great Britain),
- *Anatomical Record* (U.S.A.),
- *American Journal of Anatomy* (U.S.A.), and
- *Acta Anatomica* (Europe).

Anatomists with an interest in physical activity may publish in exercise or sports medicine related journals such as the

HIGHLIGHT
Exercise and Pregnancy

One example of research combining physical activity and the anatomical sciences is work being conducted in our laboratory (Mottola et al., 1986, 1989). We are investigating the anatomical and physiological effects of exercise during pregnancy on both maternal systems and fetal development.

Pregnancy exemplifies how the body and its systems can adapt to meet the functional physiological demands placed on them. For example, an embryo or fetus must be supplied with appropriate amounts of maternal oxygen and nutrients to grow normally. The maternal cardiovascular system adapts to this demand by expanding the arterial system to the uterus and placenta (the organ of exchange between mother and fetus) to increase both the volume of available blood and the flow of blood to the uterus.

One of the normal physiological responses to exercise in the nonpregnant state is to shunt blood from the gut to the working muscles (Lotgering & Longo, 1984; Wolfe, Ohtake, et al., 1989). Because the maternal uterus and fetus are in the gut area, an interesting question arises: Is the blood also shunted from the gut (and pregnant uterus) to the working muscles of the mother during maternal exercise? If so, can this decrease in uterine blood to the fetus affect fetal growth and development?

Another interesting aspect of maternal exercise is what happens to maternal blood glucose levels during and after exercise. The mother's working skeletal muscle uses bloodborne glucose for energy during work. One of the major energy sources of the developing fetus, however, is maternal blood glucose. The important research questions are thus how the use of maternal glucose during exercise affects fetal growth and development and whether the maternal glucose used by the mother's working muscles directly conflicts with fetal energy needs.

A third aspect of maternal exercise under investigation is the changes that occur to the mother's working joints during pregnancy. Under the influence of circulating hormones, maternal joints "loosen" to prepare for birth. This may be a problem for pregnant women who exercise during pregnancy, especially with weight-bearing, bouncing-type activities such as aerobic dance or even jogging, because the maternal joints may be more susceptible to injury.

We and other laboratories are investigating these areas of concern, but we have not yet definitively determined the answers to these questions; guidelines for women who wish to exercise during pregnancy are sketchy at best. We need more research on how the maternal systems and the fetus respond to the extra demands of exercise before we can have adequate medical prescreening and exercise contraindications, and clear prenatal fitness guidelines.

- *Canadian Journal of Sport Sciences,*
- *Medicine and Science in Sports and Exercise,* and
- *Journal of Applied Physiology.*

Undergraduate Education

Anatomy is part of the undergraduate curriculum of medical schools and science programs, as well as programs in zoology, physical education, kinesiology, human kinetics, and so on. Anatomy may be taught to students of the physical activity sciences through a medical school or faculty, especially if human cadaveric material is used for study. Such is the case in many university programs in the physical activity sciences. An undergraduate degree in anatomy does exist at the University of Saskatchewan, but in most programs anatomy forms only one part of undergraduate education.

Career Opportunities

After gaining a working knowledge and understanding of anatomy through undergraduate education, an individual interested in pursuing a career in the anatomical sciences should complete a master's or doctorate in an anatomy department. An individual who wishes to research in the combined area of anatomy and physical activity needs an undergraduate degree in the physical sciences and a master's or doctorate in anatomy. Not many anatomists conduct research in the physical activity sciences, however, so individuals interested in both may have joint positions between medicine and another department such as physical education, kinesiology, or physiology.

Career opportunities in anatomy are limitless because it encompasses such a wide array of research interests. An anatomist educated through a medical school with an advanced degree (MSc or PhD) may work in universities, hospitals, or clinical laboratories. In addition, individuals with a good anatomical background gained through an undergraduate degree in the physical activity sciences may pursue a career in athletic therapy and rehabilitation, fitness appraisal, exercise prescription, and kinesiology (see Figure 4.2).

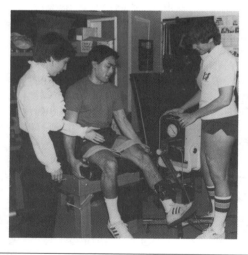

Figure 4.2 Assessment of an athletic injury and rehabilitation procedures.

Summary

Anatomy is an important part of the physical activity sciences. A working knowledge of anatomical

structure and functions is essential to understand movement and to relate movement to performance or to understand how systems work or adapt to exercise. The discipline of anatomy is thus shared by exercise physiologists, biochemists, biomechanists, medical personnel, and athletic therapists because it is the foundation of understanding how the body adapts to various changes such as disease, injury, rehabilitation, training, or pregnancy.

Because anatomy is essential to so many disciplines, anatomical research may be conducted on a large scale, such as comparing size or mass of the body and its components, or on a small, cellular level. One example of recent research that combines anatomy and the physical activity sciences is the investigation of the anatomical and physiological effects of maternal exercise on the mother and the developing fetus.

Undergraduate programs can provide a good base of anatomical knowledge, and job opportunities for those who hold an undergraduate degree in the physical activity sciences and a master's or PhD in anatomy appear to be limitless.

References and Further Readings

Anderson, J.E. (1983). *Grant's atlas of anatomy*. Baltimore: Williams & Wilkins.

Artel, R., & Wiswell, R.A. (Eds.) (1986). *Exercise in pregnancy*. Baltimore: Williams & Wilkins.

Basmajian, J.V. (1985). *Primary anatomy*. Baltimore: Williams & Wilkins.

Clapp, J.F., & Dickstein, S. (1984). Endurance exercise and pregnancy outcome. *Medicine and Science in Sports and Exercise*, **15**, 556-562.

Gauthier, M.M. (1986). Guidelines for exercise during pregnancy: Too little or too much? *The Physician and Sportsmedicine*, **14**, 162-169.

Leyshon, G.A. (1984). *Programmed functional anatomy*. Champaign, IL: Stipes.

Lotgering, F.K., & Longo, L.D. (1984, January). Exercise and pregnancy—how much is too much? *Contemporary Ob/Gyn*, **23**, 63-77.

Martin, A.H. (1985). *Introduction to human anatomy*. New York: Thieme-Stratton.

McMinn, R.M.H., & Hutchings, R.T. (1983). *Color atlas of human anatomy*. Chicago: Yearbook Medical.

Mottola, M.F., Bagnall, K.M., Belcastro, A.N., Foster, J., & Secord, D. (1986). The effects of strenuous maternal exercise during gestation on maternal body components in rats. *Journal of Anatomy*, **148**, 65-75.

Mottola, M.F., Bagnall, K.M., & Belcastro, A.N. (1989). Effects of strenuous maternal exercise on fetal organ weights and skeletal muscle development in rats. *Journal of Developmental Physiology*, **11**, 111-115.

Moore, K.L. (1985). *Clinically oriented anatomy*. Baltimore: Williams & Wilkins.

O'Railly, R. (1985). *Anatomy*. Philadelphia: W.B. Saunders.

Rohen, J.W., & Yokochi, C. (1984). *Color atlas of anatomy*. New York: Igaku-Shoin Medical.

Snell, R.S. (1981). *Clinical anatomy for medical students*. Boston: Little, Brown.

Spence, A.P. (1986). *Basic human anatomy*. Menlo Park, CA: Benjamin/Cummings.

Wolfe, L.A., Ohtake, P.J., Mottola, M.F., & McGrath, M.J. (1989). Physiological interactions between pregnancy and aerobic exercise. *Exercise and Sport Sciences Reviews*, **17**, 295-351.

Wolfe, L.A., Hall, P., Webb, K.A., Goodman, L., Monga, M., & McGrath, M.J. (1989). Prescription of aerobic exercise during pregnancy. *Sports Medicine*, **8**, 273-301.

Chapter 5

Physiology and Physical Activity

François Péronnet
Phillip F. Gardiner

The field of study known as physiology is defined as "a branch of biology that deals with the functions and activities of life or of living matter (as organs, tissues, or cells) and of the physical and chemical phenomena involved" (Merriam-Webster, *Webster's Ninth New Collegiate Dictionary*, 1983). Given such a broad definition, it is easy to imagine what a variety of subjects are investigated by exercise physiologists in the physical activity sciences. Exercise physiologists examine the responses of the various physiological systems, as well as their interactions, during exercise. We con-sider exercise a physiological challenge, to which the body's various tissues, organs, and systems adapt, and through studying the exercising body we are able to contribute knowledge that is unique compared to the study of physiology at a more general level.

• • •

Physiology is the study of the function of cells, organs, and systems. Exercise physiology looks at the responses of various physiological entities during exercise.

a

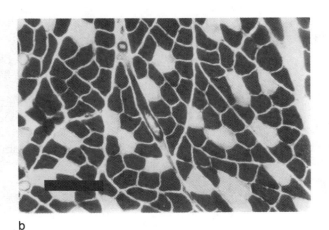

b

Approaches to research in exercise physiology include studies performed at the organism (a) and cellular (b) levels. A shows a subject performing on a rowing machine during which expired gases are being collected for analysis of energy cost. B shows a histochemical demonstration of fast (dark) and slow (light) fibers in a cross-section of rat gastrocnemius (calibration bar = 0.1 mm).

With exercise as a unifying theme, researchers are studying the various physiological systems (cardiovascular, respiratory, thermoregulatory, hormonal, nervous, and muscular) as they are taxed by the challenge of exercise. We attempt to determine what limits exercise performance of different types and how the body exceeds these limits by adapting to exercise training.

Scope of Exercise Physiology

Systems	Research Areas
Cardiovascular Respiratory Thermoregulatory Hormonal Muscular Nervous	Perturbations caused by acute exercise (for instance, after a 30-min run); mechanisms of adaptation to chronic exercise (for instance, after several months of daily running); limiting factors (what limits how far these systems can adjust to exercise); interactions among systems

We have far to go in integrating our knowledge of how these systems interact during the fatigue process and how exercise training alters the relationships between systems. It is difficult for an exercise physiologist specializing in one system to remain versed in the research advances in other systems. But we do get glimpses of how the changes in the parts affect performance in the whole at scientific conferences, where exercise physiologists studying the various systems compare and discuss their research results.

Major Concepts and Research Questions

We have divided our description of exercise physiology into two parts. First we describe current research dealing with the primary physiological movers of the exercising human: the nervous and muscular systems. Then we do the same for the physiological systems providing support for the nerve-muscle complex: the hormonal, cardiorespiratory, and thermoregulatory systems.

Neuromuscular System

The bulging muscles and strength of weight lifters and bodybuilders are an obvious illustration of how muscle tissue adapts to chronic exercise overload. During the past 3 decades, exercise physiologists have made significant contributions to our knowledge of how the neuromuscular system (the muscle and the motor nerves that innervate it and control its activation) changes when presented regularly with repeated, heavy loads (as with training with heavy weights) or with prolonged bouts of rhythmic contractions (as with endurance running, cycling, or swimming). Much of this information was the result of the use of the muscle biopsy technique, developed in the 1960s, that allowed researchers to remove and examine small samples of muscle tissue, biochemically and histologically. Thus, muscle samples from untrained and trained individuals, or from the same individual before and after acute exercise or training, could be compared. The results of these studies have allowed us to explain to some extent the basis of the *specificity principle* of exercise, the principle that the performance benefits of training are relatively specific to the type of task done in training (for example, muscles trained to give superior running performance would not provide the same high power for jumping).

Each muscle fiber (or muscle cell, of which there are many in each muscle—the human gastrocnemius, for example, has about a million muscle fibers) responds to regular training with heavy loads by increasing its content of contractile protein and thus its cross-sectional area termed *hypertrophy*. Thus, following training with near-maximum loads, which involves the use of most of a muscle's fibers, the hypertrophy of the individual fibers combines to produce greater muscle bulk and strength. Some investigators have proposed that continued high-resistance training might also increase the number of muscle fibers in the overloaded muscle (known as *hyperplasia*), although support for this idea is weak at present.

Training that uses endurance activities such as running, cycling, or swimming presents a different type of stimulus to the active muscle fibers. The load to each fiber is less (submaximal), but the contractile activity's duration is greater. The stimulus for fiber hypertrophy is weaker here than in the previous case. On the other hand, such activity improves the metabolic systems that use oxygen to provide energy to the fiber. It also promotes the

HIGHLIGHT
Carbohydrates and Fatigue

Reduced blood glucose levels and depleted carbohydrate stores caused by prolonged exercise (such as a marathon race) can cause fatigue. Ingesting dilute solutions of carbohydrates can help maintain blood glucose level and conserve carbohydrate stores. Research has suggested that it may be better to ingest fructose or glucose polymers rather than glucose. This question has been investigated on subjects working for 2 hours on a cycle ergometer. Over the 2 hours of exercise the subjects ingested either 100 g of glucose, 100 g of fructose, or 100 g of glucose polymers (Polycose) dissolved in 1,400 ml of water, or 1,400 ml of water only. The ingested carbohydrates were labeled with ^{12}C, a stable isotope of carbon, to compute their oxidation rate. The utilization rate of carbohydrates and fat from endogenous stores was computed from oxygen uptake and carbon dioxide production. Results are as follows:

	Water	*Glucose*	*Fructose*	*Polycose*
Fat utilization (g)	62	60	59	60
Carbohydrate utilization (g)	239	254	264	251
Endogenous	239	184	211	187
Exogenous	—	70	53	64

These data do not support the contention that ingesting fructose or glucose polymers is any better than ingesting glucose in terms of endogenous and exogenous carbohydrate utilization. The amount of endogenous carbohydrates utilized did not differ significantly with ingestion of glucose and Polycose and was significantly higher with ingestion of fructose. Exogenous fructose was also oxidized more slowly than glucose and Polycose (Massicotte, Péronnet, Brisson, Bakkouch, & Hillaire-Marcel, 1989).

use of lipids rather than carbohydrates as fuel and enhances both the delivery of substrates and the removal of waste products by increasing the number of capillaries surrounding each fiber. Collectively, these changes allow the muscle as a whole to contract for a longer period of time, with a more efficient use of available fuels.

Our goal is to explain these muscle-fiber adaptations at the cellular level. Researchers in the field currently apply sophisticated techniques adopted from biochemistry and molecular biology to determine the specific stimuli that promote these changes. So far, the prime candidates are the mechanical events associated with contracting muscle-tissue components as they stretch and relax and the changing concentrations of several ions and metabolic products within the muscle fiber. We are only beginning to obtain answers in this exciting field, however.

Proposed Stimuli for Muscle Changes With Training

Mechanical stresses to muscles during exercise

Accumulation of substances in muscles during exercise

Biochemical signals emanating from motor nerves or endocrine glands

We now have evidence that, to a certain degree, the enzymatic characteristics of muscle fibers govern several aspects of human muscle performance, namely, contractile speed, strength, and fatiguability. An important muscle characteristic in this regard is the relative proportions of different types of constituent muscle fibers (fast vs. slow); scientists determine this ratio using a variety of histochemical techniques. Differences exist not only between trained and untrained individuals but also among athletes in different sports. These differences appear to reflect a sport-specific optimization of muscle composition.

In the initial, primarily descriptive studies in this area researchers assumed the observed ratios of slow and fast muscle fiber to be an unalterable, genetically determined trait, but recent evidence suggests that chronic exercise training can produce changes in muscle fiber type. Though this may encourage athletes who once thought that their genetic makeup prevented world-class performance in a specific sport, the limits of adaptability for this muscle characteristic have not yet been determined. In fact, we do not yet have an unequivocal demonstration of how different proportions of muscle fiber type influence athletic performances.

Another area of interest for many exercise physiologists is neuromuscular fatigue. Among the reasons proposed for neuromuscular fatigue are that

- muscle fibers lose their ability to contract,
- motor nerves lose their ability to stimulate muscle fibers, and
- brain centers lose their ability to excite motor nerves.

Researching this topic with human subjects is difficult because the subjects' differing levels of motivation can produce different degrees of effort. As a result, many investigators have used isolated nerve-muscle preparations from animals, a technique that involves stimulating the nerve with electrical shocks to produce patterns of contractions similar to those seen in voluntary exercise and measuring both the resulting drop in muscle force and the accompanying changes in muscle biochemistry.

Although this approach bypasses many of the physiological events associated with voluntary muscle contractions, it allows researchers to pinpoint specific sites where fatigue might occur. As a result, we now know of several weak links in the chain of physiological events that extend from the spinal cord to the muscle fiber, any or all of which may cause neuromuscular fatigue under specific conditions. Though it is "reductionist," this approach to exercise physiology continues to emphasize the complexity of neuromuscular fatigue.

So far we have dealt primarily with only one side of the neuromuscular system, but the nerve portion also plays a role in the response to exercise and training. Indeed, because they share significant structural and functional relationships it is important to discuss nerve and muscle together. Motoneurons, the nerve cells that have their cell bodies in the spinal cord and send out axons to innervate groups of muscle fibers, were once thought of as being similar to electrical wire, merely transmitting commands from the central nervous system to the muscle fibers. As such, they were considered to be less important than muscle fibers or support systems in determining the limits of exercise performance. Several research groups, including our own (Jasmin, Lavoie, & Gardiner, 1988), have demonstrated that motoneurons show significant degrees of stress following exercise to exhaustion, as well as significant changes in metabolic properties in response to endurance training. We do not yet know the functional consequences of these changes. We do know that motoneurons exert a strong influence over the muscle fibers they innervate, both by controlling whether and when the muscle fibers will be activated during a voluntary contraction and by determining certain biochemical characteristics of the muscle fibers through trophic influences (the term *trophic* refers to the secretion of a chemical substance at the neuromuscular synapse that influences biochemical characteristics of the muscle fiber). Fatigue during certain types of activity may be due to failure at the level of the motoneuron, and training may strengthen this weak link.

The role of the higher nervous centers in fatigue and training is a virtually unexplored area. Researchers in the fundamental neurosciences are finding structural and chemical changes in nerve cells and their interconnections throughout the central nervous system that are related to learning and memory. Many of these concepts are spilling over into the areas of exercise training and skill development, furthering our understanding of the way in which conscious sensations of fatigue cause individuals to stop exercising. Some evidence suggests that trained individuals recruit muscle fibers differently from untrained individuals (thus implying a nervous system effect) and that their responses to the sensations of fatigue are different. In the future, researchers in exercise physiology and in motor learning may collaborate in an attempt to relate the behavioral and biochemical factors in the nervous system that are associated with voluntary fatigue and training.

Understanding the fundamental biochemical and morphological characteristics that characterize the neuromuscular system in states of exercise training and fatigue has important practical implications. Individuals working in physiotherapy and rehabilitation, for example, are looking into whether regular exercise can help restore normal neuromuscular function following cast immobilization and other types of trauma involving nerve or muscle damage. Research laboratories throughout the world are examining the possibility that regular exercise may reduce the severity of the debility accompanying several neuromuscular diseases.

Can regular exercise slow the decrease in nerve/muscle function that normally occurs during the aging process? What are the most efficient exercise programs for preventing the muscle atrophy and loss of function that occurs during prolonged space flights? These timely and important questions will require research efforts in which fundamental concepts are incorporated into practical settings. Many of these fundamental concepts have yet to be delineated.

Support Systems for the Neuromuscular System

Human movement results from neuromuscular activity. In turn, proper and continuous activity of this sort requires that the neuromuscular system possess both sufficient amounts of energy and avenues by which waste products can be continuously removed. Much of exercise physiology is devoted to the study of the various systems that perform these functions.

The choreography of these systems as they function to serve the neuromuscular machine exhibits a certain beauty; to understand this coordination of function, however, requires a solid background in the basic science of physiology. Exercise physiology provides a unique perspective from which to study the fundamental principles of physiology; indeed, several of these systems do not function fully when the organism is at rest. After all, our ancestors were compelled to exercise continuously, collecting food and defending themselves and their offspring from predators. As a consequence, the evolutionary process has bequeathed us a body that is designed for exercise, not chronic rest.

At the cellular level, three chemical pathways operate to provide energy in a complementary

fashion. Their use is governed by the power and duration demands of the muscle work.

Energy Sources for Muscle Contraction

Phosphagens (creatine phosphate, adenosine triphosphate)

Glycolysis (breakdown of carbohydrates) with accumulation of lactate

Aerobic degradation of carbohydrates and fat (plus small amounts of proteins)

The first two of these, which do not require oxygen, are termed **anaerobic metabolic pathways** and include the breakdown of phosphagens and the degradation of glycogen to lactic acid. The third is the **aerobic pathway** and employs the combustion mainly of carbohydrates and fats in the presence of oxygen.

The oxygen transport system, which includes the airways, the lungs, the blood, the heart, and blood vessels, transports oxygen from ambient air to the end user—the muscle cell. This system also transports carbon dioxide from the muscle, where it is produced in large quantities, to the ambient air, where it is expelled. Additionally, the blood brings to the muscle glucose from the liver and free fatty acids from adipose tissue.

Another task of the circulating blood is to carry away the large amount of heat produced by both muscle contraction and chemical energy released from foodstuffs. This heat is ultimately dissipated into the surrounding environment, primarily by evaporating sweat. Sweat production and evaporation in turn lead to fluid and electrolyte loss, which is in part counterbalanced by reduced diuresis. Building up adequate energy stores before and after exercise and adequately replenishing fluid and electrolytes during and following exercise require proper food and water intake; thus, exercise physiologists investigate nutrition before, during, and after exercise, as well as ways in which the various foods are processed and transformed by the gastrointestinal tract and then stored in the liver, muscles, and adipose tissue.

The description of these events is merely one chapter in the exercise physiology story. A second chapter concerns the attempt to ascertain the physiological control mechanisms by which these processes are orchestrated to meet the demands of the nerve-muscle system.

Control of Adjustments to Exercise

Circulation	Parasympathetic and sympatho-adrenal systems
Substrate mobilization	Sympatho-adrenal system, insulin, glucagon, cortisol, growth hormone, . . .
Fluid-electrolyte balance	Renin, aldosterone, vasopressin, atrial natriuretic peptide, . . .

This very complex regulation involves some local feedback mechanisms in both tissues and cells, but most of it results from the autonomic and endocrine systems, which collectively are called the **neurovegetative system** because they control the so-called vegetative functions. Many exercise physiologists study the parasympathetic and sympatho-adrenal systems and the exercise-induced release of several hormones (such as insulin, glucagon, cortisol, growth hormone, aldosterone, renin, vasopressin, and atrial natriuretic peptide) from the various endocrine glands. Indeed, investigating how the vegetative nervous centers (located mainly in the hypothalamus and the limbic system) trigger and finely regulate and tune these intricate control mechanisms according to the metabolic needs of the skeletal muscles provides a field of study in itself.

Other Systems

Finally, exercise and exercise training have direct and indirect consequences on systems and functions of the body that do not themselves directly support the neuromuscular machinery. For example, regular exercise may have positive or negative effects on the growth and maintenance of bones, tendons, and ligaments; on the reproductive systems of both females and males; and on the immune function of the body. Virtually no system or function of the body remains unaffected by exercise; consequently, none can be ignored by exercise physiologists.

The field of exercise physiology unfolds almost indefinitely from these basic problems. The responses to exercise of the various systems and functions may vary from person to person according to age, sex, race, body site concerned, health state, and environmental factors such as temperature, humidity, pressure changes (e.g., in mountain climbing or scuba diving), and changes

in gravity. Other factors include nutritional state, training state, sleep deprivation, and jet lag.

Environmental Challenge for Exercise

Altitude

Hyperbaric environment (diving)

Microgravity (space flights)

Cold

Hot and humid environment

Sleep deprivation and jet lag

Fasting and dehydration

Drugs

The various types of exercise and physical activities also induce different types of responses, as do drugs, whether used for therapeutic purposes or as ergogenic aids.

Clearly, investigating the adjustments of the various systems submitted to different types of exercises in various environmental, nutritional, and training conditions shows merit from both a theoretical and a practical point of view. Of similar value is comparative exercise physiology, which studies the adjustments to exercise in different species (horses, dogs, rats, birds, seals, and fish) and helps us understand how the evolutionary process has selected various physiological strategies in response to exercise stress.

Methods and Technologies in Physiology

Because exercise physiologists study such a wide variety of systems and functions, they need a wide variety of tools. Except for the ergometers (e.g., stationary bicycles, treadmills, rowing apparatus, and swimming flumes), which are specific to the field, exercise physiologists have "borrowed" most of the methods and equipment they use from physiology and medicine (cardiorespiratory physiology, pneumology, cardiology, endocrinology, neurology), as well as biochemistry (for instance, the assays of various substances in blood and other tissues). Thus, many innovative findings in the field come from exercise physiologists working in collaboration with colleagues in the "pure" sciences. For example, the method of indirect calorimetry (the measurement of heat production) using measurements of respiratory gas exchange, which is still widely used in exercise physiology, was first developed in the 18th and 19th centuries by scientists interested mainly in nutrition.

More recently, developments in computer technology have extended the limits of precision in measurement of all sorts. For example, computers allow researchers to analyze gas exchange breath by breath and automatically derive the kinetics of enzyme and hormone activities. Computer technology also allows the analysis of bioelectrical signals such as muscle EMG, which will help us determine the locus of fatigue and unravel the complex electrical patterns associated with the simultaneous recruitment of thousands of motor units in the exercising muscle. Researchers in our field are also applying computer techniques to the microscopic examination of tissues, precisely measuring their structural and enzymatic characteristics. The application of computer technology has rendered traditional techniques infinitely more powerful and the search more fulfilling.

Learned Societies

Researchers in many fields are becoming more interested in studies involving response to exercise as a model of physiological adaptations to natural stress. This increased interest is apparent in the activities of the many related learned societies. Presentations relating to exercise are increasingly common at the annual meetings of the Biophysical Society, Physiological Society, Society for Neuroscience, Federation of Societies in Experimental Biology (FASEB) (U.S.A.), and the Canadian Physiological Society. In addition, there are platforms more specific to experimental results in this field: the annual meetings of the American College of Sports Medicine (U.S.A.) and the Canadian Association of Sport Sciences.

Journals and Other Publications

Principal publications in which researchers present results in this field include

- *Canadian Journal of Sport Sciences*,
- *Medicine and Science in Sports and Exercise*,
- *Journal of Applied Physiology*,
- *European Journal of Applied Physiology*,
- *International Journal of Sports Medicine*,

- *American Journal of Physiology*, and
- *Canadian Journal of Physiology and Pharmacology*.

Undergraduate and Graduate Education

Exercise physiology is part of the general scientific training of the undergraduate student in physical education/physical activity sciences in virtually every program in every part of the world, but especially in Canada and United States, where this field of study has flourished for the past 25 years. A basic knowledge of exercise physiology allows the student to understand the responses of the various systems to an acute exercise session, under a variety of conditions (e.g., differences in age, sex, training states, and environments). This information helps us determine the factors that limit specific types of performance. Such information has obvious use to athletes who wish to improve their performance through diet and training.

In addition, most exercise physiology courses at the university level offer sections that provide basic knowledge of exercise as a preventive or rehabilitative intervention, applying the fundamental principles of physiology of exercise to special populations of individuals (the elderly, the sedentary, coronary patients, diabetics, pregnant women, etc.). Dealing with these populations requires basic knowledge of the physiological limitations inherent in each, as well as of exercise physiology in general. Individuals proficient in this area can design exercise programs to increase the quality of life of those who otherwise might be severely limited in their physical activity.

Career Opportunities

The career opportunities for individuals with graduate training are numerous. In North America, there are several MSc and PhD programs wherein students may specialize in exercise physiology. Graduate students in these programs are generally required to take several departmental courses at the graduate level, as well as courses in other departments (physiology, physics, biochemistry, pharmacology, and biology). An increasing number of students in the field are spending from 1 to 3 years as postdoctoral fellows in research laboratories to diversify and solidify their research skills. Several federal and provincial funding agencies provide support to such students if their academic standing is competitive. Career opportunities include university faculty positions, research positions in hospital laboratories and independent institutions, and positions in the corporate fitness field.

Summary

Although exercise physiology is one of the oldest areas of study in the physical activity sciences, many problems in the field have yet to be solved, and new ones present themselves regularly. We do not yet understand completely how all systems interact during exercise or the full extent and significance of the adaptations that occur with training. In searching for these answers, however, exercise physiologists will continue to contribute practical knowledge applicable to exercise as a recreational, rehabilitative, and preventive tool.

References and Further Readings

Åstrand, P.-O. (1986). *Textbook of work physiology.* New York: McGraw-Hill. (Available in French)

Brooks, G., & Fahey, T. (1987). *Fundamentals of human performance.* New York: Macmillan.

Exercise and Sport Sciences Reviews. Baltimore: Williams & Wilkins. (Published annually since 1973)

Gardiner, P. (1986). Exercise physiology in the 1990's: Mechanistically defining the exercise model. *Canadian Journal of Applied Sport Sciences,* **11,** 1-10.

Jasmin, B., Lavoie, P.-A., & Gardiner, P. (1988). Fast axonal transport of labeled proteins in motoneurons of exercise-trained rats. *American Journal of Physiology,* **255** (Cell Physiology, 24), C731-C736.

Lamb, D. (1984). *Physiology of exercise: Responses and adaptations.* New York: Macmillan.

Massicotte, D., Péronnet, F., Brisson, G., Bakkouch, K., & Hillaire-Marcel, C. (1989). Oxidation of a glucose polymer during exercise: Comparison with glucose and fructose. *Journal of Applied Physiology,* **66**(1), 179-183.

McArdle, W., Katch, F., & Katch, V. (1986). *Exercise physiology: Energy, nutrition, and human performance.* Philadelphia: Lea and Febiger. (Available in French)

Péronnet, F., Thibault, G., Ledoux, M., & Brisson, G. (1987). *Performance in endurance events.* London, ON: Spodym.

Chapter 6

Biochemistry and Physical Activity

Earl G. Noble
Albert W. Taylor

Biochemistry is the study of the chemical processes that occur in living matter. Biochemistry started largely as an offshoot of organic and physical chemistry and is therefore a relatively young science.

• • •

Exercise biochemistry uses chemical, histological, and morphological techniques to identify and interpret, at the subcellular to the organ level, the chemical compositions and processes responsible for exercise-induced changes.

• • •

Among the first biochemists were Liebig (1803-1873), who examined the nutritive materials in green plants, and Wohler (1800-1882), who synthesized urea, the principal end product of the body's metabolism of nitrogen. Other investigators were involved in this new field of study that attempted to elucidate the chemical composition and basic metabolism of the cell. Chevreul (1786-1889), for example, determined the composition of fat, Kossel (1853-1927) studied proteins, Fischer (1852-1919) analyzed carbohydrates, and Buchner (1860-1917) researched the concept of enzymes.

The first journal devoted to biochemistry, *Zeitschrift für physiologische Chemie*, appeared in 1879. The second, *The Journal of Biological Chemistry*, which appeared in 1906, was the first to publish in English (Harrow & Mazur, 1966).

Major Concepts and Biochemical Methods

Modern biochemistry of exercise began with the demonstration by Meyerhoff (1925) and Hill (1926) that a correlation exists between lactic acid production, oxygen consumption, and heat production in contracting muscle. Their papers reported the first major investigations attempting to relate a chemical reaction to a physiological function. Although numerous investigators continued to study this relationship over the next 30 to 40 years, few, if any, could be considered physical educators, exercise physiologists, or exercise biochemists. Nevertheless, researchers such as Dill and co-workers at the Harvard Fatigue Laboratory (Horvath & Horvath, 1973), Krogh and associates in Copenhagen (Christensen & Hansen, 1939; Krogh & Lindhard, 1919), and Palladin (1945) in Russia continued to provide impetus to this fledgling area.

It was not until the early 1960s that exercise biochemistry researchers began to appear in the physical activity sciences, often affiliated with physical education units in North America and departments of clinical physiology in Europe. To date, most important published research in exercise biochemistry has come from the U.S.A., Scandinavia, Germany, and Canada. Just as biochemistry evolved from organic chemistry and expanded to such diverse areas as genetic studies and the characterization of cellular components, exercise biochemistry evolved from exercise physiology and incorporates a broad spectrum of study of the function of the biological organism, including immunology, endocrinology, histology, histochemistry, microbiology, and enzymology (see Table 6.1). Many investigators use both physiological and biochemical techniques to see how the cell adjusts biochemically to external stressors, particularly exercise.

Major Research Questions

Typical broad concerns in exercise biochemistry might include

- fuel requirements and mobilization of fuel for exercise,
- underlying causes of fatigue during exercise, and
- the capacity of the organism to adapt to acute or chronic activity.

Table 6.1 Commonly Employed Methods and Technologies in Exercise Biochemistry

Technique	Description
Histochemistry	Staining various cellular and subcellular organelles, allowing identification of muscle fiber types and influence of exercise or training; involves microscopic analysis
Enzymology	Measurement of selected properties (especially activity) of specific enzymes; often employed as indicators of a training effect
Quantitative measures of metabolites and hormones	Measurement of intracellular or blood levels of selected metabolites (e.g., ATP, CP, glucose) and hormones (e.g., thyroid, growth hormone).
Other	Electrophoresis, chromotography, immunodetection, as well as Southern, Northern, and Western blotting.

The biochemical effects of exercise on cellular function are studied by exercise biochemistry researchers.

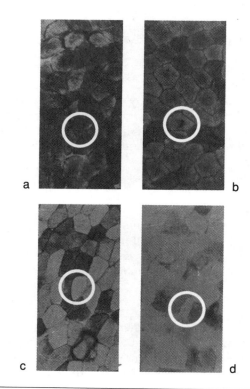

Histochemical demonstration of muscle fiber glycogen depletion following acute long term endurance exercise. Muscle biopsy samples were taken from the vastus lateralis (a thigh muscle) of a man exercising on a bicycle erogometer at 75% $\dot{V}O_2$max; at rest (a), after 30 min (b), after 60 min (c), and near exhaustion at 90 min (d). Note in a that at rest all fibers stain darkly and with a similar intensity for glycogen. Compare a to d where an almost complete loss of staining intensity occurs after exhaustive exercise. B and c indicate that this process of glycogen depletion occurs at different rates in different muscle fibers during the exercise process. Histochemical observations such as these have provided exercise biochemists with considerable information regarding the relative importance of carbohydrate versus lipid metabolism during exercise. These methods have also offered insight into the manner in which skeletal muscle is activated with exercise.

Within these broad thrusts, many specific problems have been addressed: how fat is mobilized, the relative importance of carbohydrate versus lipid metabolism, the significance of bloodborne fuels versus fuels in the muscle cells, ways to alter fuel stores, the metabolic causes of fatigue, the neuromuscular factors involved in fatigue, the adaptation of key enzymes to a chronic exercise stimulus, the causes of muscle soreness, the hormonal response to exercise, and the factors involved in muscle growth or atrophy are but a few of the areas that have been studied. Exercise biochemists investigate these problems at the subcellular, cellular, tissue, and organ levels. They observe the effects of exercise, or the response to environmental stressors, on such groups as males and females, individuals with chronic pathological conditions, elite athletes, and individuals in different age brackets.

Learned Societies

Researchers may present their scientific papers to such groups as the American College of Sports Medicine, the Scandinavian Physiology Society, the Physiological Society of Great Britain, and The Canadian Association of Sport Sciences. The organization that provides primary support for the area of study, however, is the International Group on Biochemistry of Exercise, which is sponsored by

---

HIGHLIGHT
How Training Changes Muscle

Many of the questions that exercise biochemistry attempts to solve have their origins in physiological experiments and empirical observations. Such is the case in how training changes the composition of muscle.

It has been known since the late 1800s that within a muscle tissue different kinds of muscle cells, or fibers, exist. These fast- and slow-twitch fibers (discussed in chapter 5) were identified through physiological techniques. Through biochemical experimentation, using histochemical and enzymological measures (review Table 6.1), it was found that

the slow-twitch fibers have the metabolic machinery (enzymes) that allows them to use oxygen to burn fuels (mostly carbohydrates and fats) and to conserve energy supplies. So, biochemistry told us why slow-twitch fibers are slow-contracting and fatigue-resistant:

1. Slow-twitch fibers have highly active oxidation enzymes to burn fat and hence are fatigue-resistant. Fast-twitch fibers possess more active glycolytic enzymes to utilize carbohydrates and may be less fatigue-resistant.
2. Contractile protein changes brought about by training are related to the changes in fiber type and to the contractile properties of the whole muscle.

Exercise biochemistry has sought to answer at least two important questions: Can training produce changes within a muscle fiber so that it is more aerobic? Can the proportion of slow- to fast-twitch fibers within a muscle tissue be changed? These questions have very practical implications. It is known, for example, that the average person has a composition of 50% fast-twitch, 50% slow-twitch fibers in the leg muscles, whereas successful marathoners have 50% to 100% slow-twitch fibers. Is it training that accounts for this difference, or is this type of fiber profile genetically determined?

Exercise biochemistry has shown that training will allow the fibers that are present to adapt metabolically to permit better use of the fuel supplies present and the oxygen delivered. One such adaptation is increased activity among the enzymes responsible for aerobic metabolism. But very few studies show that prolonged endurance training might cause an increase in the percentage of slow-twitch fibers. On the other hand, genetic studies show that the fiber-type profile does not completely depend upon inherited factors. The final solution awaits the development of further technical and methodological advances in exercise biochemistry.

the International Council of Sport Science and Physical Education at UNESCO. This organization holds international conferences on a regular basis (Brussels 1968, Magglinen 1973, Quebec City 1976, Brussels 1979, Boston 1982, Copenhagen 1985, London, Ontario, 1988) and attracts the top exercise biochemistry scientists from around the world. It also regularly sponsors international courses to educate interested young scientists in countries attempting to develop the field.

Journals and Other Publications

During the past 10 years a great many scientific journals have been introduced to meet the needs of investigators working in exercise biochemistry. These include

- *Canadian Journal of Sport Sciences,*
- *International Journal of Sports Medicine,*
- *Scandinavian Journal of Sports Medicine,*
- *Medicine and Science in Sports and Exercise,* and
- *Journal of Sports Medicine and Physical Fitness.*

In addition, exercise biochemistry articles are found regularly in

- *Acta Physiologica Scandinavia,*
- *American Journal of Physiology,*
- *Biochemica et Biophysica Acta,*
- *Biochemistry,*
- *Canadian Journal of Physiology and Pharmacology,*
- *European Journal of Applied Physiology,*
- *Hormone and Metabolic Research,*
- *Journal de Physiologie,*
- *Journal of Applied Physiology,*
- *Journal of Physiology,*
- *Metabolism,* and
- *Muscle and Nerve.*

Basic research in exercise biochemistry rapidly finds its way into the clinical fields of study as well, and the associated clinical journals regularly publish applied articles.

Undergraduate and Graduate Education

Canadian Programs

Although the burgeoning area termed exercise biochemistry currently has several hundred adherents internationally, Canada has fewer than 20 researchers who are members of physical education or physical activity faculties and who might place themselves in this category (Yuhasz, Taylor, & Haggerty, 1986). These individuals are strategically placed across the country, however. Currently, numerous universities offer courses in this area at the undergraduate level, and six—Alberta, Dalhousie, Laval, Montreal, Waterloo, and Western Ontario—offer PhD programs.

International Programs

As they do in Canada, a number of exercise biochemists in the United States work in departments of physical education or physical activity sciences. Undergraduate students in these departments often follow courses with a significant exercise biochemistry content, and several institutions offer the PhD. As a result, the United States is one of the leading nations in exercise biochemistry research.

Because exercise biochemistry did not evolve in Europe within physical education programs, few if any institutions offer advanced degrees or courses through the physical activity sciences. Students wishing to study exercise biochemistry are enrolled primarily in clinical physiology or medical units throughout Scandinavia and Germany, although in England physical education is starting to offer such courses. Little work in the area is presently conducted in the Orient, although China and Japan are gradually initiating study in exercise biochemistry.

Career Opportunities

Individuals with advanced degrees in exercise biochemistry teach and conduct research at universities, in clinical laboratories, and in hospitals. Given the ever-expanding education base required of most professions, however, it is expected that some basic training in exercise biochemistry will be required of individuals contemplating employment in fitness units; as high school biology, health education, and physical education teachers; and as coaches. Additionally, physiotherapists, occupational therapists, medical practitioners who prescribe exercise, and personnel in research units specializing in environmental medicine, aviation, and so on will also need this specialized training.

Summary

The more we know about adaptation to physical activity, the more we need to examine adaptation at the cellular level. Exercise biochemistry utilizes chemical, histological, and morphological techniques to identify and interpret mechanisms responsible for these exercise-induced changes. The field has grown from limited beginnings to a scientifically accepted pursuit, as demonstrated by professional and scientific societies and journals devoted to it. Students interested in the study of exercise biochemistry should develop a strong scientific background combined with an interest in the practical application of exercise modalities.

References and Further Readings

Christensen, E.H., & Hanson, O. (1939). Arbeitsfahigket und ehnahrung. *Skandinavica Archive Physiologica*, **81**, 160-175.

Exercise and Sport Sciences Reviews. (1977-1990). Vols. 1-18.

Harrow, B., & Muzur, A. (1966). *Textbook of biochemistry*. Philadelphia: W.B. Saunders.

Hill, A.V. (1926). *Muscle activity*. Baltimore: Wilkins.

Horvath, S.M., & Horvath, E.C. (1973). *The Harvard fatigue laboratory: History and contributions*. Englewood Cliffs, NJ: Prentice Hall.

Krogh, A., & Lindhard, J. (1919). XXX: The relative value of fat and carbohydrate as sources of muscular energy [30th paper in a series]. *Biochemical Journal*, **14**, 290-363.

Meyerhoff, O. (1925). *Chemical dynamics of life phenomena*. Philadelphia: Lippincott.

Palladin, A.V. (1945). The biochemistry of muscle training. *Science*, **102**, 576-578.

Saltin, B., Henriksson, J., Nygaard, E., Andersen, P., & Jansson, E. (1977). Fiber types and metabolic potentials of skeletal muscles in sedentary man and endurance runners. *Annals of the New York Academy of Sciences*, **301**, 3-29.

Yuhasz, M.S., Taylor, A.W., & Haggerty, T.R. (1986). *Acadirectory: A Canadian sourcebook for physical education and human kinetics*. London, ON: Sports Dynamics.

Chapter 7

Medicine and Physical Activity

Roy J. Shephard

Sports medicine explores the growing interface between traditional medicine and the physical activity sciences. It focuses on the value of exercise in prevention and treatment and also covers the minimization of medical and surgical complications during vigorous activity.

• • •

Sports medicine deals with all aspects of sports that have a medical import, whether a benefit (i.e., sports as therapeutic) or a detriment (i.e., sports as harmful or traumatic).

• • •

Specific therapeutic issues on the positive side of the ledger include the benefit of enhanced physical activity to lifestyle problems, exercise-induced gains of perceived health (with a resultant decrease in minor medical complaints), changes of immune function (with an altered risk of acute disease), the role of prescribed exercise in the prevention and treatment of various chronic diseases, the restoration of normal function following bed rest for medical or surgical problems, and the relief of mild psychiatric disturbances.

Therapeutic Issues in Sports Medicine

- Lifestyle problems (obesity, cigarette consumption, and substance abuse)
- Exercise-induced changes in perceived health
- Exercise-induced changes in immune function
- Prevention of chronic disease (ischaemic heart disease, hypertension, and maturity onset diabetes)

- Functional restoration following illness or injury
- Mild psychiatric disturbances (particularly anxiety and depression)

The expert in sports medicine provides advice on exercise appropriate both to individuals affected by acute disorders (e.g., upper respiratory and gastrointestinal infections) and to those with chronic medical conditions (e.g., a minor congenital heart abnormality). If the individual concerned is involved in major competition, the sports medicine practitioner may need to review and adjust medication to avoid conflicts with rules governing the "doping" of competitors.

The practitioner may also provide dietary information—whether to correct obesity, to maximize glycogen loading of the muscle fibers, to enhance muscle development, to ensure an adequate hemoglobin level, or to avoid amenorrhea and anorexia nervosa. In a hot climate, the fluid and mineral intake of competitors must also be regulated carefully to avoid either an acute or a chronic depletion of fluid and mineral reserves.

Advice Required From the Sports Medicine Expert

Exercise prescription

Review of medication

Diet

Fluid and mineral needs

Particular care is needed to guard against the medical problems that can develop when exercise is performed in unusual environments. The mountaineer faces risks of acute mountain sickness, pulmonary edema, and high-altitude deterioration, whereas the scuba diver can suffer from nitrogen narcosis, oxygen poisoning, decompression sickness, or barotrauma. Athletes encounter dangers of heat collapse, heat stroke, and hyperthermia in hot conditions and of frostbite and hypothermia in cold ones. The sports medicine practitioner must both advise athletes on the proper precautions for particular environments and treat environment-related traumas.

Environmental Concerns

High altitude (mountain sickness, pulmonary edema, high-altitude deterioration)

Diving (nitrogen narcosis, decompression sickness, barotrauma)

Heat (collapse, stroke, hyperthermia)

Cold (hypothermia, frostbite)

Finally, the sports physician and staff have major responsibilities in the prevention and acute care of athletic injuries—abrasions, lacerations, sprains, strains, and fractures.

Competence in all of the previously mentioned areas requires not only general medical proficiency but also expertise in a variety of medical specialties. The average physical activity practitioner cannot gain more than an overview of the subject by completing one or two courses in sports medicine. Nevertheless, as the person in immediate contact with the athlete, the physical activity specialist plays a key role in both prevention and treatment. Duties include

- regulation of both the athletic environment and the intensity of prescribed exercise to minimize medical problems,
- provision of emergency first aid when needed, and
- prompt recognition of conditions that require medical referral.

As research issues become more complex, specialists in fields other than medicine are making major independent contributions in such growing areas of sport science as epidemiology, nutrition, environmental physiology, and others.

Major Concepts

At one time, most physicians thought that there was a clear dividing line between health and disease. Sports medicine thus concerned itself primarily with "medical clearance for exercise"; with the development of suitable supervised programs for those with congenital abnormalities, chronic, or degenerative disorders; and above all, with the treatment of athletic injuries. The presence of disease meant the athlete could exercise only under the close surveillance of a registered medical practitioner.

More recently, however, health scientists have recognized a continuum between optimum health and clearly identifiable organic disease. On any one day, optimizing the position of a given individual along this continuum depends very much on optimizing both exercise environment and body function, areas in which the physical activity specialist has greater experience than the physician. The responsibilities of the physical activity practitioner should thus include assessing the individual client's current location on the health continuum, referring for medical advice if the client demonstrates substantial ill health, and prescribing appropriate exercise to maximize the health of all other contacts.

Everyone operates on a continuum linking frank illness with total health.

$$\text{Perceived health} \atop \downarrow$$

Illness ← -------------------------------- → *Health*

Methods and Technologies in Sports Medicine

Given the broad range of sports medicine, it is not surprising that the relevant technologies also vary. The first step in prevention is often epidemiological. For instance, the exercise scientist may carefully analyze the responses to a questionnaire that has been distributed to a large and representative population to assess the statistical significance of a reported association between disease or injury and a lack of or an excess of a certain type of activity. Other techniques help assess the environment accurately. This in itself requires competence in the use of a wide variety of equipment, including the measurement of effective air temperature and humidity by dry bulb, wet bulb, and globe thermometer; assessment of windspeed by anemometer; determination of the partial pressure of respired gases by physical or chemical methods; and an assessment of the safety of playing surfaces and protective equipment in a biomechanics laboratory.

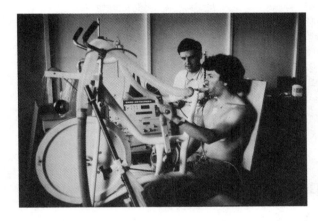

The modern sports physician must be thoroughly familiar with a wide range of exercise testing equipment. Here, the cardiorespiratory performance is being assessed during arm work—a technique applicable to individuals with disabilities of the lower limbs.

Other roles played by modern sports medicine practitioners call for more traditional medical techniques, as when the practitioner must prescribe the amount of exercise (frequency, duration, intensity, and type) appropriate to the age and physical and medical condition of the client. Standard diagnostic tools may be used to uncover functional disorders that require medical attention (e.g., an abnormal waveform in the electrocardiogram).

First aid continues to be an important part of sports medicine. The physical activity specialist must be ready to administer standard first-aid care in the event of either injury or medical emergency (for example, rewarming by body heat in hypothermia, cleaning and bandaging minor lacerations following physical injury, and providing cardiac massage in the event of cardiac arrest).

Major Research Questions

To date, major research in sports medicine has focused on applied issues. Given that ischaemic

heart disease is the major cause of death in middle-aged people, exercise scientists have invested much time in examining whether regular, endurance-type exercise can reduce the risk of either a fatal or a nonfatal heart attack. There has been equal interest in whether vigorous exercise after recovery from a myocardial infarction can improve prognosis. Parallel research has explored the possible value of endurance activity in the prevention and treatment of other chronic medical conditions while seeking also to define more precisely the optimum dose of exercise that should be recommended in various situations.

One major issue recently investigated has been the influence of work-site fitness programs upon employee health and well-being.

Epidemiological studies have examined the relative risks of injury incurred by participation in different types of sport at various levels of competition. Diving scientists have sought to develop refined tables or minicomputers to indicate the maximum allowable periods of submersion at various depths, thereby reducing the chances of developing decompression sickness. Scientists interested in mountain climbing have tested the value of acetazolamide and its analogues in the prevention of mountain sickness. Thermal physiologists have sought the optimal replacement fluid for sustained exercise under hot conditions and have applied modern analyses of heat transfer to the selection of optimal clothing fabrics for participants in summer and winter competitions. Most

HIGHLIGHT
Exercise After Heart Attack

Our laboratory recently participated in a large, multicenter study that examined the value of exercise in middle-aged patients who had already sustained a first myocardial infarction (Rechnitzer et al., 1983). Although the findings were somewhat inconclusive, they illustrate the complexities of applied research in sports medicine.

First, an epidemiologist determined an appropriate sample size for proof of the exercise hypothesis based on the expected annual incidence of fatal and nonfatal recurrences of myocardial infarction. She calculated that if exercise therapy gave rise to a clinically useful improvement of prognosis (for instance, a reduction in future "cardiac events" of 50% or more) and the number of defections from the prescribed exercise program could be held to 35% or less, a group of 375 experimental subjects and 375 controls would offer a 90% chance of demonstrating benefit with an error level of less than .05 (i.e., there would be only 1 chance in 20 that unusual data would appear to prove the value of exercise in the treatment of myocardial infarction when there was really no benefit).

Sample Size Calculation

Normal cardiac event rate: 22% over 4 years

Required proof: 50% reduction of future cardiac events

Drop-out rate: cumulative loss < 35% in 4 years

Likelihood of demonstrating effect: 90%

Statistical criterion: $p \leq .05$

Sample needed: 375 experimental   for 4 years
375 controls

The investigators defined myocardial infarction as a classic "heart attack" occurring 2 to 12 months before the study; to be included in the study, the acute event had to be documented by typical symptoms and characteristic serial changes in the resting ECG or serum enzyme concentrations. The investigators avoided the potential complicating factor of alterations in prognosis due to associated diseases by excluding all patients with a history of uncontrolled diabetes, chronic lung disease leading to a major reduction of lung volumes, and orthopedic problems that would restrict the subjects' ability to perform the prescribed fast walking/jogging program. Finally, it was decided that subjects must initially be 54 years of age or younger to allow a substantial average follow-up period prior to their death.

Despite the size of the population base (seven universities in southern Ontario, serving some 4 million people), it took several years to recruit 750 suitable postcoronary patients who were willing to accept randomized assignment in our experimental study. After the subjects gave their informed consent to all that was proposed, they were allocated to either a high-intensity endurance exercise program or a homeopathic regimen of games and light calisthenics. Including the light exercise group allowed for the possible benefit that subjects might gain from meeting as a group rather than from participating in endurance exercise as such. Four classical cardiac risk factors were assessed, and the distribution of subjects between exercise and control groups was stratified to take account of the existence of chest pain (angina), high blood pressure (hypertension), time-conscious type A behavior, and white- versus blue-collar occupation.

Experimental subjects continued the program of progressive, supervised exercise for a total of 3 to 4 years. Their clinical course was compared to that of the control subjects in terms of the incidence of recurrent myocardial infarction and of cardiac fatalities.

Unfortunately, the incidence of adverse cardiac events did not differ significantly between experimental and control groups, but we cannot immediately conclude that exercise has no value for the postcoronary patient. First, the sample size proved about five times too small to answer the question clearly, partly because the cumulative drop-out rate from the exercise classes was much higher than 35%, partly because our entry restrictions resulted in subjects with a mortality rate considerably lower than anticipated, and partly because a slow onset of training response shortened the effective period of therapeutic benefit from 4 years to 2 to 3 years. Moreover, a substantial proportion of the few patients who died over the first 4 years were those who had initially shown electrical evidence of oxygen lack in the heart muscle (an ischaemic electrocardiogram, with deep exercise-induced depression of the ST segment of the ECG). It is thus arguable that these individuals form a separate group who should have received a modified rather than a standard exercise prescription.

Finally, we had considerable difficulty in persuading subjects to remain in their group as experimental or control subjects throughout the entire study. Not only did about half of those who were assigned to the high-intensity activity program drop out of the exercise classes over the course of the study, but a substantial proportion of the control group heard of the supposed value of exercise and began significant physical activity of their own initiative. Thus, when we adopted the statistically disfavored approach of classifying patients according to objective evidence of their actual exercise behavior rather than their prescribed regimen, we saw a 28% advantage of prognosis in those who had developed a training response over those who had not.

Reasons for Study Failure

Drop-out rate higher than anticipated

Contamination of control group

Slow onset of therapeutic response

Bias in subject sample

Cardiac event rate less than anticipated

Several authors in other parts of the world have attempted similar randomized control studies of exercise for patients with myocardial infarction. The majority of investigators have shown a useful (20-30%) advantage of prognosis for those who have exercised, but no single study has been large enough to obtain conventional statistical proof of benefit (in other words, the probability that the observed benefit has arisen by chance has remained greater than 1 in 20). A larger and statistically more conclusive study is unlikely for several reasons—the pool of qualified postcoronary subjects available in any one city is insufficient to recruit the necessary 3,000 to 4,000 volunteers, the cost of such a study would be very high (probably $30 million or more), and interest has shifted from unifocal (exercise-centered) to multifocal (lifestyle-based) rehabilitation programs.

The remaining option for the investigating sports physician is to pool available studies, assuming that the protocol has been reasonably consistent from one part of the world to another. In this fashion, the exercise benefit of 20% to 30% can be confirmed, at a statistically significant confidence level (Shephard, 1988).

recently, health economists concerned about rising medical costs have begun to look at the possibility of reducing medical claims through an increase in personal physical activity.

Major Research Questions

Value of exercise in chronic disease

Risk of injury in various sports

Methods of reducing environmental hazards

Cost/effectiveness analysis of exercise

Learned Societies and Journals

The past 20 years have seen a rapid growth in the size of professional associations and societies interested in sports medicine, with a parallel growth in both society-sponsored and commercial journals dedicated to this specialty. The following are some of the journals in sports medicine:

- *Medicine and Science in Sports and Exercise*
- *Exercise and Sport Sciences Reviews*
- *Canadian Journal of Sport Sciences*
- *British Journal of Sports Medicine*
- *Médecine du Sport*
- *Sports Medicine*
- *Physician and Sportsmedicine*
- *International Journal of Sports Medicine*
- *American Journal of Sports Medicine*

Other sources include

- *Journal of Applied Physiology,*
- *European Journal of Applied Physiology,*
- *Ergonomics,*
- *Yearbook of Sports Medicine,* and
- *Cumulative Index Medicus.*

Probably the oldest professional sports medicine group is the Federation Internationale de Médecine Sportive (FIMS), which held its first meeting at St. Moritz in 1928. It has remained primarily European, and it has sustained a physician-oriented concept of sports medicine in the face of the growing competence of paramedical professionals. At least in theory, the 40 participating national federations of sports medicine require a medical qualification on the part of all full members. FIMS

sponsors 2-week postgraduate courses in sports medicine in various parts of the world, organizes a World Congress of Sports Medicine every fourth year, and produces four to six issues of the *Journal of Sports Medicine and Physical Fitness* per year. In the United States, the major sports medicine group is the American College of Sports Medicine. What started as a dinner meeting of 11 physicians and exercise physiologists in 1955 has since grown to a diverse group of more than 12,000 fellows and members, with an annual budget of $3,000,000, an annual national meeting, and substantial regional chapters. It publishes a scholarly journal (*Medicine and Science in Sports and Exercise*) and an annual collection of reviews (*Exercise and Sport Sciences Reviews*).

In Canada, the Canadian Association of Sport Sciences was formed in 1967 to bring together Canadian physicians and physical educators with an interest in sports medicine. Regular activities include an annual professional meeting and publication of the *Canadian Journal of Sport Sciences*. A second strand in the Canadian sports medicine tradition has been the Grey Cup symposium, a meeting that brings together surgeons, coaches, and trainers who have an interest in the medical aspects of team sports. There is also a Canadian Academy of Sports Medicine, which is open to members of the Canadian Medical Association with an interest in sports medicine.

Parallel national organizations can be found in other countries, each with its own house journal; for example, the British Association for Sports Medicine sponsors the *British Journal of Sports Medicine,* and its French counterpart publishes *Médecine du Sport*.

Among the growing number of commercial journals serving the specialty, *Sports Medicine* offers an excellent series of reviews 12 times per year, the monthly *Physician and Sportsmedicine* provides popular research information to the practicing physician and paramedical assistants, the *International Journal of Sports Medicine* publishes scholarly work in various subdisciplines, and the *American Journal of Sports Medicine* provides material with a focus on athletic injuries. Other journals such as the *European Journal of Applied Physiology,* the *Journal of Applied Physiology,* and *Ergonomics* carry an increasing number of contributions relevant to sports medicine. The *Yearbook of Sports Medicine* provides a useful summary of 300 to 400 major papers per year, and the *Cumulative Index Medicus* provides many helpful listings of literature (for example, the myocardial infarction section covers papers in exercise, prevention, and rehabilitation).

Undergraduate and Graduate Education

Any course in sports medicine must draw on a background knowledge of anatomy, physiology, biochemistry, and biomechanics. Sports medicine instruction in the physical activity sciences is thus deferred until the third or fourth year of an honours undergraduate program. A well-designed course integrates theoretical knowledge in the biological sciences with practical experience gained in activity classes and applies the result to specific problems of prevention and treatment in the lecture theater, in the sports medicine clinic, and in the daily prescription of physical activity for a variety of populations.

Students interested in pursuing the medical aspects of sports medicine at the graduate or professional level will need to gain sufficient experience in exercise testing and ECG interpretation to meet the requirements of certification as fitness appraisers, whereas those interested in the treatment of athletic injuries may gain additional experience as assistant to a team physician and trainer.

Career Opportunities

Many aspects of sports medicine remain strictly within the medical preserve, and the person who wishes to excel in either research or practice is well advised to gain qualifications in both medicine and physical activity sciences. However, there are also an increasing number of career opportunities for physical activity specialists who lack medical training, including the following:

- Epidemiology of sports medicine
- Environmental expert
- Government health agencies
- Industrial and commercial health promotion
- Exercise technologist
- Exercise program director
- Sales and servicing of equipment
- Books, radio and television programming
- Design of protective equipment
- Athletic therapist

The first two options listed require a fairly sophisticated academic background. The epidemiologist designing experiments in sports medicine will need proficiency in mathematics, biostatistics, and issues of study design. The scientist examining the impact of adverse environments on human

performance will commonly have a doctorate in exercise physiology.

At a more practical level, government agencies, industrial fitness programs, commercial health spas, community hospitals, and agencies selling laboratory equipment have an ever-increasing demand for those who are competent to conduct exercise tests under the general supervision of a physician, who can advise on lifestyle, who can prescribe safe and effective patterns of exercise for patients with a variety of disorders, and who can monitor body reactions to such stresses under a variety of unfavorable conditions. Some physical activity sciences graduates will devise programs and administer or teach such exercise classes, whereas others with a literary flair will write popular books or present radio and television programs covering this same information. Individuals trained in biomechanics may use their knowledge of injuries to design protective equipment such as hockey visors and running shoes.

Finally, those experienced in taping, bandaging, and treatment of minor athletic traumas will find a ready source of employment—and an ever-present client population—in the training rooms of major athletic facilities.

Summary

Issues in the interface between sports medicine and the physical activity sciences include the value of exercise in the prevention and treatment of clinical conditions and the minimization of complications from vigorous physical activity. In all of these areas, the physical activity specialist must know when to offer the athlete advice and when to refer to a sports physician. Epidemiology, environmental monitoring, exercise testing and prescription, and emergency care are all important facets of sports medicine. To date, research has mainly been of an applied nature, for example, studies to evaluate exercise as a clinically useful treatment following myocardial infarction.

Rapid growth of the specialty over the past 20 years has led to the emergence of strong national and international associations dedicated to sports medicine. There are also now many specialized journals that discuss original research and offer careful reviews of major topics in the field.

Formal undergraduate courses in sports medicine draw on knowledge in many other subdisciplines of physical activity sciences and thus tend to be third- or fourth-year options. Students electing such options may continue to medical school, or seek employment in such areas as sports epidemiology, environmental science, fitness testing and prescription, equipment design, athletic therapy, and media coverage of these various topics.

References and Further Readings

Appenzeller, O., & Atkinson, R. (1981). *Sports medicine, fitness, training, injuries*. Baltimore: Urban & Schwarzenburg.

Apple, D.F., & Cantwell, J.D. (1979). *Medicine for sport*. Chicago: Yearbook.

Bove, A.A., & Lowenthal, D.T. (1983). *Exercise medicine: Physiological principles and clinical applications*. New York: Academic Press.

Knuttgen, H., & Tittel, W. (Eds.) (1988). *Basic book of sports medicine* (2nd ed.). Lausanne: International Olympic Committee.

Masironi, R., & Denolin, H. (1985). *Physical activity in disease prevention and treatment*. Padova, Italy: Piccin.

McMaster, J.H. (1982). *The ABC's of sports medicine*. Malabar, FL: R.E. Krieger.

Rechnitzer, P.A., Cunningham, D.A., Andrew, G.M., Buck, C.W., Jones, N.L., Kavanagh, T., Oldridge, N.B., Parker, J.O., Shephard, R.J.,

Sutton, J.R., & Donner, A.P. (1983). Relation of exercise to the recurrence rate of myocardial infarction in men—Ontario Heart Exercise–Heart Collaborative Study. *American Journal of Cardiology*, **51**, 65-69.

Roy, S., & Rivin, R. (1983). *Sports medicine: Prevention, evaluation, management and rehabilitation*. Englewood Cliffs, NJ: Prentice Hall.

Ryan, A.J., & Allman, F.L. (1989). *Sports medicine* (2nd ed.). San Diego: Academic Press.

Shephard, R.J. (1988). Does cardiac rehabilitation after myocardial infarction have a favourable impact on prognosis? *The Physician and Sportsmedicine*, **16**(6), 116-127.

Sperryn, P.N. (1983). *Sport and medicine*. London: Butterworth.

Strauss, R.H. (1979). *Sports medicine and physiology*. Philadelphia: W.B. Saunders.

Strauss, R.H. (1984). *Sports medicine*. Philadelphia: W.B. Saunders.

Torg, J., Welsh, P., & Shephard, R.J. (1989). *Current therapy in sports medicine 2*. Burlington, ON: B.C. Decker.

Welsh, P., & Shephard, R.J. (Eds.) (1985). *Current therapy in sports medicine*. Burlington, ON: B.C. Decker.

Williams, J.G. (Ed.) (1976). *Sports medicine* (2nd ed.). London: Arnold.

Chapter 8

Biomechanics and Physical Activity

Benoît Roy

Traditionally, the term *kinesiology* (literally, the science of movement) was used to describe the study of the structure and function of the human musculoskeletal system. During the last two decades, however, the term *biomechanics* emerged; it is defined as the study of the structure and function of biological systems by means of the methods of mechanics (Hatze, 1974).

We are concerned here more specifically with the field of physical activity sciences and its application to sport, so perhaps we should use the definition given by Hay (1985):

• • •

Biomechanics is the science concerned with the internal and external forces acting on a human body and the effect produced by these forces.

• • •

The main purpose of biomechanics is to provide an understanding of the nature and function of human movement, whether in sport, dance, or adapted activities. The study of biomechanics establishes a frame of reference based on mechanical concepts and allows the sound and logical evaluation of the various techniques as well as the determination of underlying causes for observed effects. For teachers, whatever the student's level of skill development, it eliminates the guesswork from critical judgment. For coaches, who work with more advanced skills, a good biomechanical background is essential because it develops the careful attention to precise detail that so frequently leads to improved performance at this level.

Major Concepts

The major emphasis in biomechanics rests on mechanical concepts, but the human body is a far more complex system than are most objects encountered in traditional mechanics. We therefore must describe it as a linked mechanical model (i.e., made up of segments) with many degrees of freedom (i.e., articular joints that allow a great variety of movement). Any attempt to identify the major concepts and constructs in the field must consider the body segment parameters before the more classical mechanical concepts.

Body Parameters

Measuring human motion requires known parameters of lengths, masses, centers of mass, and moments of inertia of the body segments. Such knowledge is essential in most calculations involving either the kinematics or kinetics of human movement (these terms are defined in the next two sections).

Summary of Body Segment Parameters

Center of mass of the segments or body

Moment of inertia of the segments or body

Segmental mass and length

Anatomical joint centers

Segmental volume and density

Cadaver studies have provided most of these parameters. Unfortunately, the limited number of these studies means that they have not been representative of the average adult population with respect to age, height, weight, sex, and race.

Linear and Angular Kinematics

Kinematics is the branch of dynamics that deals with displacement, velocity, and acceleration without reference to the forces responsible for the motion. Teachers and coaches frequently describe locomotor activities (e.g., running, skating, cycling, cross-country skiing) and jumping activities (e.g., the long and high jumps) with a vocabulary made up of kinematic concepts.

Summary of Kinematic Parameters

Position

Linear and angular displacement

Linear and angular velocity

Linear and angular acceleration

Linear and Angular Kinetics

Kinetics is the branch of dynamics concerned with the forces initiating and altering motion. Forces can be internal and external. The internal forces in biomechanics come mainly from muscles and ligaments. Ground reaction forces, active bodies (e.g., a hockey defenseman), and passive bodies (e.g., wind resistance) are examples of external forces. The present and future of biomechanics depend on kinetic analysis, because it permits a deeper understanding of how and why an event takes place. The biomechanic literature frequently refers to kinetic factors when discussing activities based on either locomotor skills or jumping skills.

Summary of Kinetic Parameters

Force

Impulse (linear and angular)

Work

Power

Momentum (linear and angular)

Pressure

Mechanical energy

Mechanical efficiency

Torque or moment of force

Neuromuscular Parameters

Some elements involved in human kinetics are not easily observable. A significant portion occurs beneath the skin. Because muscles are effector organs of the nervous system, biomechanists often make reference to neuronal activity when describing and explaining the mechanical phenomena that are their principal focus. The parameters relevant at this level have to do with the timing and coordination of muscular activity. Many biomechanic articles use these concepts abundantly.

Summary of Neuromuscular Parameters

Temporal and sequential order of muscular activity

Reaction time

Premotor and motor time

Rate of tension development

Methods and Technologies in Biomechanics

Because biomechanics studies movement from the standpoint of mechanics, it must be able to measure and record that movement. The techniques commonly used allow the researcher to record a subject's (athlete or nonathlete) performance at the time of execution.

The techniques of investigation fall into three groups:

- techniques used to measure kinematic parameters,
- techniques used to record dynamic factors, and finally,
- instrumentation to analyze neuromuscular parameters.

Kinematic Measurement

Biomechanists frequently assess a subject's joint displacement or position during the execution of different skills. The following paragraphs describe some of the devices to record human movement necessary for such assessment.

Cinematography.   This method, which uses motion pictures to record human movement, has been the most popular choice over the years. Because there are high-speed films and analyzing equipment for this category, the commonly used 16-mm film provides a more accurate means of analyzing movement than the 8-mm or even Super-8 films. After the action is filmed, factors such as time, displacement, velocity, acceleration, and so on can be derived from data reduction techniques and digitization.

Optoelectric Systems.   In this system, light emitting diodes (LEDs) are placed on different body landmarks (joints, for instance) and one or more remote receivers (cameras) connected to a microprocessing system monitors the displacement of the segments of the body. A computer system is used for data processing.

Accelerometers.   These devices are used mainly in impact activities. They are inserted in protective equipment or sport implements (e.g., golf clubs or tennis racquets). Accelerometers consist of a mass suspended in a spring-damper system; the displacement of mass is sensed by an electronic system that produces an output proportional to the acceleration.

Electrogoniometers.   These devices are used to measure angular motion at the joints. They are made up of arms that are strapped to the subject's limbs and move with them. A potentiometer placed at the junction of the two arms of the electrogoniometer and positioned over the joint records the displacement of the joint; the output from the potentiometer is amplified and recorded or digitized and stored in a computer. Such a continuous record of angular position versus time provides important information about the characteristics of the joint being investigated.

Dynamic Measurement

Running, jumping, and hitting or throwing a ball all require forces to be exerted either in the body or on manipulated objects. The following devices measure such forces.

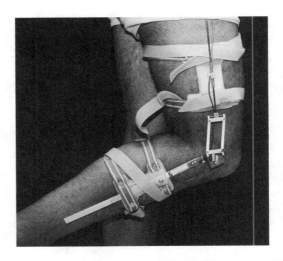

Figure 8.1   Electrogoniometer mounted for monitoring the knee joint movement.

Force Platforms.   These instruments measure forces exerted by the athlete's feet in the three components of movement and provide data to determine the instantaneous point of force application as well as the moment about a vertical axis. Transducers used in force platforms are strain gauges or piezoelectric quartzes, which convert a mechanical force into an electrical signal. An amplifier increases the magnitude of the signal, and appropriate processing is usually made with a reasonably efficient computer.

Figure 8.2   Force plate with the transducers system.

Neuromuscular Measurement

The muscles are the main sources of forces acting on the joints. By recording the electrical potential of the muscles the specialist in biomechanics can estimate the contribution of the different muscle groups to movement.

The electromyogram (EMG) gives information about the electrical signal associated with a muscular contraction. Electrodes placed over the skin (surface) or intramuscularly (indwelling) detect the average activity of a muscle. Once amplified, the signal is processed and can eventually be compared to other physiological or biomechanical signals.

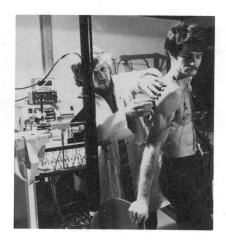

Figure 8.3 Example of surface electrodes for an EMG study.

Whatever the technique of investigation used, however, a good computing system is necessary to ensure rapid processing of information and precise and accurate analysis of the results.

Electromyography is helpful in analyzing the contributions of specific muscle groups to the performance of specific skills.

Major Research Questions

Biomechanics is diversified and covers a wide spectrum of interests, but the major research questions are of an applied nature. Methods and technologies currently used in biomechanics have been used to solve problems inherent to the human being, human activities, and human environments.

One of the most fundamental areas of research is muscle mechanics and its influence on motor performance. Occupational biomechanics covers the interaction of people and their working environments. Orthopedic biomechanics attempts to solve problems related to the behavior of bone and soft tissues (especially ligaments) under normal and clinical (pathologic) conditions. Rehabilitation biomechanics involves using the characteristic approach of the field to facilitate the reintegration to normal life of patients affected with a variety of locomotor and postural deficits. In a similar vein, gait analysis of individuals with and without prostheses also uses the biomechanical approach to solve problems related to locomotion. Finally, sport biomechanics has greatly enhanced our understanding of sport techniques.

What about the future? Modeling and optimization techniques are already flooding the literature and appear to loom large in the years ahead. Whether applied to sport biomechanics (Remizov, 1984), muscle mechanics (Herzog, 1987), or tissue mechanics (Panagiotacopulos, Pope, & Krag, 1987), optimization techniques and mathematical modeling will be used more and more to predict the outcome of athletic performance.

Learned Societies

Biomechanists have formed several associations or societies on both the international and national level. The International Society of Biomechanics (ISB) covers a wide spectrum of interest such as occupational biomechanics, orthopedic biomechanics, biomechanics of sports, and muscle mechanics. The International Society of Biomechanics in Sports (ISBS) is the only international association dedicated exclusively to sport biomechanics. Its objective is to stimulate applied sport biomechanics research.

Individual countries have their own national organizations and associations. In North America, the Canadian Society of Biomechanics (CSB) gathers specialists from across Canada and the Ameri-

HIGHLIGHT
Comparison of Two Techniques of Long Jumping

Whenever a human body becomes airborne its angular momentum may be considered constant. During the flight phase of certain sports, for example the long jump, the athlete performs rotational movements of the segments such that the trunk remains nearly upright. Herzog (1986) investigated the contributions of the various segments to proper body orientation during the flight phase of the long jump. Long jumpers were filmed while executing the "sail" jump and the "2-1/2 hitch-kick technique." Herzog then used mathematical functions to compute the whole body angular momentum about a transverse axis through the center of mass and individual segments' angular momentums about the center of mass.

The results showed that both techniques generate positive angular momentum of the whole body; that is, the body rotates forward during the flight phase. The sail jump had an angular momentum of 4.17 kgm^2/sec; the 2-1/2 hitch-kick, 11.05 kgm^2/sec. In the sail technique, the arms took twice as much angular momentum as the legs; in the other technique, the angular momentum was equally distributed between arms and legs. Herzog recommended that long jumpers generally should attempt to maximize the angular momentum of the legs, especially in the backward swing, but minimize it in the forward swing if forward rotation of the head-and-trunk segment is a problem. He also expressed the belief that the total angular momentum imparted at takeoff for the sail and hitch-kick jumps can be taken up more successfully if the arm and leg movements are executed optimally.

can Society of Biomechanics (ASB) does the same in the United States. The membership of these various societies includes biologists, engineers, ergonomists, health scientists, and physical activity specialists.

Journals and Other Publications

Proceedings such as those published by the ISB and ISBS summarize the papers presented during the scientific meetings of the sponsoring international organizations. In addition to proceedings, numerous journals and periodicals are designed to stimulate and communicate scholarly research and inquiry in the field of biomechanics. The *Journal of Biomechanics* publishes original research concerning the application of mechanics to biological problems. The papers published in this journal cover a wide spectrum, such as the dynamics of the musculoskeletal system, orthopedic biomechanics, biomechanics of human injuries, sport biomechanics, and so on. The *International Journal of Sports*

Biomechanics publishes research exclusively in the field of sport biomechanics; the research topics deal with internal and external forces affecting human movement and observed in sport activities.

Other periodicals, such as the *Canadian Journal of Sport Sciences, Medicine and Science in Sports and Exercise, Research Quarterly for Exercise and Sport*, and a few others, regularly publish articles pertaining to the topic of biomechanics.

Undergraduate and Graduate Education

Most undergraduate programs in physical activity sciences across Canada and the United States offer at least one course covering the field of biomechanics. Their content continually improves as the field advances. Over the last decade the growth of biomechanics graduate programs in a number of universities has opened new perspectives in the pursuit of excellence in that area.

Career Opportunities

A good undergraduate background in biomechanics is essential for those students interested in teaching or coaching. Physical education teachers, coaches in amateur sports, and technical directors or consultants in government agencies all need the capacity to understand and analyze human movement that a sound background in biomechanics provides. Those who are interested in advanced studies in biomechanics may eventually want to expand the frontiers of knowledge through research and teaching in an academic environment. Others may apply their knowledge of biomechanics in orthopedic clinics, occupational and rehabilitation therapy, or in the design of protective sport equipment.

Summary

Biomechanics studies the internal and external forces acting on a human body and their effects. It applies to all human movement, for example, sport, dance, or locomotion.

To evaluate human movement, the biomechanist treats the body as a system of segments and measures both their kinematic (excluding causes) parameters and their kinetic (including causes) parameters. A variety of sophisticated equipment is used, much of it electronic. Good computing systems are necessary, and computer modeling will probably play an important role in the future.

Much of biomechanics involves optimization of movement under both normal and pathologic conditions. An example of the former is the study of long-jump techniques.

Learned societies and publications in this field are readily available, both national and international, as are undergraduate and graduate programs. Career opportunities range from coaching to design of protective equipment to academic research.

References and Further Readings

Dainty, D.A., & Norman, R.W. (Eds.) (1987). *Standardizing biomechanical testing in sport*. Champaign, IL: Human Kinetics.

Hatze, H. (1974). The meaning of the term "biomechanics." *Journal of Biomechanics*, **7**, 189-190.

Hay, J.G. (1985). *The biomechanics of sports techniques*. Englewood Cliffs, NJ: Prentice Hall.

Herzog, W. (1986). Maintenance of body orientation in the flight phase of long jumping. *Medicine and Science in Sports and Exercise*, **18**, 231-241.

Herzog, W. (1987). Determination of muscle model parameters using an optimization technique. In B. Jansson (Ed.), *Biomechanics X-B* (pp. 1175-1179). Champaign, IL: Human Kinetics.

Kreighbaum, E., & Barthels, K.M. (1985). *Biomechanics*. New York: Macmillan.

Miller, D.I., & Nelson, R.C. (1973). *Biomechanics of sport*. Philadelphia: Lea and Febiger.

Panagiotacopulos, N.D., Pope, M.C., & Krag, M.H. (1987). Mechanical model for the human intervertebral disk. *Journal of Biomechanics*, **20**, 839-850.

Remizov, L.R. (1984). Biomechanics of optimal flight in ski jumping. *Journal of Biomechanics*, **17**, 167-171.

Winter, D.A. (1979). *Biomechanics of human movement*. New York: Wiley.

Chapter 9

Motor Control, Motor Learning, and Physical Activity

Ian M. Franks
David Goodman

The field of study known as motor control is concerned primarily with explaining the underlying mechanisms that lead to human motor action. Although the phrase *motor action* may seem redundant—for all human action, at least in part, is necessarily motoric—the concern here is more narrowly with purposeful, or wilful, action and excludes involuntary or reflex action. Thus, relevant research may examine how we purposefully move the arm, hand, and fingers in a very precise and controlled manner to scratch the head. Why was that particular plan of action carried out when the arm, hand, and fingers could have made almost any kind of movement? Indeed such a scratching movement may look very skillful to an engineer designing a robot to accomplish the same task.

The field of motor learning, on the other hand, studies the learning and control processes, as well as the learning variables, that lead to skillful performance. We adopt Guthrie's (1952) definition of skill as "an ability to bring about some end result with maximum certainty and minimum amount of energy" (p. 136). Thus, the ties between the two fields of study are many, and indeed, the areas are often seen as one.

• • •

The subject matter in the field of motor control emphasizes the mechanisms that lead to human motor action; the subject matter of the field of motor learning encompasses the variables that enhance motor action.

• • •

In this chapter we discuss the study of motor learning and control from a primarily behavioral perspective because the majority of the research has focused on motoric behavior that can be observed directly. Nevertheless, the relevant problems have been investigated at many levels—from cellular to behavioral—with different methodologies, and the last few years have seen increased investigation of these issues in

- neurophysiology,
- experimental psychology,
- physiology,
- cognitive science, and
- biophysics.

Life provides an immense diversity of phenomena through which scientists from different disciplines have approached the problem of how we organize, learn, and control skilled movement. Scientists have examined a wide range of skills and performers, from a concert pianist, an expert typist, and an Olympic gymnast demonstrating their masteries, to a paraplegic learning to move, a child learning to ride a bike, and a cockroach walking. Speech itself has also received consider-

This skilled performance is one of the types of behavior studied by scientists.

able attention, for it is an amazingly complex skill at which almost all of us have some degree of success.

Major Concepts

Researchers in the behavioral sciences study motor learning and control through two somewhat differing approaches. The dominant approach taken by physical educators, kinesiologists, and experimental psychologists in examining skilled action has been what is termed an **information-processing approach**, which views humans as information-processing component systems. Over the last 10 years, however, an alternate viewpoint has emerged, based primarily on the work of the Russian physiologist Nicholia Bernstein; this we term the **hierarchical approach**.

The Information-Processing Approach

The language of information processing, which has been influenced by computer models and the mathematics of control theory (Shannon & Weaver, 1949), can provide a common analytic framework for both psychology and physiology. This approach has enabled scientists to identify, isolate, and explain elementary mental processes.

The majority of all research ever conducted in the field of motor learning and control has assumed the human operator to be a component system that processes stimulus information gained from the environment. This standard approach is illustrated in Figure 9.1, which shows stimulus information passing through a series of discrete mechanisms. Meaning is extracted from the sensory stimuli at perception, and decisions are made about the appropriateness of the selected response before action takes place. Feedback, which arises from both internal and external sources, informs the system about the previous action.

Implicit within such an approach is the assumption that mental processes take time and that different component processes can take different amounts of time. Consequently, the most common dependent variable used to infer the time course of mental processes is reaction time. Figure 9.2 (see p. 74) depicts reaction time as the period between the onset of the imperative stimulus to the onset of the observed response, with this overall time divided into premotor time (central cognitive processing) and motor time (mechanical processes associated with activity in the muscles, tendons, etc.). The general methodology requires the subject to respond as quickly as possible to the onset of a stimulus, which is usually preceded by a warning signal. Variations in the stimulus display and the required movements provide the independent variables; changes in reaction time are then assumed to reflect a change in the information-processing requirements associated with these manipulated variables.

In 1868 F.C. Donders (1969) undertook one of the earliest attempts at measuring human response to stimuli. He developed a subtractive method for measuring how much time subjects take to identify a stimulus and respond to it. The basic idea is to divide reaction time into a series of additive stages

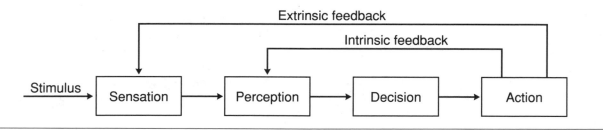

Figure 9.1 A model of human information processing. *Note.* Adapted from Whiting (1975).

HIGHLIGHT
Relative Timing Properties

A study typical of those designed to investigate the hypothesis that subjects learn the relative timing properties of a movement was recently undertaken by Franks and Stanley (in press). In this study they used a pursuit tracking task. Their subjects were asked to keep a response cursor (dot on an oscilloscope screen) aligned with a computer-generated stimulus cursor. The stimulus was programmed to move back and forth across the screen in a complex but periodic pattern that repeated every 2.5 sec. The subjects used a joystick to control the movements of the response cursor and were informed of their integrated error score at the end of each 2-min trial. This task is similar to many video arcade games. After many hours of practice the subjects were transferred to a different task in which they were asked to reproduce the complex waveform they had learned previously. This transfer task was essentially the same as the pursuit tracking task with the exception that the stimulus and response information were both removed from the oscilloscope screen (this has been called input blanking). One further modification was that the subjects were required to produce the entire movement at varying overall speeds, either faster or slower than their original learning speed. What temporal properties of the movement had been learned over the 15 days of practice at tracking 5740 cycles of this periodic complex stimulus waveform? In order to answer this question, the response waveform was analyzed, first in terms of the overall time to complete one cycle of this complex pattern (period of the waveform), and then in terms of the relative time between each response element within the pattern. A reversal in movement direction constituted a response element (seven response elements were present in one cycle of this particular stimulus waveform), and the times between these reversals were used in the analysis. The results of this study showed that, given sufficient practice, subjects will maintain the relative timing characteristics of the movement (relative time between response elements), despite variations in the overall time to complete the movement.

and develop tasks that either include or exclude one or more of these stages.

In this scheme, Task A is a simple reaction-time task requiring one stimulus and one response; thus, the only stages involved in this task are stimulus determination (is there a stimulus present?) and response programming (plan and execute the response).

Task B is a choice reaction-time task that requires not only stimulus determination and response programming but also stimulus discrimination (which stimulus should I respond to?) and response selection (match the appropriate response with the correctly identified stimulus). Finally, Task C is designed to represent the time taken for the stimulus discrimination process in addition to those processes required in Task A. Thus, subtracting Task C's reaction time from Task B's yields the response selection time. Similarly, subtracting reaction times in Task A from those in Task C yields stimulus discrimination time.

Donders's Subtractive Method

Task A: RT = Stimulus determination + Response programming

Task B: RT = Stimulus determination + Discrimination + Response selection + Response programming

Task C: RT = Stimulus determination + Stimulus discrimination + Response programming

Stimulus discrimination time = Task C − Task A

Response selection time = Task B − Task C

The notion that mental processes take time and that these processes can be isolated and measured captured the attention of many behavioral scientists and led to a number of important findings in the

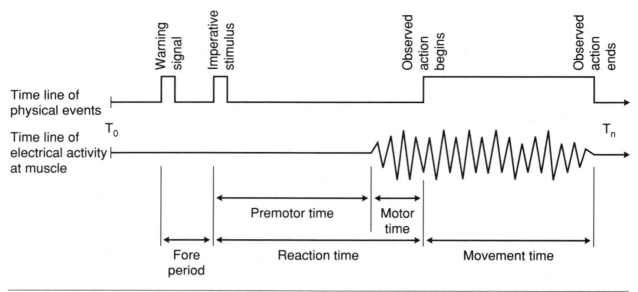

Figure 9.2 A schematic representation of the reaction time paradigm. *Note.* Adapted from Schmidt (1988) by permission.

motor domain. For instance, Merkel (1885) and later Hick (1952) and Hyman (1953) discovered a relationship between the time it takes to react to a signal (stimulus) and the number of possible signals that can occur: The more uncertain the environment, the longer it takes for an individual to make decisions about action. This is now known as Hick's Law.

Although this conceptualization of information processing has led to a wealth of information (see Schmidt, 1988, chaps. 4 and 5), it clearly oversimplifies the process of perceiving and acting. The assumption of serial processing fundamental to Donders's original studies has tended to polarize the way in which researchers have viewed human information processing (active vs. passive receiver of information). In particular, the model in Figure 9.1 describes the human as a serial processor wherein certain processes must be completed before others can begin.

The Hierarchical-Processing Approach

The hierarchical-processing approach provides an alternative to the traditional information-processing view. This approach is based largely on notions contained in papers of Nicholia Bernstein produced in the 1920s and 1930s; their translation into English in 1968 (1967 original) is generally acknowledged as the major influence in the development of this viewpoint. According to Bernstein,

a viable account of action must recognize the interaction of both muscular and nonmuscular forces. Thus, although muscles (or more properly, motor units) contract when stimulated, the system by which we act (or move) is not controlled simply by these neural commands (efference, or outflow). There is no simple one-to-one relationship between neural commands and movement outcome; rather, adjustments are made continually in the whole of the neuro-anatomical pathways. Motor control can therefore best be viewed as a system of mechanisms that interact with each other to ensure maximum flexibility in action.

Bernstein raised a number of issues with respect to the production of coordinated action. Perhaps the major one may be identified as the *degrees of freedom* problem. In producing action, a host of subunits must be controlled. If each motor unit that must contract to produce a movement is considered a single degree of freedom, the total number would be in the thousands. Individually controlling each of these elements, or degrees of freedom, would present a difficult (if not impossible) task.

Awareness of this problem led Bernstein (1967) to define the coordination of movement as "the process of mastering redundant degrees of freedom of the moving organ, in other words, its conversion to a controllable system" (p. 127). Furthermore, the Soviet school associated with Bernstein claimed that individual variables (motor subunits) are partitioned into collectives or synergies wherein the variables change both interdependently and autonomously. Handwriting provides an excellent example of this collective modification, because the movement apparatus (arm, wrist, and fingers) changes as a unit to accommodate the writing of both large or small letters. Indeed, there is an obvious appeal in this notion, and the concept of synergistic control was not new even in 1920, as indicated by the following remark by Ferrier (1886): "Every form of active muscular exertion necessitates the simultaneous cooperation of an immense assemblage of synergic movements throughout the body to secure steadiness and maintain the general equilibrium."

Thus, the cooperation of joints and muscles in a closely knit group, which we term a functional synergy, can considerably reduce the degrees of freedom of a movement. Kelso, Southard, and Goodman (1979) explored the functional synergy employed in two-handed movements. They showed the two arms to exhibit a tight relationship in movement evident in tasks requiring the hands to move to targets placed at differing distances, even when one hand had to traverse a hurdle while the other did not. The limbs apparently function as a single synergistic unit within which the component elements vary in a related manner. This view of synergies thus provides a notion of muscle groups as functional groupings of muscles, often spanning several joints, that are constrained to act as a single unit (Kelso, 1982).

The recent introduction of automobiles with both front- and rear-wheel steering offers a convenient example. Controlling the vehicle by independently steering each of the four wheels would present at best a difficult task. Consequently, engineers initially designed automobiles that had movable front wheels and fixed rear wheels. In addition, a mechanical linkage (a constraint) was established between the two front wheels so that they turned at the same time in the same direction. Some recent models also allow rear-wheel steering, but again, there is a mechanical constraint; in this case, the rear wheels turn in a fixed, though opposite, relationship to the front wheels. Control is still through a single steering wheel, and the operator need not worry about controlling the individual elements.

This hierarchical viewpoint assumes that functional linkages can operate as autonomous units. An executive subsystem uses combinations of movements constrained by these lower-level organizations. The result is a smaller number of independently controllable degrees of freedom and, ultimately, a controllable system.

Major Research Questions

Motor Control

Neither the simple information-processing model nor the hierarchical approach captures the true integrative nature of movement organization and execution. Rather, the *preparation*, *planning*, and *control* of human movement occurs in a dynamic system *interacting with the environment*. The description of such a system should be made with respect to the task in question because the interaction of the task and the environment is the critical determinant of skillful behavior.

With this in mind, we propose a model of human action that emphasizes the human need to control and operate in a changing environment (see Figure 9.3). This control is distributed rather than localized (see Pew, 1974), which allows the adoption of control strategies according to the elements of the task environment.

Environmental stimuli impinge on the senses via several possible input channels. The integration (Σ_1) of the senses occurs only after the system has been oriented toward the perception of information; that is, the system can prepare itself to receive information. Indeed, in some instances the perception of incoming information has been considerably influenced, not only by the memory of prior experience but also by concurrent perceptual activities. The main point we wish to stress here is the extremely close relationship between perception and action; in fact, many psychologists consider perceiving itself to be an action (for several excellent papers supporting this viewpoint see Shaw & Bransford, 1977).

Depending on the requirements of the task and the intentions of the subject, further cognitive processing of the environmental stimuli may be required. These processes can be conceived as being distributed throughout the system and having the potential of operating in parallel (Rumelhart & McClelland, 1986). Such task-dependent processes may involve the activation and suppression of responses in addition to the generalization and translation of codes of action. Memory and attention provide a general framework within which these processes operate.

Volitional action—movement—is initiated at the motor cortex and is the eventual result of an organized pattern of neural activity. Information about the state of the system is fed back to various summing points at several stages along the processing path, a typical feature of nested control systems.

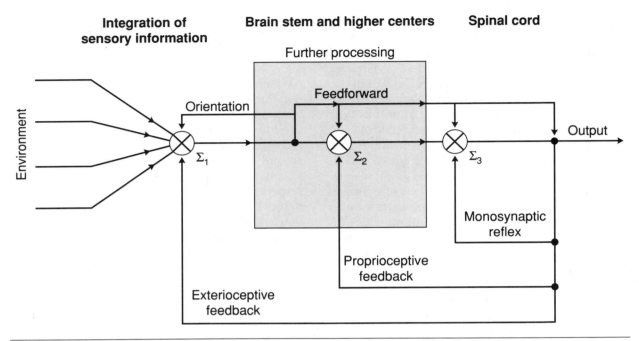

Figure 9.3   A model of human action.

Control is distributed across various levels and not necessarily through some hierarchical structure governed by a single executive controller. For instance, experiments using midbrain preparations in cats (Shik, Orlovskii, & Severin, 1968) or spinal preparation of frogs (Fukson, Berkinblit, & Feldman, 1980) have shown peripheral processing of information to be relatively intelligent. In our model, Σ_2 represents the summing point in higher centers, where meaning is given to information that is fed back, whereas Σ_3 represents the summing point at the spinal cord level. These summing points are meant only to illustrate a network of such points and do not necessarily have physiological correlates.

Another unique feature of this model is feedforward. The system must have some way to prepare itself for action and inform the various levels of control what action is likely to occur. Recently, a number of investigators have focused on the concept of preparation for action. Adapting the reaction-time paradigm, now referred to as the *precueing* paradigm, has provided some insight into advance planning for movement.

Partial information of an upcoming movement is presented to the subject by means of a precue, but subjects can determine the exact movement to make only on presentation of the imperative stimulus. Therefore, manipulating the information provided in the precue lets us examine the extent to which this information is used in the planning

and preparation for upcoming movement. There are now some preliminary data (Goodman & Datar, 1986) showing that, under certain circumstances, people can selectively prepare for movements at the spinal level—as if they potentiate certain neural pathways so that the impulse to move is acted on with expedience.

The phenomena of feedforward and preparation for action have obvious benefits. For instance, it has been shown that postural accommodation takes place approximately 60 ms prior to intended action. Rapid adjustments in movement also rely on a feedforward system; these corrections to minor perturbations can best be achieved if the intended movements are compared to actual movements during execution, and not after. For example, running over a bumpy field requires far more adjustments than the higher centers can process in the time allotted. Our view postulates that integrators (summing points) bring together information not only about the present state of the processor and the actions that have taken place but also about actions that are to occur in the future. This would explain the capacity that humans have for very fast corrective action.

Motor Learning

Schmidt (1988) provides one of the best definitions of motor learning: "A set of processes associated with practice or experience leading to relatively permanent changes in skilled behavior" (p. 438). This definition clearly implies learning to be an active process that produces consistent skilled performance.

A fundamental question that has yet to be answered concerns what is learned, and how this learning takes place. Early behaviorists struggled with this problem with little success. Karl Lashley spent 30 years searching for the site and substance of memory. He trained experimental rats to negotiate mazes and then removed portions of their brains in an attempt to remove the storage location of what they had learned. Although the overall performance of the rats was retarded, this procedure did not eradicate the learned movements. Lashley, along with his student Karl Pribram, concluded that memory for learned action is not stored in any single part of the brain but rather is distributed throughout it.

Pribram (1969) further hypothesized about the nature of the learned memory trace, stating that "the brain may exploit, among other things, the most sophisticated principle of information storage yet known: the principle of the hologram" (p. 309). Pribram considered the hologram to be an appropriate model for how the brain might store learned memories because the code of these memories is in the form of interactions that interpret frequencies and store images of the world and of the individual's own thoughts and actions. In a hologram, light waves are encoded and the resulting image that is projected then decodes the image. This may be a good analogy for how the brain decodes its stored memories. One other similarity between brain processes and the hologram is their efficiency. Like the human brain, the holographic plate can store billions of bits of information, an essential ingredient for any model of human motor learning. Finally, the holographic analogy serves not only to guide neurophysiological studies of brain processes but also to explain the mechanisms involved in formulating and developing such abstract entities as the "motor image" (a "picture" of the movement) and the "motor schema" ("rules" for the movement). It does this because the notion underlying Pribram's model—that learned experiences are distributed throughout the system—fits with our model of human action, which implies that the representation of a skilled performance probably does not reside in any one memory location.

Several studies (e.g., Franks & Wilberg, 1982; Marteniuk & Romanow, 1983) have shown that the process of learning and performing a skilled action is more constructive than reproductive. First, the system generates a movement pattern that captures the general properties of the required task. This pattern is somewhat "blurred" in that the specific details are not defined within the movement. Moreover, Franks and Wilberg (1982) showed that errors are distributed equally throughout the movement, almost as if the performer is giving an overall close approximation of the task. This generated output is then modulated by the performer using the available control systems (e.g., vision, balance, or hearing). The skilled performer has an overall mastery of the whole and on this basis constructs the details. Only after long periods of practice does the holistic motor image acquire more detail and hence reduce the system's reliance on the control process. The final result is that the performer need pay less attention to the task, thus allowing planning and anticipation of the next action.

Although the similarity is not immediately obvious, this emerging concept of how the system learns is not unlike the ideas and theories put forward by Bartlett (1932) and Schmidt (1975) regarding the motor schema. The basic premise of Schmidt's motor schema theory is that with practice people develop abstract rules (schemata) about their own behaviors. These rules are relationships between all the past actions the person has produced and the values that were used to produce those actions. The memory of these *relationships* is the key to skillful performance, not the memory for any one particular movement. What is learned, therefore, is presumably not a specific movement but the capacity to produce any one of a variety of movements that satisfy a particular relationship. This is similar to Barlett's (1932) earlier viewpoint that "together with the immediately preceding incoming impulse, [the motor schema] renders a specific adaptive reaction possible. It is, therefore, producing an orientation of the organism towards whatever it is directed to at that moment" (p. 207).

The learning of movements obviously has a direct relationship to how we orient ourselves to the environment. This orientation process (see Figure 9.3) forms a unique bond between the task environment and the human operator. The nature of this union is continually changing, and it is through this change that learning is indirectly observed.

In a discussion on the nature of learning and perception, Gibson (1966) considered the question of *what is learned*. He stated that "an observer learns with practice to isolate more subtle invariants during transformation and to establish more exactly the permanent features of an array" (p. 265). In perception, therefore, humans learn to detect invariants. In motor learning, subjects may also learn to detect the invariants of the skill they are performing. An example of such an invariant is the relative timing of response elements within a complex motor act. In order to maintain the topology (general shape) of such a movement, one must maintain its relative timing. One can, however, vary the absolute timing, while still maintaining this topology.

Bernstein, in reference to topology, has pointed out that "a function is well organized if its arguments can be separated into: 1) essential variables; and 2) non-essential variables" (1968, p. 177). Essential variables are those that preserve the topological properties of movement; these would parallel Gibson's invariants. Nonessential variables are scalar changes, for example, the overall rate or speed of a movement. Thus, in the learning of movement, *what is learned* is the essential variables (or invariants), in other words, those variables that are responsible for preserving the topology of movement.

For several years there has been evidence that the relative timing of the components of a given skilled movement remain invariant over changes in the overall duration of that movement. Original evidence for this came from some unpublished studies by Armstrong (1970, cited in Schmidt, 1988). He had his subjects repeatedly move a lever through a particular unidimensional spatial-temporal pattern. When subjects moved too quickly they nevertheless maintained invariant relative timing of the response elements within the movement. It has been proposed that this occurred because relative timing is structured into the motor program that controls the movement, whereas the overall duration is a parameter whose value can vary across instances of the movement. Thus, for each instance of the skill, a different parameter value for overall duration is assigned to the motor program. Relative timing properties were explained in this chapter's highlight.

The question of "What is learned?" when human subjects practice a continuous movement sequence appears to have at least one answer—the relative temporal properties of the response elements that make up the movement. The essence of learning (and even of life itself) may be pulling invariance (or order) out of apparent chaos. Schrodinger (1944) has argued that this is the essence of all living systems. Many of our explanations in motor control and learning have to do with the interplay of variance (entropy) and invariance (order). For example, from an information-processing viewpoint, Schmidt's (1975) Schema Theory of Motor Learning explains learning in terms of finding invariance and developing an equation that expresses what is variable and what is not variable. From an alternative perspective (hierarchical-processing approach), these action theorists postulate an equation of constraint, which also defines what is invariant and what is variable. Therefore, both viewpoints appear to converge on this issue. Two simultaneous processes are occurring, and motor learning is based on establishing an organization in which certain relationships become invariant, while others are left free to vary.

Learned Societies and Journals

The past 20 years or so have seen a major change in the nature and scope of associations and societies concerned with motor learning and control, and this is also reflected in the types of journals publishing research in the area. Although a number of national and international societies and associations now include specific sections on motor control and learning, there are two major associations in North America that have played a pivotal role. The North American Society for the Psychology of Sport and Physical Activity hosts an annual conference, the major portion of which is devoted to reports of research in motor control and learning. The Canadian Society for Psychomotor Learning and Sport Psychology is the principle academic association for those in Canada who undertake research in these fields. Both societies are open to student and professional members, and both publish bulletins as well as proceedings of their annual conferences. Scientists from various disciplines with research interests in motor control and learning have also had their work presented at international conferences such as those of the Psychonomic Society, Neurosciences, Physiological Society, American College of Sports Medicine, and the American and Canadian Alliance of Health, Physical Education and Recreation. Indeed, this underscores how scientists from a number of different areas have recently developed a keen interest in motor control and learning.

The amount of literature on the subject also attests to this interest. Although there are a number of texts written specifically for courses in the areas, two have emerged as the most prominent: *Motor Control and Learning: A Behavioral Emphasis* by R.A. Schmidt is now in its second edition, whereas *Motor Learning: Concepts and Applications* by R.A. Magill is in its third. We ourselves have developed computer software to simulate many of the classical research findings discussed in these two texts.

The first journal developed entirely for the area of motor learning and control began publication in 1969, the *Journal of Motor Behavior*. Its editorial policy at the time indicated that "the Journal publishes papers which contribute to a basic understanding of human motor behavior, broadly defined. Papers concerned with motor learning and skill performance predominate, but studies of other factors such as kinesthetic perception, fatigue, growth and maturation, and anthropometric variables as they relate to human motor behavior are acceptable." The journal now solicits "papers from various perspectives and differing levels of analysis, including physiological, neurophysiological, biomechanical, developmental, and clinical approaches" for the previously stated policy. This better reflects the changing nature of the field and the scientists from many areas now working in it.

Career Opportunities

Although there are certainly opportunities in scientific research for those trained in motor learning and control, these positions generally require considerable experience and graduate training. Rather than viewing this area as a means to an end or a particular career, we see some knowledge of the area as essential in a number of disciplines. Clearly, anyone involved in the supervision, teaching, or coaching of motor skills or related activities should have a background in the area. Similarly, a knowledge of motor-learning principles, and an understanding of motor control, is a major part of the overall preparation in the fields of ergonomics and human factors.

Summary

In this chapter, we discuss motor learning and control as fields of study in the behavioral and activity sciences and present both the traditional information-processing approach and the hierarchical approach based primarily on the writings of Bernstein. Much of the literature depicts these two views as mutually exclusive, with scientists lining up on one side or the other. We, on the other hand, feel neither view is entirely correct and have attempted a synthesis. Although this section may be somewhat speculative, we feel that these two views may not be all that different and that borrowing concepts from both will lead to a more parsimonious account of motor learning and control.

References and Further Readings

Bartlett, F.C. (1932). *Remembering*. Cambridge: Cambridge University Press.

Bernstein, N. (1968). *The co-ordination and regulation of movements*. Oxford: Pergamon Press. (Original work published 1967)

Donders, F.C. (1969). On the speed of mental processes. In W. Koster (Ed. and Trans.), *Attention and performance* (Vol. 2, pp. 131-139). Amsterdam: North-Holland Press.

Ferrier, D. (1886). *The functions of the brain*. London: Smith, Elder.

Feynman, R. (1965). *The character of physical law*. Cambridge, MA: MIT Press.

Franks, I.M., & Stanley, M.L. (in press). Learning the invariants of a perceptual motor skill. *Canadian Journal of Psychology*.

Franks, I.M., & Wilberg, R.B. (1982). The generation of movement patterns during the acquisition of a pursuit tracking task. *Journal of Human Movement Science*, **1**, 251-272.

Fukson, O.I., Berkinblit, M.B., & Feldman, A.G. (1980). The spinal frog takes into account the scheme of its body during the wiping reflex. *Science*, **209**, 1261-1263.

Gallistel, C.R. (1980). *The organization of action: A new synthesis*. Hillsdale, NJ: Wiley.

Gibson, J.J. (1966). *The senses considered as perceptual systems*. Boston: Houghton Mifflin.

Goodman, D., & Datar, R. (1986). *Planning for movement as accessed by the Hoffman reflex*. Paper presented at North American Society for the Psychology of Sport and Physical Activity, Scottsdale, AZ.

Guthrie, E.R. (1952). *The psychology of learning*. New York: Harper & Row.

Hick, W.E. (1952). On the rate of gain of information. *Quarterly Journal of Experimental Psychology*, **4**, 11-26.

Hyman, R. (1953). Stimulus information as a determinant of reaction time. *Journal of Experimental Psychology*, **45**, 188-196.

Kelso, J.A.S., Southard, D.L., & Goodman, D. (1979). On the nature of human interlimb coordination. *Science*, **203**, 1029-1031.

Kelso, J.A.S. (1982). *Human motor behavior: An introduction*. Hillsdale, NJ: Erlbaum.

Magill, R.A. (1985). *Motor learning: Concepts and applications*. Dubuque, IA: Brown.

Marteniuk, R.G. (1976). *Information processing in motor skills*. New York: Holt, Rinehart & Winston.

Marteniuk, R.G., & Romanow, S.K.E. (1983). Human movement organization and learning as revealed by variability of movement, use of kinematic information, and fourier analysis. In R.A. Magill (Ed.), *Memory and control of action* (pp. 87-117). Amsterdam: North Holland Press.

Merkel, J. (1885). Die Zeithlichen Verhaltnisse der Willensthatigkeit. *Phisophische Studien*, **2**, 73-127. Cited in R.S. Woodworth (1938), *Experimental psychology*. New York: Holt, Rinehart & Winston.

Pew, R. (1974). A distributed processing view of human motor control. In W. Prinz & A.F. Sanders (Eds.), *Cognition and motor processes*. Berlin: Springer-Verlag.

Pribram, K.H. (1969). The neurophysiology of remembering. In R.F. Thompson (Ed.), *Readings from Scientific American: Progress in psychobiology*. San Francisco: W.H. Freeman.

Rumelhart, D.E., & McClelland, J.L. (1986). *Parallel distributed processing: Explorations in the microstructure of cognition: Vol. 1. Foundations*. Cambridge, MA: MIT Press.

Schmidt, R.A. (1975). A schema theory of discrete motor skill learning. *Psychological Review*, **82**, 225-260.

Schmidt, R.A. (1988). *Motor control and learning: A behavioral emphasis* (2nd ed.). Champaign, IL: Human Kinetics.

Shannon, C.E., & Weaver, W. (1949). *The mathematical theory of communication*. Champaign, IL: University of Illinois Press.

Shik, M.L., Orlovskii, G.N., & Severin, F.V. (1968). Locomotion of the mesencephalio cat elicited by stimulation of the pyramids. *Biofizika*, **13**, 143-152.

Shaw, R., & Bransford, J. (1977). *Perceiving, acting and knowing*. Hillsdale, NJ: Erlbaum.

Schrodinger, E. (1944). *What is life? Physical aspects of the living cell*. New York: Cambridge University Press.

Whiting, H.T.A. (Ed.) (1975). *Readings in human performance*. London: Lepus Books.

Section 2

Social Science Perspectives

This section focuses on the various social science subfields of the physical activity sciences. Chapters 10 through 15 discuss psychology, sociology, anthropology, history, pedagogy, and philosophy.

Chapter 10

Psychology and Physical Activity

Albert V. Carron

It is said that someone once asked a spider how she was able to coordinate the simultaneous activity of her four pairs of legs. The spider stopped, thought about the question, and found that she didn't know how to explain it—walking was something that just seemed to happen. When she tried to resume her journey, however, she could not move. The heightened awareness of her own complexity caused her legs to tie themselves up in knots . . . and so, she died.

In defining the area commonly referred to as *sport psychology* we face a similar problem—we do not literally knot up and die, but we do have some difficulty proceeding. The difficulty arises for a number of reasons, all of which are related to the breadth and complexity of the field. For example, should the term *sport* include exercise, dance, play, and unorganized games? As another example, should sport psychology be separated conceptually from such topics as motor learning, motor control, or motor development, or can the term be used as an umbrella to represent all of these fields of research? Finally, should sport psychology be viewed as a sport science in physical education and kinesiology; as an area of professional activity in sport involved with counseling, education, and intervention; as a specialized area of science within general psychology; or as a specific type of clinical psychology? Unfortunately, the answer to all of these questions is "possibly."

Major Concepts and Research Questions

There are no easy answers to the field's questions of identity, thus the psychology of sport and physical activity has been defined by eminent sport psychologists in a variety of ways.

Definitions of Sport Psychology

"The study of the psychologic foundations of physical activity" (Morgan, 1972, p. 193).

"The science of psychology applied to athletes and athletic situations" (Singer, 1978, p. 3).

"A new field of sport science . . . concerned with both the psychological factors that influence participation in sport and exercise and the psychological effects derived from that participation" (Williams & Straub, 1986, p. 1).

Other eminent sport psychologists—those either dissatisfied with the proposed definitions or impatient with the idea of establishing boundaries around a young, emerging field—have argued that constructing an all-encompassing definition should be given low priority. This position is summarized succinctly by Rushall (1973) and Martens (1980):

- "The subject matter specialization remains to be judged by what it does" (Rushall, p. 1).
- "I do hope that we do not spend too much time trying to define the field from the podium. Instead, I hope we spend our time doing research and letting the research define the parameters of sport psychology. We are in our infancy. I am satisfied to operationally define sport psychology as what sport psychologists do" (Martens, p. 20).

If we define the psychology of sport and physical activity by what people do, two areas of emphasis must be included, sport science and professional application, both of which are undertaken in physical education/kinesiology and psychology departments. Thus, the psychology of sport and physical activity is the study and the application of the psychological correlates of human behavior and performance within the context of sport and physical activity. The "study" portion of this definition reflects the science dimension; the "application" portion, the professional activity dimension.

• • •

The psychology of sport and physical activity includes the scientific study and clinical application of the psychological aspects of human behavior and performance that occur in the domain of sport and physical activity.

• • •

Science: The Creation of Knowledge

The basic purpose of every science is to gain an understanding of behavior. Thus, geology is concerned with understanding the behavior of the earth's crust; chemistry, with understanding the behavior of chemical compounds; and psychology, with understanding human behavior.

Scientific understanding is obtained through four research stages: description, explanation, prediction, and control. Because the psychology of sport and physical activity is a young science, the overwhelming majority of research has been carried out at the description stage. Some programs of research, however, have proceeded beyond description to explanation and prediction. The following two programs illustrate the different stages of science.

Anxiety provided the focus for the first program, which was initiated by Rainer Martens (1977). On the basis of previous research in psychology, Martens developed both an overall model of anxi-

ety and a personality test to measure anxiety, the *Sport Competition Anxiety Test*. Marten's model for sport competition anxiety is illustrated in Figure 10.1.

A second program, which is in the area of group cohesion, was initiated by myself and two colleagues, Larry Brawley and Neil Widmeyer (Carron, Widmeyer, & Brawley, 1985). On the basis of research in psychology, management science, sociology, and physical education, we developed a model and a test to measure cohesiveness in groups—the *Group Environment Questionnaire*. Figure 10.2 illustrates our model for cohesion in sport teams. The first, descriptive level of research focuses on describing a phenomenon. In the case of anxiety, descriptive research establishing norms allowed the determination of whether sport competition anxiety changes with age or varies by sex (Martens, 1977). Similarly, in the case of cohesion, descriptive research provided norms that allowed us to determine whether the nature and amount of cohesiveness is different for male and female athletes competing in team (e.g., basketball) and individual (e.g., track and field) sports situations (Widmeyer, Brawley, & Carron, 1985).

In the explanation phase the scientist looks for overall patterns, developing and testing models or explanations that link the available descriptive data. Research by Passer (1983), for example, who sought to determine whether anxiety differences can be explained on the basis of differences in fear of failure, fear of evaluation, perceived competence, and self-esteem, showed that perceived competence was not related to competitive trait anxiety, that self-esteem was weakly related, and that fear of failure and fear of evaluation were strongly related to competitive trait anxiety. Similarly, Carron, Widmeyer, and Brawley (1988) conducted research to explain why some people continue (i.e., adhere) in sport and physical activity programs and others drop out. This research was based on the argument that differences in cohesion influence adherence to a program. A series of studies in elite sport, recreational sport, and fitness

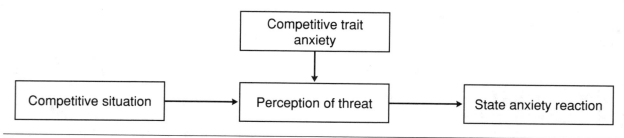

Figure 10.1 Martens's model for anxiety in sport. *Note.* Reprinted from Martens (1977) by permission.

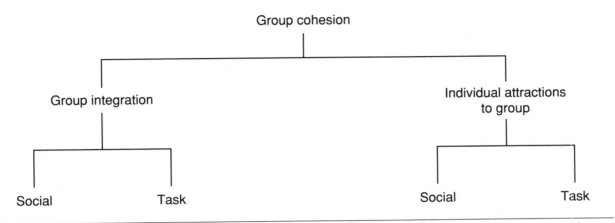

Figure 10.2   A conceptual model for cohesion in sport teams. *Note.* Reprinted from Carron, Widmeyer, and Brawley (1985) by permission.

class situations showed that perceptions of cohesiveness were strongly associated with adherence.

In the prediction phase the scientist uses a model or theory to predict outcome. One prediction that follows from the model proposed for anxiety in sport is that highly trait anxious athletes will experience greater stress prior to competitive situations than individuals possessing low trait anxiety. Gould, Horn, and Spreeman (1983) tested and obtained support for this prediction. Similarly, a prediction that follows from the model proposed for understanding group cohesion is that individuals on unsuccessful but highly cohesive teams will accept greater responsibility for the outcome than members of teams that are low in cohesion. Research by Brawley, Carron, and Widmeyer (1987) supported this prediction.

The control phase of the research process is concerned with developing methods and techniques to influence the phenomenon in question. If the results from repeated testing at the description, explanation, and prediction stages are reliable and valid, this information can be used to develop programs of intervention to improve behavior and performance in sport and physical activity. In terms of the anxiety and cohesion examples, coaches or sport psychologists might introduce programs to reduce the anxiety level of participants in sport and physical activity or to enhance the level of group cohesion on a team.

Whereas the two preceding examples illustrate attempts to gain an understanding of how psychological constructs influence human behavior and performance in the context of sport and physical activity, a number of sport psychologists attempt, through counseling and education, to help athletes achieve optimum performance. This is the profes-

sional dimension, the second purpose of the psychology of sport and physical activity.

Professional Activity: The Application of Knowledge

The basic purpose of every profession is to apply scientific and technological advances for the good of society. Thus, the medical profession applies knowledge gained from physiology, anatomy, biochemistry, and the other health-related sciences to maintain and improve the quality of human life. Education applies knowledge gained from research in psychology, sociology, and systems theory to produce more efficient teachers and hence a more knowledgeable and informed society. Similarly, sport psychology as a profession applies knowledge gained through sport science research to enhance individual and group behavior and performance in sport and physical activity settings.

The application of knowledge in the field of sport psychology involves a variety of methods, techniques, and approaches, including

- clinical counseling,
- crisis intervention,
- psychological assessment,
- performance enhancement,
- consultation and program development, and
- prevention and treatment of injuries (Nideffer, 1981).

Although all these are important, the activities most visible to the public are performance enhancement, consultation, and program development.

Terry Orlick, one of Canada's leading applied sport psychologists, has provided these services for hundreds of high-performance Canadian athletes. Orlick, who proceeds from the belief that "the greatest barriers we confront in our pursuit of excellence are psychological barriers which we impose upon ourselves, sometimes unknowingly" (Orlick, 1980, p. 11), has developed comprehensive strategies to assist and support athletes who pursue excellence (Orlick, 1980, 1986a, 1986b). These strategies include performance enhancement, mental rehearsal, goal setting, relaxation, concentration, and commitment and self-control.

An athlete can use mental rehearsal for a number of purposes—to speed up the learning process, to increase self-motivation, to plan strategies, and to reinforce (mentally) appropriate behaviors. Similarly, relaxation can also take many forms and answer a number of purposes. An athlete may have problems dealing with stress during competition or during the hours, weeks, or even months prior to an important event. Once the problem is identified, a sport psychologist might help the athlete develop a relaxation technique using meditation, progressive relaxation, biofeedback, self-hypnosis, or attention control training. Goal setting can be used to clarify performance objectives and develop appropriate training programs for a number of skills, whether physical performance, relaxation techniques, mental rehearsal techniques, or programs of commitment and self-control.

A common thread through this is the role of the sport psychologist as facilitator. The applied sport psychologist helps the athlete identify those areas where improvement is necessary and provides education and counseling to improve learning and performance.

Mental rehearsal is a psychological technique that can help an athlete attain excellence.

Learned Societies

In North America, a number of professional associations focus on sport psychology specifically or on the sport sciences in general (including sport psychology). The former group includes the North American Society for the Psychology of Sport and Physical Activity (NASPSPA), founded in 1967; the Canadian Society for Psychomotor Learning and Sport Psychology (CSPLSP), founded in 1969; and the Association for the Advancement of Applied Sport Psychology (AAASP), founded in 1986. Associations that include sport psychology as an area of emphasis include the Canadian Association of Sport Sciences, the American Psychological Association, the Canadian Psychological Association, and the American Academy of Sports Medicine.

Of these organizations, NASPSPA and CSPLSP have been most influential and important, both to individuals in the field and to the growth of the field. As Wiggins (1984) notes in outlining the history of sport psychology, "To say that the formation of NASPSPA and CSPLSP has had a significant influence on the development of sport psychology in North America would be an understatement. Since the genesis of these two organizations, there has been a proliferation of systematic research conducted in sport psychology. This research has appeared in the form of articles in sport psychology journals, conference proceedings, book chapters, and books" (p. 21).

From the time of their formation, both NASPSPA and CSPLSP have been oriented primarily toward the science dimension of sport and physical activity. The increasing number of practitioners, however, and the expanding knowledge base intensified the interest in establishing an association primarily concerned with applied sport psychology. AAASP was developed to meet this evolving need. Although still a young association, it is highly probable that AAASP will have the same impact on the professional dimension that NASPSPA and CSPLSP have had on the scientific.

Journals

A number of journals publish sport psychology research. Again, some of these are specific in content, others more general. The most important are

- *The Sport Psychologist,*
- *Journal of Motor Behavior,*
- *Journal of Sport and Exercise Psychology,* and
- *Journal of Sports Behavior.*

Other, more general publications include

- *Canadian Journal of Sport Sciences,*
- *Research Quarterly,*
- *Medicine and Science in Sports and Exercise,*
- *Perceptual and Motor Skills,*
- *Journal of Experimental Psychology,*
- *Journal of Personality and Social Psychology,* and
- *Psychological Review.*

Undergraduate and Graduate Education

Given the wide range of topics and activities in the field, it is difficult to identify the single appropriate training for a sport psychologist. One possible approach is to look at what has been (rather than what should be) the educational preparation of individuals currently practicing sport psychology. John Salmela, in an article published in *The World Sport Psychology Sourcebook* (Salmela, 1981), reported that approximately three quarters of his North American respondents were males (75% in Canada, 69.4% in the U.S.A.). The population was relatively young, with an average age of 35.6 years in Canada and 38.4 years in the United States. Training was provided in a variety of academic departments: sport science, kinesiology, or kinanthropology (21.4%); physical education (61.8%); and psychology (16.8%). The largest percentage of time during graduate education and training was spent in coursework (54.5%), followed by research (30.1%), and counseling (15.9%).

Salmela found that sport psychologists in Western and Eastern Europe spent less time on coursework (44.1% and 49.3%, respectively) and more time on research (45.3% and 31.5%, respectively) during their academic training. Their training was also more practical and less theoretical. For example, the relative emphasis placed on the theoretical aspects of sport psychology was 69.8%, 60.5%, and 54.8% in North America, Western Europe, and Eastern Europe, respectively.

To determine the specific graduate courses that individuals in sport psychology had taken, Salmela presented his respondents with 37 content areas that he then regrouped into a number of categories (see Table 10.1). The highest ranking categories, in order, were cognitive psychology, research methods, social psychology, and sport psychology. The cognitive category, with its strong emphasis on learning, ergonomics, and experimental psychology, reflects the initial emphasis on motor learning in the psychology of sport and physical activity.

Table 10.1   Academic Preparation of North American Sport Psychologists

Category	Representative courses	Rank
Cognitive	Learning psychology, experimental psychology, industrial psychology, ergonomics	1
Methods	Laboratory techniques, counseling, statistics, research methods, computing science	2
Social	Social psychology, humanistic psychology	3
Sport psychology	Motor learning, motor development, sport psychology, social psychology, sport sociology	4
Professional	General psychology, publication training, grant preparation, internship, workshops, presentation training	5
Differential	Deviant psychology, developmental psychology, psychiatry, clinical psychology	6
Biological	Perceptual psychology, neuroscience, neuropsychology	7

Note. Adapted from Salmela (1981).

The development of AAASP reflects the growing interest in the area Salmela classified as "differential"—the professional activity dimension.

Career Opportunities

Historically, the job markets for individuals with an interest and training in sport psychology have been related to their level of education. Individuals with an undergraduate degree and an area of concentration in sport psychology are similar to any other graduates with an arts or social science degree: They can elect to go into teaching, to a professional school, or into the work force. Their background in sport psychology is generally not sufficient for a career in the field, whether in the public or private sector or in a college or university. Those who earn a master's or doctoral degree may find employment in a university, to a significantly lesser degree in federal or provincial governments or their agencies (the higher degree and other related experiences rather than the sport psychology specialization are usually the reasons for employment), and to a minimal degree in the private sector as clinicians or consultants. Increasingly, sport psychologists are working in the private sector as consultants with teams and individuals.

Salmela's (1981) survey of North American professionals in sport psychology shows how individuals at the university level spend their time:

- Undergraduate teaching (33.4%)
- Graduate teaching (24.8%)
- Planning or doing research (24.8%)
- Writing and publishing (17.8%)
- Training athletes or patients (27.1%)
- Consultation (13.8%)
- Administration (19.8%)
- Other activities (2.2%)

Summary

There has always been a close association between a specialization in sport psychology and employment at the university level. University positions are not as prevalent now as they were in previous decades, however. All is not bleak, though, and the previous track record and present state of affairs of sport allow a number of predictions for the future:

- Greater emphasis will be placed on practical research and the application of the knowledge gained through research.
- Applied sport psychology will be in increasing demand at the elite levels of amateur and professional sport.
- There will be more emphasis on research and application in health psychology and in the psychology of exercise.
- Sport psychologists will be in greater demand as consultants to coaches, parents, and athletes.
- As a result of the increased applied emphasis, there will be an increasing need to use and enhance existing certification programs to provide information to consumers concerning the preparation and qualifications of individuals calling themselves "sport psychologists" (cf. Alderman, 1984; Thueson & Jarman, 1985).

References and Further Readings

Alderman, R.B. (1984). The future of sport psychology. In J.M. Silva III & R.S. Weinberg (Eds.), *Psychological foundations of sport* (pp. 45-54). Champaign, IL: Human Kinetics.

Brawley, L.R., Carron, A.V., & Widmeyer, W.N. (1987). Assessing the cohesion of teams: Validity of the Group Environment Questionnaire. *Journal of Sport Psychology,* **9,** 275-294.

Carron, A.V. (1984). *Motivation: Implications for coaching and teaching.* London, ON: Sports Dynamics.

Carron, A.V., Widmeyer, W.N., & Brawley, L.R. (1985). The development of an instrument to assess cohesion in sport teams: The Group Environment Questionnaire. *Journal of Sport Psychology,* **7,** 244-266.

Carron, A.V., Widmeyer, W.N., & Brawley, L.R. (in press). Group cohesion and individual adherence to physical activity. *Journal of Sport Psychology.*

Gould, D., Horn, T., & Spreemann, J. (1983). Sources of stress in junior elite wrestlers. *Journal of Sport Psychology,* **5,** 159-171.

Martens, R. (1977). *Sport competition anxiety test.* Champaign, IL: Human Kinetics.

Martens, R. (1980). From smocks to jocks: A new adventure for sport psychologists. In P. Klavora & K.A.W. Wipper (Eds.), *Psychological and sociological factors in physical performance* (pp. 20-26). Toronto, ON: University of Toronto Press.

Morgan, W.P. (1972). Sport psychology. In R.N. Singer (Ed.), *The psychomotor domain* (pp. 193-228). Philadelphia: Lea & Febiger.

Nideffer, R.M. (1981). *The ethics and practice of applied sport psychology.* Ithaca, NY: Mouvement.

Orlick, T. (1980). *In pursuit of excellence.* Champaign, IL: Human Kinetics.

Orlick, T. (1986a). *Coaches training manual to psyching for sport.* Champaign, IL: Human Kinetics.

Orlick, T. (1986b). *Psyching for sport: Mental training for athletes.* Champaign, IL: Human Kinetics.

Passer, M.W. (1983). Fear of failure, fear of evaluation, perceived competence, and self-esteem in competitive-trait-anxious children. *Journal of Sport Psychology,* **5,** 172-188.

Rushall, B.S. (1973). *The status of sport psychology in Canada.* Paper presented at the First Canadian Congress for the Multi-disciplinary

Study of Sport and Physical Activity, Montreal, Quebec.

Salmela, J.H. (1981). *The world sport psychology sourcebook*. Ithaca, NY: Mouvement.

Schmidt, R.A. (1982). *Motor control and learning: A behavioral emphasis*. Champaign, IL: Human Kinetics.

Singer, R.N. (1978). In W.F. Straub (Ed.), *Sport psychology: An analysis of athlete behavior* (pp. 3-15). Ithaca, NY: Mouvement.

Thueson, N.C., & Jarman, B.Q. (1985). *Predicting future trends in sport psychology*. Paper presented at the annual meeting of the North American Society for the Psychology of Sport and Physical Activity, Gulf Park, MS.

Widmeyer, W.N., Brawley, L.R., & Carron, A.V. (1985). *The measurement of cohesion in sport teams*. London, ON: Sports Dynamics.

Wiggins, D.K. (1984). The history of sport psychology in North America. In J.M. Silva III & R.S. Weinberg (Eds.), *Psychological foundations of sport* (pp. 9-22). Champaign, IL: Human Kinetics.

Williams, J.A., & Straub, W.F. (1986). Sport psychology: Past, present, and future. In J.M. Williams (Ed.), *Applied sport psychology: Personal growth to peak performance* (pp. 1-14). Palo Alto, CA: Mayfield.

Chapter 11

Sociology and Physical Activity

Barry D. McPherson
Barbara A. Brown

Individuals often enter the field of physical activity sciences because they are interested in sport, exercise, fitness, health, or physical activity. Many of the people involved with it are or were competitive athletes or highly involved in recreational sport or leisure-time physical activity; many are also avid sport consumers or fans. Indeed many of us invest a great deal of energy and enthusiasm in our participation in sport, but others may view this involvement as a trivial, "fun-and-games" part of life. Yet there is more significance to sport and our involvement with it than what we personally experience or what appears on the sports pages or in telecasts (McPherson, Curtis, & Loy, 1990).

There is another side to sport beyond the rules, techniques, strategies, physical benefits, game scores, and personalities. This back region is often hidden from the casual observer or participant and therefore constitutes a part of our social, economic, and political life to which only a few gain access and knowledge. This region includes areas such as locker-rooms, the political offices of national leaders, boardrooms, hotels, and dormitories. Here, the images, myths, and stereotypes about sport and about athletes, coaches, owners, and administrators may be shattered. Entering this back region often reveals a seamy side of sport: gambling, drug and sex scandals, cheating, discrimination, oppression, exploitation, inequality in power and control, elitism, and decisions based on political or economic considerations that may have little to do with sport per se.

One way to understand the meaning of sport in our lives and in this back region is to turn to the discipline of sociology, which seeks to describe, explain, and interpret the social structure, social interaction, and social behavior of groups. As part of their mandate, sociologists look "behind the scenes" to challenge existing myths and stereotypes and to gain a deeper understanding of specific activities and patterns that are repeated regularly in our daily lives.

Because sport may seem trivial, the sociological study of it may appear to be inconsequential as well. Surely there are more serious and important elements of everyday life that need to be researched and critiqued—religion, for example, or poverty and discrimination. Yet the sociology of sport has its place. Despite the view held by some scholars and journalists that sport is not worthy of study or analysis, sport *is* an integral component of the social, political, economic, and cultural life of North America. To see this, consider the following aspects:

- **The economic impact.** People as a group spend vast amounts of money on athletic clothing and equipment, activity instruction, memberships in athletic clubs, and attendance at and gambling on sporting events. In 1989 such transactions constituted an estimated $63.1 *billion* industry in the United States. Equally vast sums of money are invested in professional sport—the average annual salaries for professional athletes range from $200,000 to $800,000, with some superstars earning more than $1 million per year in North America.

- **The media impact.** The major television networks annually produce over 2,000 hours of sport coverage; cable networks devoted to sport (ESPN in the U.S.A. and TSN in Canada) provide round-the-clock coverage.

- **The political impact.** Sport has been used for propaganda purposes (e.g., the 1936 Olympic Games in Berlin) and as a foreign policy tool (e.g., the banning of South Africa from international competition as a sanction against its apartheid policy or the U.S. boycott of the 1980 Moscow Olympic Games in protest against Soviet military presence in Afghanistan).
- **The impact on leisure time.** Data from the 1988 Campbell's Survey on Well-Being in Canada indicate that 80% of the Canadian population spends 3 or more hours per week for 9 or more months of the year in some type of leisure-time sport or physical activity.
- **The educational impact.** Sport and physical activity are included in the elementary and secondary school curricula. In addition, sport events are an integral part of the social scene at universities, and successful sport teams, along with faculty research and alumni career success, are an integral component of the image that a university employs for recruiting students and for fund-raising.
- **The cultural impact.** Sport is a prevalent theme in art, novels, and movies (e.g., *North Dallas Forty*, *Chariots of Fire*, *The Natural*) and in advertisements (e.g., beer and clothing commercials). More important, particular sports are an integral component of the cultural heritage of some nations (e.g., baseball in the U.S.A., hockey in Canada, and soccer in many European and Latin American countries).

This relatively unsystematic evidence clearly suggests that sport and physical activity are not trivial aspects of our social, political, economic, or cultural life but instead have become important social institutions to which sociologists should devote serious scholarly attention.

Major Concepts

Sociology studies the structure of social organization and systems of human relationships and interaction. Sociologists assume that there is an underlying order and pattern to human behavior and that our behavior is, to a great extent, socially determined. Thus, unlike psychologists, who focus on individuals through such concepts as motivation and personality, sociologists are interested in social characteristics (e.g., gender or social class),

social issues (e.g., poverty, discrimination, inequality, or gender relations), and factors external to the individual (e.g., the social structure, culture, or social change), especially as they shape behavior and influence our opportunities and lifestyles.

Because sport and physical activity have become such pervasive elements in our social, political, and economic lives, the sociology of sport as a field of research and study has grown rapidly since the mid-1960s. The major purposes of this subdiscipline are

1. to discover and describe social patterns, processes, and problems associated with individual and group behavior in a sport setting;
2. to develop explanations for these patterns, processes, and problems using the theoretical perspectives and research tools of sociology;
3. to seek research evidence that will refute prevailing myths, stereotypes, and commonly held but erroneous assumptions about sport and physical activity;
4. to reveal, critique, and ameliorate problems in sport—the so-called muck-raking and debunking motifs of sociological study;
5. to utilize sport settings and groups to better understand more general aspects of social reality and social interaction, for example, using stable sport teams to study such phenomena as group interaction, group effectiveness or success, and the social processes involved in complex organizations;
6. to provide evidence on which sport and fitness policies and programs can be developed and revised; and
7. to identify and offer solutions to social problems widespread in sport and physical activity settings (e.g., drug use, violence, discrimination, cheating).

● ● ●

The sociology of sport and physical activity investigates the structure of social organization and systems of human interaction as they occur in and relate to the domains of sport, recreation, and physical activity.

● ● ●

Methods of Sociological Research

In the course of their research, sociologists use such concepts as social systems, culture and subcultures, the social structure, social differentiation, social stratification, socialization, social mobility, social conflict, social change, discrimination, class, status, gender, race, and ethnicity. In general, the work of sport sociologists involves critically observing and analyzing the social behavior and interaction that occurs in sport or physical activity settings (by players, spectators, officials, alumni, coaches, owners, or personnel of the mass media), as well as the relationships between sport or physical activity and the broader cultural and structural aspects of society in which they are situated. These concepts enable sociologists to search objectively for evidence to support or refute hypotheses, relationships, and assumptions.

Sociologists also use a variety of qualitative and quantitative research techniques and analytical procedures. The specific question under investigation determines the particular method they use. The **qualitative approach** comprises such methods as participant observation, formal interviews, and informal conversations with those in the social setting. For example, in a study designed to explain why and how behavior that is normally considered deviant and often illegal (i.e., drinking in public settings) becomes tolerated during special sporting events, one investigator spent several evenings during the week prior to the Grey Cup game as a participant observer, recording and analyzing the behavior of patrons of middle- and lower-class bars in Hamilton, Ontario—who says research can't be fun! He was interested in identifying the type of people (primarily those with a middle-class background) who became involved in what he called *legitimate deviance*, in this case, drinking in public with police approval—to a point—and in describing and explaining how and why this legitimate deviant behavior often occurs around sport events. Although it yields very detailed information, this qualitative approach to data collection is time consuming, and the investigator must be careful not to let personal biases about the outcomes intrude into the observations or interpretations.

The **quantitative approach** has been more commonly employed in the study of sport and physical activity from a sociological perspective. Typically, the scientist relies mainly on structured interviews or questionnaires to collect similar data from large groups of people, but libraries and other data archives (e.g., record books, government census reports, and bubblegum baseball cards) have also been used as sources of data. One common technique for using archival material is called content analysis. Suppose, for example, a researcher wants to know whether and to what extent women are discriminated against by representatives of the mass media in their reporting of sport events. One way of answering the question would be to complete a content analysis (for a period of many years) of the sports pages of daily newspapers, perhaps in different regions of the country, comparing the percentage of text and photographs allocated to men's and women's sport events and personalities. If the proportions changed over time, the investigator might attempt to determine whether the amount of coverage has increased since the onset of the women's movement. The major advantage of the quantitative approach is that large samples can be collected and statistically analyzed at reasonably low costs.

Professional athletes who behave violently are influencing the behavior of younger players.

Major Research Questions

Sociologists concerned with the study of sport and physical activity are currently involved in research that is directed toward a wide range of issues. The following constitutes a representative sample of the questions they ask.

- Why are members of some social groups more involved in sport than those from other groups (e.g., whites more than blacks, men more than women, and white-collar workers more than blue-collar workers)?
- Why does the perceived popularity of some specific sports vary from one society to another (e.g., baseball in America and Japan, hockey in Canada, or table tennis in China) or

---

HIGHLIGHT
Qualitative and Quantitative Approaches in Sociology of Sport Research

---

Gender Inequality on the Sport Page: A Qualitative Study

Purpose and Method. It has frequently been argued that despite increased involvement in high-level competitive sport, women athletes do not receive the same coverage and recognition in newspapers as male athletes. Theberge and Cronk (1986) conducted a study to address this question from a back region perspective of sport. One of the authors of this study worked as a copyeditor in the sport department of a daily newspaper. He unobtrusively observed and recorded the processes by which journalists function as "gatekeepers" to determine which sport events and items get published, thereby becoming "daily news."

Results and Conclusions. Theberge and Cronk (1986) concluded that "the limited coverage of women in the sport media is not due simply to journalists' biases against women's sport" (p. 195), for they found that journalists seek out what they consider to be newsworthy subjects about which they can provide reliable and accessible material. They also found the production of the sport pages to be a routinized procedure that results in standardized content and regular coverage of only certain subjects—mainly men's sport. The authors concluded that journalists assume there is greater public interest in men's sport, that the commercial nature of men's sport fosters greater accessibility to the media, and that journalists believe they are printing what their audiences wish to read. These implied assumptions become operating guidelines that ensure preferred and greater coverage of men's sport. The authors also concluded that newsworkers (in particular, editors) routinely define sport news as news about men's sport; merely increasing the number of women sport reporters therefore will not eliminate sexism in the sport news. Thus, they argue that "bias is woven into journalists' beliefs about the makeup of the news and the practices they follow to uncover the news. In turn, these beliefs and practices are outcomes of the dominance of men's commercial sport in North America" (Theberge & Cronk, 1986, p. 202).

Professional Athletes as Role Models for Violence in Hockey: A Quantitative Study

Purpose and Method. The use of violence by younger players has been an issue of repeated concern in Canadian hockey. It has been argued frequently that the reason children fight or use the stick illegally is that they are encouraged to model the behavior of the NHL players they see on television. To address this question, 604 young Canadian hockey players were asked the following question: "Have you ever learned how to hit another player illegally in any way from watching professional hockey?"

Results and Conclusions. Over half of the players, regardless of age and competitive level, responded "yes" to this question. They were then asked to describe what they had learned. Typical answers included these: "Butt-ending, spearing, slashing, high sticking, elbow in the head, sneaky elbows, how to trip properly, tripping as they go into the boards, hitting at weak points with the stick, say at the back of the legs" (Smith, 1983, p. 117). When the players were asked whether they had ever used these tactics in an actual game setting, 222 of 604 respondents said, "at least once or twice," and 90 of these 222 players reported having used the techniques five times or more. Thus, professional athletes do serve as role models for the indirect (i.e., via the mass media) learning and use of violent, rule-breaking behavior by young hockey players.

---

from one region of a country to another (e.g., basketball in the U.S. Midwest vs. the South or hockey in northern Ontario and the western provinces vs. southern Ontario or British Columbia)?

- How do sporting subcultures evolve, and what are the characteristics, meaning, and social functions of these specific subgroups within the world of sport (e.g., the martial arts, bodybuilding, aerobics, surfing, or skiing)?
- Can sport facilitate upward social mobility for those who are originally disadvantaged in society (e.g., blacks, native people, or children from lower-class families)?
- Why do some individuals become socialized and involved in sport and physical activity whereas others with the same apparent physical capabilities do not? Moreover, what governs an individual's choice of physical activity?
- How do athletes prepare for and adjust to retirement or withdrawal from competitive sport? Why do some athletes make a satisfactory adjustment to this role change while others do not?
- Is sport participation a deterrent to juvenile delinquency?
- Why and under what circumstances does violence (by players and spectators) occur in sport?
- What is the nature and extent of the interaction and correlation between sport and other basic social institutions in our society such as the family, politics, the economy, religion, the educational system, the mass media, and the law?

Journals, Publications, and Professional Organizations

In addition to consulting the books cited in this chapter's reference list, the interested student will find a wealth of material in the following journals:

- *Sociology of Sport Journal*
- *International Review for the Sociology of Sport*
- *Journal of Sport and Social Issues*
- *Journal of Sport Behavior*
- *Canadian Journal of Sport Sciences*
- *Women in Sport and Physical Activity*
- *Arena Review*

Finally, students are eligible to join the two major professional associations in this field of study: the North American Society for the Sociology of

Sport and the International Committee for the Sociology of Sport. These organizations both publish a research journal and a newsletter about professional matters, and each hosts an annual meeting where sociologists present and discuss their recent research.

Undergraduate Education and Career Opportunities

A beginning student in the sport and physical activity sciences might wonder how important this subfield of study is compared to the apparently more practical fields of sport administration, sport psychology, or exercise physiology. These fields certainly may appear to have more immediate and practical relevance at this stage, especially to someone interested in being a coach or a fitness leader. In the long run, however, anyone aspiring to be a leader, a policy maker, or an influential person in a physical activity profession will find that issues in the sociology of sport and physical activity may have significant policy and program implications at many levels: personal, career, family, organization, community, or country. Specifically, some of the more likely career opportunities for students with an aptitude and interest in this subfield of study include

- consultant or executive director of sport or fitness governing agencies within the provincial or federal government,
- coaching,
- teaching,
- private fitness or sport consultant,
- researcher,
- professor, or
- journalist.

In fact, many students with a bachelor's or master's degree and specialization in this area of study have found successful managerial, administrative, or business careers outside the world of sport, physical activity, or fitness. The student who wants to keep these options open should complete as many sociology electives as possible, particularly those focusing on sociological methods and statistics, occupations, social inequality, gender relations, organizations, the family, women, social theory, health and illness, and social change.

Sociology of sport can provide more than just a way to make a living, however. The following are some of the more personal advantages to studying sport, fitness, and physical activity from a sociological perspective:

- *You will acquire a new way of viewing and thinking critically about the world of sport and physical activity.* Rather than readily accepting what you see or are told about sport and physical activity, whether by the mass media or by fans, you will be able to observe and critically examine the total picture, including both the front and back regions. For example, sociologists as a group are less ready to accept the claim that blacks and women are underrepresented in sport because they lack the physical or mental abilities or the motivation to perform at high levels. Sociological research has provided evidence that blacks and women are less involved for a variety of social reasons; this lower level of involvement may occur either because there is overt or subtle discrimination against these groups or because they have not had the social encouragement and opportunity to acquire sport or physical activity skills at an early age. Similarly, although some journalists argue that Francophones are less involved in hockey and other sports because of language differences or a lack of interest, sociological evidence has documented that, until recently, Francophones have been discouraged from participating in sport by the strong views of the Catholic church and, more recently, through subtle discrimination by English-speaking coaches and administrators.

- *Valid sociological facts can help you understand, interpret, and perhaps even predict changes in sport and physical activity participation patterns.* For example, sociological data might help predict changing patterns of involvement by specific population segments in various forms of physical activity (e.g., an increased popularity of tennis among the lower class or a decline of the fitness movement in the middle class). If you were in the fitness business, you might then be better able to predict when interest by the adult population in particular leisure activities would rise and fall. From a business perspective you would be in a better position to make an informed decision about when to increase or decrease your investment.

- *By employing a sociological perspective, you begin to develop a social consciousness, specifically, an awareness of the social significance of sport and physical activity in our daily lives and of the social problems inherent in contemporary sport.* In short, you will be more inclined to consider both the positive and the negative social, economic, and political ramifications of sport and physical activity in our daily lives.

- *Although the sociology of sport and physical activity may not provide you with information that you can apply immediately in your personal life or your career, you may find, as others have, that 5, 10, or 15 years from now, this information may become highly relevant as you play a variety of occupational, family, or leisure roles*—as the parent of a child involved in a highly competitive youth sport program; as a sport or fitness consultant or a teacher who is requested to establish, evaluate, or revise policies or procedures; or as a manager of a fitness or racquet club with rapidly declining involvement among certain segments of your membership, perhaps because the birthrate has declined, the population is aging, leisure time has decreased, or leisure values and preferences have shifted in new directions. In short, you will have reliable and valid information, rather than hearsay or public opinion, on which to make decisions about sport and physical activity within your personal life or your career.

- *Finally, and perhaps most importantly, you should view this subject matter as you would any liberal arts or social science course that you take in university.* As with history, philosophy, or English literature, familiarity with sociology will enable you to become a more critical and analytical thinker, less inclined to accept a *single*, undocumented explanation or interpretation for an instance or pattern of social behavior. You will demand valid evidence for statements that others make and you will become skeptical of generalized opinions. You will come to question and think about what you consume and accept as fact, in both the mass media and scholarly publications. This means that you will be a better-informed and knowledgeable citizen who can creatively contribute to the decision-making and problem-solving process in a variety of sport- and fitness-related groups, associations, or organizations.

Summary

This chapter presents an abstract, macroview of the world of sport, fitness, and physical activity. These activities are conducted in a social setting and cannot be fully understood without understanding the social context in which they occur. A sociological perspective provides such an understanding of the social aspects of sport, fitness, and physical activity phenomena. This perspective fosters both analytical and critical thought about what some think are trivial or superficial elements of our social lives. A closer examination, however, indicates that these leisure activities are both pervasive and meaningful in the larger social, political, economic, and cultural contexts of groups, organizations, institutions, or societies.

Serious study of the sociology of sport and physical activity will provide analytical and methodological skills, a body of knowledge, and a way of thinking that will prove to be valuable throughout adulthood, for both personal growth and career advancement. As Peter Berger (1963, p. 20) states in his classic book, *Invitation to Sociology*, "The sociologists' questions always remain essentially the same: What are people doing with each other here? What are their relationships to each other? How are these relationships organized in institutions? What are the collective ideas that move men and institutions?" As answers are sought to these and other questions, social reality will be seen to be more complex than first imagined and will take on different meanings, some of which may be shocking and unpleasant, especially if, heretofore, they have been hidden from the official views or interpretations of society. Berger further notes that "people who like to avoid shocking discoveries, who prefer to believe that society is just what they were taught in Sunday School, who like the safety of the rules and maxims of . . . the world-taken-for-granted, should stay away from sociology" (1963, p. 24).

To those who feel comfortable with abstract thinking, who have or wish to develop a social consciousness, who are prepared to take risks in their intellectual pursuits, and who seek an intellectual challenge, we hereby extend an invitation to enter the exciting world of the sociology of sport and physical activity. Those who accept this challenge will be supported by a growing body of literature representing many different sociological perspectives and a large network of colleagues from across Canada and throughout the world. The complex population, ethical, environmental, social, leisure, and economic issues facing our global society in the coming decades will undoubtedly produce considerable social and political change in our individual and collective lifestyles. Because many of these changes will have an impact on the world of sport and physical activity, an exciting career awaits the creative practitioner, policy maker, or researcher who acquires as much training as possible in the sociology of sport and physical activity.

References and Further Readings

Berger, P. (1963). *Invitation to sociology*. New York: Anchor Books.

Boutilier, M., & SanGiovanni, L. (1983). *The sporting woman*. Champaign, IL: Human Kinetics.

Gruneau, R. (1983). *Class, sport and social development*. Amherst: The University of Massachusetts Press.

Gruneau, R., & Albinson, J. (1978). *Canadian sport: Sociological perspectives*. Don Mills, ON: Addison-Wesley.

Harvey, J., & Cantelon, H. (1987). *Not just a game: Essays in Canadian sport sociology*. Ottawa, ON: University of Ottawa Press.

Loy, J.W., McPherson, B.D., & Kenyon, G.S. (1978). *Sport and social systems*. Reading, MA: Addison-Wesley.

McPherson, B.D., Curtis, J.E., & Loy, J.W. (1990). *The social significance of sport*. Champaign, IL: Human Kinetics.

Smith, M. (1983). *Violence and sport*. Toronto: Butterworths.

Theberge, N., & Cronk, A. (1986). Work routines in newspaper sport departments and the coverage of women's sport. *Sociology of Sport Journal*, **3**, 195-203.

Chapter 12

Anthropology and Physical Activity

Susan K. Pfeiffer

Anthropology, "the study of people," holds the grand goal of studying human nature and human natural history. It differs from other social sciences in emphasizing a cross-cultural perspective. Patterns of human social behavior are observed via fieldwork (rather than laboratory experimentation), particularly with a view to their stability and commonality. Anthropology also actively seeks to understand the dynamic interaction between our biology and our behavior. Because physical activity is the product of both biological abilities and motivational or social factors, it is certainly relevant for anthropological study.

Major Concepts

A key concept for anthropologists is **adaptation**, whether it occurs through an individual's biological and social capacities or through an individual's cultural surroundings. Unlike other animals, humans routinely use their culture to modify their natural environment. Humans also rely on language to pass on information about that environment. Although we think of culture and language as social phenomena, both are rooted in the biological capacities of our species. *Homo sapiens* and human culture emerged together, interactively. Biological and cultural adaptive mechanisms thus do not act in isolation but constantly interact to allow the adaptation of human populations to different environments.

We nevertheless rather arbitrarily divide the study of human adaptation into two subdisciplines. Those anthropologists who focus on the structure and function of human societies are called social, or cultural, anthropologists; those who focus on biological adaptation are called biological, or physical, anthropologists. These two categories interact extensively, however, and whatever the disciplinary focus, anthropologists are inevitably interested in how aspects of physical activity facilitate (or hinder) adaptation.

• • •

Although the anthropology of physical activity does not exist as a subdiscipline per se, anthropologists interested in the area study the relation of adaptive strategies and cultural values to physical activity in general and sports and games in particular and attempt to reconstruct the physical activity behavior patterns of our prehuman and early human ancestors.

• • •

Methods in Anthropological Research

Anthropologists rely on fieldwork and a cross-cultural perspective to identify key themes in the natural history and survival of humankind. Doing fieldwork may mean unobtrusively watching people, sometimes as a participant-observer, or it may mean excavating archaeological sites to learn about the behavior of prehistoric people. Methods of analysis are both qualitative (subjective) and quantitative (numerically oriented), depending on the problem at hand.

Major Research Questions

Because the anthropological subdisciplines focus on different aspects of biological-social interaction, it is useful to discuss them separately.

Social Anthropology

In comparing societies, especially nonindustrialized, isolated societies, anthropologists have found many cultural universals. Table 12.1 lists the universals G.P. Murdock (1965) found when he compared 250 societies. All these cultural traits require energy beyond that necessary for basic subsistence activities such as gathering food, hunting, farming, and fishing, but human societies have always organized themselves for activities beyond those that provide for basic animal needs, activities that identify group bonds, teach the group's values, and provide enjoyment. For example, gaming pieces from prehistoric archaeological sites indicate that "playing dice" has great antiquity throughout the Old and New Worlds (Lewis, 1988). In comparing cultures, the question is not whether dance, sport, and games will be present but what functions they will serve for each society.

From an anthropological viewpoint, dance helps communicate social values, develop motor skills useful for hunting or war, and generate feelings that can be directed toward coping with environmental problems. The "rules" of who dances and how they dance may reflect and reinforce social norms. In cross-cultural studies, viewing dance as ritual, social event, or theater helps define a culture's accepted gender roles. In modern North America there are acceptable times for female dancing and acceptable times for male dancing just as there were in ancient India. The dominance of one gender or the other (in dance or in life in general) is likely to change through time as the culture changes (Hanna, 1988).

Games, including athletic competitions, can be seen as dynamic balances of our natural feelings of competition and cooperation. To anthropologists, the public confrontation of two professional boxers and the confrontation of two Greenlandic Eskimos settling their disputes with a song duel may perform similar social functions. Many of our contemporary sports clearly have their roots in the need to develop survival skills: accuracy, speed, endurance, cooperation, and control of aggression. If modern team sports can "ritualize" aggression as do stylized war games among New Guinea

Table 12.1   Cross-Cultural Universals

Age grading	Joking
Athletic sports	Kin groups
Bodily adornment	Kinship nomenclature
Calendar	Language
Cleanliness training	Law
Community organization	Luck supersititions
Cooking	Magic
Cooperative labor	Marriage
Cosmology	Mealtimes
Courtship	Medicine
Dancing	Modesty concerning
Decorative art	natural functions
Divination	Mourning
Division of labor	Music
Dream interpretation	Mythology
Education	Obstetrics
Eschatology	Penal sanctions
Ethics	Personal names
Ethnobotany	Population policy
Etiquette	Postnatal care
Faithhealing	Pregnancy usages
Family feasting	Property rights
Fire making	Propitiation of super-
Folklore	natural beings
Food taboos	Puberty customs
Funeral rights	Religious ritual
Games	Residence rules
Gestures	Sexual restrictions
Gift giving	Soul concepts
Government	Status differentiation
Greetings	Surgery
Hair styles	Tool making
Hospitality	Trade
Housing	Visiting
Hygiene	Weaning
Incest taboos	Weather control
Inheritance rules	

Note. Emphasis of physical activity universals added. Reprinted from Murdock (1965) by permission.

tribesmen, they may be very adaptive for us, indeed.

The anthropology of sport is a relatively new interest area within the discipline. Research focuses on

1. the meaning and description of sport behavior, particularly in non-Western and preliterate societies;
2. the cross-cultural definition and analysis of sport;
3. sport as a factor in acculturation, enculturation, and cultural maintenance;

4. sport as a form of human conflict and a context for issues of aggression and violence; and

5. sport as a perspective on other facets of cultural behavior (Blanchard, 1981, p. 14).

Sport can have both work and play dimensions. Even the same sport played in the same general context can be perceived quite differently by different cultural groups. To most North Americans, for example, the sport of lacrosse (or stickball) is a recreational team sport taught in schools for skills development, entertainment, or even novelty. But among the North American native people (such as the Mohawk or the Choctaw) whose ancestors invented the game, playing lacrosse is a traditional cultural activity. As such, it takes on a symbolic meaning beyond that of a recreational activity. In this context, rather than being a vehicle for playful innovation, lacrosse helps maintain cultural identity. In general, although a culture must often abandon its traditional subsistence activities when dominated by a more powerful or technologically advanced society, it may attempt to maintain its identity by perpetuating its traditional leisure activities (e.g., sports, games, and dances). Students of physical activity sciences would do well to develop a sensitivity to these ethnic differences in the cultural significance of sports and games.

Anthropology may also offer insights not only into the functions that physical activity may play within a culture but also into how people play their games. Using baseball as an example, George Gmelch has documented how players faced with risky or uncertain tasks (like pitching) perform the same sort of ritual magic that individuals in cultures around the world perform in similarly uncertain situations. Most players also observe a number of *taboos*—objects or acts whose avoidance will ward off bad luck. Fetishes, lucky numbers, and repetitive behaviors are all expected among humans regularly dealing with uncertainty.

Anthropologists have helped us see the patterns and meanings of "body language," often called **kinesics** or **proxemics**. All humans maintain a personal space, but the dimensions of that space vary by culture. Hand gestures, posture, locomotion, and rules about touching others also differ from one culture to another. In North American society for example, it is considered odd for men to hold hands while walking down the street (an act that is common in the Near East), but football teammates often pat each other's buttocks. Indeed, body language is important in athletic competitions. Facial expression and subtle movement cues can convey feelings of confidence or insecurity between opponents, and coaches are acutely aware that the outcome of a tennis match often can be predicted from the opponents' body language as they enter the courts.

Anthropologists also use physical activity to predict common psychological characteristics within a particular culture. In her classic work, *Patterns of Culture* (1934), Ruth Benedict suggested that cultures might be classified into two basic types named after the opposing cultures of Greek tragedy: Apollonian (peaceful and restrained) or Dionysian (aggressive and excessive). This basic idea has been modified and expanded through the years. In exploring such concepts, the movements and preferred activities of a culture are critical. Although two cultures may both pursue leisure activities with horses, for example, one may develop dressage, the other, rodeo. And it is easy to see different cultural values underlying the controlled, stylized dance of Bali and the open, lively movements of traditional dance in Turkey. Activities are performed within a local culture pattern, which will have its own unique coherence, continuity, and form.

In playing ball games, the Tarahumara Indians of northwestern Mexico perform feats of endurance that demonstrate this relation of a sport's form to the values of the culture in which it exists. The Tarahumara's traditional cross-country kickball races may involve a more-or-less continuous running effort for 24 to 72 hours. Experienced kickball racers are capable of energy expenditures of more than 6.94 kcal/min for 24 hours—a total of over 10,000 kcal. Their unique sport is consistent with their physically demanding lifestyle, in which rugged terrain and a harsh climate make farming and herding very challenging occupations that begin at age 5 or 6. Physical fitness and stamina thus are highly valued qualities in Tarahumara culture.

Although some motor patterns will be common to all human cultures, other patterns may be pervasive in some cultures and totally absent from others. All human societies assume that most members will walk and run, for example, but many societies place no value on knowing how to swim. We can distinguish these motor activities as **phylogenetic** (common to all) and **ontogenetic** (learned in some contexts). The timing of appearance of even phylogenetic movements can be culturally influenced, however. In traditional American Indian societies, for example, infants

Figure 12.1   An early photo of a Plains Indian (Assiniboine) mother and child. Photo courtesy of National Archives of Canada (Photo C 20815).

were "cradleboarded"—a handy aid to transport that ensured the baby would not crawl out of the canoe (Figure 12.1). This almost constant restraint appeared to early observers to retard motor development somewhat. On the other hand, infants in several African societies often show "motor precociousness," sitting up and walking earlier than Western babies. This appears to result from the traditional African mother's acts of encouragement and almost constant physical interaction during the child's waking hours (Super, 1976).

Some evidence does suggest genetic differences between groups with regard to infants' motor patterns. Daniel Freedman (1979) has documented several differences between Asiatic/Native American and Caucasian newborns, all born in the United States: Chinese and American Indian babies cry less easily and adapt more placidly to changes in position, for example. Nevertheless, Freedman emphasizes that from birth onward it is the "mother-infant unit" that determines the infant's development and that "there is no way to separate the genetic and the learned for they are permanently glued together" (p. 144).

Biological Anthropology

This subdiscipline of anthropology concerns itself with human evolution. It focuses more on biological variability than on cultural variability and tries to explain that variability in terms of adaptations. Because humankind has always been physically active, aspects of physical activity pervade the inquiry. Indeed, our species is unique in its endurance capability and its heat dissipation characteristics. Considered in conjunction with our unique reliance on the eight "essential" amino acids found in meat, these factors lead biological anthropologists to the conclusion that physical exercise was a critical feature of our ancestors' evolutionary success. These prehuman ancestors (various species of the genus *Australopithecus*) were small-bodied, with no built-in weapons such as horns or claws. To hunt successfully, they probably needed to injure their prey with a hand-held weapon and chase it until it collapsed (Bortz, 1985). Indeed, getting back to social anthropology for a moment, some argue that contemporary sports constitute efforts to re-create this ancestral hunting-gathering phase, events of accuracy and control mimicking stalking and attack and events of speed and endurance mimicking the chase (Marsh, 1988).

The biological anthropologist may focus either on reconstructing the living conditions of past populations or on the variability seen within and between living populations. Areas of interest include anatomy, genetics, biomechanics, and exercise physiology, but the social science perspective remains important here, too, for key human evolutionary adaptations have always incorporated cultural innovations. Any factors identified as variations within or between groups can be recognized only by comparison to general performance characteristics of the species. Unique features may then be explained as the result of natural selection or other evolutionary forces. Common performance characteristics are just as important as population differences in indicating our species' most fundamental evolutionary adaptations.

As a species, we have unique features: complex brains that support culture; grasping hands that make and hold tools; and upright, bipedal locomotion. We also have a unique endocrine system that gives us great endurance and probably helped our hunting ancestors cope with the reduced speed that accompanies bipedality.

Bipedal locomotion introduces evolutionarily new physical stresses to our backs and our feet, but apparently it was worth the cost. It freed our upper limbs to carry food and babies, throw weapons at prey, make tools, and hold hands. Footprints from a site at Laetoli, in northern Tanzania, show that bipedalism of an apparently human kind was established as early as 3.6 million years ago. Comparison with modern human gait has allowed us to estimate these ancestors' stride lengths, body weights, and so forth (Charteris,

Wall, & Nottrodt, 1982). Biomechanical studies of human movement help anthropologists reconstruct the transition to bipedalism and identify trouble spots where the "new design" may be imperfect.

The skeletal remains of our ancestors give us insight into the perils of excessive habitual activities, too.

Figure 12.2 shows two left humeri from a prehistoric Canadian native population. The arm bone on the right shows a growth plate prematurely fused caused by trauma to the elbow. No further growth could have occurred at this end of the bone. The humerus on the left shows how the bone normally looks at age 8 to 10 years. In Figure 12.3, the bony spurs on these tibiae show the bones' reaction to excessive strain on the patellar ligament. When the bones of a prehistoric human (or a modern forensic case) show these sorts of modifications, they give us clues to the activities the individual pursued in life.

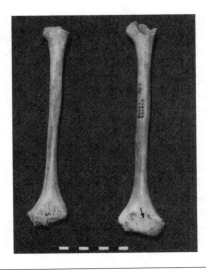

Figure 12.2 Comparison of two left humeri from a prehistoric Canadian native population; the arm bone on the right shows a growth plate prematurely fused (arrow), caused by trauma to the elbow.

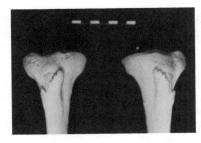

Figure 12.3 Bony spurs on tibiae.

Other examples include the tendency of ancient Inuit (Eskimo) males to show arthritic changes to the left wrist consistent with using their left hand as a pivot for a double-bladed kayak paddle. And long before "tennis elbow," ancient hunters suffered from a similar affliction we call "atl-atl elbow," after an Aztec spear-throwing device. Robust muscle markings and dense bone tissue indicate that many of our ancestral populations maintained very active lifestyles; most contemporary populations are extremely sedentary by comparison. A logical extension of this observation is that, if we are to understand the biological functioning of our ancestors, the most physically fit members of our contemporary society may offer the best model.

Today's human populations vary in body size, proportions, pigmentation, and many other biological traits. If these differences reflect adaptations to differing environments, they may show up in different performance characteristics. Studies of Olympic athletes have been invaluable in testing this idea. Research by Tanner, Carter, and others has shown the strong correlations between physique and performance—for example, people with long legs and low body weight have a mechanical advantage in track and field events. It is important that studies of physique be done carefully, however, to avoid undue racial stereotyping. During the 1930s, popular notions concerning leg structure were invoked to explain the success of black runners and jumpers. With the cooperation of 1936 Olympic champion Jesse Owens, the anthropologist and anatomist W.M. Cobb demonstrated Owens's lack of any unique anatomical features that would explain his athletic success. This and subsequent studies have demonstrated the wide overlap of racial distributions for most critical anatomical characteristics.

Besides physique, biological anthropologists also study population differences in acclimatization to environmental factors such as temperature and altitude. It is difficult to differentiate the effects of short-term acclimatization from genetically based adaptation, but populations appear to adapt differently. For example, populations have adapted to cold environments in very different ways. The Alakaluf Indians of Tierra del Fuego, who possessed a minimal material culture, may have adapted primarily by an increased basal metabolic rate. The Inuit, on the other hand, adapted with an only slightly increased metabolic rate (caused perhaps by their thermogenic diet) and extensive cultural protection: special clothing, footgear, and housing. It is impossible to hunt well with mittens on, so it is not surprising that northern populations show a rapid and efficient rewarming of their hands (called cold-induced vasodilation). Black populations, like the African-American soldiers in the Korean War, show little or no ability to rewarm their extremities, even after extended exposure. This probably reflects the tropical origin of their gene pool, in which an ability to adapt to cold stress would have had no adaptive value.

Researchers in this field of environmental adaptation are gradually acknowledging that physical activity is a critical component. Humans do not lead immobile lives, so our understanding of environmental adaptation will be flawed if it is based solely on the responses of subjects standing, sitting, or lying in cold, hot, or hypoxic (oxygen-deficient) environments. Resting skeletal muscle, for example, functions as a very effective insulator to protect core temperature, but activity increases blood flow to the muscle, which very quickly compromises its insulative characteristics. We do not yet know a great deal about cross-cultural differences in exercise physiology, but it is clear that there are intriguing differences (see Shephard, 1985; Gallow, Graham, & Pfeiffer, 1984).

Human adaptation is critical not only to adult survival but also to the survival and growth of children. Anthropologists postulate that environmental adaptation may be reflected in population differences in growth and psychomotor development. Unfortunately, the study of child growth is complicated by the fact that in many parts of the world growth is compromised by poor nutrition and health. Robert M. Malina and Peter Buschang (1985) have shown that strength and motor performance are compromised among marginally nourished children in rural Mexico. Nevertheless, their throwing performance is exceptionally good, perhaps because throwing small stones is an integral part of animal herding.

Another topic of growing interest to biological anthropologists is cross-cultural differences in disease patterns, including those diseases related to a sedentary lifestyle. Given our very active heritage, a lack of physical activity is hard on all humans, but the particular mix of diseases to which we fall prey may be influenced by the evolutionary past of our particular gene pool. Gallstones are much more common in sedentary populations whose ancestors endured a cold habitat for a prolonged period and probably result from a metabolic fat-storage adaptation. With inactivity, the adaptation becomes a maladaptation.

Biological anthropologists are likely to be involved anytime that population performance char-

acteristics must be determined: Can women (in general) operate military equipment as well as men (in general)? Are there certain population subgroups that are better suited to outdoor work in the Arctic? Do all children benefit in similar ways from physical activity?

Learned Societies and Journals

Very few associations focus on the anthropological study of physical activity. From the social perspective, the Association for the Study of Play, which publishes the journal *Play and Culture*, was created "to promote, stimulate and encourage the anthropological study of play." It shares much common ground with the biologically oriented International Society for the Advancement of Kinanthropometry. These relatively small organizations can offer important networks for the professional, but there are also a few anthropologically oriented colleagues in the large, "umbrella" organizations: the Canadian Association of Sport Sciences, the American College of Sports Medicine, and others that are discussed in other chapters in this volume.

Journals dedicated to physical activity research occasionally publish articles with an anthropological orientation, and anthropological journals sometimes publish physical-activity-oriented articles. Some of the journals that are particularly likely to yield relevant material are

- *American Anthropologist,*
- *Current Anthropology,*
- *Ethnology,*
- *Journal of Human Evolution,*
- *American Journal of Physical Anthropology,* and
- *Yearbook of Physical Anthropology.*

As yet, there is no clearly focused, well-organized interest group in "anthropology and physical activity." Although this can be frustrating for the interested student, it also means that the field is open to fresh perspectives and future developments.

Undergraduate Education

Because of the field's fledgling state, it would be unrealistic to expect full-blown undergraduate curricula built around the subject, but many physical activity programs with a social science emphasis incorporate a clear anthropological perspective.

HIGHLIGHT
Does Physical Activity Delay Maturation?

Even when environmental factors such as diet and climate are similar, children grow very differently. Each child adapts in a unique way to the challenges of daily life. Of these challenges, athletic training has aroused great interest recently. Are there analogies between the developmental retardation that anthropologists have documented in non-Western societies and the delayed maturation seen in elite juvenile athletes?

A convenient point of reference for this question is onset of menarche (first menstruation), which on average occurs later in athletes, including ballet dancers, than in the general population (swimmers are an exception). Rose Frisch, in her "critical body mass" hypothesis, suggests that of the factors proposed as causes—the psychological stress, the unusual diet, and the excessive leanness associated with elite performance—it is the latter that upsets the normal maturation mechanism.

Competitive swimmers usually have a higher proportion of adipose tissue and thus reach menarche at a "normal" age, despite performance stress, which is consistent with Frisch's idea that a certain proportion of body fat is necessary to reset the body's hormonal balance to that of a mature, ovulating female. On the other hand, people who are naturally lean (ectomorphs) naturally mature later, and it may be just these people who are selected for athletic training. That is, competitive gymnasts, runners, and ballet dancers might have been late maturers even had they not begun physical training. We do not yet know whether female athletes mature later because of some aspect of their training, or they are selected for training because they are late maturers—only more research will tell.

The best way to find out what relevant coursework is available is to speak with course counselors and professors. Programs or courses referring to *kinanthropometry* may often incorporate a biological anthropology perspective, but not always. Again, the interested student should have some exploratory discussions.

Social anthropology coursework on smaller university campuses may be subsumed within a sociology department. Biological anthropology courses are relatively rare and may on some campuses be taught in the biology faculty. Although this lack of centralization may be frustrating, it reflects the novelty of a fascinating field.

Career Opportunities

There will certainly be a need for university academicians in this area in the future. Such a career path requires at least a PhD, plus possibly postdoctoral research experience. For the undergraduate, the likely value of anthropological study is in a broadened cross-cultural sensitivity. All future physical activity professionals will function in a multicultural world in which people's unique traditions and genetic backgrounds will influence their needs and abilities. Anthropologically oriented study can improve the social skills of the planner/administrator and broaden the relevant knowledge of the sports physician.

Summary

Anthropological questions require a sensitivity about human variability and the interaction of culture and biology. Because anthropology is oriented toward the study of populations, it can help our society formulate valid generalizations about people. Its strength lies in its breadth and depth of perspective. Anthropologists consider a particular behavior cross-culturally and evolutionarily, contributing to our understanding of its origin and general function. Because people are by nature physically active, there is potential for much productive interaction between anthropologists and physical activity scientists.

References and Further Readings

Benedict, R. (1934). *Patterns of culture*. New York: New American Library.

Blanchard, K. (1981). *The Mississippi Choctaws at play: The serious side of leisure*. Champaign, IL: University of Illinois Press.

Blanchard, K., & Cheska, A.T. (1985). *The anthropology of sport: An introduction*. South Hadley, MA: Bergin & Garvey.

Bortz, W.M., II. (1985). Physical exercise as an evolutionary force. *Journal of Human Evolution*, **14**, 145-155.

Carter, J.E.L. (Ed.) (1982). *Physical structure of Olympic athletes. Part I: The Montreal Olympic Games anthropological project, vol. 16, Medicine and Sport Science Series*. Basel: S. Karger.

Carter, J.E.L. (Ed.) (1984). *Physical structure of Olympic athletes. Part II: Kinanthropometry of Olympic athletes, vol. 18, Medicine and Sport Science Series*. Basel: S. Karger.

Charteris, J., Wall, J.C., & Nottrodt, J.W. (1982). Pliocene hominid gait: New interpretations based on available footprint data from Laetoli. *American Journal of Physical Anthropology*, **58**, 133-144.

Cobb, W.M. (1936). Race and runners. *Journal of Health and Physical Education*, **7**, 1-8.

Freedman, D.G. (1979). *Human sociobiology: A holistic approach*. New York: Free Press.

Frisancho, A.R. (1979). *Human adaptation: A functional interpretation*. St. Louis: C.V. Mosby.

Gallow, D., Graham, T.E., & Pfeiffer, S.K. (1984). Comparative thermoregulatory response to acute cold in women of Asiatic and European descent. *Human Biology*, **56**(1), 19-34.

Gmelch, G. (1971). Baseball magic. *Transaction*, **8**. Reprinted in S. Friedman (Ed.), *Readings in anthropology, 1975-76* (pp. 158-161). Guilford, CT: Dushkin Publishing Group.

Hall, E.T. (1966). *The hidden dimension*. New York: Anchor Books.

Hanna, J.L. (1988). *Dance, sex and gender: Signs of identity, dominance, defiance and desire*. Chicago: University of Chicago Press.

Lewis, R.B. (1988). Old World dice in the prehistoric southern United States. *Current Anthropology*, **29**(5), 759-768.

Malina, R.M. (1983). Menarche in athletics. *Annals of Human Biology*, **10**, 1-24.

Malina, R.M., & Buschang, P.H. (1985). Growth, strength and motor performance of Zapotec children, Oaxaca, Mexico. *Human Biology*, **57**, 163-182.

Marsh, P. (1988). *Tribes*. Toronto: McGraw-Hill, Ryerson.

Morris, D. (1977). *Manwatching: A field guide to human behavior*. New York: H.N. Abrams.

Murdock, G.P. (1965). *Culture and society*. Pittsburgh: University of Pittsburgh Press.

Shephard, R.J. (1985). Factors associated with population variation in physiological working capacity. *Yearbook of Physical Anthropology*, **28**, 97-122.

Super, C.M. (1976). Environmental effects on motor development: The case of "African infant precocity." *Developmental Medicine and Child Neurology*, **18**, 561-567.

Chapter 13

History and Physical Activity

Gerald Redmond

Definitions in the social sciences that completely satisfy a majority of practitioners and researchers are notoriously difficult to obtain, though the effort to create them must be made for obvious reasons. Although there are very many opinions recorded as to what history is—ranging from Henry Ford's famous dictum that "history is bunk" to much more comprehensive and sophisticated analyses—an exact and universally accepted description remains elusive. Indeed, if the well-known historian Henry Steele Commager is correct in stating that "there are as many kinds of history as there are historians to write it" and that "each historian writes his own kind of history" (Commager, 1966, p. 15), then the existence of a diverse history of physical activity should not be surprising. The particular field of study relevant to this volume is the history of physical education and sport; given the social significance of sports in society, the field is simply referred to as sport history.

The academic study of sport has accelerated and gained international status and influence in recent years. There are now many academic associations concerned with it, as well as many professional journals and texts, conferences, and research meetings. These are complemented, in turn, by related courses in academic institutions, often in newly created departments of Sport Studies or Sport Sciences, some of which even offer degrees. Nor is this in any sense frivolous or marginal. It has been well argued for centuries that a knowledge of history is essential for a real understanding of any subject—be it art, education, politics, religion, science, or whatever—thus the history of sport (or sport history) is crucially important to the physical activity sciences and professions.

Sport history has also been difficult to define, because of varying conceptualizations of the field, but Howell's (1969) proposed definition may serve as a general guideline:

• • •

The terms **sport history** *and* **history of sport** *are not precisely the same, and may perhaps be differentiated. Any isolated study is one in sport history, whereas the accumulation of the body of knowledge, the subdiscipline, is the history of sport. Essentially, the subdiscipline, history of sport, must be concerned with a particular aspect of man's social activities—sports and games. . . . The history of sport, then, is concerned with the evolution of sport and games in culture. It deals with the past and is cognizant of movement and change. It deals with evolution of sports and games as well as their role in culture. (pp. 77-79)*

• • •

In practice, however, the distinction is not so precise, and the term *sport history* is used to describe the body of knowledge and not just an isolated study. No one would suggest, for example, that the North American Society for Sport History (NASSH) deals only with isolated studies or that the International Society for the History of Physical Education and Sport (ISHPES) concerns itself solely with the body of knowledge. The *British Journal of Sports History*, founded in 1984 and now the *International Journal of Sports History* (IJSH), has played a similarly broad role. The terms sport(s) history and history of sport are largely synonymous, therefore, and either one may may refer to the evolution of sports and games in culture.

Major Concepts

What makes this field unique is its emphasis on sport, but given the quite phenomenal status that sports enjoy in the world today such a category need be no more controversial than those of economic or military history, which along with their specialists are already well acknowledged. As Alex Natan (1958) succinctly expressed it over 30 years ago: "Never has a state risen so swiftly to world power as has sport. It has within 60 years hurried through a development for which empires have needed 5 centuries" (p. 47). Indeed, the continued absence of sporting pastimes in historical accounts would result in an intolerable imbalance and hence an inaccurate record.

Nevertheless, until recently sport has been a largely neglected topic for serious historical research. Many thought it to be an intellectually inferior vehicle for historians' attention, and some pioneering academics had to defend themselves against charges leveled at their ability or integrity. Fortunately, such indefensible snobbery has all but disappeared today as more and more historians—and academicians from other fields, as we shall see—have become involved in sport history. The current debate, however, is whether sport history constitutes a recent and separate form of research or a neglected but essential part of social history, whose practitioners are now enthusiastic to embrace it. Shunned before by history and its proponents, sport has now almost an embarrassment of suitors, a state of affairs in which physical educators have played a major, although not exclusive, role.

Methods in Historical Research

The methods of research are those of the parent discipline itself, which have been more than adequately discussed in a wide variety of sources. One particularly useful exposition is by D.B. Van Dalen (1959). In short, historians of any subject collect primary and secondary data and subject them to external and internal criticism during analysis and selection to produce a literary narrative.

This is not to imply, however, that historians must accept a methodological status quo and cannot experiment within the multidisciplinary realm of the social sciences. Indeed, as Berkhofer (1969) has argued, the historian now seeks "to achieve a more complex representation of past reality than

hitherto found in the subject" (p. 4). More and more often this involves interpreting the past through the use of various conceptual frameworks, theories, or models of human behavior, as well as the use of hypotheses, biographical and oral history methods, and quantification and sociological insights (Day and Lindsay, 1980).

History of Sport History

Basically, the study of sport history grew from three disciplines: classics, history, and physical education. In the recent and numerous "state-of-the-art" essays on the subject, most reviewers have paid too little attention to the status attained by those classicists who made sport the subject of their life's work (e.g., Gardiner, Harris, Finley, and Pleket). Gardiner, for example, enjoyed a long friendship with the famous physical educator R.T. McKenzie, who actually had hoped to publish Gardiner's opus as part of a series of physical education texts for which he was the editor. This would have met with the approval of Seward C. Staley, professor of physical education at the University of Illinois, who advocated as early as 1937 that a course in the history of sport should be included in each physical education student's professional training. In time, as Berryman (1973) has noted, "Staley influenced many colleagues and students and sport history became part of the physical educator's preparation at many colleges and universities. More important, with few exceptions, physical educators came to dominate the scholarly study of sport history" (p. 66).

Thurmond (1975) says he intends "to demonstrate the evolution of an academic discipline within the domain of physical education" (p. 10). Although this academic discipline has not flourished within physical education alone, physical educators were in the forefront of international developments during the 1960s and 1970s, organizing conferences, forming associations, editing journals, and establishing academic courses. The pace hardly slackened in the 1980s, during which decade both the Australian Society for Sport History and the British Society for Sport History were formed, and recent years have witnessed greater participation and productivity of scholars from departments of history, education, and English (e.g., Haley, 1978; Mangan, 1981; Baker, 1982; Higgs, 1982; Rader 1983).

More comprehensive reviews of the developments outlined here are available in the *Canadian*

Journal of the History of Sport and Physical Education (1970), the *Journal of Sport History* (1983), and the *British Journal of Sports History* (1984). Considering the debate over the use of more sophisticated social science methodologies, however, readers may find it ironic that few of the reviewers employ even the usual basic techniques such as questionnaires or interviews (or even correspondence) with the living scholars whose work is under discussion. Consequently, such reviews are often simply the opinion of the authors.

Canada has been well represented in the recent evolution of sport history, with some notable "firsts" to its credit. Above all the study of history of sport in Canada can be traced back primarily to one man, Howell, who developed a research program at the University of Alberta (Metcalfe, 1974). Moreover, Howell was instrumental in establishing the first doctoral program in physical education (at the University of Alberta) in Canada and the Commonwealth; his first two graduates were Allan Cox and Peter Lindsay, both of whom wrote dissertations on the history of 19th-century Canadian sport (Cox, 1969; Lindsay, 1969). Howell and his colleagues also organized the first Canadian Symposium on the History of Sport at Edmonton in 1970 (the fifth such symposium was held at Toronto in 1982) and the second World Symposium on the History of Sport at Banff, Alberta, in 1971. The Howells' book *Sports and Games in Canadian Life: 1700 to the Present* (1969) has been described as "the only book that covers the whole span of Canadian History" (Metcalfe, 1974, p. 234).

Elsewhere in Canada, the *Canadian Journal of the History of Sport and Physical Education* appeared in 1970, founded and edited by Alan Metcalfe at the University of Windsor (this became the *Canadian Journal of History of Sport* in 1981). This was soon followed by the establishment of a History for Sport and Physical Activity Committee within the Canadian Association for Health, Physical Education and Recreation (CAHPER). This committee issued a report in 1975 entitled *Sport History Canada*, which indicated that in the academic year 1973 to 1974 there were 29 courses in Canadian universities devoted solely to the history of sport and physical education.

In the same year, volume 1 of *To Know Ourselves: The Report of the Commission on Canadian Studies* (1975) strongly emphasized the significance of sport and physical culture in Canadian life and encouraged the development of Canadian sport history. In the previous year, in their introduction to *Canada's Sporting Heroes* (1974), historian Syd Wise and author Doug Fisher expressed regret over the neglect of sport by Canadian historians and paid tribute to the "pioneering work" that had been initiated in the physical education faculties of several Canadian universities. Other important works produced in Canada include Henry Roxborough's *One Hundred-Not Out* (1966); Alan Metcalfe's *Canada Learns to Play* (1987); Morris Mott's *Sports in Canada* (1989); Alan Young's *Tudor and Jacobean Tournaments* (1987); and A.J. Young's *Beyond Heroes* (1988).

In 1979, the formation of the Canadian Association for Sports Heritage (CASH) provided a forum for a membership of individuals employed primarily in the growing number of sports halls of fame and museums. A year later the first Sport History Research Methodology workshop was held at the University of Alberta, and the second at the University of Western Ontario in 1981. Two years after that the tenth HISPA (International Association for the History of Sport and Physical Education) Congress was held at Edmonton, Alberta.

The recent books and theses in the area of sport history produced by Canadian faculty and students, as well as the rising number of professional organizations and conferences, reflect improved standards and scholarship and give cause for qualified optimism. As Don Morrow (1983) states, "The years from 1972 to 1982 have represented a decade of establishment of Canadian Sport History as a viable research area: the next decade must be one of concentrated and focused development" (p. 79).

Learned Societies and Journals

A number of scholarly associations exist for individuals interested in the field. In addition to the International Society for the History of Physical Education and Sport and the North American Society for Sport History, there are organizations related to aspects of the history of sport in several nations within the Commonwealth. Both Britain and Australia have learned societies devoted entirely to the field, the British Society for Sport History and the Australian Society for Sport History. Canada boasts two organizations relevant to sport history, the Canadian Association for Sports Heritage and the History for Sport and Physical Activity Committee of CAHPER.

Beyond the regular activities of these groups, there are a variety of symposia and workshops, such as the Canadian Symposia on the History of Sport and the Sport History Research Methods Workshops.

HIGHLIGHT
To Know Ourselves: The Report of the Commission on Canadian Studies

This country has a rich and distinctive heritage in sport and physical culture. But Canadians seem smitten with cultural amnesia when it comes to this important aspect of our history and natural life. Ned Hanlan, for example, probably brought more fame and recognition to Canada than any other citizen has ever done. As the world's singles sculling rowing champion from 1880 to 1884, and the holder of the championships of Canada, England, and the United States, undefeated in 300 consecutive races, Hanlan was a legend in his lifetime. Yet even the schoolchildren of Toronto, his native city, now scarcely know his name. The prodigious feats of strength of Louis Cyr, which literally amazed the world in the 1890s, are little better known in his native Quebec. And the achievements of the four men who returned to New Brunswick from Paris, France, in 1867 after being hailed as the rowing champions of the world are almost completely forgotten. Yet the exploits of "the Paris Crew" drew far more attention in the world press than did the creation of our Canadian Confederation in the same year.

One of the ways in which Canadian educational institutions can encourage a greater knowledge and appreciation of our physical culture is through the curriculum itself. Unfortunately, the educational system largely neglects sport as an academic subject. Where social history is taught, very often sport is not included or, at best, it is passed over briefly. Women's sport and the many achievements of our female athletes are rarely acknowledged. To the extent that sport is treated at all, American sports heroes and events often receive much greater attention than do Canadian figures and events. There are encouraging signs, however, that sport is becoming more widely viewed as an important part of our culture and as a legitimate facet of Canadian studies. For example, a number of university physical education departments are now actively encouraging students to do research and to write on Canadian sport subjects. The University of Alberta and, more recently, the University of Windsor have been pioneers in this field. In addition, several universities now offer courses specifically concerned with the history and sociology of sport in Canada. Unfortunately, however, historians and sociologists generally have been unwilling to consider sport and physical culture as an area worthy of scholarly investigation. This attitude has been a serious deterrent to students and faculty members wishing to work in this field.

Sport and, more broadly, physical culture offer wide scope for Canadian studies in such disciplines as history, sociology, economics, business, and the health sciences, as well as in professional programs of physical education. There is a need for more courses in various fields of study to examine this subject, often on a cooperative, transdisciplinary basis. In addition, there is room for much more research activity and publication in this field. Many Canadian newspapers are available on microfilm, making it possible for students to do original research on sports events and to form their own opinions and interpretations about these events and the circumstances surrounding them. Audiovisual resources also offer great scope for teaching and research in this field.

The Public Archives of Canada has initiated a sport history program that involves collecting, cataloguing, and making available to researchers correspondence files, minute books, financial records, and other archival materials of many Canadian sports organizations, as well as the papers of prominent athletes, physical educators, and sports executives. [The Public Archives of Canada's name has been changed to the National Archives of Canada.] Such materials are a valuable source of information about the development of Canadian sport and of Canadian culture.

More extensive research and teaching about physical culture and sport should help Canadians to become more aware of the role of sport and of physical fitness in their lives, and of the contributions made by Canadians in this area. It should also stimulate more interest among Canadians in physical education as a profession with a vital contribution to make to the health and culture of this country.

Note. Reprinted from Commission on Canadian Studies (1975) by permission.

The student interested in this area will find many relevant articles in

- *International Journal of the History of Sport,*
- *Canadian Journal of History of Sport,* and
- *Journal of Sport History.*

In addition, journals in both history and physical activities sciences/physical education occasionally publish articles in the field.

These are examples of professional journals published in the sport history area.

Undergraduate Education and Career Opportunities

Unfortunately, the current economic difficulties in universities, to which academic programs in physical education (especially in the sociocultural or social science area) are certainly not immune, render the future of Canadian sport history less than optimistic. The expansion and improvement of what appears to be a sound foundation may not be feasible at present, and we may be in for an era of survival at best.

Comparatively, it has never been an easy area in which to obtain research grants. Moreover, the job opportunities for aspiring sport historians are limited today, both on campus and in sports halls of fame and sport associations. A genuine interest and commitment to the area, allied with personal ability, are no guarantee of related future employment—not that they ever were, but there were more opportunities and vacancies in previous years. However, the expected retirement of many of the current professors late in the 1990s and early in the next century may provide some opportunities for those now in their first year of undergraduate study.

The aspiring sport historian who is undeterred by this pessimism will need some kind of demonstrable undergraduate specialization or interest, followed by a graduate degree in the area, preferably at the doctoral level. But there should be no turning back, and no place for the faint-hearted. The courses in sport history are in the university calendars, and the subject has gained academic credibility, a status confirmed consistently by the cultural significance of sport in society. The esteemed, Pulitzer-prize-winning historian Barbara Tuchman (1981) wrote a few years ago that

> Homo Ludens, man at play, is surely as significant a figure as a man at war or at work. In human activity the invention of the ball may be said to rank with the invention of the wheel. Imagine America without baseball, Europe without soccer, England without cricket, the Italians without *bocci*, China without Ping-Pong, and tennis for no one. (p. 234)

Summary

A world without sport is unimaginable, and a present-day university without a place for sport history is unimaginative, to say the least. The cultural centrality of sport of which Tuchman speaks, together with the progress of sport history as a field of inquiry, ensures the future of sport history. Although neither sport nor history may belong exclusively to any one department or group on campus, the contributions physical educators have made to date should give people working in the physical activity sciences a significant part of that future.

References and Further Readings

Baker, W.J. (1982). *Sports in the western world*. Totowa, NJ: Rowman and Littlefield.

Berkhofer, R.F., Jr. (1969). *A behavioral approach to historical analysis*. New York: Free Press.

Berryman, J.W. (1973). Sport history as social history. *Quest*, **20**(66), 65-73.

British Journal of Sports History. (1984, May). **1**(1).

Commager, H.S. (1966). *The nature of study of history*. Columbus, OH: Charles E. Merrill.

Commission on Canadian Studies. (1975). *To know ourselves: The report of the Commission on Canadian Studies* (Vols. 1, 2). Ottawa, ON: Association of Universities and Colleges of Canada.

Cox, A.E. (1969). *A history of sports in Canada, 1868-1900*. Unpublished doctoral dissertation, University of Alberta, Edmonton.

Day, R., & Lindsay, P. (1980). *Sport history research methodology: Proceedings of a workshop held at the University of Alberta, May 28-June 1, 1980*. Edmonton, AB: University of Alberta.

Finley, M.I., & Plekett, H.W. (1976). *The Olympic Games: The first thousand years*. London: Chatto and Windus.

Gardiner, E.N. (1967). *Athletics of the ancient world*. Oxford: Clarendon Press.

Haley, B. (1978). *The healthy body and Victorian culture*. Cambridge, MA: Harvard University Press.

Harris, H.A. (1964). *Greek athletes and athletics*. London: Hutchinson.

Higgs, R.J. (1982). *Sports: A reference guide*. London: Greenwood Press.

Howell, M.L. (1969, March). Toward a history of sport. *Journal of Health, Physical Education and Recreation*, **40**(3), 77-79.

Howell, N., & Howell, M.L. (1969). *Sports and games in Canadian life: 1700 to the present*. Toronto: Macmillan.

Lindsay, P.L. (1969). *A history of sport in Canada, 1807-1867*. Unpublished doctoral dissertation, University of Alberta, Edmonton.

Mangan, J.A. (1981). *Athleticism in the Victorian and Edwardian public school*. London: Cambridge University Press.

Metcalfe, A. (1974). North American sport history: A review of North American sport historians and their works. In J.H. Wilmore (Ed.), *Exercise and sport sciences reviews* (Vol. 2, pp. 225-238). New York and London: Academic Press.

Metcalfe, A. (1987). *Canada learns to play: The emergence of organized sport*. Toronto: McClelland and Stewart.

Morrow, D. (1983). Canadian sport history: A critical essay. *Journal of Sport History*, **10**(1), 67-69.

Mott, M. (Ed.) (1989). *Sports in Canada: Historical readings*. Toronto: Copp Clark Pitman.

Natan, A. (Ed.) (1958). *Sport and society*. London: Bowes and Bowes.

New York Times. (1930, November 23), p. 25.

Rader, B.G. (1983). *American sports*. Englewood Cliffs, NJ: Prentice Hall.

Roxborough, H. (1966). *One hundred-not out: The story of nineteenth-century Canadian sport*. Toronto: Ryerson Press.

Special Review Issue. (1983). *Journal of Sport History*, **10**(1).

Sport History Canada. (1975). Windsor, ON: Canadian Association for Health, Physical Education and Recreation (CAHPER).

Thurmond, R.C. (1975, October). Sport and physical education historiography. *Journal of Health, Physical Education and Recreation*, pp. 10-12.

Tuchman, B. (1981). *Practicing history: Selected essays*. New York: Alfred A. Knopf.

Van Dalen, D.B. (1959). The historical method. In M.G. Scott (Ed.), *Research methods in health, physical education and recreation* (pp. 465-481). Washington, DC: American Alliance for Health, Physical Education and Recreation.

Wise, S.F., & Fisher, D. (1974). *Canada's sporting heroes*. Don Mills, ON: General.

Young, A. (1987). *Tudor and Jacobean tournaments*. Dobbs Ferry, NY: Sheridan House.

Young, A.J. (1988). *Beyond heroes: A sport history of Nova Scotia* (Vols. 1 and 2). Hansport, NS: Lancelot Press.

Chapter 14

Pedagogy and Physical Activity

Jean Brunelle
Marielle Tousignant

In general, pedagogy concerns the art, science, and profession of teaching. As an academic area it focuses on two related areas:

1. *Research on teaching*, which examines the impact of teacher action on student learning
2. *Research on teacher education*—that is, on the professional preparation of those who teach—which delves into the impact of university professors' actions on prospective and inservice teachers' learning

Although pedagogy has long been considered a "bag of tricks," systematic investigation has produced a rapidly growing body of knowledge that provides a great deal of reliable information in these areas.

● ● ●

The pedagogy of the physical activities sciences investigates both the impact of teachers' action on students' learning in the natural settings wherein teaching of physical activities occurs and the strategies whereby individuals prepare themselves to undertake such teaching.

● ● ●

Major Concepts

Researchers in pedagogy study an integrated construct, commonly called *teaching*, that includes the three phases of the teaching-learning process: planning, instruction, and evaluation (see Figure 14.1). After Dunkin and Biddle (1974) published their version of Medley's teaching model, numerous authors have used these concepts (further categorized as presage, context, process, and product) in the course of their writings. In doing so, they have helped reduce the confusion surrounding the field's essential elements. In studying the pedagogy of physical activity, for example, our research team in the Department of Physical Education at Laval University has adapted the Dunkin and Biddle model. As Figure 14.1 shows, this adaptation outlines five major variables and highlights some of the specific aspects of the teaching-learning process currently under scrutiny in the field.

Research on teacher education is conducted through either of two major theoretical perspectives (Bain, 1990). First, the behavior analysis framework, which searches for laws of human behavior, fosters research on how to develop effective teacher training programs. Second, the theory on occupational socialization provides a conceptual framework for investigating the factors that initially influence people to choose a career in physical activity, for example, significant others (coaches, teachers, or family members), personal experience as a participant or leader, or desire to work with children or to remain associated with sports. Other elements of interest to this perspective are the factors responsible for teachers' perceptions and actions during their formal professional preparation programs and their experiences as professionals.

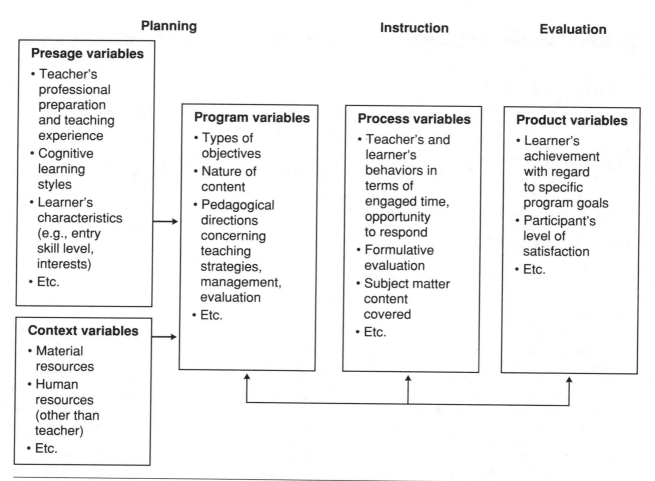

Figure 14.1 A comprehensive model showing the variables associated with the three dimensions of the teaching-learning conditions. Reprinted from Tousignant, Brunelle, and Godbout (1987) by permission.

Methods and Major Research Questions

Unfortunately, the study of teaching has had a rather difficult time getting off the ground. The rigorous but artificial techniques of traditional scientific research proved a blind alley. Progress in understanding the complex teaching-learning process emerged only when researchers stopped trying to test theoretical hypotheses under laboratory conditions and instead focused their efforts on observing teacher-learner interaction as it occurs in natural settings. Various research methods are used.

Quantitative Research

Quantitative methods in the field of pedagogy have revolved around what Rosenshine and Furst (1971) identify as the descriptive-correlational-ex-

perimental loop. During the last two decades, many studies of teaching used a *descriptive analytical* approach to identify, name, classify, and count the various phenomena that occur during the teaching-learning process, for example, academic learning time, engaged time, waiting time, teacher feedback, enthusiasm, and managerial procedures.

Some observational instruments that use a predetermined set of categories have been derived from classroom research. For example, the Academic Learning Time System, a physical education system developed by Daryl Siedentop at the Ohio State University to determine the time a student spends actively learning a task, was derived from the Beginning Teacher Evaluation Study at the Far West Laboratory in California. In addition, a variety of systems specifically designed for describing and discussing motor-learning activities are now available, and a compendium has been published of these specialized instruments (Darst, Zakrajsek, & Mancini, 1989). Numerous descrip-

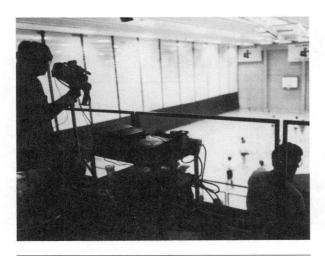

Videotaping classroom teaching is one way of collecting information that can later be used in the analysis of the teaching-learning process.

tive analytical studies have provided the research community with an extensive array of information on what "goes on" in the various settings where physical activities are taught (Siedentop, 1983).

Improved descriptive techniques have led to more sophisticated research designs focusing on teaching effectiveness. The specific purpose of *correlational studies*, also called process-product research, is to identify teaching variables related to learner achievement. In a nutshell, the issue here is what makes a good teacher. Whereas previous research looked for personal characteristics of good teachers, recent studies have shown the most influential variables to be the types of available learning conditions.

Teaching is often viewed as a craft learned primarily through apprenticeship; pedagogy has long been considered an art rather than a science. The process-product studies investigating the relations between what happens in the classroom (process) and how much students learn (product) have provided substantial information about what can be considered effective teaching (Siedentop, 1983; Wittrock, 1986). In physical education, for example, correlational studies have been conducted to describe the relationship of both a learner's engagement and rate of successful practice trials to motor achievement, as well as to investigate the links between various teacher behaviors, student characteristics, class size, and type of class organizations to student engaged time.

Besides using these descriptive methods, researchers in pedagogy also use more rigorous *experimental designs* to test the effect of specific types of learning conditions on students' behavior and achievement. For example, studies have tested the effect of various instructional methods (direct instruction, peer teaching, or the problem-solving approach) on student engagement and learning. In teacher education, a number of experimental studies have investigated the effectiveness of various means to improve teaching, such as increasing the quality of feedback or reducing a learner's waiting time. This research has established beyond question that, under the proper conditions, student and professional teachers can develop new behaviors, modify old patterns of teaching, and adapt generic models to the particularities of their context without elaborate or expensive training (Siedentop, 1986).

Qualitative Research

Pedagogy specialists also use *qualitative approaches* to better understand how the teaching-learning process operates in the real world of teaching physical activity and in the training of teachers. They use techniques derived mainly from anthropology and ethnography, sociology and ethnomethodology, and psychology and phenomenology (Locke, 1989).

Qualitative researchers gather detailed and in-depth descriptions of what teachers and learners think and do. They spend many hours observing and interviewing people involved in the context of interest. Unlike researchers who use descriptive analysis, qualitative researchers do not enter the world of the participants with a set of predetermined categories to code what is happening. To understand the social reality from the participant's point of view, they immerse themselves in the natural context being investigated and gather information that reflects its particularities and complexity.

The literature of this approach covers a wide variety of phenomena, yielding, for example, rich descriptions of teachers' planning strategies that indicate teachers do not plan according to theoretical models, as well as descriptive accounts of how students accomplish learning tasks that show learners to have numerous ways to avoid the tasks while appearing not to. In addition, detailed portraits of how boys and girls are treated have illustrated that equity remains an issue worth attention, and qualitative research on the process of learning to teach has yielded information and raised complex questions about the factors influencing socialization of individuals as teachers.

HIGHLIGHT
The Benefits of Peer Evaluation

A 3-year project conducted by several members of our research group at Laval University provides a good example of a study that helps explain what constitutes effective teaching. The goal of a project by Godbout, Desrosiers, Brunelle, and Spallanzani (1988) was to describe the effect of three teaching strategies on learners' behavior and their learning gains. The components of this study of the effect of three teaching strategies are outlined as follows:

> The purpose was to test the effect of three teaching strategies on student behavior and learning gains during a 4- to 6-week teaching unit devoted to learning specific motor skills.
> The independent variables were three teaching strategies that used different ways of constructively evaluating the learners.

Strategy	*Evaluation*
A	The teacher gave the type of feedback physical education teachers usually give.
B	In addition to teacher feedback, the learners learned to evaluate their own performance.
C	Systematic evaluation from the peers provided the formative (constructive) evaluation.

The dependent variables, the measures used to assess the effect of the three strategies during the experimental teaching unit, were

- the *quantity* and *quality* of student active learning time and
- the *amount of gains* made by the learners during the unit.

The results indicate that

- students' active involvement in the formative evaluation process leads to a lower percentage of active learning time, especially when a peer evaluation strategy is used;
- the students actively involved in the evaluation process learn as well as, if not slightly more than, the others, despite a reduced active learning time; and
- some students find it difficult to interact with their peers in an evaluation context, which suggests the need to develop such social skills before implementing peer evaluation programs.

Professional Organizations

This is a very exciting time for researchers in pedagogy, especially those studying physical activity. The field of study has seen steady progress and an increasingly well-organized network of professional organizations through which to disseminate research results. Scientific and professional associations that frequently include sessions related to research on teaching in the program of their annual conferences include the following:

- Association Canadienne française pour l'avancement des sciences (ACFAS)
- Canadian Association for Health, Physical Education and Recreation (CAHPER)
- Canadian Association of Sport Sciences (CASS)
- American Alliance for Health, Physical Educa-

tion, Recreation and Dance (AAHPERD)

- National Association for Sport and Physical Education (NASPE)
- International Council for Health, Physical Education and Recreation (ICHPER)
- Association internationale des écoles supérieures d'éducation physique (AIESEP)

The Association internationale des écoles supérieures d'éducation physique (AIESEP) annual meeting has become the largest international gathering of specialists in research on physical activity pedagogy. Since the Madrid meeting in 1978, which boasted the first session on teaching analysis, pedagogy-related research has become the major theme at AIESEP conventions (e.g., Audiovisual Means in Sports, Macolin, Switzerland, 1979; Better Teaching of Health and Fitness, Boston, 1982; the Physical Education Teacher and Coach Today, Heidelberg, 1986; Physical Education and Coaching: Present States and Outlook for the Future, Trois-Rivières, 1987).

Several international meetings on physical activity have featured keynote speakers from the pedagogy subfield, for example, the International Congress of Physical Activity Sciences, Québec, 1976; the VII Commonwealth and International Conference on Sport, Physical Education, Recreation and Dance, Australia, 1982; the International Symposium of Research in School Physical Education, Finland, 1982; and the International Council for Health, Physical Education and Recreation, Vancouver, 1987. The Sport Pedagogy section of the Olympic Scientific Congress held in 1984 in Eugene, Oregon, and the Adelphi-AIESEP 1985 Conference in New York are considered outstanding events in the history of pedagogy of physical activity. Some of the most important publications in this field have emerged from such conferences.

Pedagogy specialists have developed special interest groups, such as CAHPER's Research on Teacher Education in Physical Education group, which began in 1983. Pedagogy specialists have been very active in NASPE and in associations within AAHPERD. Recently, the prestigious American Educational Research Association agreed to create a special interest group under the rubric of Research on Learning and Instruction in Physical Education.

Journals and Other Publications

Various journals have published papers about the pedagogy of physical activity. Some of these jour-

nals focus on physical activity and some on education. The following are some of the most important.

Education

Teaching and Teacher Education
Journal of Teacher Education
Australian Journal of Teaching Practice
Canadian Journal of Education
Revue des sciences de l'éducation

Physical Activities

Journal of Teaching in Physical Education
Research Quarterly for Exercise and Sport
Journal of Sport Psychology
QUEST
Canadian Journal of Sport Sciences
Revue des sciences et techniques des activités physique et sportives

Undergraduate Education

All undergraduate programs aimed at preparing professionals to teach physical activity include courses somewhat related to pedagogy (e.g., in methods and curriculum). Unfortunately, the content of these courses often falls far short of the state of knowledge in current pedagogy research. A vast majority of teacher educators base their courses not on contemporary research but mostly on the traditional ways physical educators behave and on their beliefs as framed by personal experience. Moreover, many teacher educators, as well as future teachers, assume that knowing the subject matter (i.e., the physical activities themselves) is a necessary and sufficient condition for effective teaching. Consequently, the knowledge gained from pedagogical research does not appear directly relevant to many preservice teachers and teacher educators.

Other teacher educators, however, have a more positive attitude toward using pedagogy research in professional preparation. They believe that teachers should learn to be reflective practitioners who use research conclusions to identify their own working hypotheses, test them in their particular teaching context, and assess their contribution to improving learning conditions.

One of the most prevalent current research topics in undergraduate courses concerns how learners' behavior (while learning) affects the learning process. Thus, the notion of active learning time and its related components (success, rate, waiting time, organizational time) are widely used to help teachers examine how their teaching strategies influence student behavior.

Other research topics found in teacher training classes include effective management, interpersonal relations associated with classroom climate, and teacher planning. In a related but slightly different context, knowledge gained from studies of the teaching-learning process is useful in designing learning experiences for prospective teachers, who need to find out about teaching through "experiential" learning.

Career Opportunities

People skilled in pedagogical research methodology can seek a teaching or coaching position in a variety of institutions depending on their experience, knowledge, and skill in performing particular physical activities and working with specific populations (for example, elementary or secondary school students, athletes, handicapped people, adults, or senior citizens). Furthermore, such a person is especially well qualified to play the role of supervisor or resource person in charge of improving the quality of teaching-learning conditions in the various contexts wherein physical activities are taught (e.g., schools, sport federations, and health centers).

Finally, despite cutbacks in education budgets, individuals with a doctoral degree and a specialization in sport pedagogy can find employment as university professors. Indeed, the field's increased recognition in various physical education departments is exemplified by an entirely new phenomenon: Many of the qualification lists posted in announcements of vacant university positions now specify specialized preparation in pedagogical research.

Summary

The field of research in physical activity pedagogy is barely 25 years old; nonetheless, it has become a productive research area. New and exciting results have contributed to a better understanding of how manipulating learning conditions affects partici-

pants' gains in skills and knowledge about physical activity. Despite the complexity of the phenomenon under scrutiny, the major concepts involved are now operationally defined, and a variety of research methods are used to illuminate the main features of effective teaching. Researchers have created a network that allows for an effective dissemination of the results, leading to an improvement in the current research effort and to strategies that put research results into practice.

References and Further Readings

Bain, L. (1990). Physical education teacher education. In W.R. Houston, M. Haberman, & J. Sikula (Eds.), *Handbook of research in teacher education*. New York: Macmillan.

Barrette, G.T., Feingold, R.S., Rees, C.R., & Piéron, M. (Eds.) (1987). *Myths, models, and methods in sport pedagogy*. Champaign, IL: Human Kinetics.

Darst, P., Zakrajsek, D., & Mancini, V. (1989). *Analyzing physical education and sport instruction* (2nd ed.). Champaign, IL: Human Kinetics.

Dunkin, M.J., & Biddle, B.J. (1974). *The study of teaching*. New York: Holt, Rinehart & Winston.

Gage, N.L. (1985). *Hard gains in the soft sciences: The case of pedagogy*. Bloomington, IN: Phi Delta Kappa Center on Evaluation, Development and Research.

Godbout, P., Desrosiers, P., Brunelle, J., & Spallanzani, C. (1988). The effect of three formative evaluation strategies on the learning of selected motor skills. In H. Rieder & U. Hanke (Eds.), *The physical education teacher and coach today* (Vol. 2, pp. 200-206). Köln, Germany: Bundes Institut für Sport Wissenschaft.

Hawley, W.D., Rosenholtz, S., Goodstein, H., & Hasselbring, T. (1984). Good schools: What research says about improving student achievement. *Peabody Journal of Education*, **61**(4), 1-178.

Locke, L.F. (1982). Research on teaching physical activity: A modest celebration. In M.L. Howell & J.E. Saunders (Eds.), *Proceedings of the VII Commonwealth and International Conference on Sport, Physical Education, Recreation and Dance* (pp. 189-198). Brisbane: University of Queensland Press.

Locke, L.F. (1986). The future of research of pedagogy: Balancing on the cutting edge. *The American Academy of Physical Education Papers*, **20**, 83-94. Champaign, IL: Human Kinetics.

Locke, L.F. (1987). Research and the improvement of teaching: The professor as the problem. In

G.T. Barrette, R.S. Feingold, C.R. Rees, and M. Piéron (Eds.), *Myths, models, and methods in sport pedagogy* (pp. 1-26). Champaign, IL: Human Kinetics.

Locke, L.F. (1989). Qualitative research as a form of scientific inquiry in sport and physical education. *Research Quarterly for Exercise and Sport*, **60**(1), 1-20.

Piéron, M., & Cheffers, J. (Eds.) (1982). Studying the teaching in physical education. *Proceeding of the AIESEP*. Liège, Belgium: Umieti de Liège Press.

Piéron, M., & Graham, G. (Eds.) (1986). *Sport pedagogy*. Champaign, IL: Human Kinetics.

Rosenshine, B., & Furst, N. (1971). Research in teacher performance criteria. In B.O. Smith (Ed.), *Research in teacher education* (pp. 37-72). Englewood Cliffs, NJ: Prentice Hall.

Siedentop, D. (1983). *Developing teaching skills in physical education* (2nd ed.). Palo Alto, CA: Mayfield.

Siedentop, D. (1986). The modification of teacher behavior. In M. Piéron & G. Graham (Eds.), *Sport pedagogy* (pp. 3-18). Champaign, IL: Human Kinetics.

Telema, R. (Ed.) (1983). *Research in school physical education*. Uimahalli, Finland: The Foundation for Promotion of Physical Culture and Health.

Templin, T.J., & Olson, J.K. (Eds.) (1983). *Teaching in physical education* (Big Ten Body of Knowledge Symposium series, vol. 14). Champaign, IL: Human Kinetics.

Templin, T.J., & Schempp, P.G. (1989). *Socialization into physical education: Learning to teach*. Indianapolis: Benchmark Press.

Tousignant, M., Brunelle, J., & Godbout, P. (1987). Methodological trends in Laval University's research on teaching physical education. In C. Paré, M. Lirette, & M. Piéron (Eds.), *Research methodology in teaching physical education and sports* (pp. 57-86). Trois-Rivières: Département des sciences de l'activité physique, Université du Québec à Trois-Rivières.

Wittrock, M.C. (Ed.) (1986). *Third handbook of research on teaching*. New York: Macmillan.

Chapter 15

Philosophy and Physical Activity

Klaus V. Meier

The term *philosophy* has a rather wide application in everyday use. We need to narrow it somewhat before we can see what significance philosophy has for the study of sport and physical activity and how it is useful to sport and exercise science students. Thus, this chapter opens with a brief discussion of what the discipline of philosophy entails, what philosophers attempt to do and just how they go about doing it, and what its issues are.

Philosophy may be characterized as "the art of wondering"—in fact, one noteworthy introductory text to the discipline uses this phrase as its title (Christian, 1973). It takes to heart the Socratic assertion that the unexamined life is not worth living. Philosophy is a major part of the eternal and ever-vibrant search for truth, inviting humanity to question, think, and speculate in the pursuit of wisdom. It is a probing, critical discipline whose practitioners carefully describe and systematically inquire into various aspects of human experience and the world. Philosophy involves efforts to construct a well-grounded and accurate picture of reality within which the diverse elements of human knowledge, experience, and aspirations will find their proper place.

● ● ●

The philosophy of sport seeks to define the essential characteristics of sport and to determine its meaning and value for human experience.

● ● ●

The philosophy of sport limits its range of inquiry into the nearly universal and historically extended involvement of humans in sport, play, and games. Undertaking such an investigation from the perspectives of the various contemporary philosophic orientations, positions, and investigative methodologies can help clarify and explain the nature, purpose, meaning, and significance of these phenomena.

First, one thing must be made clear. In the rigorous sense in which the term is employed throughout this chapter, philosophy is not simply "having a point of view" or expressing a personal opinion on a specific matter. It entails instead vigorous descriptive and "root" reflection; its business is to ascertain what justifiable grounds may be presented to uphold a particular position, and it requires careful and systematic construction of a well-formulated and substantiated set of assertions and beliefs. This is not always an easy or a comfortable task. Indeed,

> philosophy is both inviting and forbidding. Reflection on the world and on oneself in the world is part of commonsense existence, yet radical, *root* reflection, which is the mark of true philosophizing, is on the far side of daily life. There is nothing more commonplace than "philosophy" and nothing rarer than philosophy. (Natanson, 1970, p. 1)

Consequently, philosophy is a venture not for those who have closed minds or entrenched personal opinions, but rather for those who still demonstrate a capacity for wonder and an enthusiasm for "creative disturbance." Instead of pursuing constriction or closure, philosophy questions, appraises, and debates to provide expansion and illumination.

Philosophers engage in critical scrutiny and dialogue to achieve clarity, by examining basic presumptions and assumptions, premises and ideas, derived positions, and conclusions. Thus, debate and conflict within philosophy should not be viewed negatively but rather as demonstrations of continuing growth and as necessary components in the process of clarification and knowledge attainment. In essence, then, philosophy is both a challenge to all that has preceded and a stimulus to future inquiry.

Methods in Philosophical Research

Philosophy employs numerous methods and ways of inquiring about all facets of reality and the human condition, including sport, adding to its richness and productivity through diverse approaches rather than methodological singularity.

The conceptual analysis of terms and the things they represent (e.g., sport, games, and play) is one such approach. Because philosophy seeks clear thought, precise terminology, and valid reasoning structures, it often uses various techniques of critical and linguistic analysis—sometimes with a degree of rigor and order similar to that of mathematics—to determine meanings and to test the usefulness of definitions, to eliminate ambiguities and irregularities, to challenge presuppositions, and to appraise full argument structures.

In addition, philosophy also avails itself of precise and basic descriptive procedures to great benefit. Phenomenology, which entails a delineation and systematic investigation of phenomena as they present themselves to the senses and human consciousness, is a particularly beneficial way to unearth and analyze the sport experience and its lived meaning for participants.

The philosophy of sport uses numerous other orientations and techniques, including, to mention but a few, hermeneutical (interpretive) inquiry, critical and dialectical phenomenology, Marxist and critical theory, and structural analysis. Any attempt to encapsulate these particular methods and their underlying world views in a few sentences would likely do more harm than good, however. By reading some of the many accessible studies that use these techniques interested students can become familiar with how philosophers go about their tasks and also develop their own personal abilities of critical thinking. In the end, this is the only way to learn philosophy, which is essentially a "do-it-yourself" activity.

Major Topics of Inquiry

In turning to the specific area of concern, let me note that this brief chapter addresses the philosophy of physical activity as exemplified in sport, games, and play; I deliberately do not address exercise, dance, or physical education. This is because the philosophical problems associated with exercise are usually subsumed in discussions of sport, games, and play; the literature on the philosophy of dance is so vast as to warrant a separate chapter; and the philosophy of physical education centers on pedagogical concerns that also warrant separate consideration to an extent precluded here. Largely for the sake of brevity and convenience, I will generally use the term *sport* to refer to the relevant physical activities of sport, games, and play. Any exceptions will be clear from the context.

The Nature of Sport, Games, and Play

It has frequently been observed that classification is a precursor to understanding. To analyze, clarify, and understand sport, games, and play and their significance for an individual or for societal functions, it is necessary to decide what activities fall within each category and to specify the interrelationships among these three forms of human activity. Such efforts illuminate as well as facilitate discourse and, thereby, further research. You can get some idea of the difficulty inherent to the task of classification from the following representative questions:

- Which activities should properly be covered by magazines such as *Sports Illustrated* or a television program entitled the "Wide World of Sports"?
- Are major league baseball and tiddlywinks both sports?
- Are any or all of the following activities games, sports, or both: automobile demolition derbies, surfside frisbee throwing, jogging, marathon running, mountain climbing, aikido, tai chi, ice dancing, chess, bridge, roulette, automobile cruising, tag, "ring-around-the-rosie," solitaire, playing the stock market, and playing the role of Hamlet?
- And finally, into what category should we put refrigerator carrying, "buffalo chip" throwing, or even making love?

You could easily think of similar questions.

Before any meaningful work can be done toward

resolving competing claims about the moral, social, or artistic importance of the values in sport or how best to conduct it, it is necessary to be clear about its essential nature. Therefore, a philosophical examination of the basic structure of sport, games, and play, including a delineation of the necessary and sufficient conditions of these diverse enterprises, is a basic and important undertaking.

Philosophy, of course, does more than just analyze. Such deliberations are a means, not an end; that is, they lay the groundwork for the subsequent examination of important issues, ranging from questions about the personal meaning of sport, to deliberations concerning appropriate ways of acting within specific sports situations.

Sport and Metaphysics

The branch of philosophy known as **metaphysics** focuses mainly on concerns about the basic structure or ultimate nature of reality, including the fundamental constitution or essence of things, humankind, or even the world itself. Metaphysics examines reality from the standpoint of human existence and thus investigates what it means to be, and the inherent possibilities possessed by, a human being engaged in the world.

The philosophy of sport as pursued from a metaphysical orientation thus discusses the meaning and significance of human participation in sport, games, and play. The first question is whether these activities are merely trivial diversions or peripheral concerns of very inferior status—perhaps even totally meaningless—or whether they may embrace important components located at the very center of life. The overwhelming majority of the existential literature on sport, for example, contends that these enterprises are of singular merit and consequently attempts to explore the inherent meanings and personal rewards of sport and leisure activity.

In contrast to participation in forms of sport, games, and play that are uninformative, mechanical, strictly utilitarian, or even demeaning, open and aware engagement may result in vibrant moments during which a player can actualize personal possibilities. Such moments are opportunities to engage in an absorbing and delightful transcendence of everyday functionality, to luxuriate, openly and completely, in play as a joyful occurrence—an expression of freedom, potential, and self-actualization. In other words, the sport offers a forum in which the player's creativity may be used to construct freely a personally significant symbolic world. There is a considerable body of philosophical literature that attests to the meanings awaiting discovery in open sports and true play experiences, both in individual participation and during interpersonal interactions. In addition, sport possesses many other expressive features and functions; for example, confronting the challenges posed by sport not only permits the release of individual subjectivity but also assists the development of a conception of personal identity.

The foregoing sets the stage for a question that inevitably arises, namely, what is the attraction of risk sports? Why do people deliberately place themselves in dangerous sport situations, up to and including confrontations with possible death? Why do mountain climbers, freestyle skiers, skydivers, and race car drivers voluntarily and enthusiastically seek out these activities and walk the "feather edge of danger"?

Philosophy provides one answer (psychology, by the way, another), which is that such activities, despite their potentially devastating risks and costs, provide overwhelming individual rewards and very meaningful personal responses to the confrontation with finitude. In fact, many studies in the area celebrate the apparently "useless" and argue forcibly that sport, games, and play are very important human phenomena that, in individuals who are open to the positive possibilities inherent in responsive participation, both permit and facilitate the development of self and the attainment of true authentic existence.

Ethics and Sport

Philosophy also deals with the study of values and questions of proper or ethical conduct in human affairs. This area of philosophic concern, properly termed **axiology**, examines arguments about the kinds of evaluative and moral issues that arise in all facets of our daily lives. What is at stake here are issues of direction, justification, and guidance for appropriate principles of conduct and actions, for example, whether there are values—or even moral laws—that are objective and universal. Ethical theory, therefore, concerns itself with expressions of preference between better or worse, with statements of appraisal, and with judgments of approval or disapproval and the rightness or wrongness of specific actions, states of affairs, or postulated ends.

Ethics is a normative enterprise concerned not so much with how people *do act* in certain circumstances or situations but rather with arguments about how they *ought to act*. Sport and its associated phenomena yield many morally contentious issues; fortunately, value theory provides a rich harvest of pertinent recommendations. The following list presents some of the problems, issues, and questions concerning appropriate and inappropriate conduct within sport situations.

- Just what types of agreements, promises, contracts, or obligations does a player enter into, either implicitly or explicitly, by agreeing to "play by the rules"?
- What are the requirements and forms of "sportsmanship"? In other words, how should an athlete treat competitors?
- What moral imperatives operate in sport; that is, what is "fair play" or "justice" in sport?
- How is the "spirit of play" preserved or enhanced in athletic competitions?
- Do penalties or other sanctions restore equilibrium and maintain both the rules and the integrity of the game?
- What is entailed in deception, deliberate rule violation, and cheating? Is there such a thing as "the good foul," and how may it be justified?
- Is winning everything, or is it unimportant?
- What are athletes' rights, and what are the limits of a coach's authority in regulating the lives of athletes?
- What is the propriety of blatantly or surreptitiously using performance-enhancing drugs such as steroids or techniques as blood doping? What moral problems result from the recent "urine transfusion" techniques designed to avoid chemical detection?
- What are the merits and demerits of permitting gambling in and on sports by spectators, coaches, and players? Should athletes be permitted to bet on the outcome of contests in which they are engaged?
- Is it wrong for a school, university, or even an entire society to reward and positively reinforce participation in violent sports such as football and hockey? Should bullfighting, dogfighting, and cockfighting be legalized in North America? Should gladiatorial contests, perhaps to the death, be permitted among consenting adults?
- How does one ensure equity (not just equality) in sport; in other words, do such actions as separate but equal programs ensure that females are treated fairly in sport?

Sport and Social-Political Philosophy

The social-political philosophical analysis of sport broadens the issues considerably from concerns about individual athletes or teams to a macrocultural perspective. This is a complex area of inquiry, requiring extensive knowledge of philosophy, sociology, politics, and economics; it is intimidating in the amount of relevant material but exciting in its significance and its prospects.

The simple question of whether sport mirrors society is disposed of rather easily, but more complex queries remain, for instance, whether the specific political or economic orientations and mechanisms reflected in sport merit support, criticism, or demands for change. An extremely wide range of questions arise concerning the use of sport by various states and forms of government—capitalist democracies, socialist democracies, state bureaucratic entities, and dictatorships—for social indoctrination and other national and international ends. The discussions may have wide-ranging ramifications: The issues concerning the propriety of using sport to sustain or challenge political ends are often transformed into discussions and debate about the wisdom or necessity of supporting existing institutional and regulatory control mechanisms, if not about the overall thrust or even the very nature of the state itself.

Sport Aesthetics, and Other Concerns

The general sphere of the theory of value includes aesthetics as well as ethics and social-political philosophy. Whereas ethics addresses questions of what is good and how people ought to act and social-political philosophy deals with questions about the common good, aesthetics concerns itself with beauty or the beautiful, especially in works of art, and with questions of taste and standards of value in judging art.

Modern aesthetic theory has focused predominantly on two areas of inquiry: first, the nature and significance of works of art; and second, the processes of producing and experiencing art works. In this context, the primary issue for the philosophy of physical activity is the legitimacy of including various forms of sport production, experiences, or contemplation within either or both of these two areas.

Artists have long considered sport to be a worthy *subject* capable of evoking an aesthetic experience in the viewer, but this is at best a secondary issue.

What is of commanding interest is whether sport is, in and of itself, an art form; that is, does sport fulfill the criteria applied to readily acknowledged art forms such as sculpture, painting, and dance?

The relevant philosophical literature ranges widely from completely rejecting the entire idea to making strong claims of identity between sport and art. Everyone admits that sport has dramatic possibilities; that is, it has numerous occurrences that are spectacular, emotionally satisfying, euphoric, tragic, and perhaps even cathartic. These "great moments" are long remembered by athletes and spectators alike. To claim that a sport contest *has* such aesthetic elements or values, however, is not necessarily to contend that it *is* an artistic enterprise.

Philosophers frequently suggest that a fruitful and necessary distinction may be made between *purposive* and *aesthetic* sports. The writers claim that the aesthetic element is largely incidental in competitive sports such as football and volleyball—if not absent altogether. Rather than any aesthetic concerns, the point of these activities is to accumulate enough points to outscore the opponent or opponents. In other sports, such as springboard diving, figure skating, and gymnastics, the elements of form, style, and grace are integral components that count substantially in the judging of the events. Consequently, these sports clearly lay claim to aesthetic components as significant central elements. The matter does not end here, however; there is also the further distinction between *aesthetic* and *artistic*. Although sports at times demonstrate aesthetic elements, this does not imply that they are works of art, artistic in nature, or properly included within the classification of the performing arts. There is still a great deal of controversy in this area.

The foregoing are only some of the more popular issues in the philosophy of physical activity. There are many other interesting areas of inquiry that can be only briefly itemized here:

- The philosophy of embodiment, which focuses on the *mind–body* problem—from dualistic and mechanistic structures to phenomenological explications of the lived body—as applied to sport
- Those aspects of epistemological inquiry into the origins, nature, and limits of human knowledge that touch on skill acquisition, cognitive mechanisms, differences between propositional and procedural knowledge (knowing that vs. knowing how), as well as action theory
- Alternative directions in sport studies, including sport and religion, the theology of play, Eastern movement disciplines, and altered states of consciousness, as well as "peak experiences" and "inner games" in sport

Learned Societies and Publications

The philosophy of sport, although older than many of the areas discussed in this book, is still a very young field; in fact, its major impetus and ensuing growth occurred largely within the last two decades. Helping to precipitate this growth were some noteworthy works in the philosophy of sport that started to appear in the late 1960s. The seminal monographs by Slusher (1967), Metheny (1968), and Weiss (1969), for example, led to other important efforts in the field, including the publication of two important anthologies, one edited by Gerber (1972) and one by Osterhoudt (1973).

The early 1970s also saw the philosophy of sport start to become the focal point at several formal and important scholarly meetings. The most auspicious occurrence in the development of the entire field occurred late in 1972, when the Philosophic Society for the Study of Sport (PSSS), the first scholarly society devoted exclusively to this area, was officially formed. This society, although based in North America, exerts continuing worldwide influence; since 1980, annual meetings have been conducted in Germany, England (twice), and Japan, as well as in North America.

In addition to the PSSS, at least three other North American associations schedule philosophy of sport sessions on a regular basis as part of their annual meetings: the American Alliance for Health, Physical Education, Recreation and Dance (AAHPERD), the Canadian Association for Health, Physical Education and Recreation (CAHPER), and the National Association for Physical Education in Higher Education (NAPEHE). The journals and published proceedings of these associations frequently offer pertinent material.

More than anything else, however, the most important factor in the growth of the field has been the *Journal of the Philosophy of Sport* (*JPS*), founded in 1974 under the auspices of the PSSS. Since its inception, *JPS* has been the premier source of research publication, directing and dominating the field and providing a handy barometer to its development. The 50-page "PSSS Bibliography on the Philosophy of Sport, Games, and Play," published in *JPS* in 1987, incorporates more than 1,000 relevant entries; this is certainly the most comprehensive listing currently available.

A great many worthwhile studies in the philosophy of sport also appear in a variety of other publications. *Quest* and *Sportswissenshaft* sometimes offer pertinent reflective essays, and social-political philosophy is at times covered by such vehicles as the *Sociology of Sport Journal* and the *Journal of Sport and Social Issues*. Mainstream philosophy journals that have published noteworthy relevant papers include *Ethics, Man and World,* and *Philosophy Today*. Finally, *The Philosopher's Index* provides an extremely beneficial and comprehensive source of annotated references to relevant papers published within all philosophical journals throughout the world.

Two anthologies are worthy of both mention and consultation. Morgan and Meier's *Philosophic Inquiry in Sport* (1988), the newest and most comprehensive in the field, contains definitive essays on all of the issues and major sections discussed in this chapter. Vanderwerken and Wertz's *Sport Inside Out* (1985) is a large, valuable collection that uses many literary pieces to help clarify selected philosophic issues.

In addition to these works, Thomas's (1983) very accessible introductory text provides a handy overview of the entire area. In addition, there are individual monographs that address particular philosophic aspects in considerable depth. Suits (1978) presents the still-definitive work on the nature of games, and Hyland's (1984) piece is a significant contribution to play theory. Specific ethical concerns form the focal points of works by Keating (1978), McIntosh (1979), Fraleigh (1984), and Simon (1985). Finally, monographs by Arnold (1979) and Best (1978) are worth looking at, as is Kleinman's (1986) recent anthology.

Summary

The importance of philosophy to the rest of the physical activity sciences, research, and professional practices should by now be clear. Put very simply, the philosophy of sport, play, and games is the *essential foundation* on which all else is built, including all of the other disciplines described in this book. Fortunately, this admittedly audacious claim is easily supported.

It is not intuitively obvious that there is any merit in dedicating several hours each day, perhaps for a decade or longer, to such apparently useless and trivial activities as dribbling a basketball up and down a hardwood court or swimming endless repeats in a 25-meter pool. Such activities are not automatically worthwhile; indeed, they open the participant to charges of nonproductive and wasteful behavior. What possible significance can there be in spending 10 years of highly intensive training attempting to take 5/100s of a second off the world record for the 200-meter breaststroke?

Thus, it may seem as if sport, games, and play are in serious need of apology. Scientific or social scientific disciplines cannot provide this, however, because they are not equipped to handle questions of value. Justification and significance are of the utmost importance here; until these concerns are answered the rest simply does not matter, whether it is determining the best techniques of biomechanical analysis, the best methods of skill acquisition, optimum efficiency in a sport skill, the optimum training program, or the maximum age of participation. All of these issues are hollow and insignificant if the primary questions are not resolved; if sports have no justifiable meaning, all these activities are empty, if not absurd.

In addition, philosophy provides guidance for other areas of sport studies, not only for such aspects as ethical treatment of subjects, regulation of research design, and proper conduct within sports ventures but also in matters of direction, procedures, and importance, both currently and in the future.

Further, developing the critical thinking skills essential to philosophy will enhance both the productivity and the quality of results among students and researchers in all areas of sport studies; in other words, the positive transfer is substantial.

Although the practice of philosophy, like play, may often seem to be its own reward, its diligent application to extrinsic concerns can form the basis of significant change in both procedures and positions. Thus, the philosophy of sport is an enterprise with limitless potential and significance to the entire field of physical activity studies.

References and Further Readings

Arnold, P.J. (1979). *Meaning in movement, sport and physical education*. London: Heinemann.

Best, D. (1978). *Philosophy and human movement*. London: George Allen & Unwin.

Christian, J.L. (1973). *Philosophy: An introduction*

to the art of wondering. Corte Madera, CA: Rinehart Press.

Fraleigh, W.P. (1984). *Right actions in sport: Ethics for contestants*. Champaign, IL: Human Kinetics.

Gerber, E.W. (Ed.) (1972). *Sport and the body: A philosophical symposium*. Philadelphia: Lea & Febiger.

Hyland, D.A. (1984). *The question of play*. Lanham, MD: University Press of America.

Keating, J.W. (1978). *Competition and playful activities*. Washington, DC: University Press of America.

Kleinman, S. (Ed.) (1986). *Mind and body: East meets west*. Champaign, IL: Human Kinetics.

McIntosh, P. (1979). *Fair play: Ethics in sport and education*. London: Heinemann.

Meier, K.V. (1987). Games, sport, play. In *Proceedings of the PSSS conference on the philosophy of sport held in Tsukuba, 1986*. Tsukuba, Japan: University of Tsukuba Press.

Metheny, E. (1968). *Movement and meaning*. New York: McGraw-Hill.

Morgan, W.J., & Meier, K.V. (Eds.) (1988). *Philosophic inquiry in sport*. Champaign, IL: Human Kinetics.

Natanson, M. (1970). *The journeying self: A study in philosophy and social role*. Reading, MA: Addison-Wesley.

Osterhoudt, R.G. (Ed.) (1973). *The philosophy of sport: A collection of original essays*. Springfield, IL: Charles C Thomas.

Postow, B.C. (Ed.) (1983). *Women, philosophy and sport: A collection of new essays*. Metuchen, NJ: Scarecrow Press.

Simon, R.L. (1985). *Sports and social values*. Englewood Cliffs, NJ: Prentice Hall.

Slusher, H.S. (1967). *Man, sport and existence: A critical analysis*. Philadelphia: Lea & Febiger.

Suits, B. (1978). *The grasshopper: Games, life and utopia*. Toronto: University of Toronto Press.

Thomas, C.E. (1983). *Sport in a philosophic context*. Philadelphia: Lea & Febiger.

Vanderwerken, D.L., & Wertz, S.K. (Eds.) (1985). *Sport inside out: Readings in literature and philosophy*. Fort Worth: Texas Christian University Press.

Weiss, P. (1969). *Sport: A philosophic inquiry*. Carbondale, IL: Southern Illinois University Press.

Part III

The Application of Knowledge: Service Areas of the Physical Activity Sciences

Part III introduces the reader to the working environments of the physical activity specialist. Familiarity with these will help in making career choices from among the various service areas of the field.

Part III begins with an overview of the service areas, along with their most important characteristics (chapter 16). The next 11 chapters (17-27) analyze important work settings in terms of objectives and activities of the area, available resources, professional organizations, career opportunities, and other related topics. In order, the service areas considered in this part include: physical education in a school environment, high performance and coaching, leisure and recreation, outdoor activities, dance, fitness, the aging population, the disabled population, therapy and rehabilitation, program management, and the workplace.

Chapter 16

The Service Component of the Physical Activity Sciences

Paul Godbout

Jacques Samson

Gilles Bérubé

As is evident in the first two parts of this book, research developments in the physical activity sciences are important because humans engage, in great numbers and in many ways, in physical activity. The phenomenon was already there to be experienced and seen, and so it was bound to be studied.

At the same time the quality and complexity of human physical activity evolved beyond the limits of natural and spontaneous motor activity, generating a need for expertise, counsel, support, and professional services. For a long time, though, the systematic practice of physical activity seemed to be mostly the lot of the healthy young and physically gifted. Professional services were therefore primarily focused on teaching physical education in school and coaching athletes. As discussed in chapter 2, the search for proper methodologies within these services led to the current form of the physical activity sciences. In turn this new and sharper focus shed light on how physical activity contributes to the quality of life at a time when an increasing number of adult people were seriously considering becoming more active.

Taking into consideration the interaction depicted in Figure 1.1 (chapter 1) and the growth of research activity alluded to in chapter 3 (Science and Physical Activity), in this chapter we try to analyze why and how *physical education* as an area of professional service has also expanded to the point that the term no longer covers even the bulk of professional practices related to physical activity.

There is more to any particular professional practice than merely its functions, and future practitioners should give some thought to the underlying facets. For example, besides offering professional services, the practitioner will eventually join some professional group or may even help develop one. Such phenomena demonstrate that professional practices do not (or at least no longer) appear spontaneously; their implementation requires that various conditions be met. That is what this chapter is all about.

Variables Affecting Professional Practice

People engage in physical activity in such a variety of contexts that it is difficult to distinguish the needs met by or associated with it. New combinations of needs and services appear all the time. Nevertheless, it seems worthwhile to examine the most significant variables associated with the rise and development of professional practices. These variables are neither mutually exclusive nor necessarily of the same order, and the list is far from exhaustive, but serves only to underline the considerable potential for the development of professional practices.

Variables

Unalterable characteristics, particularly the age of individuals

Conditions prevailing on a temporary or permanent basis, such as pregnancy, cardiovascular problems, obesity, mental disability, physical disability, social maladjustment, and others

Motives for which people engage in physical activity, such as health, wellness, education, leisure (recreation, play), art, work, performance, self-realization, and others

Types of physical activities, including such categories as sport, outdoor activity, dance, fitness exercises of all kinds, and, more comprehensively, games and play, as well as physical activity related to occupation

Contexts in which people relate to physical activity, for example, schools, municipalities, industries, hospitals, governmental agencies, prisons, sport clubs, private agencies, retirement homes, and so on, which thus are sometimes the specific locus of professional practice (e.g., coaching for a sport club)

Processes by which people relate to physical activity—usually the primary involvement of people in physical activity, but also indirect (spectator) involvement requiring information about sport

Levels of implementation (in its largest sense) of physical activity programs, which always have many (often unobvious) requirements associated with them (e.g., facilities, equipment, objectives, instructional strategies, personnel)

Which combination of the above elements best describes the type of work you would like to do or the type of population you would like to work with?

Developmental Characteristics of Professional Practice

Everyone agrees that professional practice consists of using knowledge and skills to render services in specific contexts. It is, however, no longer useful to define a professional practice solely on the basis of direct contact between professionals and the public. Whereas traditional professional organizations understandably tend to retain traditional labels for their identification, newer or more flexible institutions have come up with myriad names to designate professional practices related to physical

Table 16.1   Designations for Specialized Programs in Professional Preparation Curricula Related to Physical Activity

Adapted physical education	Adult fitness
Agency recreation	Aquatic specialization
Athletic administration and coaching	Athletic training
Business/physical education	Cardiac rehabilitation
Coaching	Commercial recreation
Commercial sports	Community health
Community physical fitness	Community recreation
Corrective therapy	Dance
Dance education	Dance performance
Early childhood physical education	Dance therapy
Elementary physical education	Exercise physiology
Exercise program directors	Exercise science
Exercise science and health fitness	Health education
Health education teacher	Health spa
Industrial recreation	Intramural sports
Kinesiological sciences	Leisure sciences
Leisure studies and recreation	Leisure studies
Motor behavior and sport humanities	Motor development therapy
Movement and sport sciences	Outdoor recreation
Physical education for corrective institutions	Physical education for the aging
Physical education for the exceptional	Physical education for industry
Physical education for special students	Physical fitness specialist
Pre-atheletic training	Pre-occupational therapy
Pre-physical therapy	Professional golf management
Public recreation	Research training
Recreation and park administration	Recreation
Recreation services administration	Sport(s) administration
Sport(s) broadcasting	Sport(s) clubs
Sport(s) community and public relations	Sport(s) journalism
Sport(s) management	Sport(s) marketing and retailing
Sport(s) medicine	Sport(s) physiology
Sport(s) social-psychology	Sport(s) studies
Sport(s) studies and management	Sport(s) writing
Therapeutic and church recreation	Therapeutic recreation
Urban community physical education	

Note. Compiled from the National Association for Sport and Physical Education (1982) and Considine (1979).

activity. For instance, a limited survey of titles of professional preparation curricula offered by universities in North America tabulated at least 69 different names (see Table 16.1). In fact, it's not clear whether such diversity in labels indicates creativity or chaos.

An area of professional practice must meet several conditions to gain recognition (Kroll, 1982). The most critical ones appear to be

- a specific area of intellectual endeavor,
- an application of knowledge to provide services, and
- a continuous flow of new data from related fields of study or from a given subfield.

The satisfaction of these conditions eventually leads to a coherent body of knowledge, interpreted with reference to specific populations in specific contexts so as to meet people's needs. In a way, this process might be called the reorganization of a functional body of knowledge or, in other words, the development of a theory of practice. No matter what the topic, the constituent body of knowledge for a professional practice usually exhibits the following characteristics:

- An analysis of the needs of the people concerned
- Established terminology specifying the objectives of the relevant physical activity programs
- Specific methodology ensuring the proper use of physical activity in light of the objectives pursued
- General rules (developed on the basis of experiments or experience) ensuring proper environments for the programs
- Proposed instructional strategies that account for variations in people's characteristics, the objectives of the programs, the types of activity involved, and the context in which the program takes place
- Evaluation strategies to verify success in the pursuit of objectives
- An identification of specific vocational skills relevant to the habitual interactions between the practitioner and the participants in the program

The flow of new knowledge from various physical activity sciences subfields to professional practice has important consequences. For instance, the fast growth of some subfields and the richness of the resulting knowledge (both in terms of quality and diversity) can fragment an area of professional practices, producing specializations that will best meet the diversified needs expressed by consumers or anticipated by professionals; developments in physical fitness and wellness are good examples of such a phenomenon.

Consequences of Increasing the Social Impact of Physical Activity

Since the beginning of the 1980s, numerous papers and reports have cited both the considerable increase in the proportion of North Americans engaging in regular physical activity and the social impact of this trend (*Fitness and Lifestyle in Canada*, 1983; Bouchard & Landry, 1985; "America Shapes Up," 1981). According to these sources, the phenomenon has yet to reach its peak. As suggested by the Canada Fitness Survey (1983), the regular practice of physical activity is likely to become the social norm, if it is not already. This massive increase in the physically active population and the evolution of the social meaning of physical activity bear consequences for professional practices, including the following four.

1. The proliferation of private and public organizations offering programs of physical activity of all kinds may force some practitioners to reexamine their traditional role; Brunelle (1981) and Lawson (1982), among others, suggest this in connection with physical educators in the school system.

In the future, physical education teachers can no longer assume to be the sole (and in some cases the main) source of influence on students in terms of physical activity.

2. Better-informed people ask for more specific and competent services. At the same time, a greater number of individuals express the same needs. Together, these two phenomena make it possible, if not necessary, to offer increasingly specific programs. Thus, general areas of professional practice are fragmenting into a series of subareas. For example, physical fitness now comprises aerobic dancing, Nautilus programs, aquatic conditioning, and so on; the same fragmentation can be observed in dance, outdoor activity, adapted physical activity, and others.

In the future, physical activity specialists must be prepared to carry professional preparation beyond the traditional general format of physical education, recreation, or health education.

3. Regular physical activity is increasingly recognized as playing a major role in the development or recovery of well-being in conjunction with other lifestyle components. The implications for professional practices are at least twofold. On the one hand, physical activity specialists collaborate with others to develop, for instance, diet-exercise programs, stress management programs, and so on. On the other hand, specialists such as dietitians, nurses, health educators, and recreation specialists are paying more attention to physical activity. Up to a certain point, clear-cut frontiers separating professional territories are eroding.

In the future, physical activity specialists will face tough job competition from graduates who were not traditionally involved in physical activity programs.

4. Finally, as physical activity becomes an important social focus, practitioners from various fields have begun to gravitate around the

concept in the discharge of their professional duties; this is increasingly the case for lawyers, journalists, writers, marketing specialists, and so on. Such a phenomenon will very likely bring about new areas of professional practice.

In the future, the wide social impact of physical activity will create full-time employment opportunities in areas that hitherto only occasionally touched on the field.

Differences Among Physical Activity Specialists: Practitioners and Scientists

The considerable increase in the number of people engaged in physical activity programs, the growing ramifications of organizations planning or offering such programs, and the refinement of direct and indirect services supporting these programs have brought about differentiation in the roles of physical activity specialists. Figure 16.1 identifies four such roles.

The first, and obvious, category consists of specialists who interact directly with people participating in given physical activity programs. In a second category are the specialists who assume one or more of the following roles: development, implementation, and evaluation of programs; de-

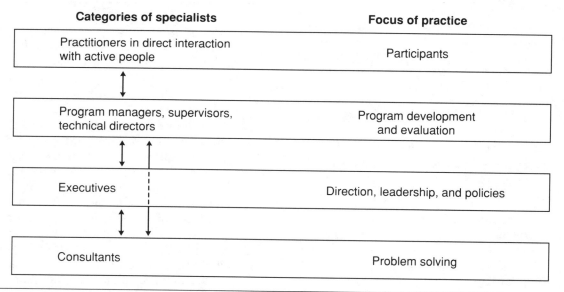

Figure 16.1 Roles of physical activity specialists in the context of professional services.

velopment and evaluation of instructional strategies; development, implementation, and assessment of product evaluation strategies; and program management. These managers offer support to practitioners "in the field," who implement and regularly apply the physical activity programs. Thus, individuals in these two categories interact frequently, if not constantly. A third category involves specialists who might be defined as policy planners and executives. These individuals provide leadership and determine the programs and strategies with which the managers deal.

Finally, a fourth category consists of a growing number of highly specialized professionals who are not specifically associated with any given physical activity program but who are available for expert advice and services; these consultants actually fall outside the organizational structure of professional practice. They generally are incoming and outgoing satellites temporarily called on for their expertise, which may have been developed within a given subfield of study related to the physical activity sciences (e.g., exercise physiology, human movement engineering, sport psychology) or within any other field of study not primarily concerned with physical activity (e.g., equipment or facilities design, law, marketing, etc.). Which of these levels appeals to you? Involvement at the second through fourth levels will likely require graduate studies.

So far, however, we have not addressed the relationship between physical activity practitioners and physical activity scientists. Figure 16.2 illustrates this relationship. The right-hand side of this figure is a reduced replica of Figure 16.1 that represents the differentiation of professional practices; it also represents *the application of knowledge*. The left-hand side of the figure represents the *static aspect* of the physical activity sciences, that is, the body of knowledge already available in the various subfields described in part II of this book.

Finally, the center part of the figure illustrates the role of the specialized organizations and people linking the two so that the domain of the physical activity sciences can function as a whole. This domain comprises the *dynamic aspect* of the physical activity sciences, namely, the search for knowledge as well as the development of theories of professional practices. It also includes the important function of professional preparation, which draws on these dynamic functions. Physical activity scientists should be involved in all three roles. Some migrate (mostly on a temporary basis) toward professional areas as consultants.

Current and Emerging Areas of Professional Practice

This book attempts to identify major current or emerging areas of professional practice, each of which opens the way to a number of specific careers. Some of these careers are more developed than others, but clusters of practices can be identified that rely basically on some common or at least partially shared body of operational knowledge. Specifically, the next several chapters discuss the following areas of professional practice related to physical activity:

- Childhood
- High performance
- Leisure and recreation
- Outdoor pursuits
- Dance
- Fitness
- The elderly
- The physically and developmentally disabled
- Therapy
- Program management
- The workplace environment

Anyone trying to describe the reality of the professional world soon discovers that the areas overlap. This might be important to the professions but should not concern more general institutions because knowledge, whether fundamental or applied, belongs to everyone. Moreover, labels must be used to designate areas, but they are less significant than the area's functional description. When reviewing this list of professional practice areas, the reader should keep one thing in mind: In spite of struggles over identity, whatever names may be adopted to identify some professional practices, millions of individuals all over the country participate in physical activities, and their number increases year after year. If we in the physical activity sciences and professions do not find unique and valid ways to meet their needs, others will. It is up to you to meet that challenge!

Summary

The popularity of physical activity and an explosion of knowledge in the physical activity sciences have shattered the traditional boundaries of professional practices areas such as physical education, coaching, and physical fitness. Whereas this

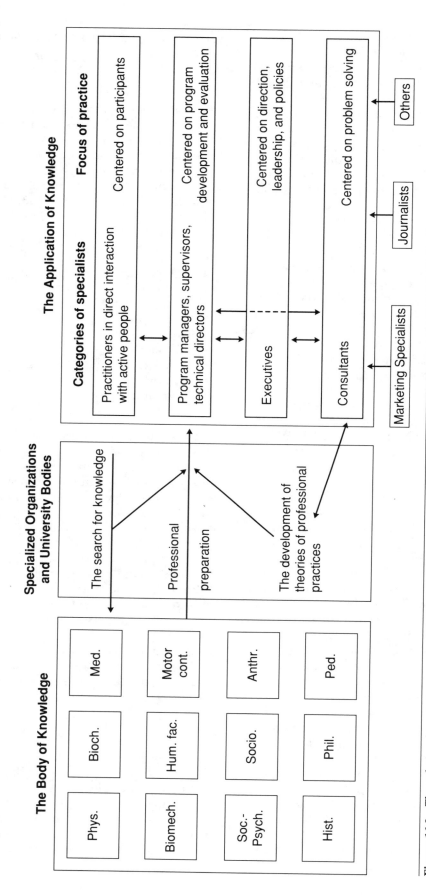

Figure 16.2 The relationships between practitioners and scientists associated with the physical activity sciences.

creates many career openings in specific need-oriented professional areas, it also opens the way to outside competition from young professionals traditionally associated with other service areas.

Although the drastic expansion of the physical activity sciences has made it necessary to differentiate the roles of physical activity specialists, the practitioner and the scientist remain partners in pursuit of better services for an active mankind; the former draws on the relevant body of knowledge and professional experience to provide direct support to active people, and the latter answers questions about how these people relate to physical activity. So far, this partnership has led to the opening of numerous new service areas related to physical activity.

As a physical activity undergraduate student, it is your privilege to choose your future place in the field and your responsibility to prepare for the competition you will face. In doing so, remember that the scientific knowledge we have developed is there for all. The choice may well be as simple as using the knowledge or losing your job.

References and Further Readings

America Shapes Up. (1981, November 2). *Time*, pp. 94-106.

Bouchard, C., & Landry, F. (1985). La pratique des activités physiques [The practice of physical activity]. In J. Dufresne, F. Dumont, & Y. Martin (Eds.), *Traité d'anthropologie médicale* (pp. 861-904). Sillery, PQ: Presses de l'Université du Québec.

Brunelle, J. (1981). La socialisation des étudiants dans le rôle de participants à des activités physiques: Un moyen de revigorer l'intervention pédagogique en milieu scolaire [Student socialization in the role of participants in physical activity: A means for reinforcing pedagogy in the school]. *La Revue québécoise de l'activité physique*, **1**(1), 49-52.

Canada Fitness Survey. (1983). *Fitness and lifestyle in Canada*. Ottawa, ON: Author.

Considine, W.J. (Ed.) (1979). *Alternative professional preparation in physical education*. Reston, VA: American Alliance for Health, Physical Education, Recreation and Dance.

Kroll, W.P. (1982). *Graduate study and research in physical education*. Champaign, IL: Human Kinetics.

Lawson, H.A. (1982). Looking back from the year 2082. *Journal of Physical Education, Recreation and Dance*, **53**(4), 15-17.

National Association for Sport and Physical Education. (1982). *Directory of undergraduate physical education programs*. Reston, VA: American Alliance for Health, Physical Education, Recreation and Dance.

Chapter 17

Physical Activity in Childhood and Youth

A.E. Wall
Greg Reid

The physical activity and fitness needs of children have been a concern of school systems throughout most of the 20th century. Indeed, school physical education programs initially provided the only systematic and organized means to meet the physical activity needs of children. A recent proliferation of community-recreation-based instructional programs and competitive leagues has further contributed to the physical well-being of children and youth, but these programs are sometimes implicitly restricted to fairly affluent and skilled performers. School physical education programs, which include all Canadian children, regardless of ability, social background, or family income, remain the primary vehicle for physical activity. This chapter focuses on the physical activity programs for children and youth offered within the Canadian elementary and secondary school systems.

Unlike physical activity programs in the community, school-based physical education is a public enterprise that must adhere to the goals and objectives established by provincial authorities and school boards. Hence, these programs require systematic learning and incorporate key curriculum objectives. This constraint, together with the demand that school physical educators teach all children (in fact, the recent trend is toward integrating persons with disabilities), constitutes much of the challenge faced by physical educators in the public school system (Reid & Wall, 1987).

Physical educators are expected to maintain the social values of the school, which often constrain behavior more than the values that guide participation in community recreation programs. Furthermore, school physical education programs are expected to be broadly based to meet the activity and instructional needs of all children and youth. Thus teachers are expected to establish learning environments in which pupils acquire not only a degree of physical fitness but also physical skills, knowledge, and appropriate attitudes.

Because provincial ministries control education, school physical education programs and curricula vary greatly across Canada. In some provinces, for example, specialists in physical education are the norm in elementary schools, whereas elsewhere a classroom teacher may be responsible for instruction. The time allotted to physical education also differs across the provinces, although the Canadian Association for Health, Physical Education and Recreation recommends at least 30 minutes per day for elementary school programs and up to 60 minutes per day for secondary programs. Despite these differences, most programs include an instructional component for all children during regularly scheduled class periods, an intramural component for older children at lunchtime or after school, and, for the more skilled high school students, an interscholastic program of athletics.

The school physical educator's duties may even include concerns outside the school setting.

Physical educators are increasingly encouraged to facilitate student involvement in existing community programs. Essentially, the teacher counsels students about programs that are congruent with the individual's interests, skills, and aspirations.

• • •

In general, school-based physical educators are responsible for developing, in all students throughout the elementary and secondary grades, physical fitness, physical skills and knowledge, and appropriate attitudes, as well as providing advice on various athletic and physical activity programs and on lifestyle choices as they relate to physical well-being.

• • •

Major Concepts

The broad mission of school physical eduction is to contribute to the optimal well-being and physical development of each individual. More specific goals include developmental changes in the areas of

- skill acquisition,
- physical fitness,
- social and emotional control, and
- leisure awareness.

What Does It Mean To Be Physically Educated?

Skill Development

- Acquiring a repertoire of culturally normative physical skills
- Learning concepts of skill acquisition
- Controlling emotions in the physical activity environment
- Recognizing personal capabilities and weaknesses
- Knowing how to learn and control skilled performance

Fitness Development

- Understanding the key components of physical fitness (including muscular strength and endurance, aerobic and anaerobic power, flexibility, etc.) and how they develop

- Appreciating basic fitness principles, including heart rate, overload principles, interval training, etc.
- Knowing ways to monitor and improve physical fitness

Social and Emotional Development

- Developing the concept of fair play and sportsmanship
- Understanding competitive and cooperative activities and knowing the difference between them
- Appreciating other people's physical abilities and interacting appropriately with people with different abilities
- Developing and nurturing one's physical self-concept
- Controlling aggression in competitive situations
- Coming to grips with winning and losing in sport situations

Leisure Awareness

- Appreciating one's own interests, skills, and fitness level
- Being familiar with physical activities available in the community
- Understanding the demands of different tasks and performance environments
- Wisely using community-based physical activity programs to meet one's own needs
- Selecting intelligently from a physical activity menu

Because children's physical activity needs change as they mature, there is a significant shift in the emphasis of physical education objectives from lower to higher grades. As Figure 17.1 shows, during the early elementary school years the emphasis of the physical education program is mainly instructional, with a strong focus on skill development, a positive introduction to physical activity, and to a much lesser extent an introduction to fitness activities. The content of the program would include basic gymnastic movements; catching, throwing, and other ball skills; turning, chasing, and tag games; and dance. In his study of the factors that enhance the development of talent, Benjamin Bloom (1985) reports that these early years should emphasize fun, plenty of progressive practice opportunities, and positive support from teachers and parents.

The later elementary school years have been called the golden years of skill learning. As Figure

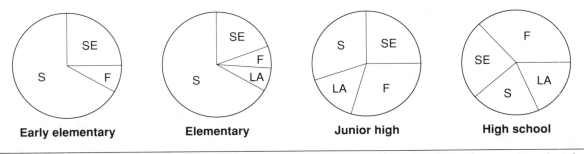

Figure 17.1 Changes in program emphasis during the school years. *Note.* S = Skill development; SE = Social-emotional development; F = Fitness development; LA = Leisure awareness.

17.1 shows, the emphasis in grades 4 to 6 is on skill acquisition, positive social-emotional development, and fitness. Through a well-balanced instructional and intramural program, physical educators help children acquire a repertoire of culturally normative skills that will allow them to be active in a variety of physical activity options throughout their lives. During these years children enjoy playing lead-up games to traditional sports, being challenged with fitness activities, engaging in track and field and swimming events, and consolidating their gymnastics and dance skills. During this period children should be encouraged to become aware of how they spend their leisure time and the importance of being active.

The junior high school years present to physical educators the challenge of wide individual differences in development. The physical growth changes that occur at puberty make the adolescent period a rather turbulent one and render difficult—and important—the demand that physical education programs meet the needs of all children.

Participating in sport and fitness activities while in school leads to more leisure-time options later in life.

As Figure 17.1 shows, the instructional program will have somewhat less emphasis on skill development, more time for physical fitness activities, and a continued attempt to help youngsters develop a positive physical self-concept. Furthermore, sound intramural and interscholastic programs must provide challenges and participation opportunities for all children, including those with disabilities. Such programs can provide a wide range of benefits. The Canadian Intramural Recreation Association (1985) has created a student leadership development program that encourages student management of the intramural program. Macintosh (1990) has described the changes of interscholastic sport programs in Canada over the past decade and encourages us to maintain those programs within school physical education rather than allow them to be taken over by community- or parent-run organizations.

In addition to such physical activity participation objectives, physical educators must help students appreciate their relevant strengths and weaknesses and encourage them to select extracurricular activities that they enjoy, both within and outside the school. Students in this age range begin to realize the importance of an active lifestyle and to recognize that their own personal decision processes can affect the quality of their leisure time.

The program balance changes again during the high school years, with less emphasis on skill development and much more emphasis on fitness development, social-emotional control, and leisure awareness. In this period, students need to be given ample opportunity to select their participation opportunities. Special attention must be given to developing skills in "carry-over" activities that will likely play a role in adulthood, such as swimming, cycling, camping, golf, and cross-country skiing. Thus at this stage, the physical education instructional program should provide opportunity for the self-selection of activities and include information on how to examine one's own strengths and weaknesses, the factors that limit participation in various activities, and the participation opportunities available within the community. It is at this time that physical educators must determine if they have been able to physically educate their students. Does every student have a repertoire of skills, an understanding of fitness training principles, a positive social and emotional self-concept, and an awareness of how to choose an active lifestyle? Successful programs will let us answer ''yes'' to these questions.

Major Trends in Physical Education

Daily Quality Physical Education

The Daily Quality Physical Education Program is an important initiative of the School Physical Activity Programs Committee of CAHPER. Stemming from a concern about the lack of daily physical education in many schools and the need for better quality control of such programs, this group of professionals identified seven key elements that underlie sound physical education programs. The Daily Quality Physical Education Program is a sound example of a professional initiative that identified a need in our field, examined the factors that related to it, and proposed steps to solve it.

In collaboration with Fitness Canada, CAHPER produced a series of seven booklets in which leading authorities in the field addressed the previously mentioned key factors for sound daily physical education programs, making clear recommendations on

- meeting the needs of children,
- fostering positive attitudes,
- facilitating maximum participation,
- developing physical fitness,
- handling competition,
- preparing qualified teachers, and
- optimizing the use of facilities and equipment.

We encourage you to read all of these booklets; for your convenience we have selected and edited quotations from this bilingual series that underscore the fundamental principles of quality daily physical education (see Highlight).

This program has not been universally embraced, however, and opponents have questioned the value of ceding academic time to physical education. Nevertheless, the research evidence clearly indicates that physical skill and fitness improvements do not jeopardize the academic progress of children (Shephard, 1982; Sinclair, 1983).

Good physical education classes ensure that all students are provided an opportunity to be active.

Integrating Persons With Disabilities Into Physical Education

In collaboration with Fitness Canada, the Adapted Programs Special Interest Group of CAHPER held an important symposium on the physical activity needs of persons with disabilities in October 1986. The Jasper Talks Symposium on strategies for change in adapted physical activity brought together professionals and volunteers interested in persons with disabilities to examine the current situation and plan future initiatives.

Some key recommendations were generated at the Jasper Talks. The importance of fostering integration in physical activity programs was a central theme, along with the need for more extensive and intensive professional and volunteer leadership development. Special attention was given to the way in which school and community physical activity programs could facilitate the integration process.

Following the Jasper Talks, Fitness Canada formed a National Adapted Physical Activity Committee. The committee met to discuss means to implement the recommendations of the Jasper Talks Symposium and formulate a Blueprint for Action. The blueprint stresses the importance of developing responsive communities that offer physical activity options to meet the interests and needs of all Canadians.

Vision of Physical Activity for Canadians With Disabilities

The Canadian Summit on Fitness, June 1986, described the vision of the fitness movement as follows:

> The vision of fitness by the year 2000 depicts a society that values well-being as fundamental and an integral part of day-to-day life. Canadian social structures, the family, the schools, the workplace, the health care system, will all enthusiastically embrace and reward daily physical activity and behaviors which contribute significantly to health and well-being. Regular physical activity and optimal well-being will be ingrained as important and widely accepted values in Canadian society (in effect, a Canadian "cultural trademark"). (Physical Activity for Canadians, 1987)

To include individuals with disabilities in this movement and meet their additional physical activity needs, the following key points were added to the vision of the Summit.

- Create self-empowered individuals who have the knowledge, skill, and support to accept responsibility and make independent decisions for a full, satisfying lifestyle
- Focus on the individual's interests, abilities/skills, fitness level, and social-communication capabilities
- Facilitate participant-centered activity based on the needs and choices of the individual
- Provide equal opportunity and access to quality programs, services, and resources
- Ensure availability of a full continuum of programs
- Establish a community-based coordinated infrastructure that includes collaboration and communication among all levels and sectors of Canadian society
- Create a network of competent and enabling advocates, support persons, and leaders
- Foster awareness and support of individuals with disabilities by all Canadians
- Provide readily available support resources, research, and current information

---

HIGHLIGHT
Key Factors in Daily Quality Physical Education

The Needs of Children (CAHPER, 1985d)

Provide a balanced program of games, dance, gymnastics, aquatics, and outdoor pursuits to develop and improve physical skills.

Include activities in the intramural and the instructional program that stress particular fitness components.

Provide a variety of activities that will contribute to the development of coordination, agility, balance, speed, power, and rhythm for all students, able or disabled.

Organize activities and set guidelines to involve leadership and group decision making by the students.

Create an atmosphere that fosters mutual respect, sportsmanship, and equality of opportunity.

Teach facts and knowledge related to movement during the activity session.

Stimulate cognitive growth by teaching rules and game strategies through active participation.

Ensure that the social atmosphere in each class contributes to the self-worth and confidence of each student.

Fostering Positive Attitudes (CAHPER, 1985f)

Provide a safe and supportive learning atmosphere to encourage participation.

Offer a variety of activities that are fun, interesting, and challenging to encourage maximum participation.

Include activities that challenge students to express their creativity and individuality.

Do not substitute intramural and interscholastic programs for a balanced instructional program.

Do not use physical education as a reward for good behavior.

Schedule special events that allow parents, teachers, and students to share the benefits of physical activity.

Maximum Participation Principles (CAHPER, 1985c)

Design a program starting with a foundation of basic physical skills that initiates the cycle of fun and satisfaction, increased skill, and more fun and satisfaction.

Encourage maximum participation by providing activities suited to the maturity level of the students.

Make enough equipment readily available. Include equipment suitable for persons with disabilities. Avoid lineups and placement of equipment that tend to produce a "follow the leader" type of organization.

Keep instructions brief and to the point; keep everyone active.

Modify rules, equipment, facilities, and activities to increase student participation.

Elimination games reduce participation for some individuals; keep everyone involved.

Developing Physical Fitness (CAHPER, 1985e)

Provide continuous vigorous activity during a portion of each lesson to improve cardio-respiratory fitness.

Teach the students to stretch muscles and tendons safely and effectively.

Provide stretching activities during the cool-down phase of the lesson in order to speed up recovery and to reduce stiffness after exercise.

At the secondary school level, teach safe methods and proper progressions in weight training. Remember specificity—you get what you train for.

Make effective use of a battery of fitness tests to enhance the fitness program.

Use fitness testing as one phase of the fitness program, not the program itself.

Teach the importance of rest and relaxation as part of a long-term commitment to an active lifestyle.

Discuss the influence that tobacco, alcohol, and other drugs have on fitness and lifestyle.

Competition (CAHPER, 1985a)

Provide adequate fundamentals so that competition does not interfere with specific skill development.

Help the individual or the team set realistic short- and long-range goals.

Group participants homogeneously for drills and games.

Emphasize teamwork, sharing, interacting, and communicating to achieve group success in competitive situations.

Encourage students to recognize, appreciate, and accept each individual and his or her positive contribution in competition.

Simplify competition at the intramural level to promote participation, satisfaction, and enjoyment.

Communicate your positive expectations to students regarding sincere effort and set a realistic standard of performance according to their abilities.

Qualified Teachers (CAHPER, 1985g)

Use a variety of teaching styles and methods appropriate to the program content and to the needs of all students.

Monitor and examine your teaching effectiveness and remember that the gymnasium is a place for action, not lecturing.

Ask a consultant for resources, ideas, and workshops.

Take advantage of professional upgrading, development, and support services.

Join national, provincial, and regional physical education associations, coaching associations, and sport interest groups to share in the benefits available.

Contact community agencies and service groups such as the Heart Association, Cancer Society, Associations for Community Living, Lung and Respiratory Diseases Association, YM/YWCA, Health Service Centres, Participaction, etc. to utilize their resources.

Facilities and Equipment (CAHPER, 1985b)

Determine the nature and extent of available indoor and outdoor facilities. Establish an equipment inventory.

Determine what safety considerations are necessary to offer the intended program.

Discuss with community leaders the potential for sharing facilities such as church halls, rinks, pools, ski facilities, tennis courts, bowling alleys, track and field facilities, orienteering routes, etc.

Modify, adapt, and be creative in the use of equipment to extend the program and to integrate the child with limited abilities.

Establish a procedure for regular care and maintenance of supplies and equipment.

Teach students proper methods for handling equipment to protect not only the student but also the equipment.

Note. This material is extracted from seven booklets in a series entitled *Daily Physical Education: Part of a Quality Program*, produced by the Canadian Association for Health, Physical Education and Recreation (CAHPER), Ottawa, 1985. Used by permission.

Professional Societies and Journals

Physical education teachers are usually members of a provincial-level professional teachers association or union. Such organizations may have a unit devoted to physical education that supports teachers by analyzing or creating new curricula, developing workshops, or promoting physical activity for students. More commonly, an independent professional physical education association will exist for these purposes. By forming these associations teachers maintain professional contacts and ensure continued professional growth.

National organizations emerge when professionals believe there is a need to communicate and share common concerns across provincial boundaries (Gurney, 1983). The Canadian Association for Health, Physical Education and Recreation (CAHPER) is the major national professional organization concerned with physical education for children and youth. Its mission is to provide leadership that will foster a physically active lifestyle for all Canadians. CAHPER began in 1933 as the Canadian Physical Education Association through the efforts of Dr. A.S. Lamb of McGill University. The early years of the organization saw a continual struggle to develop and expand its influence. Members often felt greater allegiance to provincial bodies, in part because education in Canada is under provincial jurisdiction, yet, for over 50 years CAHPER has remained faithful to Dr. Lamb's challenge to "strive to develop a national consciousness for the full and complete education of the individual" (Gurney, 1983, p. XI).

Today CAHPER has a strong national presence. It publishes topical books and videos, produces six journal issues per year, supports an annual convention, celebrates excellence with nationally recognized awards, and lobbies with relevant federal government agencies to advance its mission. In addition CAHPER initiates and promotes programs of national interest, for example the Jasper Talks (Reid & Wall, 1987), the Quality Daily Physical Education Program, the Canadian Physical Activity Week (held annually in May), and the Canadian Fitness Awards Program.

CAHPER members can become active with a variety of special interest groups. Each of these groups remains congruent with the mission of CAHPER in areas such as adapted programs, dance, fitness, school physical education, and measurement. The groups develop and promote programs unique to their perceived needs, such as preparing position papers, facilitating research, publishing newsletters, soliciting journal articles, and fostering conference presentations.

Many provincial physical education associations are affiliated with CAHPER, and there are many student CAHPER associations promoting important professional and social functions in the university setting. In fact, there are annual regional student conventions that address the needs of the young professional. Membership and contribution to organizations such as CAHPER are important components of professional growth.

Professional physical educators should also have access to important journals to keep up-to-date with changing perspectives, new initiatives, and novel practices. The journals of particular interest to teachers are

- *CAHPER Journal*,
- *Journal of Teaching in Physical Education*,
- *The Physical Educator*,
- *Journal of Health, Physical Education, Recreation and Dance*,
- *Adapted Physical Activity Quarterly*, and
- *Canadian Journal of Sport Sciences*.

Undergraduate Education

The development of school-based physical education teachers begins, no doubt, with the positive experiences they enjoyed when they were students themselves, but the formal process of professional preparation begins at university.

There are essentially two models of university education for teachers in Canada. The first model involves a degree program that emphasizes the physical activity sciences, as discussed in part II of this book; many of these programs also provide some specialization. The degree obtained is often a BA or BSc, and the professional preparation required for teaching in the schools follows the basic degree. This latter phase, which emphasizes pedagogical concerns, physical skill development, and student teaching experiences, occurs at a teachers college or university. It usually requires a year's study beyond the first degree and results in a teaching certificate. The second model incorporates the physical activity sciences and professional preparation courses into a single degree program, usually called a BPE or BEd. Thus, in a given semester, students in such a program might follow science courses in anatomy and motor learning, as well as professionally oriented courses in curriculum development, teaching methodology, and basketball. On completion of the program the student is awarded both a degree and a teaching certificate.

Because education is a provincial matter in Canada, students are certified to teach only in the province in which they studied. Some provinces, however, have reciprocal relations that allow students to be certified in one province and work in another. In other cases, a teacher from outside a given province may apply to teach there on the condition of following specified courses leading to that province's certification.

School physical education teachers are supported by a network of consultants, associations, and publications. Large schools boards often hire an experienced professional who functions as a consultant for physical educators. The consultant fosters cooperation among the practitioners, listens and responds according to their needs, and facilitates professional development by encouraging, supporting, and expanding their teaching skills. Unfortunately, in times of severe budget constraint, consultants are sometimes not replaced after departure, thus removing crucial support for practicing professionals.

Career Opportunities

The job market in school physical education is tied to the number of children enrolled in the public and private educational systems. Since the peak number of "baby boomer" students in the middle to late 1960s there has been a steady decline, which appears to have leveled only recently. Although forecasts differ among the provinces, the number of students enrolled in school should increase slightly throughout the 1990s, when the baby boomers' babies reach school age. This phenomenon, coupled with predicted retirements, suggests a modest need of teachers in the years to come, including specialists in physical education.

Job opportunities also depend on hiring policies concerning specialists in physical education. As noted previously, some provinces and school boards do not place specialists in the elementary schools. A change in this policy would create many new teaching positions.

Not all the relevant factors are beyond the prospective physical education teacher's control, though. Specialized skill certification in specific sports from the Coaching Association of Canada can make it easier to find a position in a secondary school, as will a teaching certification from a provincial education ministry. Further, as bilingual school programs expand across Canada, the physical educator who can teach in French is also likely to be in a more favorable position to secure employment. Finally, there is always a need for teachers in remote areas of Canada; such opportunities should be viewed as challenging and important experiences for the young professional.

Summary

Teachers of physical education have the exciting challenge of promoting a physically active lifestyle for children and youth. We have described the current goals of physical education and how they change in emphasis across the various levels of education. Furthermore, there are impressive program initiatives throughout Canada designed to meet the needs of society as it moves toward the 21st century; daily quality physical education and the integration of persons with disabilities are only two. The professional growth of teachers requires a lifelong pursuit of knowledge and skills augmented by university study, professional organizations, and publications.

References and Further Readings

Bloom, B.S. (1985). *Developing talent in young people*. New York: Balantine.

Canadian Association for Health, Physical Education and Recreation. (1985a). *Competition*. Ottawa, ON: Author.

Canadian Association for Health, Physical Education and Recreation. (1985b). *Facilities and equipment*. Ottawa, ON: Author.

Canadian Association for Health, Physical Education and Recreation. (1985c). *Maximum participation*. Ottawa, ON: Author.

Canadian Association for Health, Physical Education and Recreation. (1985d). *The needs of children*. Ottawa, ON: Author.

Canadian Association for Health, Physical Education and Recreation. (1985e). *Physical fitness*. Ottawa, ON: Author.

Canadian Association for Health, Physical Education and Recreation. (1985f). *Positive attitudes*. Ottawa, ON: Author.

Canadian Association for Health, Physical Education and Recreation. (1985g). *Qualified teachers*. Ottawa, ON: Author.

Canadian Intramural Recreation Association. (1985). *Teacher's guide for student leadership development*. Ottawa, ON: Author.

Gurney, H. (1983). *The CAHPER Story*. Ottawa, ON: Canadian Association for Health, Physical Education and Recreation.

Macintosh, D. (1990). Interschool sport programs in Canada. *CAHPER Journal*, **56**, 36-40.

Physical activity for Canadians with a disability: Blueprint for action. (1987). Ottawa, ON: Fitness Canada.

Reid, G., & Wall, A.E. (Eds.) (1987). The Jasper Talks [Special issue]. *CAHPER Journal*, **53**.

Shephard, R.J. (1982). *Physical activity and growth*. Chicago: Yearbook Medical.

Sinclair, G. (1983). A daily physical education pilot project. *CAHPER Journal*, **49**, 22-26.

Chapter 18

Physical Activity and High Performance

Norman Gledhill

The term *high performance* is used by Sport Canada, a federal agency in the Fitness and Amateur Sport Branch, to describe competitive sport at the highest international level. The high-performance sport system comprises the training and competitive programs of athletes who are ranked in the top 16 in the world in individual sports or in the top 8 in the world in team sports, together with the support personnel who work with those athletes (coaches, administrators, sport scientists, and medical and paramedical professionals). Sport Canada previously used the term *elite* to identify these athletes, but it proved inadequate. Although the high-performance support system focuses on international athletes, it occasionally embraces highly competitive "recreational" athletes and even individuals who are employed in physically demanding occupations. In fact, these latter groups are receiving increasingly more attention from exercise scientists and fitness professionals.

• • •

The high-performance sport support system is composed primarily of personnel who provide support services to international athletes. Such services are increasingly being extended to recreational athletes and individuals employed in physically demanding occupations.

• • •

Major Concepts

The Canadian Association of Sport Sciences (CASS) is a voluntary organization of professionals involved in the study and application of science in relation to sport and fitness. It promotes sport and fitness research and the application of scientific knowledge to sport and fitness, organizes scientific meetings, and publishes the *Canadian Journal of Sport Sciences*. Affiliated provincial associations, such as the Ontario Association of Sport and Exercise Science, are being developed. Members of CASS who are involved in the high-performance support system include exercise physiologists who work with athletes to enhance their training and monitor their fitness; sport biomechanists who provide athletes and coaches with advice on technique, such as the ideal takeoff angle to maximize force production; sport psychologists who work with athletes to optimize their mental preparedness; and sport nutritionists who provide athletes with information on optimal diet. Although the majority of work done by most sport scientists is accomplished during the training period, sport psychologists frequently travel to major competitions to work with the athletes.

The medical, physiotherapy, and athletic therapy personnel involved in high-performance support treat the athletes at their training sites and also accompany them to major competitions. Although the physicians in this group often are trained and experienced in sports medicine, many are general practitioners. There is a network of such physicians, physiotherapists, and athletic therapists across Canada, who are referred to as "dedicated" practitioners; these individuals give priority to treating high-performance athletes in chosen sports and are occasionally requested to accompany the athletes to international competitions. They generally receive the applicable health insurance payment for treatments performed in their clinics, but their services are provided voluntarily when they travel either domestically or internationally with the athletes—the sport organization pays for their out-of-pocket expenses.

In addition to the dedicated practitioners and therapists who travel with teams in chosen sports, a separate group of physicians, physiotherapists, and athletic therapists is selected to travel with and treat the entire Canadian contingent at major competitions such as the Olympic and Commonwealth Games. Interested individuals must apply for these positions, and there is considerable competition. The medical team must have physicians and therapists of both genders and include an orthopedic specialist and manual and manipulative therapists; all must be bilingual. The team lives in the village along with the Canadian athletes, and the medical clinic often becomes a social focal point for the athletes. In addition, the host country at major games staffs a "polyclinic" with physicians, physical therapists, and other health professionals to treat athletes who are not accompanied by medical and sport therapy personnel from their own country.

Major Trends in the High-Performance Support System

The extensive development of high-performance sport in the past decade has opened a whole new vista of professional opportunities for practitioners and researchers in the physical activity sciences. Both biological and social scientists now help apply scientific knowledge and deliver scientific services in the high-performance system. Even scientific and medical associations, which were formed solely to serve the professional needs of their membership, have become involved in the provision of high-performance support services. Moreover, the expanding possibilities for involvement in this area

will likely offer many additional interesting and challenging new career opportunities to graduates of programs in the physical activity sciences. Although a large proportion of the jobs in the high-performance area require postgraduate training, there are also many interesting support positions held by people with undergraduate degrees.

Nonathletic High Performance

In recent years, the high-performance support system has been extended to include individuals in physically demanding occupations. Many occupations involve tasks with inherent physical demands, and in some jobs the demands are considerable. Strenuous physical demands affect worker productivity and also increase the likelihood of accidents and injuries. More than just the workers' well-being can be at stake, however; public safety depends on proper job execution in occupations such as firefighting or the RCMP's Elite Intervention Squad.

Workers who apply for jobs known to be physically demanding should possess the physical capacities necessary to meet the demands. Consequently, ergonomic studies are being conducted in a variety of occupations to determine the associated physical demands. Based on the findings of

Firefighters performing a task with heavy physical demands. *Note.* Photo by the *Toronto Star*. Copyright by the Toronto Star Syndicate.

HIGHLIGHT
Testing High-Performance Athletes

A specific example of sport science support in the high-performance system is the physiological assessment of athletes' strengths and weaknesses in those fitness components important to successful performance in their chosen sport. This information is used as baseline data for designing appropriate training programs and evaluating the effectiveness of intervention programs. It also provides the athlete and coach with a better understanding of their sport. The usefulness of the assessment depends very much on the validity and reliability of the tests employed. The test items must be relevant to the sport, measuring fitness components that could limit performance in it, and the tests must elicit behavior as similar to the actual performance in the sport as possible. In addition, assessments are occasionally used to identify potential talent and to predict performance, but they are of limited value in this regard.

High-performance athletes have their fitness monitored year-round at accredited testing laboratories located across Canada; these high-performance testing centers provide interesting career opportunities.

World figure skating champion Brian Orser undergoing testing in the High Performance Laboratory at York University.

This assessment generally involves sophisticated laboratory procedures, and because Canadian athletes live and train in all areas of the country it is economically more feasible to have them tested in locally situated laboratories. A major concern, however, is quality control and comparability of results from these laboratories. For this reason, Sport Canada, the funding agency for national sport programs in Canada, requested that CASS develop a program to standardize testing protocols across the country and accredit acceptable laboratories involved in the testing of high-performance athletes.

In pursuing this goal, CASS's first step was to publish a manual entitled *Physiological Testing of the Elite Athlete*, in which MacDougall, Wenger, and Green (1982) catalogued standardized protocols for a variety of physiological measurements. The second step was to develop and implement a laboratory accreditation program aimed at identifying laboratories with both the necessary equipment and the competency to conduct a representative battery of protocols with an accuracy within a predetermined tolerance.

Accreditation inspections were made of laboratories across Canada by teams located in two regional centers. Directors of laboratories that did not initially pass all the requirements were later offered another chance to readminister those tests in which they had deviated from the established tolerances. Twenty-five laboratories were eventually accredited; these are now the laboratories to which National Sports Organizations are directed and the only laboratories that can be reimbursed with Sport Canada funds for conducting high-performance athlete assessments. Reaccreditation is scheduled to occur every 3 years.

---

these studies, protocols will be developed to validly assess the applicants' capability to meet the relevant physical demands and to monitor the incumbents' ongoing ability to do so.

The initial task in these ergonomic studies is to gain a clear understanding of what these jobs specifically require from incumbents and supervisory personnel, possibly via the use of time-motion analyses. The next step is to identify and evaluate precisely, both at the worksite and in the laboratory, the physical demands of the various job requirements. The final step is to develop and validate an assessment battery that both addresses the physical demands of the job and complies with the principles embodied in Equal Rights Legislation through appropriate evaluation criteria and standards of acceptability. The resultant screening protocols typically involve job-specific performance tests embodying the limiting physical demands of the job, general tests of fitness that are specific to the physical requirements of the job, and a medical evaluation to screen for contraindications. Often, it is necessary to evaluate the impact of implementing the screening protocol on job incumbents and applicants, especially as it relates to Equal Rights Legislation.

A prominent example in the field of applied ergonomics, and one that offers additional opportunities for careers, is that of defense science research. The Department of National Defense has established research laboratories across Canada in which investigators examine such topics as human performance under operational conditions, environmental stress and human effectiveness, physical protection against natural environments, and diving/aerospace life sciences. Several academic disciplines are represented in these research teams, and physical activity science practitioners are notable among them. These defense scientists, whose research projects occasionally take them to Canadian Forces bases in foreign countries, hold civil service appointments with all the attendant benefits.

Professional Societies

The high-performance athlete support system provides optimal medical, paramedical, and sport science assistance to Canada's top athletes so that they can compete at their highest potential. The provision of such services to high-performance athletes is coordinated by the Sport Medicine Council of Canada (SMCC). The Council's membership includes four "provider" groups:

- the Canadian Association of Sport Sciences (CASS),
- the Canadian Academy of Sports Medicine (CASM),
- the Sport Physiotherapy Division of the Canadian Physiotherapy Association (SPD), and
- the Canadian Athletic Therapist Association (CATA).

The SMCC's membership also includes a number of "user" groups (athlete representatives, Coaching Association of Canada, Canadian Olympic Association, Commonwealth Games Association, National Sport Organizations' Technical Council, and the Canadian Interuniversity Athletic Union). The user groups bring their sports medicine needs to the Council and the provider groups attempt to meet these needs.

Journals

There are several journals that publish material relevant to the high-performance support system.

The orientation of these journals ranges from medical to physiological to therapy-centered. The interested student should look at the following:

- *Medicine and Science in Sports and Exercise*
- *Exercise and Sport Sciences Reviews*
- *Journal of Applied Physiology*
- *Journal of the Canadian Athletic Therapists' Association*
- *Canadian Journal of Sport Sciences*
- *Sports Medicine*

Undergraduate and Graduate Education

Sport Scientists

Members of CASS must have a minimum of a master's degree in the physical activity sciences, and to qualify for a position as a university faculty member, a doctorate is generally required. The corresponding educational requirements are 4 years for an undergraduate degree, 2 years for a master's degree, and an additional 3 years for a PhD. To gain specific expertise in the high-performance area the student should select a graduate supervisor who works in the high-performance support system. There are many interesting positions in high-performance sport for holders of master's degrees, such as running a high-performance athlete testing laboratory; these individuals often supervise assistants who have bachelor's degrees. Not all sport scientists complete their entire education in the physical activity sciences, however. For example, to legally use the term *sport psychologist*, the practitioner must have a degree in psychology; those individuals who work in this area without this qualification are termed *sport behavior professionals*.

Sport Physicians

The physicians who work with high-performance athletes are primarily general practitioners and orthopedic specialists who have gained particular experience in sports medicine. Medical school is a 4-year program (there are some 3-year programs), and although most candidates complete a 3- or 4-year degree before admission to medical school, it is possible to enter medical school after completing 2 years of university. The medical internship requires another year, more or less, and specialization in orthopedic surgery requires an additional 3-year residency. At present, the government does not recognize a specialization in sports medicine, but qualified physicians can train in sports medicine at the Sports Medicine Clinic at the University of British Columbia. Other centers have plans for similar training programs, and CASM is currently lobbying for the creation of a government-recognized sports medicine residency and specialization.

Sport Physiotherapists

Members of SPD must be graduates of a 4-year program in physiotherapy who have also completed specialized postgraduate training in sport therapy, rehabilitation, and counseling to athletes. SPD hosts national symposia and an annual congress, provides a 5-level postgraduate sports injury specialization educational system to its members, and encourages the development and publication of research and clinical studies in the area of sport physiotherapy.

Athletic Therapists

Members of CATA are graduates of a university or community college program in the physical activity sciences. In addition, they have completed a 1,200-hour clinical and practical internship and passed a certification examination. Certified athletic therapists treat sport-related injuries through comprehensive programs in prevention, acute treatment, and follow-up rehabilitation. CATA provides continuing education for its members through regular publications, workshops, symposia, and an annual national convention.

Career Opportunities

The most extensive high-performance involvement of physical activity science practitioners and researchers is in the sport science support program. The involvement of sport scientists is normally coordinated through the medical or scientific committees of the National Sports Organizations (NSOs). These committees provide a wide range of services to the NSOs, such as

- ensuring priority treatment by dedicated physicians and sport therapy personnel for carded athletes at their normal site of training;

- making recommendations regarding medical and sport therapy personnel for domestic, international, and Olympic competitions;
- providing carded athletes with optimal allied health resources such as fitness testing, sport psychology counseling, and nutritional counseling;
- correlating and sharing with other countries any medical and scientific information pertaining to sports;
- promoting, initiating, evaluating, and, in certain cases, funding, research projects pertaining to sports;
- maintaining a data base on athletes' medical, fitness, and training information;
- developing and implementing an educational program for coaches and athletes on medical or scientific aspects of the sport;
- assisting the NSOs in applying for grants from Sport Canada to fund medical or scientific initiatives; and
- assisting the NSOs in conducting antidoping education programs and implementing doping controls.

There is considerable need for the expertise of sport scientists on these committees.

There are also career opportunities for physical activity science practitioners among the "user" groups on the SMCC. The Coaching Association of Canada (CAC), for example, provides an extensive program of professional development and support services for beginner to elite coaches; to fulfill this mandate, the CAC employs a number of highly trained professionals who are responsible for developing, implementing, and administering the various programs. Similarly, the technical directors and executive directors of NSOs and provincial sport organizations (which coordinate high-performance sport science services for the athletes and coaches in particular sports and provide many related services that parallel those of the CAC), often have backgrounds in the physical activity sciences. Many of Canada's full-time elite-level coaches hold undergraduate and graduate degrees in the physical activity sciences that help them in orchestrating sport science support services for their athletes.

Summary

The multifaceted high-performance support system provides considerable opportunity for the involvement of practitioners and researchers from the physical activity sciences. This relatively new area of career opportunity is both interesting and challenging.

The Sport Medicine Council of Canada coordinates the provision of high-performance support services through professional associations of sport scientists, physicians, and paramedical personnel. Medical, physiotherapy, and athletic therapy practitioners treat high-performance athletes during training and accompany them to major competitions. Sport scientists, who generally—but not always—hold at least a master's degree, help high-performance athletes deal with performance-related concerns such as fitness, mental preparedness, and nutritional status. The day-to-day involvement of sport scientists in the high-performance support system is often directly overseen by the medical or scientific committees of the National Sport Organizations.

One area of the high-performance support system in which physical activity sciences practitioners work is the fitness assessment of high-performance athletes. These athletes are tested year-round at centers across Canada. In addition, high-performance testing services have been extended to individuals applying for or working in physically demanding occupations, which indicates a trend that should increase employment opportunities in this area.

References and Further Readings

Coaching Association of Canada. (Updated annually). *Coaching theory: Levels one, two and three* (National Coaching Certification Program). Ottawa, ON: Author.

MacDougall, D., Wenger, H.A., & Green, H. (1982). *Physiological testing of the elite athlete.* Ottawa, ON: Mutual Press. Revised as MacDougall, D., Wenger, H.A., & Green, H. (1991). *Physiological testing of the high-performance athlete.* Champaign, IL: Human Kinetics.

Chapter 19

Physical Activity, Leisure, and Recreation

Leonard M. Wankel
Judy M. Sefton

Debate continues in the scholarly literature over the operational definitions of recreation and leisure. Whereas some authors use leisure in an objective sense to refer to unobligated time (Kraus, 1984; Shivers, 1980), others define it as an experiential "state of being" characterized by a perception of freedom and intrinsic interest (e.g., Neulinger, 1981). In a like manner, recreation is viewed either as voluntary participation in activities during discretionary time (Kraus, 1984) or as an experiential state characterized by positive feelings and free choice (Gray & Greben, 1974).

Perspectives of Leisure and Recreation

Perspective	Leisure	Recreation
Objective	Discretionary time	Voluntary activity
Subjective	State of mind; perceived freedom and intrinsic interest	State of mind; choice, enjoyment, recuperation

Major Concepts

• • •

The general convention within the field of practice, however, is to accept a discretionary time definition of leisure and an activity definition of recreation.

Leisure *is unobligated or discretionary time—the free time that remains after the demands of work, maintenance, and family and social obligations have been met;* **recreation** *refers to the activities* *voluntarily performed during leisure. Sport and physical activity thus constitute one important subset of recreational activities.*

• • •

The perception of freedom is an important aspect of our definition; hence, time made available through external coercion such as unemployment, sickness, or injury is not leisure, nor does an activity, whether passive or active, count as recreation unless the individual has voluntarily chosen to participate in it during leisure. This chapter deals with sport and physical activity as recreational activity, that is, as voluntarily participated in during leisure. Outdoor recreation pursuits, dance, and prescribed programs for special populations (i.e., therapeutic recreation) are also important subsets of the overall recreation field that involve considerable physical activity. These areas are the subject of other chapters (chapters 20, 21, and 23 and 24, respectively).

The Service Area

Just as *education* has been narrowed in some contexts to mean the formal school system, so *recreation* often refers to the field of service delivery encompassing agencies, personnel, and programs involved in providing recreation opportunities. The recreation delivery system, however, is not as neatly packaged as the education system, and involves a number of public, quasipublic, private, commercial, and voluntary agencies. Figure 19.1 illustrates five different sectors involved in recreation service delivery and identifies typical agencies within each sector.

A given agency may provide recreation services as its primary mandate (e.g., the Parks and Recreation Department or the Minor Sport Association) or as a secondary service to its employees (e.g., employee recreation program) or clients (e.g., recreation services in such institutions as schools, hospitals, and penal institutions). Although agencies within the various sectors may cooperate extensively in the provision of overall recreation services within a given area, they define their mandates for providing recreational opportunities quite differently. Because recreation is viewed as an essential social service in the Canadian public sector, public tax funds are allocated to finance recreation services for the general welfare of the public. This perspective is reflected in the resolution passed by the 1974 Canadian Conference of Provincial Recreation Ministers: "Recreation is a

social service in the same way that health and education are considered as social services and [its] purpose should be: (a) to assist individual and community development, (b) to improve the quality of life, and (c) to enhance social functioning" (Alberta Recreation and Parks, 1983, p. 4). Sport and physical activity programs are justified within public recreation agencies on the basis of their contribution to these social goals.

The public recreation system in Canada involves federal, provincial, and local levels of government. At the national level, the Federal Ministry of Fitness and Amateur Sport is responsible for federal government involvement in sport and physical activity. Much of the ministry's work is carried out through two divisions, Sport Canada and Fitness Canada. Sport Canada is responsible for federal initiatives pertaining to high-level international sport, whereas Fitness Canada is responsible for fitness and recreation.

At the next lower level, each provincial government maintains a department responsible for recreation services. Although these departments are structured and staffed in various ways, their general mandate is to provide overall leadership for recreation services in the particular province. This primarily indirect leadership involves the provision of funding, leadership development, and information services; provincial-enabling legislation cedes to local municipalities the responsibility for providing public recreation services at the local level.

Local public recreation agencies adopt one of two major approaches to program delivery. A *social planning orientation* is a centralized approach to program delivery in which agency personnel maintain considerable responsibility for organizing and overseeing the program leadership. The professional staff, although soliciting information from the public to be served, plays the leading role in program planning and execution. A *community development approach*, on the other hand, is an indirect approach to programming. The professional recreation agency assumes the role of a facilitator, assisting community groups to offer recreation opportunities by providing major facilities, financial assistance, and consultation. Community volunteers, however, assume the major responsibility for determining program direction and type. In fact, even in a social planning orientation volunteers provide much of the actual leadership (e.g., league organization and coaching).

Quasipublic, private, commercial, and voluntary agencies vary in their funding and their particular service orientation. Essentially quasipublic agen-

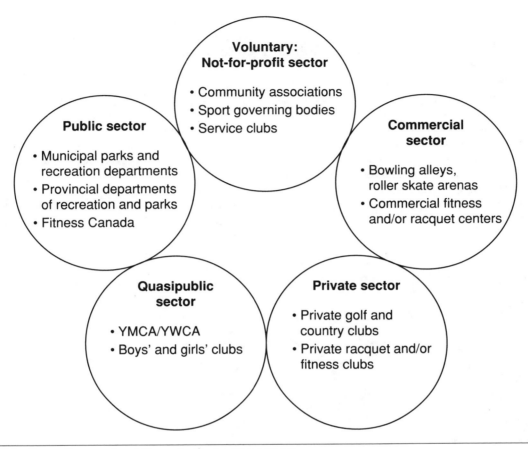

Figure 19.1 Recreation service delivery in the various sectors.

cies like the YMCA/YWCA, which depend to a considerable degree on public grants for their funding, adopt the same social need perspective of recreation that public agencies use. They may, however, focus their programs on a more restricted target population. Private clubs (e.g., golf or racquet clubs) offer a desired service to their members; commercial agencies, like any business, are designed to yield an income. Such facilities as bowling alleys, fitness centers, and roller-skating rinks sell their services on a market basis to make a profit for the owners.

Voluntary agencies vary tremendously in how and to what extent they provide recreation services. At one extreme, an agency might only provide limited funding for a program (e.g., service club sponsorship of a given sport team); at the other, it might be the principal agency for organizing and providing recreation opportunities in a community (e.g., the community league system in Edmonton, Alberta).

The voluntary sector also includes the sport governing bodies responsible for overseeing competitions within various sports. In Canada, most sports are governed by a hierarchically structured sport governing body system. Each sport has a National Sport Organization responsible for planning the sport's operation on the national level and for interfacing with the international sport organizations that govern the sport's international competitions. The provinces and territories in turn have their own provincial or territorial sport organizations for the various sports; these organizations oversee the operation of their sport in the province or territory. Similarly, a local association for a sport supervises the conduct of that sport at the local level. The larger sport organizations may also have regional sport associations (e.g., the Northern Alberta Curling Association or the Alberta Swimming Association Southern Region) that organize local and provincial competitions at an intermediate level.

Any sport program in which successful competitors may proceed to higher level competitions comes under the aegis of this sport governing body system. At the local level, however, there may be a number of other recreational sport agencies that are not affiliated with the formal organizational system. A municipal recreation agency, for example, may operate an adult volleyball program independently of local or provincial volleyball associations; such a program might use modified rules or operate without certified officials. Similarly, a number of agencies (private, public, or voluntary) or groups of individuals might also organize recreational sport programs (e.g., old-timers hockey, women's basketball, youth floor hockey) independent of the official sport governing bodies. At the most informal level of organization, a number of agencies may operate "drop-in" programs, where participants play a sport on a pickup team.

Some sport programs operate outside the Canadian sport governing body system.

U.S.A. and Other Countries

The recreational sport/physical activity delivery system in the United States resembles the Canadian system in many ways. The overall system can be partitioned into the same sectors, with a variety of public, quasipublic, private, commercial, and voluntary agencies providing recreation services. There is, however, less government involvement at the national level in the U.S.A. and there are no agencies comparable to Sport Canada or Fitness Canada. Also, the organization for public recreation at the local level is more diverse. Murphy and Howard (1977) state that

the administration of recreation services by local governments is characterized by a great

deal of diversity . . . the administrative authority for recreation can vary tremendously from state to state and from city to city. State enabling laws have allowed community recreation services to be administered by a variety of units of local government: city, county, township or special district. . . . It is not uncommon, therefore, to find in the same community two and sometimes three legally authorized public sponsored recreation agencies. (p. 135)

Generally, countries in other parts of the world do not have elaborate public recreation systems like those in North America. Government involvement in Europe is limited largely to the provision of facilities, and the provision of activities is left to an extensive sport club system. These clubs may be affiliated with particular businesses or industries or formed specifically to provide leisure or recreation services for members. They may offer only one sport or a variety of activities. Recreation leadership in Europe is generally voluntary.

Public recreation facilities and programs are not well established in the developing parts of the world; however, as industrialization progresses there is a tendency to adopt some of the North American approaches to recreation services (Westland, 1985).

Major Trends in Leisure and Recreation

Population surveys conducted in Canada and the United States in the 1970s and early 1980s document a trend toward more widespread participation in vigorous physical activity (Wankel, 1988). Although these overall trends are encouraging, examining the relevant figures for various groups within the population reveals a number of problem areas:

The level of leisure-time physical activity in Canada is, in general, quite high when measured in terms of total time and consistency of participation. However, the active population is not a representative cross-section of the total population: it tends to be younger, better educated, more often single, working in managerial or professional occupations and living in the west. (Canada Fitness Survey, 1983, p. 10)

In interpreting such group differences it is important to ask to what extent they reflect differential program opportunities and barriers. With this in mind, we will examine four trends in recreational program delivery that have been part of the overall movement toward greater involvement in sport and physical activity over the past decade.

The Proliferation of Organized Youth Sport Programs

The past 20 years have witnessed a continued expansion of organized youth sport programs in North America. A variety of sports have followed Little League baseball in establishing highly structured leagues for different age levels. According to Valeriote and Hansen (1986), approximately 2.5 million Canadian youths between ages 6 and 18 years participate in organized sports, of which 73% are males. Information from other Western countries indicates similar high overall participation rates with more males than females participating (see Campbell, 1986; Martens, 1986; Robertson, 1986). Despite the popularity of these programs, they have been subjected to a number of criticisms.

Large dropout rates have led critics to question some of the leadership practices in youth sports, especially a perceived excessive emphasis on winning and disregard for the enjoyment or fun of the participants; discriminatory coaching practices that give little playing opportunities to less-skilled participants; and, in the particular case of hockey, too much emphasis on violence.

Research has generally supported these concerns. Vaz (1974) and Smith (1975), for instance, have documented the important role that violence plays in hockey. A number of researchers have provided evidence that fun is the primary motive for youth sport involvement, and, contrary to a popular adult stereotype, winning is not of major importance (Gould & Horn, 1984; Wankel & Kreisel, 1985). Studies of sport participants indicate that simply doing the skills of the sport, learning and displaying competence in the skills, and the excitement of a challenging contest contribute to an enjoyable sport experience (Fry, McClements, & Sefton, 1981; Pooley, 1980; Sefton & Fry, 1982; Wankel & Kreisel, 1985). A recent season-long study of hockey and ringette participants indicated that personal performance was the major factor contributing to fun in a game (Wankel & Sefton, 1989).

A number of coaching development programs have been initiated as a means of improving sport

programs. These programs are discussed in the highlight.

Broadening Opportunities for Females in Sport and Physical Activity

Although more than twice as many boys participate in youth sport programs, the number of girls participating in community programs has increased dramatically in the past decade (Martens, 1986; Valeriote & Hansen, 1986). This represents an increase not only in the number of participating girls but also in the variety of sports in which they participate.

This increased involvement is consistent with the overall trends for female involvement in physical activity. Canada-wide surveys indicate that, whereas more males than females participated in physical activity in 1976, by 1981 the percentages were nearly equal (Canada Fitness Survey, 1983). Similarly, a 1980 Gallup poll indicated that in the U.S.A. nearly as many women (70%) as men (71%) engaged in some form of daily exercise. Some evidence, however, indicates that males exercise at a higher intensity level than do females (Fitness Ontario, 1984).

Although it has become acceptable for females to engage in a much broader range of physical activities and sports, many inequities still exist. Females have fewer program opportunities than males, and these programs generally receive less publicity and funding. A lack of women in influential coaching and administrative positions, together with a lack of media attention to women's sports, results in a serious lack of sport role models for young girls.

An issue that periodically arises in attempts to redress these inequities is whether girls should be allowed to play on boys' teams when they are not provided with challenging competition on girls' teams. Although court rulings have generally allowed males-only restrictions in certain sport programs, integration has proceeded successfully in many recreational sport programs. Because such programs include participants of diverse size and skill levels and because many female participants are stronger and more skilled than many males, there seems little compelling argument for maintaining segregated recreational programs.

Along these lines, Hall and Richardson (1982) have recommended an innovative approach to provide equal opportunities for males and females across the whole spectrum of competition levels. These authors advocate a combination of integrated and segregated programs. Where basic physiological differences between the sexes do not disadvantage one sex then integrated programs should prevail; where one sex has a distinct advantage separate programs should be offered. The principle that "the disadvantaged can move up" should be followed, however. Where opportunities for challenging competition at one's ability level is not available in a segregated program, individuals from the disadvantaged sex group should be allowed to move up to challenge for positions in the appropriate advantaged program. On the other hand, the converse would not hold. Athletes from the advantaged programs would not be allowed to move down to occupy positions in the disadvantaged program.

Increased Opportunities for Older Adults

Organized program opportunities for older adults have also increased. Although ageist stereotypes still exist, considerable progress has been made in broadening the scope of activities considered appropriate for older people. The developing popularity of old-timers hockey programs and senior's and master's competitions in such sports as track and field, swimming, and curling indicates that many older adults can benefit from sports. As with youth sport programs, these adult programs cut across a wide spectrum of skill levels and range from strictly community-based programs to highly structured international competitions.

Although exemplary organized program opportunities for older adults are available, they are not commonplace. For older adults, as for adults generally, the predominant forms of recreational activities are informal and individual (Canada Fitness Survey, 1983). More important, many older people are not involved in any regular activity.

Age continues to be the single most important factor distinguishing between active and sedentary Canadians (Canada Fitness Survey, 1983). The results of the Campbell's Survey of Well-Being in Canada indicate that a greater percentage of older adults, 65 years or more, were active in 1988 than had been the case in 1981. Further research is required to determine whether or not this reflects a basic shift away from the generally negative association of age and activity involvement. Current demographic projections add significance to this fact. According to a recent Statistics Canada report (Stone & Fletcher, 1986), the percentage of Canadians 65 years and older will have increased at a rate 3 times that of the general population during the period 1981 to 1991. These trends, to-

gether with the limited program opportunities currently available for this age group, make this an extremely important and challenging area for future recreation leaders. Not only must new, exciting programs be developed for aging populations, but this age group must be educated about the benefits of activity and how to establish a healthy, active lifestyle. Educating the general public about the importance of lifelong physical activity should be an important part of this educational thrust.

Privatization and User-Fee Charges in Public Recreation

Government attempts to control public expenditures in recent years have resulted in trends toward reduced public recreation services and increased user fees. To a degree, private and commercial services have filled the void by offering a wider range of recreation services, but the costs for these services often make them inaccessible to lower income groups. As a consequence, there has been a tendency for fitness and physical activity programs to become increasingly income segregated.

The Fitness Boom

In the 1970s the media were full of reports about the so-called fitness boom. As we have already mentioned, however, this trend, albeit encouraging, affected only a part—and a relatively affluent part—of the population.

The boom is in large part illusory. To begin with, it's much more of a factor in some social, economic and age groups than others. The much ballyhooed growth in the number of private health clubs and employee fitness programs has been paralleled by a less widely recognized decline in the availability of traditional fitness programs in parks, recreation departments and, above all, schools. This shift in emphasis from the public to the private sector is reflected in the fitness boom demographics: participants in it are more likely to be rich than poor, executives than blue collar workers, white than non-white, college graduates than high school graduates, adults than children. The myth that the boom is a democratic phenomenon has been nurtured in part by the gratifying increase in the number of women participating in it. But women have moved into fitness activities largely to the extent that they've advanced into the upper middle class, to which the boom is geared. (Kirshenbaum & Sullivan, 1983, p. 63)

In addition to the tendency of private and commercial agencies to cater to the more profitable high-income groups, public and quasipublic agencies have moved toward self-supporting programs, so that they, too, increasingly exclude lower income groups.

Thus, another major challenge facing recreation leaders in the future will be to broaden programming approaches, rendering sport and physical activity truly available to all income groups. Innovative methods of delivering programs and promoting activity involvement will be required.

The National Coaching Certification Program trains all levels of coaches. *Note.* Image used by permission of the NCCP.

Professional Societies and Journals

In Canada, the Canadian Parks and Recreation Association (CPRA) is the national organization most closely allied with recreation leadership. It maintains a national office in Ottawa with an executive director, convenes an annual national conference, and publishes a bimonthly journal, *Recreation Canada*, designed to keep individuals involved in the field aware of current developments. A second national organization, the Canadian Association for Health, Physical Education and Recreation (CAHPER), is the appropriate organization for those interested in physical activity, especially as it relates to activity in the school system; it publishes the bimonthly *CAHPER Journal*. CAHPER places little emphasis on recreation, however, and does not attract many members with a recreation orientation.

Most Canadian provinces have their own provincial associations designed to facilitate communication among members and to assist in leadership development and improved service delivery. The usual organizational structure is an elected board of directors and an appointed executive director. These associations typically hold annual conferences and publish regular bulletins or newsletters. Both CPRA and these provincial

---

HIGHLIGHT
Coaching Certification Programs

In Canada, the National Coaching Certification Program, which was initiated in Ontario in 1972, was implemented nationally in 1977. It provides training in the underlying theory, technical, and practical aspects of coaching for beginner through international level coaches. In the United States a number of different organizations are involved with youth sport leadership development programs, including

- the American Coaching Effectiveness Program (ACEP), Champaign, IL;
- the Youth Sports Institute at Michigan State University;
- the North American Sport Institute, Kernersville, NC;
- YMCA Youth Sports Training Programs; and
- the National Youth Sports Coaching Association, endorsed by the National Recreation and Park Association (NRPA).

Participation in these programs is essentially voluntary, however a number of organizations are beginning to require that their coaches attain a specified level of certification. Little systematic evaluation of the effects of these programs has been carried out, but they are generally considered useful in providing basic coaching information to volunteers who have had a limited background in coaching.

associations are quite diverse organizations accommodating both professional and lay members. Many provinces have several organizations that serve specific interest groups within the overall recreation field.

Although occasional research reports might be presented at CPRA or published in *Recreation Canada*, the main initiative for recreation and leisure research in Canada has come from elsewhere. The Canadian Association for Leisure Studies was established in 1981 to promote the development of leisure research in Canada. It convenes a Canadian Congress on Leisure Research every 3 years and circulates an occasional newsletter. Also relevant are the two Canadian journals devoted to recreation and leisure research: the *Recreation Research Review*, published quarterly by the Ontario Council on Leisure, and *Leisure and Society*, a bilingual journal published twice annually at the Université de Trois Rivières. In addition, the *Journal of Leisurability*, which is published quarterly by Leisurability Publications, focuses on leisure, disability, and human service issues.

The national association for recreation in the United States has been more directly involved with education and research in the recreation and leisure field than has been the case in Canada. The National Recreation and Park Association (NRPA) sponsors an annual national conference and publishes a journal geared to the recreation practitioner, *Parks and Recreation*. In addition, the American Academy for Park and Recreation Administration publishes the *Journal of Park and Recreation Administration*. Unlike the CPRA, the NRPA established an educational section (the Society of Professional Recreation Educators) that sponsors a leisure research symposium at the annual conference. The NRPA also publishes a research journal, the *Journal of Leisure Research*, and the *Journal of Therapeutic Recreation*, a quarterly publication that focuses on issues and research in the specialized subfield of therapeutic recreation. *Leisure Sciences* is also published in America.

On a more cosmopolitan level, the International Recreation Association was formed in 1956. This organization, which was renamed the World Leisure and Recreation Association in 1973, has sponsored a number of conferences throughout the world and has assisted a number of countries in developing their own recreation organizations (Westland, 1987). It also publishes the journal *World Leisure and Recreation*. Two other significant journals in the recreation and leisure field, *Leisure Studies* and *Leisure, Recreation and Tourism Abstracts*, are published in Great Britain.

In addition to the mainstream recreation and leisure journals in Canada and the United States, there are a number of specialized publications in various sport and activity areas that are valuable resources for recreation leaders (e.g., *Tennis Today*, *Golf Digest*, *Track and Field News*). In addition, a number of other agencies such as the YMCA/YWCA, Boys and Girls Clubs, and the Federation of Fitness Leaders in Business also publish magazines that provide useful information on a variety of topics.

Undergraduate Education

There is no generally required certification for employment in the recreation field; rather, the qualifications for a specific position are set by the hiring agency. As a consequence, individuals with a broad range of formal education backgrounds find employment in recreation agencies. Such individuals typically have a strong participation background and have worked as a volunteer leader prior to moving into a paid position.

Within the public recreation sector, the general practice is to hire individuals with a pertinent academic background. The pattern in Canada has been for recreation and leisure studies university programs to develop out of previously established physical education programs. Although in a number of universities recreation courses remain within the physical education program, the field's development has led to a greater number of separate recreation and leisure studies programs. These large, independent programs emphasize such areas as recreation management, outdoor recreation, recreation for special groups, and therapeutic recreation. Graduates of these programs are sought after for a diverse range of recreation jobs.

For specialized positions more directly related to sport or physical activity leadership, it is often unclear whether a physical education or a recreation graduate is most appropriate for a given position. In these cases, the hiring decision is usually based on which individual has the most appropriate experience, personal characteristics, or other qualifications, not the individual's degree.

University programs in physical education and recreation have not been developed in other countries to the extent that they have in North America. In most European countries, recreation leaders tend to be educated generally in the social sciences. In recent years, however, European universities have developed more specialized university programs in physical education and recreation and leisure studies (Westland, 1985).

Career Opportunities

Just as there is a wide variety of agencies, activities, and program formats involved in the recreational sport delivery system, there is tremendous variety in the type of leadership provided and in the career opportunities available. Indeed, this variety will likely increase in the future.

Most municipal boards within the public sector in Canada employ a professional recreation director. In smaller communities, the director may be the only paid employee beyond the maintenance and support staff. Typically, physical activity and sports are major components of the program offerings in these communities; thus, these recreation directors spend much of their time organizing and administering sport competitions and leadership clinics. To a lesser extent they may also provide direct leadership in selected activity areas. In larger communities, where more resources are available, the staff may be more numerous and specialized, including an overall sport director, a fitness coordinator, an outdoor pursuits director, various athletic facilities managers, and perhaps supervisors for programming in specific activities and for particular populations.

Provincial government recreation departments, or the departments responsible for these services, typically have a number of consulting or supervisory positions pertaining to sport and physical activity services. In some provinces, the pertinent governmental departments have established separate agencies (e.g., SaskSport, Alberta Sport Council) to assist in providing sport opportunities. Whether these positions are in a government department or an "arm's length" organization, they generally require a sport background and some expertise in the physical activity or sport area, as well as management skills; more and more, a degree in recreation administration or physical education is required for these positions. In the quasipublic sector, such agencies as the YMCA/YWCA and the Boys and Girls Clubs also hire individuals with recreation or physical education degrees. The specific degree that is considered most relevant will depend on the particular position and the degree of specialization with the agency.

Many universities, colleges, and schools employ individuals to offer recreational physical activity programs as well as more elite competitive programs. For employment in a school system individuals generally must have an education degree, with an appropriate specialization in physical education or recreation, and have special skills in the particular activities to be emphasized (e.g., intramural sports administration, outdoor pursuits, or aquatics). In some provinces, individuals with recreation degrees may be employed as recreation coordinators in schools that have been designated as community schools. At the college or university level specialized training specific to the particular job responsibilities is usually required.

Sport or social clubs in the private sector hire staff to manage their facilities and to provide organizational and direct program leadership. The particular job description for a specific club or association will determine what qualifications are required; however, in many cases a physical activity or sport background together with some training in administration is considered appropriate. Similarly, commercial agencies such as fitness centers and bowling alleys also employ individuals for varying combinations of activity program leadership and general organizational and managerial responsibilities. Although workers in these fields come from a broad variety of backgrounds they increasingly have a college or university education in recreation or physical education.

The position of recreation or fitness director for larger businesses and industries constitutes a growing field of opportunity. As with their commercial club counterparts, these positions typically entail a variety of leadership positions, but some expertise in the fitness area is generally a priority. Another growing employment area is that of therapeutic recreation personnel within such institutions as hospitals, nursing homes, and remand centers, where the emphasis is on more specialized expertise relevant to the particular institution and the population being served.

In the voluntary sector, a number of professional positions have been established within the sport governing bodies at both the national and provincial levels. Most sports at the national level now employ both a technical director who has particular expertise in the sport and an executive director who has administrative competencies to look after the organization's business functions. A similar pattern has developed at the provincial level, especially for the major sports.

A prominent trend within the recreational and leisure services field has been to greater diversity in program offerings and a more complex system, with more agencies involved in providing recreation services. This trend will lead to an increasingly diverse range of career opportunities for individuals with specialized education in recreation and leisure.

Summary

Physical activity and sport form an important component of recreation and leisure services, regardless of the type of agency or the particular clientele involved. Widely diverse career opportunities are available to individuals who combine training in sport and physical activity sciences with the study of recreation and leisure. The field presents many exciting opportunities as well as difficult challenges. The task of fostering active, healthy lifestyles to enhance general well-being and quality of life will become even more important with the rapid technological advances of postindustrial society. How to meet this challenge given the reality of increased economic pressures, rising unemployment, and an aging population will require dynamic and innovative leadership.

References and Further Readings

Alberta Recreation and Parks. (1983). *Sport development policy*. Edmonton, AB: Author.

Campbell, S.C. (1986). Youth sport in the United Kingdom. In M. Weiss & D. Gould (Eds.), *Sport for children and youths* (pp. 21-26). Champaign, IL: Human Kinetics.

Canada Fitness Survey. (1983). *Fitness and lifestyle in Canada*. Ottawa, ON: Fitness and Amateur Sport.

Farrel, P., & Lundegren, H.M. (1983). *The process of recreation programming: Theory and technique* (2nd ed.). New York: Wiley.

Fitness Ontario. (1984). *Physical activity patterns in Ontario: Winter patterns*. Toronto: Ministry of Tourism and Recreation.

Fry, D., McClements, J., & Sefton, J.M. (1981). *A report on participation in the Saskatoon Hockey Association*. Saskatoon, SK: SaskSport.

Gould, D., & Horn, T. (1984). Participation motivation in young athletes. In J.M. Silva & R.S. Weinberg (Eds.), *Psychological foundations of sport* (pp. 359-370). Champaign, IL: Human Kinetics.

The Gallup Poll. (1980). *Sports*, pp. 109-111.

Gray, D., & Greben, S. (1974). Future perspectives: An action program for the recreation and parks movement. *California Parks and Recreation*, **30**, 16.

Hall, M.A., & Richardson, D.A. (1982). *Fair ball: Towards sex equality in Canadian sport*. Ottawa, ON: Canadian Advisory Council on the Status of Women.

Kirshenbaum, J., & Sullivan, R. (1983, February 7). Hold on there, America. *Sports Illustrated*, pp. 60-74.

Kraus, R. (1984). *Recreation and leisure in modern society* (3rd ed.). New York: Appleton-Century-Crofts.

Martens, R. (1986). Youth sport in the U.S.A. In M. Weiss & D. Gould (Eds.), *Sport for children and youths* (pp. 27-33). Champaign, IL: Human Kinetics.

Murphy, J.F., & Howard, D.R. (1977). *Delivery of community leisure services: An holistic approach*. Philadelphia: Lea & Febiger.

Neulinger, J. (1981). *To leisure*. Boston: Allyn & Bacon.

Orlick, T., & Botterill, C. (1975). *Every kid can win*. Chicago: Nelson-Hall.

Pooley, J. (1980). Drop-outs. *Coaching Review*, **3**(15), 36-38.

Robertson, I. (1986). Youth sport in Australia. In M. Weiss & D. Gould (Eds.), *Sport for children and youths* (pp. 5-10). Champaign, IL: Human Kinetics.

Seefeldt, V., Blievernicht, D., Bruce, R., & Gilliam, T. (1978). *Joint legislative study on youth sport programs. Phase II: Agency-sponsored sports*. Lansing: State of Michigan.

Sefton, J.M., & Fry, D. (1982). *A report on participation in competitive swimming*. Saskatoon, SK: Canadian Amateur Swimming Association (Saskatchewan Section).

Shivers, J. (1980). *Recreation leadership: Group dynamics and interpersonal behavior*. Princeton, NJ: Princeton Book.

Smith, M.D. (1975). The legitimation of violence: Hockey players' perceptions of their reference groups sanctions for assault. *Canadian Review of Sociology and Anthropology*, **12**, 72-80.

Smoll, F., & Smith, R. (1984). Leadership research in youth sports. In J.M. Silva & R.S. Weinberg (Eds.), *Psychological foundations of sport* (pp. 371-386). Champaign, IL: Human Kinetics.

Sopinka, J., Nicholas, C., and Van Kiekebelt, D. (1983). *Can I play? Report of the task force on equal opportunity in athletics* (Vol. 1). Toronto: Government of Ontario.

Stone, L.O., & Fletcher, S. (1986). *The seniors boom.* Ottawa, ON: Ministry of Supply and Services.

Valeriote, T., & Hansen, L. (1986). Youth sport in Canada. In M. Weiss & D. Gould (Eds.), *Sport for children and youths* (pp. 17-20). Champaign, IL: Human Kinetics.

Vaz, E. (1974). What price victory? An analysis of minor hockey league players' attitudes toward winning. *International Review of Sport Sociology,* **2**, 33-53.

Wankel, L.M. (1988). Exercise adherence and leisure activity: Patterns of involvement and interventions to facilitate regular activity. In R.K. Dishman (Ed.), *Exercise adherence: Its impact on public health* (pp. 369-396). Champaign, IL: Human Kinetics.

Wankel, L.M., & Kreisel, P.S. (1985). Factors underlying enjoyment of youth sports: Sport and age group comparisons. *Journal of Sport Psychology,* **7**, 51-64.

Wankel, L.M., & Sefton, J.M. (1989). A season-long investigation of fun in youth sports. *Journal of Sport and Exercise Psychology,* **11**, 355-366.

Westland, C. (1985). Leisure and recreation: An international perspective. In T.L. Goodale & P.A. Witt (Eds.), *Recreation and leisure: Issues in an era of change* (pp. 373-390). State College, PA: Venture.

Westland, C. (1987). I.R.A.-W.L.R.A., 1956-1986, Thirty years of service: An historical perspective. *World Leisure and Recreation,* **29**, 1, 9-13.

Wiggins, D.K. (1987). A history of organized play and highly competitive sport for American children. In D. Gould & M. Weiss (Eds.), *Advances in pediatric sport sciences* (Vol. 2, pp. 1-24). Champaign, IL: Human Kinetics.

Chapter 20

Physical Activity and Outdoor Pursuits

Georges-André Nadeau

The use of the outdoors to keep physically fit, for excitement, or for learning is a remarkable and fast-growing phenomenon in our society. Canadians and Americans place a high value on the outdoors, and more than half engage in some form of outdoor activities. This takes in a wide range of activities. The relevant sense of *outdoor pursuits* depends on the emphasis that a program places on social needs and interest. Because of this diversity, the notion encompasses outdoor education/recreation, education *in* and *for* the outdoors, and education dealing with the outdoors (Donaldson & Goering, 1970; Grenier & Quenneville, 1987; Smith, Carlson, Masters, & Donaldson, 1963).

The outdoors is a natural habitat for plants, animals, and people: Its quality—and thus the quality of our life—is threatened as never before. Acid rain, toxic chemicals, and radioactive wastes pollute our air and water, placing an inestimable burden on our natural environment and diminishing our lives (President's Commission on American Outdoors, 1986). No more can we take the outdoors for granted.

The term *outdoor pursuits* refers to a holistic, direct, and sensory approach to learning and education through outdoor exploration and adventure (Ford, 1981); it also refers to all physical and noncompetitive activities in which the individual uses direct contact with the natural environment to acquire knowledge, skills, and values in an educational, recreational, or cultural setting. Outdoor activities, such as hiking, camping, skiing, orien-teering, canoeing, and cycling, are increasingly seen as a foundation for a healthy lifestyle (Corporation Plein-Air 2000, 1985). They also offer unique opportunities for exploring and improving human relations.

The following definition was derived from a survey among a group of over 100 experts in North America and Europe:

● ● ●

The learning process of outdoor pursuits offers opportunities for direct experiences in the acquisition of: (a) sound concepts and knowledge concerning human and natural resources; (b) lifetime skills permitting health, "wellness," and a creative, healthy, and refreshing way of living; and (c) positive attitudes reflecting the harmony of man with nature. (Nadeau, 1976, p. 136)

● ● ●

The outdoors thus provides important elements for a healthy, productive, and enduring society. Because of the term's unclear background and various definitions, however, the previously mentioned survey also investigated and ranked the general objectives of outdoor education.

1. To provide the individual with unique opportunities for the development of personal creativity and initiatives
2. To provide a meaningful setting for the development of attitudes

Outdoor activities like this can provide people with a solid foundation for healthy living.

3. To develop awareness, appreciation, and understanding of the natural environment and man's relation to it

4. To help realize the full potential of the individual for optimum development of the mind, body, and spirit

5. To provide a context within which the child's socialization can materialize by providing additional opportunities for social group life

6. To enable students to develop new outdoor skills and interest, and provide a basis for a lifetime of meaningful living

7. To use wisely and protect the natural environment

8. To provide outdoor settings that will make teaching more creative

9. To provide unique opportunities for behavioral changes by means of the particular setting offered by the outdoors

10. To contribute to the fostering of better teacher-student relations through direct outdoor experiences

11. To provide an opportunity for direct learning experiences by a faster implementation of the school curriculum in many areas

12. To utilize surroundings and community resources for education to the best advantage of the curriculum (Nadeau, 1976)

Major Concepts

In general, three major concepts define many of our outdoor programs.

In the *learning process concept* outdoor pursuits are seen as an interdisciplinary learning process arising from a series of organized activities held in the outdoors. This approach exploits the potential of the natural setting to contribute to physical and mental development. By increasing the awareness of interrelations with nature, a program can modify attitudes and behaviors toward the natural environment. Such programs typically embody the discovery approach to learning, which requires the use of all the senses.

The *outdoor activity concept* is found primarily in education for outdoor recreation. This approach is used in outdoor living and camping programs that provide opportunities to acquire basic skills, attitudes, and appreciation of outdoor recreation pursuits. For example, the camp-centered setting includes leisure time activities such as camping, backpacking, archery, rafting, mountaineering, snowshoeing, and fishing. Other related activities such as outdoor cooking, primitive living, survival, crafts, and nature study may also be part of such programs (Ministère du Loisir, de la Chasse et de la Pêche, 1985).

Snowshoeing is one of the activities a participant in an outdoor recreation program might learn.

The *environment concept* refers to an ecological exploration of the interdependence of living things. This approach contributes to the development of an ethic illustrating humanity's temporary stewardship of the land (Ford, 1981). The purpose of this type of program is to explain our function in the universe and show how to ensure the quality of the natural environment, now and for future generations. It includes nature study, field trips, and nature-related excursions of all kinds.

Major Trends in Outdoor Activities

Several historical phases marked the evolution of the use of the outdoors. John Kirk, as cited by Ford (1981), identified the following eight phases of the outdoor education/recreation movement.

1. The trend toward *naturalism* in education from 1823 to the 1920s, which emphasized a *back to nature* philosophy, as seen in the writings of Rousseau and Pestallozzi
2. The *time of growth* in the 1920s and '30s, with the influence of camp life and the work of L.B. Sharp and Vinal in the '20s
3. The *recreational phase* of the 1940s, with an emphasis on outdoor-living skills
4. *The curriculum-oriented school programs* of 1950 to 1960
5. The *social-living* phase of the 1950s, which emphasized individual growth, group interaction, and social adjustment
6. The *ecology phase* of the 1960s, with its changing attitudes and values toward the natural environment, during which many camp programs became available in schools
7. The *environmental education* phase of the 1970s, which emphasized *leisure education, adventure programs,* and *special populations*
8. The *holistic approach* of the 1980s, which has demonstrated a trend toward teaching the intelligent use of the outdoors for recreation and environmental purposes in urban as well as in wilderness areas (Ford, 1981, pp. 45-47)

Many interesting programs have been developed, in schools as well as in camps and recreational settings, to provide individuals with sound outdoor experiences and to educate them about the potential humans have to irreparably harm the natural environment. New, multidisciplinary environmental outdoor education projects emphasize various concepts to develop knowledge and positive attitudes toward nature, including Project Learning Tree, Project WILD, Outward Bound schools, the National Outdoor Leadership School, and the MIMN (Modèle d'Intervention en Milieu Naturel).

Professional Societies

A student interested in the outdoor education field may want to contact the outdoor education/recreation division of large, nonprofit organizations such as the Canadian Association for Health, Physical Education and Recreation (CAHPER) or the American Alliance for Health, Physical Education, Recreation and Dance.

Numerous professional organizations are very active in promoting the use of our natural resources at local, provincial/state, and national levels. These include the National Audubon Society; the National Wildlife Federation, with its special program for children (Ranger Rick); the Wilderness Society; the Nature Conservancy; the Sierra Club, and others. Many other professional groups are involved in outdoor education, including the National Recreation and Park Association, the Conservation Education Association, the National Service for Youth Foundation, and the National Camping Association, among others. In addition local organizations and clubs often conduct outdoor programs and workshops for children and adults.

Finally, as a result of both the highly touted "fitness boom" and the recent trend toward ecological awareness, there has been a proliferation of private and public organizations offering outdoor activities of all kinds. These groups typically provide information as well as program opportunities.

Journals and Other Publications

There are several relevant professional journals, magazines, and periodicals, many of which charge a reduced fee for students. In most cases, newsletters provide the most current information and news in the field. The most important monthly or bimonthly publications are

- *Journal of Health, Physical Education, Recreation and Dance (JOHPERD),*

HIGHLIGHT
Modèle d'Intervention en Milieu Naturel and Project WILD

MIMN: A New Teaching Model in the Outdoors

At Université Laval in Quebec City, a new model for teaching in the outdoors, MIMN (Modèle d'Intervention en Milieu Naturel), helps explain the teaching process in natural settings through four phases: planning, organization, implementation, and control. Adapted from the Dunkin and the Biddle teaching model (1974), the MIMN adds new components specific to the outdoors, integrating a systemic approach to operationalize and evaluate the effectiveness of learning and teaching in the outdoors. In the past few years, the university has offered many courses incorporating this model, and student response has been positive. Based on behavioral objectives, this model can be adjusted to different levels of learning, providing appropriate teaching strategies to answer the learner's needs and improving the learning/teaching process (Nadeau, 1985).

Future outdoor leaders found that this new model enabled them to better isolate and analyze their teaching strategies and, most of all, allowed them to take into account parameters such as the physical, biological, and climatic environment. Many outdoors specialists in the school community who experienced this model are convinced that it provides opportunities to innovate in the outdoor education curriculum and to better understand the educational process involved.

Project WILD

Project WILD is an interdisciplinary program that, through its implementation process and curricular materials, emphasizes wildlife to create students' awareness of their responsibility to the environment. Since its establishment in the United States in 1984, Project WILD has reached over 100,000 teachers in 40 states and 12,000 Canadian teachers in 6 provinces. Two studies conducted by national and state leaders provide strong evidence that the 81 activities prepared for young people from kindergarten to high school contribute to the growing field of knowledge of outdoor/conservation education.

Project WILD is a quality program that emphasizes the natural environment as a way to understand our responsibilities to all living things. The goal of this program is to develop awareness, knowledge, skills, and commitment that will result in responsible behavior and constructive actions throughout the United States and Canada (Western Regional Environment Education Council, 1986).

- *Journal of the Canadian Association for Health, Physical Education and Recreation* (CAHPER),
- *Journal of Outdoor Education,* and
- *Parks and Recreation.*

In 1973, the American Association for Health, Physical Education and Recreation published *Research in Outdoor Education: Summaries of Doctoral Studies,* vol. 1, which contains 117 studies. The second volume, published in 1978, contains 121 additional dissertation summaries, and the third publication, in 1980, adds another 115 for a total of 353 (Hammerman, 1986-87).

The bibliography of dissertations in ecoeducation compiled for the American Alliance for Health, Physical Education and Recreation by Swan and Mackay (1985) contains over 900 citations.

Undergraduate Education

The number and type of training programs at the university level give eloquent testimony to the importance of the outdoors. Institutions throughout North America have experimented with programs that take individuals and resource materials into the outdoor environment to more effectively meet curricular objectives. In addition, outdoor pursuit programs incorporate various models and approaches.

Anyone planning to work in outdoor education should consider general leadership preparation in four main functions: teaching, leadership, counseling, and administration. The course curriculum in outdoor education should include the following components or characteristics:

- Basic philosophy
- Principles and values of outdoor education
- Outdoor leadership
- Skills in outdoor experiences in all types of environments
- An understanding of human growth and development and of the learning and teaching process
- Knowledge of and skills in communications and human relations
- Knowledge of and skills in outdoor activities and sports for year-round programs

In addition, a working knowledge of management principles and skills can help in contacts with private organizations and businesses, recreation and conservation groups, youth and senior citizen groups, land managers, manufacturers, and basic retailers. Finally entrepreneurship knowledge is a must, as are medical skills and safety knowledge and a sound training in cooperating with public and private organizations.

Career Opportunities

Outdoor pursuit careers fall into four major categories: teacher, counselor, leader, and administrator. Career opportunities are diversified further as to their target populations, for example, the general public, the aged, and the handicapped.

Employers expect to hire a decision maker who has not only an educated approach to curriculum development for year-round programs from kindergarten to college level but also basic skills in working with a teaching model that includes contemporary teaching techniques and methods for outdoor experiences. They also look for a well-motivated generalist with a broad and sound vision of the attendant duties.

Most positions require appropriate training in an area of specialization through provincial agencies, a bachelor's degree in outdoor education/recreation, or both (Cousineau, 1978). If a candidate exhibits a high degree of expertise and leadership skill, academic experience may be considered nonessential. Most positions are in elementary, secondary, and high schools; outdoor education centers/camps; community centers; public organizations dealing with education, recreation, or leisure activities; government agencies dealing with provincial/state and federal services (park or forest services); and government-sponsored agencies or private organizations.

Summary

North Americans put a high value on the "great outdoors," whether as a means to physical fitness, excitement, or education. *Outdoor pursuits* implies a holistic, direct, and sensory approach to learning and education through outdoor exploration and adventure. The three most important objectives of outdoor education are to find unique opportunities for the development of personal creativity and initiative; to find a meaningful setting for the development of attitudes, awareness, appreciation, and understanding of the natural environment and humanity's relation to it; and to help people realize their full potential of mind, body, and spirit.

The three major concepts that define outdoor programs are the *learning process concept*, exemplified in programs wherein an interdisciplinary learning process results from a series of organized outdoor activities; the *outdoor activity concept*, which is exemplified primarily in outdoor activities used as practice or training; and the *environmental concept*, which refers to an ecological exploration of the interdependence of living things. The major trend of the 1990s is toward a holistic approach in teaching the wise use of the outdoors for recreation and environmental purposes, in both urban and wilderness areas.

A student interested in the outdoor education field should contact a professional society and read the relevant journals and other publications. Outdoor service careers fall within four major roles: teacher, leader, counselor, and administrator. The different positions require appropriate training in the area of specialization through provincial agencies, a bachelor's degree in outdoor education/recreation, or both. Career opportunities are mainly in schools, camp communities, government-sponsored agencies such as park or forest services, or private organizations.

References and Further Readings

American Alliance for Health, Physical Education and Recreation. (1978). *Research in outdoor education: Summaries of doctoral studies* (Vol. 2). Washington, DC: Author.

American Association for Health, Physical Education and Recreation. (1973). *Research in outdoor recreation: Summaries of doctoral studies* (Vol. 1). Washington, DC: Author.

Corporation Plein-Air 2000 et Regroupement des Organismes nationaux de loisir du Québec. (1985). *Symposium Plein-Air 2000. Rapport des conférences et ateliers secteur plein-air.* Laval: Info-Loisir.

Cousineau, C. (1978). *Revue et analyse critique de la recherche relative aux programmes d'aventure de plein-air.* Communication présentée au congrès annuel de l'Association canadienne-française pour l'avancement des sciences (ACFAS), Ottawa.

Donaldson, G.W., & Goering, O.H. (1970). *Outdoor education: A synthesis.* ERIC/CRESS Report.

Dunkin, G.N., & Biddle, B.J. (1974). *The study of teaching.* New York: University Press of America.

ERIC/CRESS. (1977). *Directory of outdoor education degree programs in higher education.* Las Cruces, NM: National Educational Lab.

Ford, P.M. (1981). *Principles and practices of outdoor/environmental education.* New York: Wiley.

Grenier, J., & Quenneville, G. (1987). *Long sentier . . . petits portages: Les fondements du Plein-Air.* North Hatley, Québec: Les Éditions C and C.

Hammerman, W.M. (1986-87). The impact of outdoor education on American education. *Journal of Outdoor Education, 21,* 4-14.

Ministère du Loisir, de la Chasse et de la Pêche (1985). *Étude sur le loisir des québécois.* Québec: Gouvernement du Québec.

Nadeau, G.-A. (1976). *Outdoor education as seen through a Delphi survey of selected groups of experts in the Province of Quebec, Canada, U.S.A., and overseas and implications for the outdoor education curriculum at Laval University, Quebec.* Unpublished doctoral dissertation, Michigan State University, East Lansing.

Nadeau, G.-A. (1985). Modèle d'intervention en milieu naturel (MIMN). In *Colloque Franco-québécois/pédagogie des actions de restaurations.* Conference given at Bergerac, France.

President's Commission on American Outdoors. (1986). *Report and recommendations to the president of the United States.* Washington, DC: U.S. Government Printing Office.

Smith, J.W., Carlson, R.E., Masters, H.B., & Donaldson, G.W. (1963). *Outdoor education* (2nd ed.). Englewood Cliffs, NJ: Prentice Hall.

Swan, M., & Mackay, B. (1985). *TAFT campus occasional paper XV.* Doctoral dissertation, Northern Illinois University, DeKalb.

Western Regional Environment Education Council. (1986). *Project WILD: Elementary activity guide and secondary activity guide.* Boulder, CO: Western Association of Fish and Wildlife Agencies.

Chapter 21

Physical Activity and Dance

Magdeleine Yerlès
Madeleine Lord
Martine Epoque

Dance is taught across Canada and the United States in a variety of contexts, by a diversified corps of specialists, and under varied forms and styles. It is taught in private studios or dance schools, in leisure centers, in public schools, in physical fitness centers, in dance academies, and in dance departments at colleges and universities. It is taught by dancers, dance teachers, physical educators, physical fitness specialists, and primary school teachers. It is taught under varied forms such as folk, social, tap, and ethnic dance, and as a performing art it often involves a great variety of styles such as ballet, modern dance, or jazz. Clearly dance is kaleidoscopic and not a single, well-delineated area of practice. Undergraduate students in the physical activity sciences are thus faced with a series of questions ranging from the sublime to the mundane: What is dance? What is dance for? Should and how can I become a specialist in dance? Will I be able to earn a living with dance?

Dance has long been part of undergraduate physical activity education in North America. A quick glance at the *Physical Education Gold Book* (1982) confirms the persistency of this trend, for there is generally at least one dance specialist within the college or university physical activity sciences departments throughout the United States and Canada. The very name of the American professional association—the American Alliance for Health, Physical Education, Recreation and Dance—provides eloquent testimony of the presence of dance within the professional universe of

physical activity specialists, and dance teachers have been instrumental in developing dance as both an art form and an educational experience. Occasionally, these dance specialists freed themselves from the tutelage of physical education and became actively involved in the development of dance departments.

Major Concepts

The concept of dance has different meanings for various people, but one of dance's essential characteristics is movement.

The Nature of Dance

Movement. Dance is movement in the same way as sport is movement; that is, dance uses a wide range of motions that may be defined in terms of structured space and time. Movement in itself does not distinguish dance from sport, but does distinguish it from other forms of art, for example painting or music.

Communication. Human movement has two fundamental aspects that may be conceptualized as two poles of a functional continuum. On one end of the continuum, human movement allows for survival, for example, insofar as it constitutes activities such as hunting and fishing or, more narrowly, aiming, catching, paddling, or swimming. At this end of the continuum, movement

The creation of movements designed to express a state of mind, a belief, a feeling, or an idea is the essence of dance. *Note.* Photo by Denis Poulin. Reprinted by permission.

is essentially instrumental or utilitarian. Outdoor activities and physical fitness activities relate to this pole of the continuum. At the other end of the continuum, human movement allows for communication of a state of mind, an emotion, an intention, a prayer, or an idea. Movement is here essentially expressive and dance belongs to this pole of the continuum to the extent that it centers on communication through movement.

In sports, all movements are means to the ultimate end of demonstrating an individual or collective superiority over an opponent; in this sense, all its movements are instrumental. Nevertheless, human movements in sports are not always devoid of intended communication. In gymnastics, synchronized swimming, or dance skating demonstrating superiority requires movements to be expressive and translate an idea, an intention, or an emotion. In this sense, these sports also incorporate expressive movement, but in dance *all* movements are expressive.

Essence. The essence of sport lies in the reduction of uncertainty about the outcome. At least ideally, all contestants have an equal chance of winning at the outset of a competition; at the end, there are only winners and losers (Jeu, 1987). The structure of the movements within the competition and the choice of the appropriate amount of energy ex-

pended are dictated by the quest to affect the chances in favor of one side as efficiently as possible. In dance, however, the structure of movement and energy expended are dictated by the quest for the most perfect expression of significance. The nature of dance resides in the carefully crafted motor expression of a state of mind, a belief, a feeling, or an idea.

The Functions of Dance

People dance for many different reasons and use any number of dance forms. Dance may fulfill different functions that vary according to age, gender, socioeconomic status, and culture. Dance may fulfill a religious function and, as a form of ritual, allow for direct communication with the divine. It may fulfill a cultural function, either as an art form (i.e., choreographic works) or as a folk form (i.e., traditional dances). Dance may play an economic function through the creation of part-time or full-time employment in the artistic, educational, or leisure fields. Dance may serve an educational function when taught in schools and provide recreation under its social forms such as rock-and-roll or the cha-cha. Finally, as a means of emotional release or reeducation, dance may serve a therapeutic function.

• • •

As an area of professional practice related to the physical activity sciences, dance involves teaching organized movement experiences as a means to a range of diverse objectives, including psychomotor development, recreation, self-expression, mental health, and artistic expression.

• • •

Major Trends in Dance

Four of the functions of dance are directly linked to trends in professional practice: the recreational, therapeutic, artistic, and educational functions.

Dance in Education

Dance is currently taught in primary and secondary schools as part of physical education or art programs. Through the years, dance was successively presented as a form of healthy exercise, a way to develop good posture and sound sensory motor ability; it was also presented as a privileged means to develop creativity and personality through the integration of affective, cognitive, and motor dimensions in artistic expression.

Although its place in the public curriculum was first as movement form, dance is now construed more and more as an art form. In this context, it is approached as a creative art experience rather than as a technique or a style to be learned. The child's natural movement potential is actualized and refined through basic technical and improvisational experiences. Rather than using routines to learn set forms of movement, children learn how to invent and vary movements through manipulating spatial, temporal, and energetic components. Through composing, performing, and appreciating, children learn how to create, perform, and share their visions of the world. Creative dance education thus could be defined summarily as a set of organized movement experiences for the learning of artistic expression.

Dance as Recreation

Adolescents, adults, and older persons dance in their free time for a variety of motives. They may dance for the sheer pleasure of dancing, for relaxing, for establishing social relationships, for acquainting themselves with or maintaining a cultural heritage, or for maintaining physical fitness. Dance forms such as social (or ballroom) and folk are well suited to serve recreational purposes, but theatrical dance forms such as ballet, modern dance, and jazz also constitute popular forms of recreational dancing.

Dance as Therapy

Mental health is a fairly recent concern of dance professionals. Although dance therapy began in the 1940s with the innovative work of Marian Chace at the St. Elizabeth Hospital in Washington, DC, it did not begin to flourish until the 1960s, when it benefited from the influence of the human relations training movement and the resurgence of research in nonverbal communication. Dance therapy is discussed further in a Highlight.

The basis of dance therapy is movement interaction. *Note.* Photo reprinted by permission of Claire Schmais.

Dance as an Art Form

As an art form, dance was born in the 20th century, when "the cry of gesture," the art of the ephemeral, was finally accepted. It was in this century that dance progressively freed itself from music and theater and ceased to be a supporting art (*art d'accompagnement*). Although dance has not yet inspired any widespread cultural movements, as

---

HIGHLIGHT
Mental Health and Dance Therapy

Dance therapy is a form of psychotherapy in which movement interaction is the primary means for accomplishing therapeutic goals. Although their work was first confined to hospital settings, dance therapists are becoming more and more involved in health community centers, private clinics, specialized schools, prisons, and rehabilitation centers. The scope of dance therapy is now moving toward the broader picture of movement therapy and tends to open the area of professional practice toward the educational concerns of the mentally and physically disabled and the elderly. Whereas the United States requires a master's degree for professional practice in this field, no formal training is yet offered in Canada.

Created in 1966, the American Dance Therapy Association is the main professional organization in this sector. This association plays a leadership role, setting professional standards and publishing the *Newsletter* and the *American Journal of Dance Therapy*. The National Dance Association of AAHPERD has also encouraged and supported the efforts of dance therapists by publishing a monograph focusing on the nature and theoretical bases of dance therapy and on the professional training of dance therapists (Mason, 1974).

---

music, painting, and sculpture have, the recent development of visual technologies will now allow it such a leadership role.

The 20th century witnessed an extraordinary explosion in the number and quality of choreographers from all styles, including Maurice Béjart, Pina Baush, Merce Cunningham, Robert Joffrey, Paul Taylor, Trisha Brown, Lucinda Childs, John Neumeier, Jerry Kilian, Judy Jarvis, and Brian Mc-Donald. Further, as dance cannot exist without dancers, the realization and diffusion of choreographic works required the training of highly skilled dancers who were able to render the subtleties of each creator's style. This vitality of the dance professional milieu and the increased visibility of dance on television and in the press supported dance educators in their efforts to convince governmental and school authorities of the place of dance in school and university curricula. It is now possible for children to receive an initial training in dance in primary schools and to pursue their formal studies and dance professional training at college and university levels. The following is a list of some Canadian colleges and universities offering dance programs.

- Collège Montmorency (Laval, PQ)
- Collège Saint-Laurent (Montréal, PQ)
- Collège de Rivière-du-Loup (PQ)

- Concordia University (Montréal, PQ)
- Dalhousie University (Halifax, NS)
- George Brown College (Toronto, ON)
- Grant MacEwan College (Edmonton, AB)
- McMaster University (Hamilton, ON)
- Simon Fraser University (Burnaby, BC)
- University of Alberta (Edmonton, AB)
- University of British Columbia (Vancouver, BC)
- University of Calgary (AB)
- Université de Montréal (PQ)
- Université du Québec à Montréal (PQ)
- University of Saskatchewan (Saskatoon, SK)
- University of Waterloo (ON)
- University of Winnipeg (MN)
- York University (Toronto, ON)

Formerly, our physical education departments used to attract dancers in the same way they attract athletes. These dancers acquired a scientific and professional training in human movement and a diploma that legitimated their use of dance as a subject matter in physical education. In a way, these dancers had no other choice and endured through the programs while fighting for specificity. Those dancers who did not wish to pursue formal studies at the university level typically pursued their specific training in a private *académie* under the aegis of a master, becoming first professional dancers and, after long years on stage, perhaps choreographers or masters of dance.

Professional Societies

The national associations for health, physical education, and recreation in Canada and in the United States both have dance divisions that provide the major focus for the educational applications of dance.

Since its creation in 1965, CAHPER's Dance Division has played a leadership role in the educational context through the guidelines it provides for dance programs at the elementary and secondary school levels and through the involvement of its members with professional education in dance. In addition to its own publications, the division keeps a dance column in the monthly magazine *CAHPER Journal*; it also holds conferences and workshops throughout the country.

In the United States, the National Dance Association—one of the seven divisions of AAHPERD—plays a very similar role. Several of its publications deal with topics such as the educational function of dance, dance curricula, dance for the handicapped, and professional training in dance. This group holds a yearly national conference and regularly provides a dance section to the *Journal of Health, Physical Education, Recreation and Dance*.

Myriad local, provincial, national, and international associations exist with regard to dance as recreation.

As mentioned in the Highlight to this chapter, the American Dance Therapy Association is the main professional body for individuals involved with therapeutic dance. Its activities include setting professional standards and publishing a newsletter and a journal.

Dance in Canada is the most active association in the area of artistic production. Its annual conference, which recently took the form of a Canadian dance festival, is a unique opportunity to assess the state of the art in Canadian theatrical dance. The association provides highly specialized workshops for professional dancers, choreographers, and dance administrators. It publishes a quarterly magazine entitled *Dance in Canada*, which has the Canadian dance stage as its main focus and which occasionally features articles on education, administration, and research.

The American Dance Guild is the most important national organization for dance educators, writers, and performers in the United States: Its monthly *Newsletter* and its *Job Express Registry* are the major media offering information about the dance world activities and job opportunities. In addition, the association publishes *Dance Scope* every semester, maintains a library of contemporary dance publications, operates a book club to market relevant publications to its members, and holds national conferences on dance.

Physical activity sciences have played, and will keep playing, a leading role in expanding the body of knowledge on dance. Scientific and applied knowledge developed in such fields as physiology of exercise, sports medicine, biomechanics, motor learning, pedagogy, and sociology is currently taught by specialists from the physical activity sciences in dance departments. Quite a few of these researchers are members of the international interdisciplinary organization called CORD, the Committee on Research in Dance.

Journals and Other Publications

In addition to the *CAHPER Journal* and the *Journal of Health, Physical Education, Recreation and Dance*, many other journals and publications cover dance and dance-related topics. The following list divides the most prominent by area of specialization.

Physical Activity Sciences/Research
- *Dance Research Journal*
- *Dance Chronicle: Studies in Dance and Related Arts*
- *Kinesiology for Dance*
- *Movement and Dance*
- *Dance Notation Journal*

Education
- *Dance Research Journal*

Recreation
- *Dance Teacher Now*
- *Dance Scene*
- *Folk Dance Scene*
- *Dance*

Therapy
- *Newsletter of the American Dance Therapy Association*
- *American Journal of Dance Therapy*

Art
- *Dance in Canada*
- *Newsletter of the American Dance Guild*
- *Dance Scope*

Undergraduate Education

Dance will probably remain part of Canadian undergraduate programs in the physical activity sciences, but the emphasis of dance courses will be different from what it used to be. Because of the growing acknowledgment of dance as an art form, our students will be exposed increasingly to courses centered on composition, performance, and appreciation, that is, on the principles underlying artistic expression through movement. Students will thus be required to get a formal training in ballet or modern dance prior to their specialization into dance as an educational experience.

A full mastery and understanding of dance as a creative art is an essential competency for dance educators; their training program should not differ fundamentally from that of professional artists. Both need experiences in technique, structured improvisation, free improvisation, composition, performance, and appreciation, though dance educators need not meet the technical and creative standards of the professional dance stage. Dance educators need not be virtuosi but nevertheless should be artists in the full sense of the word.

In the public education system dance is taught either by art specialists or by physical activity teachers. In both cases, it is likely that the teaching of other movement or art forms will be required as part of the teaching load. Art education is not a priority in most North American educational systems; consequently, governmental standards regarding physical education and art programs, their time allotment, and the competences of the professionals who should implement them exist only in some states or provinces (e.g., in Québec). Even so, current practices and socioeconomic constraints sometimes prevent the implementation of these standards.

Career Opportunities

In terms of career opportunities, graduates who have a prior experiential knowledge of dance will be well trained for several occupations.

Some may find employment as dance educators working in primary or secondary schools within physical education or art programs or in the recreational sphere with children, adolescents, adults, and the elderly, with an emphasis on either creative or aerobic dancing. The current number of job opportunities for school-based dance educators is limited. However, considering the mean age of the public education personnel and a growing understanding and concern for the arts in our society, it is possible that a greater number of openings will become available in the near future. Clientele imperatives dictate the current strong emphasis on the learning and interpreting of dance styles in settings such as school or university sport facilities, municipal recreational centers, fitness centers, and private studios. Although aerobic dancing might be a fad, a number of part-time employment opportunities are currently open to graduates who are both dance and physical fitness specialists. Very little control is exerted, however, on professionals working in the recreational areas and, besides the mastery of a specific dance style, no further competencies in dance or teaching are formally required.

Others may find themselves coaching professional dancers. Training for "new dance" is more and more demanding and requires the careful planning of training sessions and performance. This is a new venture, but a viable option.

Choreographers can find positions in gymnastics, synchronized swimming, dance skating, or any sport that requires an expressive quality of movement during performance. This is another relatively new area of practice, but also worth trying.

Finally, individuals who go on to do research in any subfield of the physical activity sciences may choose to focus on dance-related topics.

Summary

It is likely that graduates in the physical activity sciences who wish to work in dance will increasingly be thrown on their own resources to acquire additional training in any particular form or style of dance, especially if they wish to work in dance as a performing artist or as a dance educator. Far from being merely a means to the ends of physical education, dance has reached a high degree of autonomy and legitimacy both as an art form and as a formal curriculum of colleges and universities and is rapidly approaching the status of music or theater in art and education. This does not mean, though, that the cross-fertilization of the physical activity sciences and dance is over, but only that each contribution will be more and more different from what it used to be.

References and Further Readings

Beatty, P. (1986). *Form without formula: A concise guide to the choreographic process.* Toronto: Press of Terpsichore.

Cheney, G., & Strader, J. (1975). *Modern dance.* Boston: Allyn and Bacon.

Febvre, M. (Ed.) (1987). *La danse au défi* [A challenge to dance]. Montréal: Parachute.

Hawkins, A.M. (1988). *Creating through dance.* Pennington, NY: Dance Horizons Books.

Hayes, E.R. (1981). *A guide to dance production: "On with the show."* Reston, VA: American Alliance for Health, Physical Education, Recreation and Dance.

Jeu, B. (1987). *Analyse du sport* [The analysis of sport]. Paris: Presses Universitaires de France.

Kraus, R., & Chapman, S.A. (1981). *History of the dance in art and education* (2nd ed.). Englewood Cliffs, NJ: Prentice Hall.

Livet, A. (Ed.) (1978). *Contemporary dance: An anthology of lectures, interviews and essays with many of the most important contemporary American choreographers, scholars and critics.* New York: Abberville Press.

Lord, M., & Bruneau, M. (1983). *La parole est à la danse* [Dance, it is your turn to speak]. Sainte-Foy, PQ: Laliberté.

Mason, K.C. (Ed.) (1974). *Dance therapy.* Washington, DC: American Alliance for Health, Physical Education, Recreation and Dance.

Morgenroth, J. (1987). *Dance improvisations.* Pittsburgh: University of Pittsburgh Press.

Physical Education Gold Book. (1982). Champaign, IL: Human Kinetics.

Sorrell, W. (1981). *Dance in its time: The emergence of an art form.* Garden City, NY: Anchor Books.

Chapter 22

Physical Activity and Fitness

H. Arthur Quinney

One of the most dynamic and rapidly changing areas of practice for physical activity professionals is the one broadly defined as "fitness." The past 20 years have witnessed a worldwide explosion of participation in physical activity for the purpose of increasing fitness and health. The profession is only now catching up in the training of new leaders to service this growth. Coupled with the lack of legislation governing provision of fitness services in Canada, this rapid growth of consumer demand has caused a wide diversity of public and private involvement in the fitness field.

Fitness training involves the use of physical activity to increase the functional capacity and efficiency of the body. Other outcomes that are generally accepted goals of fitness activities are

- caloric expenditure,
- weight management,
- stress management,
- social interaction,
- decreased risk of ill-health,
- enhanced self-image, and
- "feeling good."

Many fitness activities also provide an opportunity to enjoy the natural environment.

Fitness activities include a broad range of opportunities with highly structured classes at one end of the continuum and individually selected, unstructured physical activities at the other end. The type of activity chosen is far less important to the result than the commitment to be physically active on a regular and frequent basis. The major goal of the fitness field is to ensure that the opportunity to be physically active is easily available to all.

• • •

At its most rudimentary level, professional practice in the field of fitness involves on-the-floor fitness instruction to produce health benefits; more typically, it involves training other fitness personnel and designing and administering programs that provide easily available opportunities for physical activity.

• • •

Major Concepts

Most of the major policy decisions that have shaped the field of fitness have been made at the federal and provincial levels, but the actual delivery of programs and services occurs at the local level. By providing facilities and programs municipal (city, county) governments have had a major impact on fitness activity opportunities. In addition, the private sector and not-for-profit organizations such as the YMCA/YWCA have developed significant programs and services that both complement and compete with public-sector programs.

If a physically active lifestyle is to be an easy and attractive choice, a wide variety of physical activities must be available. Many people prefer formal, highly structured fitness classes; these programs are offered in a variety of settings. Others prefer structured recreational sport programs as their mode for regular physical activity. In fact, middle-aged and older adults are increasingly involving themselves in recreational sports and athletics such as swimming and ice hockey. The majority of Canadians, however, indicate that their main involvement in physical activity for fitness is through totally unstructured activities such as walking, gardening, swimming, and cycling (Canadian Fitness and Lifestyle Research Institute, 1990).

The opportunity for social interaction is an important benefit of physical activity.

Nonprofit organizations such as the YMCA and YWCA traditionally have led the development and provision of fitness programs in most Canadian communities, but the increased demand for fitness programs soon brought educational institutions, municipal recreation departments, and private, profit-driven companies into the fitness marketplace. Fortunately, the influx of quick profit, private operators into fitness seen in the 1970s has abated, leaving the industry with more professionally oriented businesspeople who want to provide high-quality fitness services for the public.

One of the major markets for the private sector is employee fitness consulting and programming. The workplace is now regarded as a very important component of the delivery system for fitness in Canada. Indeed, this relatively new area of focus has become so important that chapter 27 is dedicated to a discussion of it.

Major Trends in Fitness

Several pivotal events have influenced the evolution of the fitness field in Canada. Perhaps the most significant was the publication of a working document by the former Federal Minister of Health and Welfare Marc Lalonde (1974) entitled *A New Perspective on the Health of Canadians*. This report emphasized the links of physical activity and other lifestyle elements to good health. In many ways, this document legitimized the role of the fitness professional by giving importance to the positive health outcomes of a lifestyle that includes regular physical activity. Paffenbarger (1984) has now demonstrated that physical activity is a stimulus for other positive health-related behaviors. Essentially, if we can motivate people to increase their exercise patterns, a number of other lifestyle behaviors also change for the better.

Another key concept emphasized in this document is self-responsibility for good health. This "taking control" philosophy sent a clear message that prevention is the long-term solution to the health care problem. A 1987 document published by National Health and Welfare, *The Active Health Report*, reemphasized this and many of the other important points made in the Lalonde document and presented strategies to reduce health risk through exercise and other positive lifestyle behaviors.

In June 1986, The Canadian Summit on Fitness brought together 190 fitness professionals, government representatives, and academicians to develop a vision for fitness in Canada for the year 2000.

The vision of fitness by the year 2000 depicts a society that values well-being as fundamental and an integral part of day-to-day life. Canadian social structures, the family, the schools, the workplace, the health care system, will all enthusiastically embrace and reward daily physical activity and behaviors which contribute significantly to health and well-being. Regular physical activity and optimal well-being will be ingrained as important and widely accepted values in Canadian society (in effect, a Canadian cultural trademark). (Fitness Canada, 1986, p. 14)

The mission of the Canadian fitness movement is to mobilize individuals, industry, and social institutions to develop the physical environments and social norms leading to physical activity and optimal well-being as an integrated part of Canadian life. (Fitness Canada, 1986, p. 16)

The delegates to the conference made it clear that the concept of fitness must be viewed from a holistic perspective in that the physical/biological component is only one aspect of total well-being. This view is consistent with the integrated concepts of the "wellness" philosophy that is currently receiving wide acceptance.

Delivery of high-quality professional fitness services requires a broad perspective on the interrelationships of different aspects of total fitness; for example, any consultation regarding physical activity patterns must include reference to nutrition. Thus, the fitness professional must be able to place exercise in context with all the lifestyle behaviors that contribute to optimal function. This does not mean that the fitness specialist must also be a registered dietician, psychologist, physician, exercise physiologist, philosopher, and vocational counselor (though it might help). A basic, working knowledge in these areas is essential and must be included in professional preparation, but it is also important to know when to refer a client to a specialist in another area.

A close working relationship between these allied health professionals is equally essential. The fitness professional is a new addition to the health delivery system whose ability to make a meaningful contribution may be greeted with some degree of cynicism. Experience has shown, however, that hard-working fitness specialists who demonstrate a high level of expertise soon become accepted members of the team.

Fitness Canada has recognized and responded to the importance of broadening the scope of fitness through the introduction of a conceptual model entitled Active Living. Active living is viewed as

- a way of life,
- part of a lifelong developmental process, and
- a contribution to well-being and improved quality of life.

Many other societal trends have an impact on the fitness field and will continue to direct and redirect our programs and services. For example, a softening of the very prescriptive approach to fitness activities has led to the emergence of personal physical activity counseling. A similar recent innovation is the personal fitness trainer; one-on-one physical activity programs are growing in popularity for those who can afford this service.

One of modern life's most pervasive trends is ongoing technological development, which continues to reduce the requirement for physical activity in our daily lives so that we must deliberately build it into our schedules. Technology can also provide attractive physical activity opportunities, however, through interactive games that require movement or exercise machines that provide immediate feedback.

Another trend in the fitness field has been an increase in the level of fitness knowledge of the public. Fitness professionals successfully provided information about fitness and lifestyle, creating a higher level of understanding about fitness principles, but this has required that they be able to answer sophisticated questions.

Finally, environmental awareness has begun to affect everything in our lives, including physical activity. A prime example of this is the use of "appropriate technology" in transportation. People increasingly are cycling and walking not as recreation but as ways of getting places. This has necessitated the construction of safe and attractive pathway systems in urban centers.

Trends in Fitness

- Less rigid approach to physical activity for fitness
- Personal physical activity counseling
- Personal fitness trainers
- High-tech equipment and clothing
- Better informed participants
- Environmental awareness (e.g., cycling/walking)

Demographic factors also have significant impact on the fitness field. In the next few decades fitness professionals will have to provide services to a population with an increasingly large percentage of older individuals. In addition, a trend toward early retirement will give people who are already committed to an active lifestyle more time to be more involved in physically active leisure pursuits.

Professional Societies

Although a number of provincial and regional professional fitness associations exist, no national association has a clear claim to the title of *the* national fitness professional association. The two national associations that offer the most direct leadership are the Canadian Association for Health, Physical Education and Recreation (CAHPER) and the Canadian Association of Sport Sciences (CASS). Beyond these two organizations, the Canadian Parks and Recreation Association and the Canadian Public Health Association also touch on aspects of fitness.

FITNESS APPRAISAL
CERTIFICATION AND ACCREDITATION
A NATIONAL PROGRAM OF THE

CANADIAN ASSOCIATION
OF
SPORT SCIENCES

THE PROGRAMS OF THIS
ASSOCIATION ARE FUNDED IN PART
BY
FITNESS CANADA

CASS's Fitness Appraisal Certification and Accreditation Program functions in every province. *Note.* Image reprinted by permission of the Canadian Association of Sport Sciences.

Many Canadian fitness professionals, however, look to American associations for leadership. The American College of Sports Medicine, the Association for Fitness in Business, the National Strength Coaches Association, and the National Wellness Institute all attract a large number of Canadian members.

Journals

Because there is no commonly accepted fitness association in Canada, professionals rely on journals from all the associations listed in the previous section:

- *American Journal of Health Promotion*
- *CAHPER Journal*
- *Canadian Journal of Public Health*
- *Canadian Journal of Sport Sciences*
- *Medicine and Science in Sports and Exercise*
- *National Strength Coaches Association Journal*
- *Physician and Sportsmedicine*
- *Research Quarterly for Exercise and Sport*

A number of very informative newsletters are also available on a provincial and regional basis. The only national newsletter that has survived for any length of time is the *Fitness Report*, which provides Canadian fitness professionals with valuable information about current events, professional development opportunities, new resources, and job opportunities.

Undergraduate Education

The steady growth in the demand for fitness services in Canada has provided a level of stability encouraging to both full-time professionals and part-time workers. A new professional can look forward to a career in fitness with the potential to contribute to society in a very meaningful way. Although there is still a significant role in fitness for the volunteer and part-time worker, the well-trained fitness professional will be the cornerstone on which this field will grow and develop.

An ongoing concern in many professional groups and universities has been the best curriculum to prepare fitness professionals. In August 1987 the National Wellness Institute convened a wellness/health promotion/fitness curriculum focus meeting to address this issue by developing a curricular structure that could be recommended to universities and colleges interested in training fitness professionals. The outcome of this meeting was a consensus on both the knowledge and skills necessary for professionals in fitness and health promotion.

I   Knowledge base
   A Health
      • Assessment and evaluation
      • Environmental literacy
      • First aid/CPR
      • Nutrition and weight control
      • Stress management
      • Substance abuse/smoking cessation
      • Personal and emotional self-development (mental health)
   B Fitness
      • Assessment and evaluation
      • Exercise principles and foundation
      • Physiological testing
      • Exercise prescription
   C People and populations
      • Consumer awareness
      • Aging
      • Special populations
      • Human growth and development
      • Social awareness
      • Lifestyle/values
II Professional skills
      • Communication skills
      • Computer literacy
      • Professional orientation
      • Philosophy, values, ethics
   A Methods and skills in human behavior and human behavior change
      • Teaching methods/learning styles
      • Communication
      • Counseling
      • Human relations
      • Organization cultural change
   B Program development and evaluations
      • Programming and program evaluation
   C Supervision and administration skills
      • Facilities and equipment
      • Finance
      • Liability and insurance
      • Marketing and promotion

The delegates also agreed that practicum experience is an essential part of professional preparation that can place all the student's knowledge and skills in a realistic context.

Unfortunately, few, if any, Canadian university programs can now meet this suggested curriculum completely. On the positive side, several Canadian universities are moving to implement curricula that can meet these guidelines. For now, undergraduate students who wish to pursue a career in the fitness field should choose courses that cover the suggested knowledge base and professional skills as much as possible.

Undergraduates should also be aware of the fitness certification and accreditation programs available in Canada. Several initiatives have recently been undertaken in Canada to provide a level of quality control/consumer protection in the Canadian fitness industry.

In addition to providing its Fitness Appraisal Certification and Accreditation (FACA) program (see Highlight) CASS has worked with the American College of Sports Medicine to offer the Preventive and Rehabilitative Exercise Specialist Certification program in Canada. These programs are now an integral part of the FACA program and are designed to recognize competence in exercise testing, prescription, and leadership among professionals working with persons who have medical limitations (American College of Sports Medicine, 1986).

Fitness Canada and the Interprovincial Sport and Recreation Council have played the prominent role in the development of guidelines for the training of fitness leaders. This multilevel training recognition program is delivered on a provincial level (as is the CASS program). The first level of the fitness leadership program, called the Basic Fitness Leader, is designed to provide and certify the minimum level of knowledge and skill requisite to leading fitness classes. To gain this recognition the individual must attend a training session and successfully complete written and practical exams.

Individuals staffing the courses for Basic Fitness Leaders must satisfy the requirements of Trainer of Fitness Leaders. One requirement to work in this capacity is an undergraduate degree, which means that this is an appropriate position for the fitness professional.

The second level of recognition in the program is the Specialist Fitness Leader. Currently, five areas of specialization training have been developed or are in advanced stages of preparation:

1. Dance fitness
2. Fitness for the older adult
3. Music and fitness
4. Strength training
5. Youth fitness

Candidates must successfully complete a certification course and a written examination, as well as

HIGHLIGHT
The Fitness Appraisal Certification and Accreditation Program

In 1981, the Canadian Association of Sport Sciences (CASS) initiated a Fitness Appraisal Certification and Accreditation (FACA) program. This program has two thrusts:

1. to recognize competence in fitness appraisal and counseling on an individual basis, and
2. to accredit fitness centers that meet minimum standards for personnel and equipment on an institutional basis.

The widely accepted FACA program functions in every province.

The program currently certifies fitness appraisers at two levels, the Standardized Test of Fitness Appraiser (STFA) and the Certified Fitness Appraiser (CFA), and also certifies STFA Course Conductors. STFA certification recognizes only a very basic competency and does not presume any level of professional status. The STFA is trained to administer the Canadian standardized test of fitness and to interpret it in a very rudimentary fashion. The CFA is the first level of recognition of professional competence. Individuals seeking CFA certification must have an undergraduate degree as well as additional training and experience. In many cases, employers advertising for fitness professionals require CFA certification.

---

have practical leadership experience and athletic first aid and CPR training.

Trainers of Specialist Fitness Leaders must be certified Trainers of Fitness Leaders with additional training and experience. Again, this is the primary role of the professional in the program.

Career Opportunities

At the present time, volunteers and part-time non-professionals deliver a large portion of the fitness services in Canada. The YMCA/YWCA, municipal recreation, and educational sectors all rely heavily on volunteer or part-time instructors. This reflects both a perceived inability to pay instructors at a level that would attract professionals and a market situation in which services have been provided for so long a time at such a low rate that programmers think consumers will not pay more for them.

Only a very small number of professional physical activity specialists earn a living through on-the-floor fitness instruction. In general, the role of the more highly trained professional is to train fitness leaders, supervise programs, and market, promote, and administer fitness centers. Status as a CASS Accredited Center, which appears to be

a desirable designation, requires that a Certified Fitness Appraiser be on staff. Fitness professionals are also finding full-time employment in the fitness appraisal and counseling service area where there is a greater concern for liability. The legal liability issue will undoubtedly influence organizations to hire more highly trained and skilled personnel.

At the present time payment for fitness services is the direct responsibility of the consumer. There has been some investigation with respect to accessing health care system funding, but this does not appear to be likely. There is, however, a definite movement in some provinces to seek official recognition as an allied health profession. The status resulting from such recognition would define a working mandate for fitness professionals and a minimum level for their training.

Graduates of undergraduate programs that offer specialization as fitness professionals have gained employment in the fitness field in a variety of settings:

- Corporate fitness/wellness programs
- YMCA/YWCA
- Government departments/municipal recreation departments
- Fitness resource centers
- Workers compensation programs

- Fitness clubs, spas
- Private consulting
- Educational institutions (colleges, universities)
- Medical screening/hospital-based programs

Summary

In many ways, Canada has been an international leader in the development of a fitness conscious society. The role played at the national level by Participaction and at a more local level by a number of provincial programs has contributed greatly to the current high profile of fitness in Canada. The central role of physical activity in promoting positive health and lifestyle behavior will be a major factor in the continued thrust to promote fitness and will require even higher levels of training for fitness professionals in Canada.

References and Further Readings

American College of Sports Medicine. (1986). *Guidelines for exercise testing and prescription* (3rd ed.). Philadelphia: Lea & Febiger.

Ardell, D.B. (1986). *High level wellness*. Berkeley, CA: Ten Speed Press.

Canadian Fitness and Lifestyle Research Institute. (1990). *Campbell's survey on well-being in Canada: Highlights report*. Ottawa, ON: Author.

Epp, J. (1987). *The active health report: Perspectives on Canada's health promotion survey 1985*. Ottawa, ON: Government of Canada.

Fitness Canada. (1972). *Proceedings of the national conference on fitness and health*. Ottawa, ON: Government of Canada.

Fitness Canada. (1978). *Guidelines for fitness centre and health clubs*. Ottawa, ON: Government of Canada.

Fitness Canada. (1984). *Guidelines for the training and recognition of fitness leaders in Canada*. Ottawa, ON: Government of Canada.

Fitness Canada. (1986). *Fitness . . . the future: Report on the Canadian summit on fitness*. Ottawa, ON: Government of Canada.

Fitness Canada. (1987). *Guidelines for the training of specialist fitness leaders*. Ottawa, ON: Government of Canada.

Fitness Canada. (1988). *Canadian fitness sourcebook: Organizations and resource materials*. Ottawa, ON: Government of Canada.

Lalonde, M. (1974). *A new perspective on the health of Canadians*. Ottawa, ON: Information Canada.

Paffenbarger, R.S., Hyde, R.T., Wing, A.L., & Steinmetz, C.H. (1984). A natural history of athleticism and cardiovascular health. *Journal of American Medical Association*, **252**, 491-495.

Chapter 23

Physical Activity and the Elderly Population

David A. Cunningham

Donald H. Paterson

Human aging and the increasing proportion of the population who are over age 65 are topics of growing concern in most industrialized societies. The numbers of persons 65 years and over may reach 20% of the population by the year 2020; this would constitute a doubling of their numbers in the next 30 years (Piscopo, 1985). This fact and the attendant problems of caring for large groups of elderly persons have motivated a greater interest in the health and physical fitness of the elderly.

The role of physical activity in maintaining health and vigor into old age is currently a high-priority research area whose findings are being translated into service programs. This process is the base from which to develop effective activity programs for seniors that comprise an appropriate mix of aerobic, strength, and flexibility components. It's not enough for these programs merely to exist, however; it is crucial that their leadership must provide a strong enough appeal for the elderly that a sizable proportion of them become involved. Psychology and sociology of sport will play an important role in this latter task.

The challenge to those working in the field of physical activity and aging is to develop fitness activities and programs that maximize the physical potential of a large segment of the elderly population and thus promote greater health and a more active and independent lifestyle.

A suitable goal for our society may be the "rectangularization of mortality and morbidity" de-scribed by Fries (1980), which entails a reduction in mortality rates from birth to old age and in time for chronic convalescence. Were this concept realized, an active, healthy population would function well into its ninth decade, followed by a very short period of functional deterioration and then death (Figure 23.1). The importance of improving health status among the elderly cannot be over-stated: An increase in the years of healthy living and independence must accompany the large increase in those surviving to older age if the health care systems are to provide for those in older age ranges.

Professionals working with older people should bear in mind a distinction between what is called normal and successful aging. For example, many age-related changes such as blood pressure and body weight increases are reported in Western industrial nations but are seldom observed in traditional agricultural societies. The changes normally observed with aging in an industrialized society may be linked to other factors such as type of diet and lack of habitual exercise; although normal, they may not be successful when compared with other societies.

The role of exercise as a potential moderator of aging may be masked in the normalized data. If this proves to be true (the jury is still out on this issue), exercise would constitute a way to reduce functional losses and maintain vigor in old age, and activity programs would be an integral

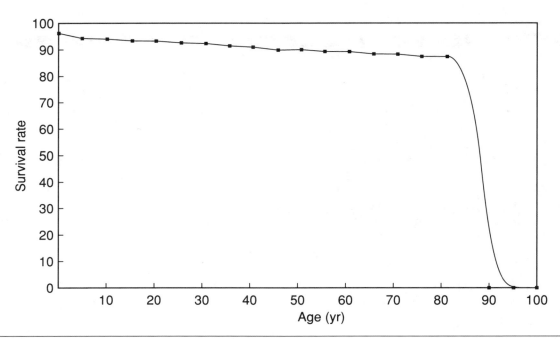

Figure 23.1   Age and survival rate. Hypothetical, ideal representation of a healthy population. *Note.* Adapted from information appearing in *The New England Journal of Medicine.* "Aging, Natural Death, and the Compression or Morbidity" by J.F. Fries, 1980, *NEJM,* **303**, p. 131. Copyright 1980 by the Massachusetts Medical Society. Adapted by permission.

component of successful aging. The challenge to those who work and study in the field of physical activity and aging would thus be to create a better understanding of the physical and physiological performance capacities and limitations in the elderly. Development of the relevant programs will require input from professionals in sports medicine and biomechanics to ensure that activity components are suitable to the elderly individual.

Above all else, health promotion and disease prevention are central to any plan that might result in a scheme for successful aging. Thus, developing strategies to motivate and encourage a behavior change among older men and women toward a prevention approach will be a mark of successful programming in this area.

● ● ●

The goal of physical activity sciences profession-als working with the elderly is to promote contin-ued good health and self-sufficiency by designing and implementing effective and appealing activity programs for the aged population.

● ● ●

Major Concepts

The evolving field of study in physical activity and the elderly is outlined in Figure 23.2. Descriptive studies are necessary to increase our understand-ing of the physical abilities and limitations of the elderly compared to younger persons and to estab-lish normal standards for physical fitness in the elderly. Research in this area includes comparisons of physiological functions and anatomical differ-ences among persons of different age groups.

An important concept in developing activity programs for seniors is the extreme variability of physical capability within the population. Each participant's activity must be individually ad-justed and monitored. The elderly and the very young do not relate well to age-specific categoriza-tion; it is not hard to find exceptions in data sets showing the typical age decline (see Figures 23.3 and 23.4). Many older persons are active, and some have attained levels of physical fitness and sport achievement formerly thought restricted to the young. Figure 23.5 presents times achieved for a marathon race by individuals ages 10 to 80 years to illustrate the performance level some elderly persons have attained.

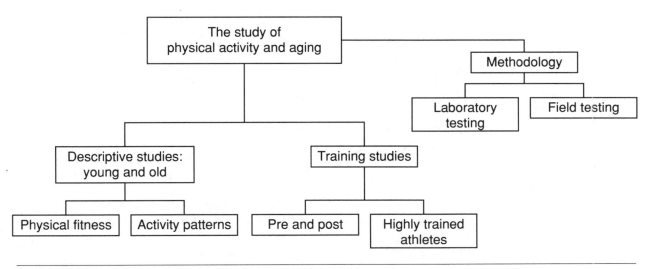

Figure 23.2 Physical activity and aging: The scope of the field.

Despite this wide dispersion in capabilities and performance in the elderly, facilitating a healthier and more active lifestyle in a large proportion of elderly men and women means that the exercise leader must know the daily requirements and normal activity patterns of old people. Determining these norms is important for understanding age-related loss of function. Regular daily activity is an important factor in maintaining optimum health; for example, it reduces the incidence of coronary heart disease. (That is, physical activity has been shown to be inversely and causally related to the incidence of coronary heart disease.) The intensity and frequency of participation in physical activity declines with age, however, and in the elderly may reach levels associated with health risk and loss of muscle strength and endurance. The age-related loss of physical fitness in the elderly may be explained in part by this observed decline in the frequency and intensity of customary physical activity among the elderly.

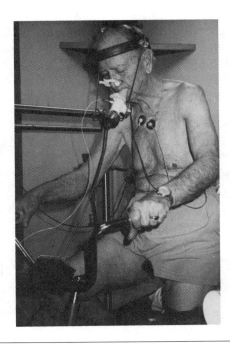

This elderly athlete is being tested on a cycle ergometer.

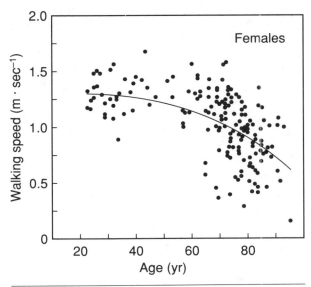

Figure 23.3 Age and normal walking speed for females. *Note.* Adapted from Himann et al. (1988) by permission.

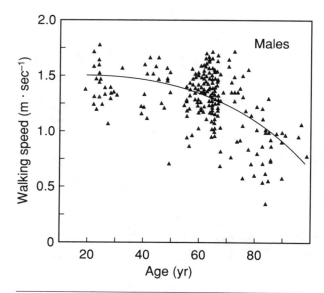

Figure 23.4 Age and normal walking speed for males. *Note.* Adapted from Himann et al. (1988) by permission.

Customary daily activity in the elderly has been measured in different ways. The method of body-borne tape recorders measures heart rate by bipolar chest leads and activity level by an impact switch attached to the foot. Activity has also been determined by questionnaire; this subjective method of assessing activity is the more typical technique and can be adopted easily by the practitioner in the field. One potential problem concerning the elderly, however, is that these questionnaires rely on the ability of the respondent to recall past activities.

The Minnesota questionnaire of leisure activity constitutes one of the best examples of this method.

A study of the first year of retirement showed no change in the activity levels of men from many different types of working environments (both blue- and white-collar occupations) (Cunningham, Rechnitzer, Howard, & Donner, 1987). For those men in the study who were involved in an exercise program, however, a significant increase in high-intensity activity was found (Table 23.1). The study suggests that future programs should include vigorous, relatively high-intensity structured exercise rather than merely an encouragement to ''be more active.'' Further research is needed, however.

In addition to incorporating high-intensity exercise, activity programs for older men and women should reflect the degree of differences between the young and old. There is no doubt that old age brings loss of function and stamina. Maximal oxygen uptake (a measure of the maximal capacity of the heart and muscle function), or $\dot{V}O_2max$, declines with age ($.46$ ml $\cdot$ kg^{-1} $\cdot$ min^{-1} $\cdot$ year^{-1} for men and $.30$ for women, or about 10% per decade for men and 8% per decade for women). This decrement can be explained in part by reduced levels of activity and in part by other factors attributed to aging, including

- increases in body fatness,
- lack of motivation to exercise vigorously and reach maximal levels, and
- problems with disease that preclude vigorous exercise.

Physiological determinants of gas transport capacity are also affected by age. Maximal heart rate declines slowly with advancing years and can be approximated by the equation

Maximal heart rate =
220 beats $\cdot$ min^{-1} − age in years.

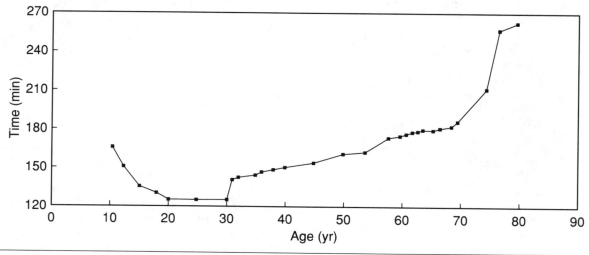

Figure 23.5 Age and approximate times to run a marathon for males.

Table 23.1   Time Spent in Leisure Activities at Light, Moderate, and High Intensity for 1 Year Following Retirement

Group	Baseline (min/day)	1 year (min/day)	P
Light (< 3.5 Mets[b])			
Activity[a] (n = 111)	261 ± 153	381 ± 163	.09
Control (n = 105)	253 ± 103	420 ± 216	
Moderate (3.5 to 4.9 Mets)			
Activity	101 ± 83	160 ± 99	.53
Control	102 ± 82	152 ± 126	
High (> 4.9 Mets)			
Activity	65 ± 110	138 ± 150[c]	.01
Control	48 ± 60	85 ± 116	

Note. All values are means plus or minus standard deviations. Values are min/day for the year preceding the test day. *P* refers to the 1-year comparison with the value at baseline constant. From "Exercise Training of Men at Retirement: A Clinical Trial" by D.A. Cunningham, P.A. Rechnitzer, J.H. Howard, and A.P. Donner, 1987, *Journal of Gerontology*, **42**, p. 20. Copyright © The Gerontological Society of America. Used by permission. (Note that values from the original table have been rounded to the nearest whole number.)

[a]Activity group participated in a thrice weekly aerobic exercise program for 1 year; the controls carried out their normal activities.

[b]The energy expended at rest is defined as one Met unit. A metabolic rate of 4 Mets represents an exercise intensity equivalent to 4 times the energy expended at rest.

[c]This value of 138 min/day is significantly different from the baseline mean value of 65 min/day, and with the control values held constant.

Exercise practitioners should remember, however, that submaximal heart rates do not similarly decline. For example, it has been shown that heart rate does not decline very much from age 20 to 95 years at normal walking speed, although the speed itself declines across age. Therefore, although the maximal value is reduced by about 18% from ages 25 to 65 (190 to 155 beats · min⁻¹) the submaximal value to perform a standard exercise task remains unchanged, though the task itself is reduced. Obviously, if the power output were held constant, the heart rate would increase, indicating the relatively greater intensity of activity.

A number of cross-sectional studies have documented a progressive decline in strength with age. Longitudinal studies have confirmed this finding. Decline in muscular strength appears to be related to a decrease in the amount of regular physical activity, particularly that of a vigorous nature. More specifically, loss in muscle strength is closely related to loss in muscle tissue mass; when age groups are matched in terms of lean body mass or muscle cross-sectional area, the difference between the groups decreases or disappears.

Because motivation is a factor in muscular exertion, researchers sometimes use electrical stimulation of tissues to control for motivational variations between the young and old. The contractile force of the calf muscle decreases gradually up to the latter part of the sixth or first part of the seventh decade of life; thereafter, it appears to decrease very rapidly. Men between the ages of 67 and 71 years reach only about 70% of the force produced by 21-year-old men. This age, at which muscle strength is most rapidly lost, is also the age at which normal walking speed decreases, as was shown in Figures 23.3 and 23.4. Studies using an isokinetic measuring device to measure contractile force of muscles involved in the typical daily activity of walking have allowed comparisons between the strength of young and old at different speeds of contraction. At the slowest speeds of movement the elderly did very well and produced forces only slightly less than those produced by the younger men. At the fastest speeds the young produced significantly greater forces. Thus, at slow speeds little loss of force is found in muscles habitually used in everyday activities, but as early as age 60 years there will be large losses in faster movements, facts with obvious implications for exercise programming for older men and women.

Measures of short-term (less than 1 minute) anaerobic power output in the elderly have received little attention. In a cycling test of all-out effort, the peak power (first 5 s of exercise) and the mean power (averaged over 30 s of exercise) achieved by active elderly men (age 69 years) were 70% of the values for young men (age 30 years). Post-exercise measurement of blood acid (lactate) similarly showed values 30% lower in the elderly. Arm cranking showed similar differences between the young and the elderly.

Major Trends in Research on Training Elderly People

Training studies of elderly populations provide important information that will allow us to create exercise programs to maximize the physical potential of the older person. As with studies on younger persons, training periods range from 3 months to a year, with before and after measurements of performance. These studies compare maximal exercise capacity, submaximal endurance, cardiovascular function, muscle size, and body composition in a training group with the same parameters in a nontraining control group. In addition, valuable insight into the effect of long-term training may be obtained by comparing elderly elite athletes with sedentary old persons. Such individuals are increasingly available because the number of elderly persons involved in athletics has grown in recent years with the development of masters competitions.

The progressive decrease in heart and muscle function ($\dot{V}O_2$max) with age (8% to 10% per decade) has been described earlier. In young healthy subjects endurance exercise training can produce large increases in $\dot{V}O_2$max (approximately 20%). In the elderly the situation has not always been as clear, though recent studies have consistently shown that appropriate exercise training of the elderly increases $\dot{V}O_2$max.

In a study of 220 subjects who were randomly assigned to an exercise program or control, the exercise group showed a 12% increase in $\dot{V}O_2$max with endurance training over a 1-year period. Further, the individual level of improvement in the exercised group was negatively correlated with pretraining $\dot{V}O_2$max: Those with the lowest $\dot{V}O_2$max at the start of the program had the greatest gains over the year. Thus, improvements of 30% to 40% have been found with persons with initial values of $\dot{V}O_2$max of 24 to 25 ml · kg^{-1} · min^{-1}.

Interestingly, most of the changes reported after 1 year were evident in the first 6 months. Substantial gains apparently can be achieved in endurance fitness in as little as 6 months—maybe earlier. The elderly improve their $\dot{V}O_2$max with training over a time course similar to that observed in younger subjects.

The improvement in the cardiovascular fitness of the elderly is also seen in cross-sectional studies that compare masters athletes to both younger persons and nonathletic elderly. These active older athletes have $\dot{V}O_2$max values over 50% greater than the sedentary controls, but these differences are probably due in part to genetic factors as well as to activity levels.

The elderly can also increase their capacity for submaximal work. Some research has shown a 15% increase in $\dot{V}O_2$ at a submaximal heart rate of 125 beats · min^{-1}, 3% more than the 12% increase at $\dot{V}O_2$max; other studies have found even greater changes. This has important implications for the elderly for their daily activity is most often performed at light to moderate exercise intensity. Recent research has shown submaximal exercise endurance to increase as much as 180% following a 2 to 3 month program of endurance exercise (Figure 23.6), with $\dot{V}O_2$max increased approximately 10%. This level of improvement is very significant, for it means that the elderly can have independent and active lives until very old age.

Strength training programs for the elderly are not common. One study of older men in training programs observed subjects in a program of static and dynamic exercise over 12 weeks and found that voluntary strength measurements increased. Generally, it appears that maximal voluntary con-

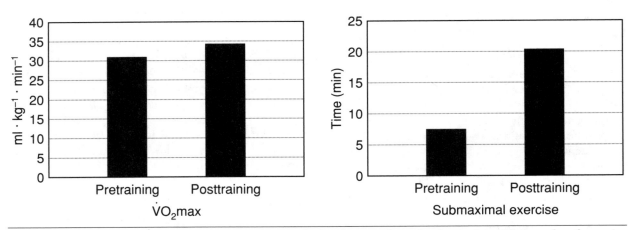

Figure 23.6 Changes in $\dot{V}O_2$max and time-to-fatigue during heavy submaximal exercise with 9 weeks of exercise training in elderly men.

HIGHLIGHT
Adapting Test Protocols for Elderly People

Studies of aging and physical activity have been severely limited by a lack of appropriate testing methodology. In both laboratory and field testing, traditional test protocols do not allow for the low work capacities and special problems of the elderly. Because many old people are not physically able to travel to a laboratory site, the development of simple field tests is essential. There have been some excellent recent developments in fitness testing of the elderly, including

- the measurement of maximal oxygen uptake ($\dot{V}O_2$max) using ramp tests (continuously increasing work rate) and breath-by-breath gas analyses to establish a true plateau in $\dot{V}O_2$ as the objective criterion of a maximum test rather than relying on the subject's decision to terminate exercise,
- a test of self-selected walking speeds in which subjects walk an 80-meter course at what they consider to be a "normal" and "rather fast" pace (this field test of cardiorespiratory fitness has shown chosen walking speed in the elderly to be slowed, particularly after age 60 years (Figures 23.3 and 23.4), and changes in speed perception to be affected by a program of endurance training of the elderly)
- the use of electrical stimulation of muscle to determine contractile properties during isometric force generation and allow assessment of muscle strength independent of motivational influences, and
- a field measure of strength applicable in weaker populations that uses a modified blood pressure cuff and aneroid pressure meter to record forces.

Adequate field tests are essential if exercise programs are to be adjusted to the aerobic fitness of the elderly individual. Self-selected walking pace may provide just such a test. In this test, the elderly subject is asked to walk at three different speeds: slow, normal, and fast. The measured speed is highly related to individual level of vigor. It may also represent the internal *speed-o-stat*, a measure of cardiorespiratory fitness.

A large (220 subjects), recently completed study of fitness in elderly retired men found that the exercising men improved their fitness about 12% over 1 year whereas nonexercisers showed no change in fitness (Cunningham et al., 1987). In addition, the exercise group showed significant increases in self-selected walking speeds and level of daily physical activity. Retirement from work in itself resulted in lowered blood pressure, increased type-B personality, and lowered blood cholesterol.

---

traction (MVC) in both isometric and isotonic exercise increases in the elderly following a period of strength training. Most strength training studies have been of very short duration, however, often less than 3 months. Longer training programs have shown that even older individuals can increase muscle mass.

Professional Societies

Relatively few organizations or societies focus solely on the development of research and pro-

grams in aging, although more appear each year. In Canada the most important organizations in the field are the Canadian Association on Gerontology and the Canadian Geriatrics Research Society. In addition, the Canadian Association of Sport Sciences is active in fitness and aging, and although this is not its primary mandate this association probably has the greatest specific interest in the area. Finally, the Canadian Association for Health, Physical Education and Recreation deals with aging and physical activity from an applied perspective.

In the U.S.A., the American College of Sports Medicine is the major group with an interest in activity, exercise, and health. As are other scientific groups, ACSM is developing a greater interest in the elderly and the aging process and offers leadership certification at various levels of expertise that can be very useful in running activity programs with older men and women.

Journals and Other Publications

Specialty journals devoted to work related to age and aging are not numerous, however several publications do provide good references in this area, including

- *Journal of Gerontology,*
- *Age and Ageing,* and
- *Canadian Journal on Aging.*

Several journals specialize in sports and exercise:

- *Canadian Journal of Sport Sciences,*
- *European Journal of Applied Physiology,* and
- *Journal of Sports Sciences.*

The American College of Sports Medicine publishes an annual review of exercise sciences (*Exercise and Sport Sciences Reviews*) that has included studies on aging. Reviews that include information on aging and exercise are also published in a journal called *Sports Medicine.*

Undergraduate Education

Universities and colleges have responded to the growing interest in exercise in the elderly by developing new programs or courses within existing structures. In addition, many universities have developed research centers or study groups devoted to specific aspects of aging.

Career Opportunities

The job market should expand considerably in this area as the numbers of and interest in the elderly expand. The 1990s and beyond will see great development of exercise programs for the elderly, providing ample employment opportunities for fitness program directors, trained fitness appraisers, and exercise leaders who understand the unique program requirements of the elderly.

Summary

Studies of activity and aging have not been carried out in any great numbers; the available research has produced considerably conflicting evidence about their relation, but it has demonstrated that cardiorespiratory fitness, strength, and flexibility can be improved in men and women in the seventh and eighth decades of life. (For a more extensive treatment of this topic see Shephard, 1987; Holloszy, 1987; Fitzgerald, 1985; Landin, Linnemeir, Rothbaum, Chappelear, & Noble, 1985; Bassey, 1985).

The research findings from this area of study can help planners design optimal exercise programs for the elderly and provide a method of analyzing physiological control systems through observation of physiological responses. The opportunity for leadership roles in development of model programs for the elderly is thus an exciting prospect for those beginning studies in the physical activity sciences.

References and Further Readings

Aniansson, A., Grimby, G., Rundgreu, A., Svanborg, A., & Orlander, J. (1980). Physical training in old men. *Age and Ageing,* **9**, 186-187.

Bassey, E.J. (1985). Benefits of exercise in the elderly. In B. Isaacs, (Ed.), *Recent advances in geriatric medicine.* (pp. 91-112). Edinburgh: Churchill Livingstone.

Bassey, E.J., Davies, C.T.M., & Kirby, C. (1983). The relation between daily walking activity and maximal isometric force of triceps surae in male and female elderly subjects. *Journal of Physiology,* **334**, 35P.

Cunningham, D.A., Montoye, H.J., Metzner, M.L., & Keller, J.B. (1968). Active leisure time activities as related to age among males in a total population. *Journal of Gerontology,* **23**, 551-555.

Cunningham, D.A., Morrison, D., Rice, C.L., & Cooke, C. (1987). Ageing and isokinetic plantar flexion. *European Journal of Applied Physiology,* **56**, 24-29.

Cunningham, D.A., Nancekievill, E.A., Paterson, D.H., Donner, A.P., & Rechnitzer, P.A. (1985). Ventilation threshold and aging. *Journal of Gerontology,* **40**, 703-707.

Cunningham, D.A., Rechnitzer, P.A., & Donner, A.P. (1986). Exercise training and the speed of self-selected walking pace in men at retirement. *Canadian Journal of Aging*, **5**, 19-26.

Cunningham, D.A., Rechnitzer, P.A., Howard, J.H., & Donner, A.P. (1987). Exercise training of men at retirement: A clinical trial. *Journal of Gerontology*, **42**, 17-23.

Davies, C.T.M., & White, M.J. (1983). Contractile properties of elderly human triceps surae. *Gerontology*, **29**, 19-25.

Fitzgerald, P.L. (1985). Exercise for the elderly. *Medical Clinics of North America*, **69**, 189-196.

Fries, J.F. (1980). Aging, natural death and the compression or morbidity. *New England Journal of Medicine*, **303**, 130-135.

Helewa, A., Goldsmith, C.H., & Smythe, H.A. (1981). The modified sphygmomanometer—an instrument to measure muscle strength: A validation study. *Journal of Chronic Diseases*, **34**, 353-361.

Himann, J.E., Cunningham, D.A., Rechnitzer, P.A., & Paterson, D.H. (1988). Age related changes in speed of walking. *Medicine and Science in Sports and Exercise*, **20**, 161-166.

Holloszy, J.O. (1987). Aging and exercise: Physiological interactions. *Federation Proceedings*, **46**, 18-23.

Landin, R.J., Linnemeir, T.J., Rothbaum, D.A., Chappelear, J., & Noble, R.J. (1985). Exercise testing and training the elderly patients. *Cardiovascular Clinics*, **15**, 201-218.

Marsh, G.D., Paterson, D.H., Cunningham, D.A., & MacKesy, D. (1987). Aging and short-term exercise capacity. *Canadian Journal of Sport Sciences*, **12**, 14P.

McDonagh, M., & Davies, C.T.M. (1984). Adaptive response of mammalian skeletal muscle to exercise with high loads. *European Journal of Applied Physiology*, **52**, 139-155.

Patrick, J.M., Bassey, E.J., Irving, J.M., Blecher, A., & Fentem, P.H. (1986). Objective measurements of customary physical activity in elderly men and women before and after retirement. *Quarterly Journal of Experimental Physiology*, **71**, 47-58.

Piscopo, J. (1985). *Fitness and aging*. New York: Macmillan.

Powell, K.E., Thompson, P.D., Caspersen, C.J., & Kendrick, J.S. (1987). Physical activity and the incidence of coronary heart disease. *Annual Review of Public Health*, **8**, 253-287.

Rinder, L., Roupe, S., Steen, B., & Swanborg, A. (1975). Seventy-year-old people in Gotenburg: A population study in an industrialized Swedish city. *Acta Medica Scandinavica*, **198**, 397-407.

Rodeheffer, R.J., Gerstenblith, G., Becker, L.C., Fleg, J.L., Wersfeldt, M.L., & Lakatta, E.G. (1984). Exercise cardiac output is maintained with advancing age in healthy human subjects: Cardiac dilatation and increased stroke volume compensate for diminished heart rate. *Circulation*, **69**, 203-213.

Rowe, J.W., & Kahn, R.L. (1987). Human aging: Usual and successful. *Science*, **237**, 143-149.

Seals, D.R., Hagberg, J.M., Hurly, B.F., Ehsani, A.A., & Holloszy, J.O. (1984). Endurance training in older men and women: Part I, cardiovascular response to exercise. *Journal of Applied Physiology*, **57**, 1024-1029.

Shephard, R.J. (1987). *Physical activity and aging*. Beckenham, UK: Croom and Helm.

Taylor, H.L., Jacobs, D.R., Jr., Schucker, B., Kinedsen, J., Leon, A.S., & Debacker, G. (1978). A questionnaire for the assessment of leisure physical activities. *Journal of Chronic Disease*, **31**, 741-755.

Thomas, S.G., Cunningham, D.A., Rechnitzer, P.A., Donner, A.P., & Howard, J. (1985). Determinants of the training response in elderly men. *Medicine and Science in Sports and Exercise*, **17**, 667-672.

Vandervoort, A.A., & McComas, A.J. (1986). Contractile changes in opposing muscles of the human ankle joint with aging. *Journal of Applied Physiology*, **61**, 361-367.

Chapter 24

Physical Activity for People With Physical and Developmental Disabilities

Robert D. Steadward
Laurie D. Clifford

For quite some time, professionals involved in the care of persons with physical and developmental disabilities have known that a physically active lifestyle provides benefits critical to their well-being. Consequently, a field of study dealing specifically with all aspects of physical activity programming for these groups has developed on both national and international levels.

The area of study that deals with physical activity and its relation to persons with physical and developmental disabilities is referred to as **adapted physical activity**. The majority of textbooks available on this subject emphasize the educational component and the instructional setting involved in providing programs for this population; consequently, they use the term **adapted physical education**. Adapted physical education focuses on recognizing, identifying, and remediating motor (movement) problems associated with both learning and performance and developing instructional strategies for dealing with the physical and psychological consequences of these problems.

A recent trend has been to broaden the scope of the field by going beyond the educational component. Thus, the term *adapted physical activity* was coined to include all aspects of physical activity in relation to persons with disabilities. Broadhead (1983) suggests that adapted physical activity

"means far more than mere activities which can be adjusted to suit the needs of individuals and heterogeneous groups" (p. 330); rather, it "is a mutidimensional area of concern" (p. 332).

• • •

Adapted physical activity includes sports, recreation, and fitness activities, as well as educational programming for the physically challenged. The field of study encompasses knowledge and techniques from the areas of motor learning/skill acquisition, biomechanics, psychology of sport, and exercise physiology as these relate to the special psychological and medical needs of persons with disabilities.

• • •

Major Concepts

The aim of adapted physical activity is to provide persons with disabilities the same opportunities to develop sports, fitness, physical education, and recreation skills that are available to the able-bodied population. Although physiological adaptations result in anyone who exercises, the benefits derived from fitness are especially important to persons who must overcome or compensate for a disability (e.g., paraplegics who rely totally on their upper body for mobility must ensure that their functional muscles are as fit as possible merely to carry out regular daily activities independently). The social and psychological benefits of participation in physical activity are also very important for this population. Everyone deserves opportunities to develop feelings of well-being, to be accepted by one's peers, and to participate in self-chosen activities.

Major Trends in Adapted Physical Activity

One of the most pressing issues in adapted physical activity is the role of integration and segregation in programming. Many have argued that opportunities for participation in integrated physical activity settings with nondisabled students, co-workers, and friends are crucial for healthy social development. On the other hand, segregated programs may provide disabled persons important opportunities to develop the basic skills required for successful participation in integrated situations. Furthermore, segregated programs provide fair and equal competition by incorporating activities designed specifically for persons with disabilities (e.g., wheelchair rugby and goal ball).

This segregation/integration dichotomy is often illustrated as a continuum of program options; ideally, individuals with disabilities should be placed in the least restrictive environment. Consequently, this schema suggests that integration is the ultimate programming goal.

Segregation/Integration in Schools

In Canada children with physical and developmental disabilities may be placed in segregated schools or in segregated classes within regular schools, or they may be integrated (mainstreamed) into regular classrooms for one period or for the entire day. A questionnaire circulated by Watkinson and Bentz (1986) revealed that although the majority of the responding teachers thought students with disabilities were more likely to benefit from participation in integrated classes than from segregated programs, they questioned the inclusion of these students in regular physical education. For example 45.7% claimed that their

Teachers disagree on whether it is better for disabled students to be in segregated or mainstream physical education classes.

students with disabilities would benefit more from segregated physical education classes than from integrated physical education.

Segregation/Integration in Sports

To date, the sports field has forgone the benefits of programming in the least restrictive environment in favor of ensuring that persons with disabilities have appropriate sporting opportunities. Local, provincial, national, and international organizations for the disabled are currently responsible for the coordination and administration of segregated sports competitions for the physically and developmentally disabled. Even so, individuals training for these competitions often integrate themselves into able-bodied clubs (e.g., cerebral palsy and amputee athletes are often members of regular swim clubs).

A recent trend across Canada has been to integrate able-bodied players into disabled sports (i.e., reverse integration). Given the large distances between Canadian population centers and the limited number of eligible competitors, it is frequently difficult for national caliber disabled team-sport players to train together. As a result, the Canadian Wheelchair Basketball League includes both disabled and able-bodied players. This increases the opportunity for persons with disabilities to participate in wheelchair basketball by making it easier to field the necessary number of players. Consequently, the caliber of wheelchair basketball has improved for both able-bodied and disabled players.

Demonstration sports performed by athletes with disabilities have been included within the most recent international and Olympic able-bodied competitions (e.g., the 1986 World Swimming Championships in Madrid, the 1987 World Track and Field Championships in Rome, the 1988 Calgary Winter Olympics, the 1988 Seoul Summer Olympic Games, and the 1990 Commonwealth Games in Auckland). Mass media coverage of these championships has increased public awareness of and respect for the high standards of performance, dedication, and effort amateur athletes with disabilities bring to their training.

Segregation/Integration in Coaching

The National Coaching Certification Program in Canada has begun to address the coaching needs of persons with physical and developmental disabilities by including an adapted physical activity addendum to the swimming and basketball technical manuals. This may lead, in the foreseeable future, to the development of specialized training facilities and to the employment of professional coaches to train Canada's national caliber disabled athletes.

Professional Societies

Canada has a very extensive network of associations, societies, and organizations that promote various facets of adapted physical activity. At the grassroots level each disability group has local, provincial, or national advocacy associations or societies that address the importance of appropriate recreational and leisure activities (e.g., Northern Alberta Brain Injury Society). Local sports clubs for disabled persons have been organized in cities all across Canada (e.g., Ottawa Royals Wheelchair Basketball Club).

The Canadian Special Olympics organization serves the needs of athletes with mental handicaps. Both provincial and local clubs provide sporting competitions that emphasize fun and participation. The INAS-FMH is the international organization that governs sport for athletes with mental handicaps outside North America.

Sport associations for athletes with physical disabilities exist in most provinces. These associations are governed by the six National Sport Organizations for the disabled: Canadian Wheelchair Sport Association (CWSA), Canadian Amputee Sports Association (CASA), Canadian Blind Sports Association (CBSA), Canadian Association for Disabled Skiers (CADS), Canadian Deaf Sports Association (CDSA), and Canadian Cerebral Palsy Sports Association (CCPSA). These six organizations are affiliated with—or at least recognized by—an umbrella organization, the Canadian Federation of Sport Organizations for the Disabled (CFSOD). CFSOD represents Canada's interests internationally through the International Sport Organization for the Disabled (ISOD) and the International Paralympic Committee.

Nationally, an adapted physical activity special interest group operates as part of the Canadian Association for Health, Physical Education and Recreation (CAHPER). Among other responsibilities, this special interest group reviews and judges the acceptability of adapted physical activity related submissions to the *CAHPER Journal*. Adapted physical activity representation is also available at each of the 10 provincial health, physical education, and recreation associations.

Journals and Other Publications

Textbooks, bound conference proceedings, and manuals are popular avenues for disseminating information regarding programs and research in adapted physical activity. To date, the *Adapted Physical Activity Quarterly* is the lone professional journal specific to this field of study, but physical education and sport journals such as the *CAHPER Journal*, *Research Quarterly*, *Perceptual and Motor Skills*, the *Journal of Physical Education, Recreation and Dance*, and the *Canadian Journal of Sport Sciences* provide issues or sections pertaining to adapted physical activity. Magazines designed for athletes and coaches involved in disabled sports, such as *Palaestra* and *Sports 'n Spokes*, publish program and research articles for the lay reader.

Because there is a strong medical element in the field of adapted physical activity many medical journals publish relevant articles. These journals include

- *American Journal of Disabilities in Childhood,*
- *Clinical Sports Medicine,*
- *Paraplegia,*
- *Scandinavian Journal of Medicine,*
- *Science and Medicine in Sport,*
- *Physician and Sportsmedicine,*
- *Canadian Journal of Rehabilitation Medicine,*
- *American Journal of Rehabilitation Medicine,* and
- *Scandinavian Journal of Rehabilitation Medicine.*

HIGHLIGHT
Program Initiatives
for Canadians with Disabilities

In October 1986 the Adapted Physical Activity Special Interest Group of CAHPER, Fitness Canada, and the University of Alberta cosponsored the Jasper Talks, a symposium that reviewed the status of adapted physical activity in Canada and suggested strategies for future development. Fitness Canada then established an Advisory Committee on Physical Activity for Canadians with Disabilities, which developed the Blueprint for Action, a plan for ensuring that the importance of and opportunity for a physically active lifestyle is recognized by Canadians with disabilities. Goals for achieving this objective include improving delivery systems, organizational planning, program and leadership development, public awareness, and research. This committee is now working toward these goals.

Rick Hansen's Man in Motion World Tour has given three initiatives the potential to affect adapted physical activity in Canada:

1. National Access Awareness Week is a federally legislated week organized as a means of educating the Canadian public regarding both the needs and the achievements of persons with disabilities. In addition to employment, transportation, education, and housing, recreation/physical activity has been identified as a component necessary to make a community accessible. Canadian communities are evaluated annually as to how well they meet the needs of their disabled constituents in these five areas.
2. The Premier's Councils on the Status of Persons with Disabilities are mandated to address the issues affecting persons with disabilities. To date, they have been incorporated in New Brunswick, Alberta, and British Columbia.
3. The Rick Hansen Man in Motion Legacy Fund is the proceeds from his world tour; 10% is allocated to programs that increase the public awareness of Canadians with disabilities.

As these three initiatives heighten the awareness of Canadians regarding the lifestyles of persons with disabilities, professionals in adapted physical activity will be called on as the resource people, program developers, and researchers to develop and provide services and generate relevant knowledge.

A recent initiative in adapted physical activity has been the incorporation of the Alberta Sports Centre for Athletes with Disabilities. Housed within the Rick Hansen Centre at the University of Alberta, Edmonton, this is the first training center in North America designed to meet the athletic needs of competitors with disabilities. State-of-the-art training facilities, physiological and psychological testing and monitoring, and nutritional counseling are available on an ongoing basis to Alberta's disabled athletes.

Another initiative has been the creation of the International Paralympic Committee (IPC), which is responsible for organizing the Paralympic and Multi-Disability World Games and World Championships. In addition to its other goals, the IPC seeks integration into the international able-bodied sports movement of sanctioned sports (rather than demonstration sports) for athletes with disabilities. Canada was instrumental in the creation of this organization; R.D. Steadward, a professor at the University of Alberta, was elected the first president of the IPC in Dusseldorf, September 1989.

Undergraduate Education

Most Canadian university degree programs in physical activity sciences now offer at least one undergraduate course in adapted physical activity, though the content of these courses may vary significantly from institution to institution (e.g., survey courses highlighting disability conditions to program courses that emphasize practicum situations). Unfortunately, very few of these are required courses. Consequently, a very large number of professionals graduate from Canadian universities unprepared to meet the challenges of working with persons with physical and developmental disabilities. Watkinson and Bentz (1986) report that very few Canadian teachers have any significant professional training in adapted physical activity at either the preservice or inservice levels. An important step forward would be to require physical education and education students to complete at least one adapted physical activity course.

A number of Canadian universities offer specialization "routes" in adapted physical activity within their undergraduate physical education degree programs. Graduate programs at both the master's and doctoral level are also available.

Career Opportunities

There are a number of career opportunities available for persons trained in adapted physical activity. Graduates of this area traditionally have pursued teacher training and have obtained teaching positions in segregated schools or classes for the physically or developmentally disabled. Recreation positions in residential institutions have also been frequent avenues of employment. Persons who have completed graduate work in the field have become faculty members of universities and community colleges or held supervisory positions in associations and institutions.

More recently, adapted physical activity graduates have also obtained positions as consultants for local and provincial parks and recreation departments and as program administrators for the YMCA/YWCA, community leagues, and specialized centers (e.g., Variety Village in Toronto, Ontario). Many have also become program developers for auxiliary hospitals and extended care facilities, as well as executive, technical, and program directors for provincial and national disabled sports associations. Recreation positions are also available

in most of the local and provincial societies for specific disabilities. Finally, rehabilitation institutions such as Workers Compensation hire exercise therapists as part of their rehabilitation team; these positions are very appropriate for graduates who have both an adapted physical activity and a physiology specialization.

At the present time, the Edmonton Public School Board has two adapted physical activity consultants. An increased number of positions of this type in other school districts across Canada would help teachers implement the integration process. Persons interested in this field should apply directly to boards of education or consider creating their own private clinic or consulting service.

Although they do not as yet exist, the establishment of provincial and national training centers for disabled athletes would further expand employment opportunities by opening up salaried positions in coaching, research, and program development.

Summary

The field of study that addresses the physical activity needs of persons with physical or developmental disabilities is referred to as adapted physical activity. Because professionals in this field believe that all Canadians have the right to experience the benefits of a physically active lifestyle, they strive to educate the public, empower persons with disabilities regarding advocacy, improve programs and service delivery systems, develop leadership opportunities and conduct research.

The importance of integration is an unresolved issue in the field. Although placement within the least-restricted environment is generally conceded to be the best program solution, many physical educators remain unprepared to meet this integration challenge. The International Paralympic Committee is working toward the full inclusion of sanctioned events performed by athletes with disabilities into the present system of able-bodied Olympic and World Games.

References and Further Readings

Berridge, M.E., & Ward, G.R. (Eds.) (1987). *International perspectives on adapted physical activity*. Champaign, IL: Human Kinetics.

Bleck, E.E., & Nagel, D.A. (Eds.) (1982). *Physically handicapped children: A medical atlas for teachers* (2nd ed.). New York: Grune & Stratton.

Broadhead, G.D. (1983). Research directions in adapted physical activity. In R.L. Eason, T.L. Smith, & F. Caron (Eds.), *Adapted physical activity: From theory to application* (pp. 329-341). Champaign, IL: Human Kinetics.

Fait, H.F., & Dunn, J.M. (1984). *Specialized physical education: Adapted, individualized and developmental*. Philadelphia: Saunders.

Goodman, S. (1986). *Spirit of Stoke Mandeville: The story of Sir Ludwig Guttmann*. London: Collins.

Guttmann, L. (1976). *Textbook of sport for the disabled*. Oxford: Alden Press.

Sherrill, C. (1986a). *Adapted physical education and recreation: A multidisciplinary approach* (3rd ed.). Dubuque, IA: Brown.

Sherrill, C. (Ed.) (1986b). *Sport and disabled athletes: The 1984 Olympic Scientific Congress Proceedings* (Vol. 9). Champaign, IL: Human Kinetics.

Walsh, C.M., Holland, L.J., & Steadward, R.D. (1985). *Get fit: Aerobic exercises for the wheelchair user*. Edmonton, AL: University of Alberta.

Walsh, C.M., Hoy, D.J., & Holland, L.J. (1982). *Get fit: Flexibility exercises for the wheelchair user*. Edmonton, AL: University of Alberta.

Walsh, C.M., & Steadward, R.D. (1984). *Get Fit: muscular fitness exercises for the wheelchair user*. Edmonton, AL: University of Alberta.

Watkinson, E.J., & Bentz, L.J. (1986). *Cross Canada Survey on mainstreaming students with physical disabilities into physical education*. Ottawa: Queens Press.

Chapter 25

Physical Activity and Therapy

David J. Magee

Sport therapists use knowledge about the effects of physical activity on the human body both in the prevention and treatment of athletic injuries and in the conditioning that follows. Thus, the sport therapist may be, and often is, involved in various aspects of the athlete's training and conditioning as well as in the treatment of injuries. In the United States, the sport therapist is referred to as an athletic trainer; in Europe, the term *trainer* means a coach.

Major Concepts

The sport therapist is a professional in an area of applied practice who must not only have an intimate knowledge of several areas but also be able to integrate them to provide effective care to the athlete. Specifically, the therapist must have a strong background in anatomy, kinesiology, biomechanics, and physiology to understand the structures of the body, how they function, and how the various body systems work together to enable an athlete to reach maximum potential.

• • •

The sport therapist applies knowledge from various biological, medical, and social scientific disciplines to prevent and treat sports-related injuries, rehabilitate injured athletes, and educate and advise athletes and coaches about matters concerning injury and physical activity.

• • •

Knowledge of therapeutic exercise, exercise as an activity, motor skills, movement analysis, nutrition, and exercise physiology provide the needed bases for understanding the stresses placed on the body by sports and how exercise must be adapted to enable the athlete to function optimally. Sport therapists use exercise not only to bring athletes to peak levels of performance but also to restore them to maximum levels of fitness following an injury. In addition, sport therapists are often responsible for screening and conditioning programs.

An understanding of pathology and the various conditions that can affect the body in a way relevant to sporting activity is essential. The therapist must be able to distinguish between the normal and the pathological state and provide ways to avoid or ameliorate injury, for example, by demonstrating proper fitting of equipment or modifying that equipment to meet an individual athlete's needs or to protect an injury.

Two primary areas of concern in sport therapy are bandaging and taping and primary care, or first-aid, techniques. The therapist, who is often the first individual to see the athlete following an injury, must have a strong working knowledge of cardiopulmonary resuscitation techniques and first-aid procedures to deal with potentially life-threatening or catastrophic events. The therapist must recognize the severity of different injuries and administer the appropriate first aid to the injured athlete. Because athletes commonly play while injured, the sport therapist must exhibit speed and proficiency in providing support for an injured part, for example, by means of tape, bandages, splints, braces, or other supportive devices.

As the primary care individual the sport therapist often deals with acute injuries and ensures that further medical assessment is obtained as soon as possible. The sport therapist closely observes all athletes during practice and games for signs of potential injuries or anything else that might require referral to a physician. The sport therapist also has the responsibility of inspecting the playing areas for potential hazards and correcting them if any are present.

Efficiency in all areas of care will require competency in the various therapeutic techniques and modalities that will enable the therapist to treat the athlete efficiently and effectively, to provide the best possible environment for healing, and to safely return the athlete to competition as quickly as possible.

Sport therapists must be prepared to act as an educator and counselor not only for athletes but for coaches and parents. Thus, knowledge of health, psychology, and human relations plays an important role in the therapist's position.

The sport therapist must keep appropriate records of injuries, treatments given, and all matters concerned with the physical health of the athlete, such as medical histories and physical fitness tests. Documentation has become especially important in this age of litigation. Besides playing bookkeeper the sport therapist often plays a manager's role, too, supervising and maintaining the training and treatment facilities by keeping them adequately supplied and equipped and in an orderly and sanitary state and supervising and providing clinical and practical experience for student and assistant therapists.

Above all else, sport therapists treat athletic injuries. Injuries are just as debilitating, cause just as much pain, bleed just as much, and take just as long to heal in an athlete as in the average citizen, only athletes are highly trained, motivated individuals. As previously stated, the sport therapist is often the first person to see an injury after it happens, which is the best time to determine what is wrong because there is no swelling, no spasm, no reflex inhibition, and pain has not yet set in.

Highly trained and motivated athletes may sometimes appear to be hypochondriacs. Because they are training and competing at such a high level, everything must be "just right." Athletes are often concerned about minutes, seconds, or less, so the therapist must be prepared to do everything possible to prepare the athlete for competition physiologically and psychologically. When treating any injury, however, the player's physical welfare must be placed above all other considerations. Pressure from coaches, management, parents—sometimes even from the athlete—must be ignored.

Arnheim, in his excellent introductory text *Modern Principles of Athletic Training* (1985), showed the proportions of a sport therapist's activities to be as follows:

- Prevention, 18%
- Recognition and evaluation, 24%
- Management and treatment (first aid), 22%
- Rehabilitation, 20%
- Organization and administration, 9%
- Education and counseling, 7% (p. 30)

Given that rehabilitation accounts for only 20% of a therapist's time the job does not primarily involve working in a clinical setting treating athletes. Thus, the sport therapist does not play the traditional role of a physical therapist. A great deal of the sport therapist's time is spent "on the sidelines" in all types of weather, waiting for something to happen: "hours of minimal activity interspersed with moments of sheer terror" is an appropriate description of the practicing sport therapist's job.

The role of a sport therapist can be very rewarding and gratifying, but it involves a lot of time and effort and a great deal of sacrifice. The hours are long and irregular, and the profession is not all fun and glory as it might first appear. The sport therapist is there to serve the athlete and must be available when needed. Indeed, though it is a rewarding occupation, it is one that few people have the perseverance and dedication to pursue for their entire working life.

Professional Societies

There are two organizations that are primarily concerned with sport therapy in Canada, the Canadian Athletic Therapists Association and the Sports Physiotherapy Division of the Canadian Physiotherapy Association.

Both organizations work to advance and improve the area of sport therapy. They foster improved working relationships among their various members as well as with medical and other paramedical groups involved in sports medicine. Both groups have developed educational and technical skills standards for people seeking certification as an athletic therapist or sport physical therapist. Both groups also work to provide the best possible injury prevention, treatment, and care for all athletes and sport participants. In so doing, they promote interest in the field of sport therapy and encourage people to actually participate in sports and to work toward ensuring proper care of athletes. At the present time, however, only physical therapists need be licensed to practice in the province in which they reside. Athletic therapists are working toward formal standing as a recognized profession at the provincial level, but they have not yet obtained this status anywhere in Canada.

The Canadian Athletic Therapists Association (CATA) sets educational standards for athletic therapists in Canada. Becoming a CATA-certified athletic therapist requires the successful completion of a written and practical exam; individuals may attempt the exams once they have met criteria involving either a formal education program or on-the-job learning. The Canadian Athletic Therapists Association defines the certified athletic therapist as "an individual holding a recognized university or college degree in Biological Sciences. The individual will have followed an approved course and have successfully passed a comprehensive examination in the area of prevention, immediate care, and treatment of those conditions common to and inherent to sport" (Canadian Athletic Therapists Association).

In the United States, the National Athletic Trainers Association established procedures for certifying athletic trainers and began their certification exam in 1970. To qualify to take this exam, the candidate must complete an approved undergraduate or graduate curriculum in athletic training, a physical therapy program, or an apprentice period.

The second group concerned with sports therapy in Canada is the Sports Physiotherapy Division of the Canadian Physiotherapy Association, which admits only physiotherapists. Any physical therapist who wishes to specialize in sport physical therapy can do so through the Sports Physiotherapy Division's education program. This program offers an avenue whereby members can upgrade their skills and knowledge in the field of sport physiotherapy and sports medicine.

The program, which is designed to ensure that Canada's competitive and recreation athletes receive a nationally uniform quality of care from sport physiotherapists, has five levels. The first level is simply a statement of support of and commitment to the structured education system that demonstrates interest in becoming a sport physical therapist. The requirements for this level are a St. John's Ambulance Standard First Aid course or equivalent and a basic cardiopulmonary resuscitation certificate.

The level 2 physiotherapist is capable of working independently at an athletic competition. The areas of concentration for this level are protective equipment, basic taping techniques, orthopedics and biomechanics, exercise physiology, sport physiotherapy, and sport injuries.

The level 3 individual is capable of looking after the total needs of an athletic team. The Sports Physiotherapy Division considers an individual who has reached this level to have demonstrated sufficient competence to be called a sport physiotherapist. The areas of concentration include equipment and supplies, orthopedic conditions and athletics, science of athletics, exercise physiology, and pharmacology and sports.

Competency at level 4 involves experience in administration, consulting and international work, for example, as a chief therapist at a major game. Individuals at this level are called specialists in sport physiotherapy and must possess a master's degree in physical therapy or related field. The areas of concentration for level 4 include orthopedic medicine, advanced exercise physiology, health and communicable diseases, nutrition, and growth and development.

All four of these levels require successful completion of written and practical/oral examinations. The final level, level 5, is an honorary title given in recognition of service to the Division. This honorary title can only be given if the individual has completed the first four levels.

Sport Therapy Organizations

In Canada

- Sports Physiotherapy Division, Canadian Physiotherapy Association (SPD)
- Canadian Athletic Therapists Association (CATA)
- Sport Medicine Council of Canada (SMCC)
- Address for all of the above:
  Place R. Tait McKenzie
  1600 James Naismith Drive
  Gloucester, Ontario
  K1B 5N4

In the United States

- American College of Sports Medicine (ACSM)
  401 West Michigan Street
  Indianapolis, IN 46202

- Sports Physical Therapy Section, American Physical Therapy Association
1111 North Fairfax Street
Alexandria, VA 22314
- National Athletic Trainers Association (NATA)
1001 E. Fourth Street (P.O. Box 1865)
Greenville, NC 27835-1865

Journals and Other Publications

Over the last few years, there have been a number of journals developed to enable the therapist to keep current with new developments in sport therapy. The following journals are some of those most commonly used:

- *American Journal of Sports Medicine*
- *Journal of Orthopedic and Sports Physical Therapy*
- *Sports Medicine*
- *Physician and Sportsmedicine*
- *International Journal of Sports Medicine*
- *Clinical Journal of Sports Medicine*

Undergraduate Education

There are two types of sport therapists in Canada, the athletic therapist and the sport physical therapist. Many individuals have qualifications in both areas, but each type has a distinct educational path to it.

The ideal sport therapist has a background in physical education as well as the technical skills needed to be a physical therapist. Thus, the "best" individual will be trained in both areas. Individuals will sometimes earn an undergraduate degree in both fields, one after the other, or they may earn an undergraduate degree in one area and then enter a diploma program or do graduate work in the other.

In Canada, the bottleneck in this system is the physical therapy component. There are 13 physical therapy schools in Canada, all of which operate quota programs. The largest of these schools only take approximately 65 to 70 students per year; the smallest take approximately 20 students. The entrance requirements to these schools is thus very high—an academic average around 80+% is the norm. Many potential sport therapists do not have such high grades. If they do not, they can do one of three things.

Part of sport therapists' early training involves learning to palpate specific muscles.

First, they can enter a physical education program and work to improve their academic average; should they achieve this, they can transfer to a physical therapy program, completing their physical education degree on a part-time basis while in the physical therapy program. This concept has been developed at the University of Saskatchewan, where in a 6-year process the student obtains a baccalaureate in physical education as well as in physical therapy. Having both degrees demonstrates the individual's knowledge both of sports and of how therapy might be applied to highly trained individuals.

The second possible avenue is to complete a physical education program that includes a strong sport therapy component in it. In this case, the student would also work toward certification in the Canadian Athletic Therapists Association. An example of this type of program is seen at the University of Alberta, which offers an "athletic therapy route." The following types of courses are offered in this route:

- Introduction to athletic therapy
- Scientific basis of athletic injuries
- Advanced athletic therapy, methods, and techniques
- Practicums in athletic therapy techniques
- Nutrition
- Pharmacology
- Health education
- Biomechanics
- Sport psychology
- Introduction to research

The third alternative is to complete a physical education degree and then complete a diploma program in athletic therapy at Sheridan College in Ontario or Concordia College in Quebec or go to the United States and complete a master's degree in athletic training.

Career Opportunities

The individual interested in becoming a sport therapist must remember that the hours are not regular. They are long, as the sport therapist tends to be "the first one in and the last one out," and the busiest times are those when others have leisure time to take part in sports—in other words, in the afternoons, evenings, and weekends. Thus, the individual who wants to work in this area must be prepared to work not only during the day but also on afternoons, evenings, and weekends and not only for competitions but also for practices.

The individual who holds degrees in both physical therapy and physical education has the advantage in terms of employment prospects. In Canada, very few organizations other than professional teams or universities and colleges can afford to have sport therapists on full-time staff. Thus the sport therapist does a lot of work either on a volunteer basis or at a rate of pay too low to live on. Anyone who holds a physical therapy degree, however, can work in a private practice or hospital, maintaining the relevant technical skills and applying for positions as they become available. The experience gained as a working physical therapist increases the chances of getting such a position.

The individual who goes through the athletic therapy route will find it more difficult to obtain jobs in the area of sport therapy—not impossible, only more difficult. This state of affairs reflects not so much the training or the value of these individuals, who are very valuable and make a significant contribution to the area of sport therapy, but rather the competitive job market: It is simply difficult to obtain a full-time position as an athletic therapist in Canada today.

Other areas of employment must be developed to increase the "employability" of athletic therapists in Canada. One of the more promising developments is the faculty/trainer concept, wherein a school either hires a certified athletic therapist who is qualified to teach subjects such as physical education or trains a teacher on the staff as an athletic therapist. This position would require a person who is every bit as knowledgeable and has the same credentials as a therapist working with a college or professional team. Part of the individual's duties would be to act as an athletic therapist for 2 to 3 hours per day; the individual would teach the rest of the day. This model has been successfully used in the United States, but whether school boards in Canada will be prepared to look at this type of program in the age of budgetary restraint is another question.

Summary

Although sport therapy is a very demanding profession, it is also a very rewarding one, ideal for the individual who wants to deal directly with athletes in a "hands-on" setting. There is more money to be made as a physician, sport scientist, or a teacher in the school system, but these occupations do not provide the intimate contact with athletes that sport therapy entails. Job satisfaction is easy to come by in the profession.

On the negative side, however, the profession does involve long hours, often very little recognition, and low pay, all of which can add great stress to family life if not handled properly.

References and Further Readings

Arnheim, D.D. (1985). *Modern principles of athletic training*. St. Louis: Mosby.

Canadian Athletic Therapists Association. *Certification documentation*. Gloucester, ON: Sport Medicine Council of Canada.

Canadian Physiotherapy Association, Sports Physiotherapy Division. *Education level system*. Gloucester, ON: Sport Medicine Council of Canada.

National Athletic Trainers Association. (1982). *Professional preparation in athletic training*. Champaign, IL: Human Kinetics.

Porter, M., Noble, H.B., Backman, D.C., & Hoover, R.L. (1982). The faculty athletic training program: A model. *Physician and Sportsmedicine*, **10**, 85-89.

Wilson, J. (1980). Bridging the gap between physiotherapists and physical education. *New Zealand Journal of Physiotherapy*, **8**, 33-35.

Chapter 26

Physical Activity Program Management

Terry R. Haggerty

P. Chelladurai

Many organizations operate sport, exercise, dance, and play programs to meet the physical activity needs of individuals and groups. These organizations include intercollegiate athletics, fitness clubs, intramurals, sport clubs, resorts, minor sport organizations, professional sport teams, school physical education programs, dance troupes, and municipal recreation programs, all of which can be labeled physical activity programs. To be effective, these programs must make organized efforts to obtain the necessary human and material resources and to transform these resources into programs that satisfy the needs of the organization's constituents. This process involves management.

The field of study concerned with the management of physical-activity-related organizations is generally called *sport management* or *sport administration*. (In most instances the terms *management* and *administration* are considered synonymous; we use the term *sport management*.) Haimann and Scott (1974) defined management as "a social and technical process that utilizes resources, influences human action, and facilitates change in order to accomplish an organization's goals" (p. 6). In short, a sport manager helps determine what a program should be doing and how it should be done and attempts to steer the efforts of individuals inside and outside the organization to meet organizational goals.

A knowledge of sport management techniques can benefit not only the managers of physical activity programs but also coaches, research lab directors, teachers, fitness consultants, and staff at all levels of an organization; to varying degrees, all these positions can use management concepts.

Major Concepts

Although management is a complex and dynamic process, we will describe its basic elements by analyzing its four main functions:

- Planning
- Organizing
- Leading
- Evaluating

The important roles of

- communicating information and
- decision making

are also highlighted.

• • •

Sport management uses decision-making and communication techniques to plan, organize, lead, and evaluate sport programs of all kinds and at all levels, from professional sports teams to public, quasipublic, and private physical activity organizations.

• • •

Planning

Planning is the process of deciding now what to do later, how best to do it, who should do it, and when to do it. Such decisions are the basis of management activity. Filley, House, and Kerr (1978) identify the following planning steps:

- *State the goals (ends).* For example, a manager of a physical activity program involving elderly adults might state the program's main goal to be encouraging daily physical activity in the older adult.
- *Identify the constraints.* This step involves considering factors that may limit methods of achieving goals (e.g., available facilities, weather, legal issues, resources).
- *Generate alternative means to achieve goals.* This requires brainstorming to list as many viable alternatives as possible. In the case of programs for the elderly, some options might be an exercise class held at your organization's facility, a session at a central location, an aquatics-based exercise program, recreational sports such as golf or bowling, and walking tours.
- *Specify performance criteria to evaluate the alternatives.* This step resembles the second, for it involves identifying possible criteria by which to evaluate the alternatives and decide among them. Some examples are cost, enjoyment, risk, scientific basis, and so forth.
- *Select the best alternative.* Once the evaluation criteria are selected they are applied to the alternatives to determine the best option. In this step, the manager may use quantitative decision-making techniques such as decision tree analysis, cost-effectiveness analysis, or break-even analysis.
- *Prepare a document that presents the results of the planning process.* To clarify and explain the plan you should specify (a) the goals being sought, (b) the means to those goals, (c) the responsibilities of organizational members and units, (d) the standards to be maintained, and (e) the controls that will monitor the process. The plan is a predetermined course of action (or set of them) and becomes the premises for future decisions.

Organizing

Organizing, another main function of management, involves breaking down activities that support the planning process into clearly defined

Planning is an important component of the managing process.

tasks, hiring and promoting appropriate personnel to carry out these tasks, and establishing authority relationships among the various positions doing the tasks.

For example, the management of a professional baseball team might divide the program's goal-directed activities into scouting, recruiting, contract negotiations, marketing, and technical aspects such as budgeting, purchasing, and accounting. Once the tasks are outlined, detailed job descriptions established, and individuals assigned to carry out these tasks, management can focus on motivating, guiding, and directing the staff; these latter processes involve leadership.

Leading

Leadership is the process of influencing or motivating group members to achieve organizational goals. It is one of the most difficult and complex managerial functions because it attempts to channel the efforts of many people with different goal preferences and orientations. Effective leaders are able to link an individual's personal goals with those of the organization. They impress on the members how their personal goals can be achieved through attaining the organizational goals.

The complexity resides largely in the situational nature of management, which requires the successful manager to use different leadership behaviors in various situations. For example, the leader of a volunteer minor sport organization works with people who do not seek economic benefit for their efforts. Volunteers are motivated for a variety of reasons such as helping others, cultivating friendships, learning new skills, gaining work experience, and effectively using leisure time. Effective leadership behavior and style in a volunteer situation differ from those used with paid employees of a profit-oriented fitness club.

Evaluating

This managerial function typically focuses on one important aspect of organizational effectiveness—goal achievement. The manager assesses the program by comparing actual organizational performance with the desired performance standards set in the planning process, changing the program if necessary to increase the probability of achieving the goals.

This process of evaluation can also be viewed as a process of control. In management control, standards are set, the process operates, and the results are constantly compared with the original standards; whenever necessary, corrective action is taken to decrease the discrepancy between actual and desired behavior. The operation of any control system, such as a room thermostat, follows a similar approach. The notion of control, which is a major and universal element in all management processes, led Eilon (1979) to state that "without control there can be no management" (p. 14). Control requires information on a system's intended and actual states and on ways to decrease any discrepancy between the two. Eilon (1979) notes that "no decision making, no purposeful control, no comprehension of what is happening in the world is possible without information" (p. 14). An effective manager must deal with a flood of information that, if the modern trend continues, will only increase.

Communicating Information

The main management functions of planning, organizing, leading, and evaluating require the communication of information. Members of a management team require clear and concise information to formulate goals (desired performance), assess actual performance, and select the activities that will decrease the discrepancy between actual and desired organizational states. Whereas information is the basis for all decisions in management, communication is the vehicle for that information, linking people together to achieve a common purpose. Many managers have noted that a main prerequisite to organizational effectiveness is the communication of the right information to the right

unit at the right time. Eilon (1979) aptly notes that "information flow in a communication network is the lifeline of a business enterprise; it is like blood flowing through the veins and arteries of the body."

Unfortunately, most managers attempt to process too much information. This leads to situations of information overload or even worse—"information anxiety." Given that the amount of available information now doubles every 5 years, it is quite likely that one of a manager's biggest challenges is, and will continue to be, to filter the really important information needed for decision making from the flood of meaningless data.

Deciding

The planning, organizing, leading, and evaluating that constitute management all require good decision making. Many authors view decision making as the central process underlying all management activity. Simon (1976) says that "the task of deciding pervades the entire administrative organization as much as does the task of doing—indeed it is integrally tied up with the latter" (p. 1).

Decision making can be simply defined as the selection of a preferred course of action from two or more alternatives. It involves the following four steps:

- Problem determination
- Development of alternatives
- Analysis of the alternatives
- Selection of the best alternative

Decision making is at the core of planning. In fact, comparing the steps just listed for decision making to those listed earlier for planning shows the latter to be a special case of the former.

Major Trends in Program Management

Sport management is a relatively new field that has tremendous potential for capable women and men. Sport management university programs in Canada and the United States continue to be developed and improved. Lipsey (1989) aptly remarks that "one of the most interesting and important trends that has paralleled the dynamic growth of sports marketing has been the growth of the number of colleges and universities offering degree programs in sports marketing and/or sports management'' (p. 367). It is difficult to predict whether these new graduates will find interesting entry-level positions in physical activity organizations.

The outlook seems encouraging on the academic level, however. Recent reports indicate that the 1990s will experience a shortage of PhD graduates in a number of fields. Given the increase in new undergraduate and graduate programs, there undoubtedly will be a demand for qualified faculty members to teach in sport management programs.

Professional Societies

Sport management students, theorists, and practitioners can learn about new management techniques and stay in touch with colleagues with similar interests by joining professional associations and by reading management texts and journals. One of the most important professional organizations in this field is the North American Society for Sport Management (NASSM). The purpose of NASSM is to promote ''the theoretical and applied aspects of management theory and practice specifically related to sport, exercise, dance, and play as these enterprises are pursued by all sectors of the population'' (Zeigler, 1987, p. 5). This society organizes an annual conference and publishes the *Journal of Sport Management*.

Besides NASSM, many of the major physical activity associations have management special interest groups. A partial listing includes

- the Canadian Association for Health, Physical Education and Recreation (CAHPER),

HIGHLIGHT
Using Computers in Professional Sport Administration

Computer technology has advanced in several stages, each marked by cheaper, more powerful, and easier-to-use microcomputers than the last. Some organizations have managed to keep up with this change whereas others have been slow to adapt. A recent study (Haggerty, 1990) described and analyzed the use of computers in professional sports. Professional baseball, basketball, football, and hockey teams were surveyed to determine what computers, printers, software, and training methods they used. This information will assist professional sport managers evaluate their own computer environment and help students better prepare themselves for entry-level positions in professional sports.

The results indicated that football teams were the greatest mainframe users (92.9%); the percentages of baseball, basketball, and hockey teams using mainframes were 53.9%, 62.5%, and 37.5%, respectively. The teams also showed great variability in the number of microcomputers they used. Teams had few of the newer 80386 processor machines and nearly equal numbers of AT-style 80286 computers and the older 8088 machines. Few teams used Apple Macintosh computers.

The software programs used most frequently were Lotus 1-2-3 for budgeting (53%) and WordPerfect for word processing (33% teams), but altogether a great variety of software was used for most tasks. Most teams relied on a knowledgeable staff member for training computer users and hardly ever used commercial videos or tutorial programs. The most frequently mentioned problem areas were: user training, improving performance by keeping abreast of technological changes (especially networks), and scarce resources.

The findings suggest that professional sport managers need to focus on better user training and consider using consultants to help them with their concerns about networks, compatibility, upgrades, and improving performance. Given the variety of software used, there was no clear choice for programs that students should learn. However, based on the areas of concern, a knowledge of networks and of the most popular MS-DOS business and education programs such as WordPerfect and Lotus 1-2-3 are advisable.

- the American Alliance for Health, Physical Education, Recreation and Dance (AAHPERD),
- the National Intramural-Recreational Sports Association (NIRSA),
- the Canadian Intramural Recreational Association (CIRA),
- the Canadian Association of Sport Sciences (CASS),
- the National Association of College Directors of Athletics (NACDA), and
- the College Athletic Business Managers Association (CABMA).

Journals and Other Publications

Sport management and management journals that often include articles of interest to physical activity managers include the following.

Sport Management Sources
- *Athletic Administration*
- *Athletic Business*
- *Canadian Journal of Sport Sciences* (CJSS)
- *Journal of the Canadian Association for Health, Physical Education and Recreation*
- *Fitness Management*
- *Journal of Physical Health, Education, Recreation and Dance* (JOPHERD)
- *Journal of Sport Management*
- *Quest*
- *Research Quarterly for Exercise and Sport*
- *Parks & Recreation*

General Management Journals
- *Academy of Management Journal*
- *Academy of Management Review*
- *Administrative Science Quarterly* (ASQ)
- *Behavioral Science*
- *Educational Administrative Quarterly* (EAQ)
- *Harvard Business Review* (HBR)
- *Journal of Educational Administration*
- *Management Science*
- *Organizational Behavior and Human Performance*
- *Personnel*
- *Public Administration Review*

Other Sources

In addition to the previously listed information sources, managers can search the annual proceedings of the relevant associations, *Dissertation Abstracts*, the *ERIC* data base, and *SIRC* (Sport and Recreation Index—a comprehensive international data base of sport-related literature based in Ottawa). These sources can be readily accessed via a computer search of major commercial information services by a knowledgeable librarian.

Undergraduate Education

Many Canadian universities now offer some type of sport management program of studies at the undergraduate or graduate level. Some universities have several sport management faculty members and a complete set of course experiences; others are more limited in their scope. In America, the National Association for Sport and Physical Education (NASPE) recently formulated a plan to accreditate sport management programs that meet basic guidelines.

For sport management programs at Canadian universities students can refer to the *Acadirectory: A Canadian Sourcebook of Physical Education, Kinesiology, and Human Kinetics* (Yuhasz, Taylor, & Haggerty, 1986). Students interested in a listing of sport management programs in the United States should refer to *The Sports Market Place* (Lipsey, 1989).

Career Opportunities

Because physical activity organizations constitute one of the largest sectors of the economy, there are many career opportunities for qualified physical activity managers. Parks and Quain (1986) identify the following six general career areas:

1. The physical fitness industry
2. Sport promotion
3. Sport marketing
4. Sport organization management
5. Sport directing
6. Aquatic management

Soucie (1986) identifies the following 10 areas and associated job titles:

Career Opportunities
1. *Professional sport*—manager, publicity director, marketing and promotion agent, ticket manager
2. *Amateur sport*—executive director, technical director, program supervisor, or coordinator in sport governing bodies
3. *Commercial enterprises*—production and marketing manager of sports equipment

4. *Private clubs*—management careers in fitness, tennis, squash, and racquetball centers, as well as in outdoor centers, summer camps, and youth centers
5. *Facility management*—sport facility managers or sport facility planning consultant
6. *Educational institutions*—sport directors at the high school, college, or university level
7. *Municipal recreation departments*—managing sports programs for children, the handicapped, the elderly, and so forth
8. *Private agencies*—managing sport programs in centers for the aging, YMCA/YWCA, corporations, and so forth
9. *Governmental agencies*—managing sport programs in agencies such as Sport Canada, Fitness Canada, state-operated agencies, and so forth
10. *Professional associations*—managing sport and physical activity delivery systems in professional associations such as CAHPER, AAHPERD, CIRA, and so forth

In addition, DeSensi and Koehler (1989) note that growth is anticipated in

- telecommunications;
- sport and fitness centers for the aging;
- hotel, airport, hospital, and conference fitness centers;
- the travel and cruise industry;
- and sport retail merchandising.

Summary

Sport management is a varied, exciting, and dynamic field that offers many opportunities for qualified young men and women who appreciate physical activity. Sport management careers allow individuals to maintain strong links with physical activity organizations and contribute to their effectiveness. DeSensi and Koehler (1989) provide sound advice for an individual planning for a career in sport management when they suggest a carefully chosen curriculum, affiliation with existing professional organizations (e.g., NASSM), professional contacts, and creative self-promotion. In addition, volunteer and work-related experience is highly valued in the workplace.

References and Further Readings

Chelladurai, P. (1985). *Sport management: Macro perspectives*. London, ON: Sport Dynamics.

DeSensi, J.T., & Koehler, L.S. (1989). Sport and fitness management: Opportunities for women. *JOHPERD*, **60**(3), 55-57.

Eilon, S. (1979). *Management control*. Oxford: Pergamon Press.

Filley, A.C., House, R.J., & Kerr, S. (1976). *Managerial process and organizational behavior*. Glenview, IL: Scott, Foresman.

Haggerty, T.R. (1990). *The administrative use of computers in professional sport organizations*. Manuscript submitted for publication.

Haimann, T., & Scott, W.G. (1974). *Management in the modern organization* (2nd ed.). Boston: Houghton Mifflin.

Lipsey, R.A. (Ed.) (1989). *The sports market place 1989*. Princeton, NJ: Sportguide.

Parks, J.B., & Quain, R.J. (1986). Sport management survey: Employment perspectives. *JOHPERD*, **57**(4), 22-26.

Simon, H.A. (1976). *Administrative behavior*. New York: Free Press.

Soucie, D. (1986, July). *The sport administrator: An administrative professional or a professional administrator*. Paper presented at the annual CAHPER conference, Charlottetown, PE.

Yuhasz, M.S., Taylor, A.W., & Haggerty, T.R. (Eds.) (1986). *Acadirectory: A Canadian sourcebook of physical education, kinesiology, and human kinetics*. London, ON: Sports Dynamics.

Zeigler. (1987). Sport management: Past, present, future. *Journal of Sport Management*, **1**(1), 4-6.

Chapter 27

Physical Activity in the Workplace

Art Salmon

Joyce Gordon

What do ALCAN, Bell Canada, NASA, General Foods, General Motors, XEROX Corporation, and McDonald's Restaurants have in common? At first glance these corporate giants might seem to share nothing other than their huge success. There is another similarity, however; all these companies—and 50% of North America's other largest corporations—have implemented physical fitness and lifestyle enhancement programs at the workplace. In Canada an estimated 1000-plus companies have an on-site fitness facility.

Percentage of Canadian Businesses With Organized Fitness Programs

Region	100-499 employees	500 or more employees
Canada	13	14
Atlantic Canada	11	34
Quebec	8	27
Ontario	13	11
Prairie Region	19	33
British Columbia	17	4

Source: Reprinted from Canadian Chamber of Commerce (1986, p. 5).

There are several reasons for the growth in corporate fitness programming. Most senior executives would probably justify fitness programs by citing needs to increase corporate morale, decrease absenteeism and employee turnover, improve employee health, and augment corporate image. Although the reasons may be varied, there is no doubt that in the last 15 years the implementation of employee fitness programs by business and industry has provided significant potential employment opportunities for those interested in careers in the exercise sciences. In this chapter we examine the area of employee fitness programming and determine what constitutes adequate preparation for a professional in the employee fitness field.

● ● ●

Workplace-based physical activity sciences practitioners are responsible for the design, implementation, management, and day-to-day operation of physical activity programs within business and industry.

● ● ●

Major Concepts

The notion of introducing exercise programs in the workplace is not a radical new idea. The Bell Telephone Company of Canada initiated exercise breaks for its office employees as far back as the 1920s. (Some have argued that the armed forces have been using a form of employee fitness to prepare service personnel for combat for hundreds of years.) Only in the past few years, however, has sport science research indicated that fitness and health promotion programs at the work site may offer more benefits than simply improved physical fitness.

In 1972, the Department of National Health and Welfare hosted the National Conference on Fitness and Health. The delegates to the conference provided the federal government with 24 recommendations for policy and action related to fitness and health. The 22nd recommendation reads as follows: "It is recommended that the federal government identify, define and publicize an incentive program which would encourage employer groups to adopt physical recreation and fitness programs" (Health and Welfare Canada, 1974, p. 128).

More specifically, the conference recommended that the federal government provide information to employers concerning the advantages of physical recreation programs and assist them in devising methods to implement such programs. The conference also suggested that a pilot research project be undertaken to demonstrate the effectiveness of implementing corporate fitness programs at the work site. In response to the recommendations, Fitness Canada, in conjunction with the University of Toronto and the Toronto YMCA, designed and conducted a comprehensive research project at the Canada Life Assurance Company. The "Canada Life Study" (Cox, Shephard, & Corey, 1981) and a subsequent 10-year follow-up study (Walker, Cox, Thomas, Gledhill, & Salmon, 1989) are invariably cited in discussing the numerous advantages of implementing a fitness program at the work site.

In releasing the Active Health Report in 1985 (Health and Welfare Canada, 1987), the Minister of Health and Welfare remarked that it was time Canadians took responsibility for their own health and no longer disregarded good health habits with the expectation that the medical system would make them well again if they became ill. The motivation for his comments was the increasing cost of medical care in this country: In the province of Ontario the cost of health care is a staggering $27 million per day, or about 30% of the provincial budget. These escalating costs are giving rise to a severe health care crisis, yet statistics indicate that much of the disease and premature death is directly related to inappropriate lifestyle habits, which are relatively inexpensive to change. Heart and blood vessel disease, cancer, and alcohol-related disorders are the leading causes of morbidity and mortality in the United States and Canada.

According to the U.S. National Institutes of Health (1981), out of 1,000 randomly selected employees

- 200 to 250 will be overweight,
- 300 will have lower-back injuries,
- 290 will smoke cigarettes,
- 100 to 150 will have alcohol or other drug problems,
- 160 to 250 will be hypertensive and unaware of it, and
- 500 will not get enough regular exercise.

The business and industry sector is recognizing that poor health and fitness translates into poor human performance, lower productivity, and increased labor costs. The 1978 Canada Life Employee Fitness Study provided data concerning the cost-effectiveness of implementing an employee fitness program at the workplace (Cox, Shephard, & Corey, 1981). Among the findings reported were

- a 22% reduction in absenteeism among the regular exercising group;
- a drop in employee turnover from 15% to 1.5% within the exercising group; and
- a saving of $250,000 per year, as estimated by Canada Life based on 28% participation in the program.

Major Trends in Workplace Fitness

The 1985 Active Health Report asked 11,000 Canadians 109 questions about their health habits. The most frequent response (29%) to the question "What is the single most important thing you have done in the past year to improve your health?" was "get more exercise" (Health and Welfare Canada, 1987). In addition, when Canadians were asked what they thought to be the most important step they could take to improve their health, 41% responded by saying they should exercise more. There is a willing and receptive audience out there that needs only to be offered safe and effective programs. Nor are businesses unresponsive. Pyle (1979) estimates that 50,000 companies in the U.S.A. have instituted workplace fitness programs. In Canada, the Canadian Chamber of Commerce survey (1987) suggested that by the year 1990, 25% of companies with over 100 employees will offer fitness programs to their employees.

Growing numbers of employers are providing worksite fitness programs. *Note.* Photo reprinted by permission of The Canada Life Assurance Company.

If these new programs are to be a success, however, they must be managed by knowledgeable, highly trained physical educators. Rick and Karen Danielson (1979) of Laurentian University in Sudbury have reported strong leadership as the key ingredient in the development of an employee fitness program. Appropriate preparation for such leadership includes several elements.

First of all, anyone considering a career in the employee fitness field must read and understand the relevant research. One of the most challenging aspects of an employee fitness coordinator's job is the preparation and presentation of program proposals to potential corporate clients. This often requires a written submission followed by a verbal presentation to senior corporate executives, who will ask detailed questions about the recommended course of action. A clear rationale based on sound reasoning is required for success.

In addition to an adequate knowledge of the fitness field, some courses on business techniques are advisable, especially business writing and financial analysis. An employee fitness coordinator works in a world very different from that of hospital-based kinesiologists or school-based physical education teachers. A fitness coordinator in the corporate environment can expect to play many roles, including educator, trainer, planner, staff supervisor, exercise class leader, fitness appraiser, exercise counselor, promoter, researcher, and evaluator. In a 1982 survey, Patton, Corey, Gettman, and Graf (1986) asked corporate fitness

directors to rank their major responsibilities. The 10 most often identified were

1. communication with clients and program participants,
2. program development,
3. participant motivation,
4. lifestyle counseling,
5. program management,
6. staff supervision,
7. public relations inside and outside the company,
8. program evaluation,
9. finance and budgeting, and
10. equipment purchase and maintenance.

An unpublished research project undertaken by the Ontario Fitness Council in 1987 reviewed the job descriptions of current employee fitness coordinators and found the following common characteristics and job requirements:

Staff Supervision

- Interview, hire, and dismiss staff
- Coordinate program and staff
- Evaluate staff
- Provide on-site project leadership

Exercise Class Leadership

- Assess group needs
- Plan and teach classes
- Tape music
- Provide guidance to participants
- Demonstrate safety techniques
- Be a role model

Program Management

- Operate daily program
- Design program activities
- Plan and monitor budget
- Purchase and maintain equipment
- Maintain clean facilities
- Communicate with staff and participants
- Cooperate with other departments
- Meet with other health-related groups
- Coordinate fitness advisory committee
- Maintain and update policies and procedures
- Write reports

Promotion

- Develop and implement marketing strategies
- Develop and maintain library of resources
- Coordinate special events
- Write articles and design newsletters/posters
- Perform public relations work with outside sources

- Represent company at conferences and professional events
- Promote the company fitness program in the business community

Fitness Assessment

- Supervise or conduct participant fitness tests
- Interpret test results
- Develop safe procedures
- Consult with medical director
- Recommend action to appropriate party for high-risk subjects

Staff and Volunteer Training

- Recruit, develop, train, and retain staff and volunteers
- Instruct participants
- Evaluate impact of learning experiences
- Develop and present educational programs

Program Planning

- Establish goals for the program
- Design programs
- Organize and coordinate resources
- Schedule activities

Program Evaluation

- Design program evaluation procedures
- Perform statistical analysis
- Interpret results
- Convey reports to management

Accountability

- Maintain confidential records concerning health
- Ensure confidentiality

An employee fitness coordinator directing a program in a corporate setting usually will be part of a health care team. The medical director or the head of personnel services is most often responsible for the overall program. This means that the fitness coordinator's direct supervisor may have little or no training in the exercise sciences and will rely on the coordinator to ensure that the programs are conducted in a safe and proper manner. This also means that part of the fitness coordinator's job will be to educate the supervisor and senior management regarding the steps necessary to ensure a safe and effective program.

Professional Societies

The last decade has seen a trend toward certification in the fitness field. A public increasingly interested in physical fitness has demanded assurances that those individuals providing exercise advice and counseling are adequately trained. As a result, several groups and organizations have begun offering certification programs in the exercise sciences; the American College of Sports Medicine, the National Wellness Association, the Canadian Association of Sport Sciences, and the YMCA/YWCA are but a few of the organizations currently training and certifying fitness leaders and instructors. In addition, in response to the growing number of corporate fitness leaders, specialty organizations like the Association for Fitness in Business and the National Employee Services Recreation Association have established themselves to assist their members in the corporate environment. These organizations and certification programs can help demonstrate to potential employers that an individual has the capabilities to direct physical fitness programs safely and effectively.

Certification training is only one way to obtain the background necessary to meet the demands of working in the employee fitness field. Becoming actively involved in the profession is a key step in remaining contemporary as the field grows and matures. Networking with other fitness professionals, joining and actively participating in professional health/fitness/exercise science associations, and attending regional and national meetings are absolutely essential for keeping up with the field. The individuals who take the time and make the effort to share ideas and discuss new and changing trends in employee fitness programming with their peers will be contributing to the field and ensuring their professional growth.

Journals and Other Publications

Staying current in issues related to the health aspects of fitness and sport requires regular reading of the relevant professional journals. The following journals publish material related to physical activity in the workplace, among other topics, and can be of help in preparing term papers and reports:

- *American Journal of Health Promotion*
- *Physician and Sportsmedicine*
- *Medicine and Science in Sports and Exercise*
- *Canadian Journal of Sport Sciences*

In addition, some helpful books are listed in the References and Further Readings section at the end of this chapter.

HIGHLIGHT
Health and Fitness Programs
at Northern Telecom

The Digital Switching Division of Northern Telecom in Brampton, Ontario, is firmly committed to the idea that the health and well-being of its 4,500 employees are important. An array of voluntary programs offered through its health center, fitness department, and human resources department back up Northern Telecom's commitment. For a number of years Northern Telecom's health center has taken a proactive role in developing optimal employee well-being through its employee assistance program (EAP), health assessments, and hearing and vision tests, along with weight control and smoking control courses and back-care awareness.

In February 1988, a 1,500-square-foot fitness center opened its doors to all workers and retirees. The center boasts state-of-the-art exercise equipment, an aerobic area, locker and shower areas, a fitness assessment laboratory, and offices. A spacious multipurpose area is used for tai chi, aerobic classes, blood donor clinics, and educational seminars. The completion of a fitness assessment is the only prerequisite for membership.

Three months after the initial opening of the fitness center, an in-house physiotherapy clinic staffed by a registered, licensed physiotherapist began operation. Assessments and treatments are provided for both work- and nonwork-related injuries and conditions and rehabilitation programs requiring exercise are prescribed in the fitness center with fitness staff supervising programs.

August 1988 saw the implementation of daily stretch breaks in the plant. An initial pilot group of 55 employees soon grew into a plant-wide program. As part of the stretch program employees gather twice daily to participate in a 6-minute exercise routine designed to alleviate stress and minimize work-related injuries. A full-time exercise specialist leads the exercise breaks, trains volunteer instructors, designs promotional incentives, and is involved in employee lifestyle education projects. More recently the health center has initiated stretch breaks and a comprehensive back-care program for office workers. Two full-time physical education graduates develop and implement these new programs. The following table illustrates the integrated network of services provided through Northern Telecom's Wellness Program (Marsden, 1988).

The Integrated Health Network

Health Center	PURPOSE	Fitness Center
• Stretch breaks in plant	FITNESS	• Aerobic classes • Individual programs • Sport leagues
• Employee assistance counseling • Cessation courses	SMOKING CESSATION	• Policy development and support
• Awareness seminars • Physiotherapy clinic	BACK CARE	• Exercise prescriptions for back health
• Weight-loss programs • Nutritional counseling	NUTRITION	• Exercise and weight control education • Nutrition counseling • Cafeteria food input

- EAP program
- Courses for upper management

- Modified work program
- Immunization clinics
- Health assessments

STRESS
REDUCTION

PREVENTION
AND
REHABILITATION

- Tai chi courses
- Stress survey

- Lifestyle assessments
- Fitness assessment
- Rehabilitation exercises

Undergraduate Education

Within the employee fitness field job skills focus mainly on three areas: programming, human resource management, and facility management. These in turn require training in a variety of areas.

Above all, a sound grounding in exercise physiology and the social sciences is essential for an employee fitness coordinator, who, as the in-house corporate fitness professional, is expected to either provide or be able to obtain qualified personnel and services in such diverse areas as research, fitness assessment, exercise prescription, lifestyle counseling, and on-floor fitness leadership. Graduates who have a broad formal background combined with experience obtained in a fitness facility will be well prepared to assume these roles.

Leading a safe, effective fitness program is no accident—it requires solid training. *Note.* Photo reprinted by permission of The Canada Life Assurance Company.

In addition to the knowledge and skills learned in a traditional physical education undergraduate program, however, business skills such as budgeting, marketing, and proposal writing can prove valuable. These skills often can be obtained in introductory night courses at a community college. Managerial courses and psychosocial courses dealing with group dynamics are also helpful preparation for the challenges associated with supervising subordinate staff.

Many universities offer certification courses in fitness assessment, first aid, and fitness leadership. In particular, it is a good idea to complete the certification program in fitness assessment offered by the Canadian Association of Sport Sciences and the fitness leadership certification program offered by the relevant provincial ministry responsible for physical fitness and recreation. These certification programs are rapidly becoming requirements for employment in the employee fitness field.

Career Opportunities

New graduates generally start as a fitness staff member and, depending on facility size, move on to a coordinator's position and then to program director. Involvement in the corporate fitness environment can open many doors, however, and moving not up but over to a new company can provide the opportunity for broadened experience in various corporate and industrial cultures. Fitness professionals in the field are also moving into closely aligned professions such as human resources, training and development, and occupational health and safety. In addition, there has been a recent trend for fitness professionals to move out of the profession and into marketing and sales as their business and interpersonal skills develop.

Skills acquired in program, facility, and resource management are easily transferable and applicable to managerial positions in the corporate world as well as in the health and fitness field. Government agencies, sports governing bodies, professional associations, municipal recreation departments, and nonprofit agencies like the YMCA and YWCA look for well-trained physical educators with good management skills.

Finally, those with an entrepreneurial spirit may start a consulting business. This generally requires several years of working as a fitness programmer and then passing these responsibilities on while developing new clients. Many employee fitness consultants have achieved success by developing a strong business plan and taking on the challenge of providing direct service to clients, and many find the rewards of developing their own business very satisfying.

Summary

Workplace physical fitness and wellness programs are rapidly expanding as business and industry recognize that healthy, physically fit employees are more productive employees. Research continues to document the benefits that workplace fitness facilities can provide not only to the worker but also to the employer. This trend offers a significant alternative for students considering careers in the exercise or health sciences. Program, facility, and human resource management skills are essential attributes for anyone who desires to pursue a career in this emerging field. In addition, a solid background in the exercise sciences is needed along with business and managerial skills to successfully conduct the variety of duties associated with the workplace fitness environment.

References and Further Readings

Bouchard, C., Shephard, R.J., Stephens, T., Sutton, J.R., & McPherson, B.D. (1990). *Exercise, fitness, and health: A consensus of current knowledge.* Champaign, IL: Human Kinetics.

Canadian Chamber of Commerce. (1986). *Fitness and health promotion by Canadian business.* Ottawa, ON: Fitness and Amateur Sport Canada.

Cox, M., Shephard, R.J., & Corey, P. (1981). Influence of an employee fitness programme upon fitness, productivity and absenteeism. *Ergonomics*, **24**, 795-806.

Danielson, R.R., & Danielson, K.F. (1979). Leadership. In *Proceedings of the Ontario Employee Fitness Workshop* (p. 109). Toronto: Ontario Ministry of Culture and Recreation.

Health and Welfare Canada. (1974). *Proceedings of the National Conference on Fitness and Health.* Ottawa, ON: Department of Health and Welfare.

Health and Welfare Canada. (1987). *The active health report—perspectives on Canada's Health Promotion Survey 1985* (Report No. H-39-106/1987E). Ottawa, ON: Ministry of Supply and Services.

Marsden, V. (1988, Summer-Fall). Integrating fitness and health promotion programs. *Work and Well-Being Quarterly*, pp. 5-10.

National Institute of Health. (1981). *Cardiovascular primer for the workplace.* Bethesda, MD: National Heart, Lung and Blood Institute.

O'Donnell, M.P. (1984). *Health promotion in the workplace.* New York: Wiley.

Patton, R.W., Corey, J., Gettman, L., & Graf, J.S. (1986). *Implementing health/fitness programs.* Champaign, IL: Human Kinetics.

Pyle, R.L. (1979, Fall). Performance measures of a corporate fitness program. *Human Resource Management*, pp. 26-30.

Walker, J., Cox, M., Thomas, S., Gledhill, N., & Salmon, A. (1989). Canada Life—corporate fitness 10 years after. *Canadian Journal of Applied Sport Sciences*, **14**(4), p. 142.

Part IV

The Future: Emerging Trends in the Physical Activity Sciences

Part IV, the final section of the book, includes two chapters that outline some of the emerging trends from the perspectives of research (chapter 28) and program and service (chapter 29). For some readers, the pursuit of knowledge as a researcher in one of the field's scientific foundations may become a career goal. Chapter 28 presents some of the requirements, as well as some of the opportunities, for a career in the physical activity sciences as a scientist.

The majority of students, however, seek a career as a practitioner in one of the service areas of the field. Chapter 29 provides an overview of the conditions that will most likely prevail in the near future. The expected changes in programs, policies, and required services that are described in this chapter indicate where the field is going and the best sort of training to make a significant contribution as a physical activity practitioner with some type of special expertise.

The future of the field offers numerous challenges and promises for both researchers and practitioners. Reading this book should adequately prepare the student to think seriously about ways and means through which to contribute best to society as an active member of the field. The continuous and creative growth of the physical activity sciences and professions, as we enter the next millennium, will be in direct proportion to the talent and dedication of undergraduate and graduate students who are trained as imaginative scholars and creative practitioners.

Chapter 28

The Future of Research in the Physical Activity Sciences

Claude Bouchard

Barry D. McPherson

Albert W. Taylor

Previous chapters in this book have discussed the important role that the scientific method plays in furthering the knowledge base in the physical activity sciences and have described several subfields of the physical activity sciences in terms of current research activities, the use of specific methods, and the professional organizations and journals that disseminate research results. It should be clear by now that research is an essential component of the physical activity sciences. Creation, verification, and dissemination of knowledge are absolutely vital for the growth of the subfields and for the initiation of valid and creative practices or policies. This chapter considers the immediate future for the research component of the field of study and addresses the fundamental questions that need to be answered in any attempt to forecast evolution in the field over the next 5 to 10 years.

From Research to Knowledge to Practice

The physical activity sciences have grown rapidly since the early 1900s. Compared to other fields, however, the knowledge base has not expanded as rapidly, and in many respects, research in the physical activity sciences lags behind. The body of knowledge in this field is, by most criteria of assessment, quite limited and not very sophisticated. One reason for this deficiency was the paucity of active scientists working in the field prior to the 1970s. Indeed, until the mid-1960s most scientific publications in North America were produced by only a few dozen scientists. Teaching, coaching, administration, and sports skill instruction were the main responsibilities of most faculty in American and Canadian universities. Research and related scientific activities generally were perceived as unessential or unnecessary by physical education leaders and administrators.

Nevertheless, research was a major preoccupation for a small number of individuals who contributed much to the evolution of the field. These contributions, and some of the consequences, have been discussed by Kroll (1982) and McPherson and Taylor (1980); these publications contain excellent accounts of the field's move from a professional practice orientation to a scientific and scholarly one.

Since the late 1970s both the quantity and quality of research in the physical activity sciences have increased. For instance, a growing number of faculties have become involved, part-time or full-time, in research; research qualifications are required for faculty positions; research funding for scholars in the field has become more available; specialized research journals have appeared in most of the subdisciplines; and more scientific papers are published. In general, however, the quality and quantity of scientific activity in the field remains below that of other disciplines. Only about 400 of the approximately 600 Canadian faculty members in the field have a doctoral degree; of these, fewer than 200 actively engage in research, and only about 40 to 50 publish regularly in scholarly journals. In the meantime, other fields of study are experiencing exponential growth in both the number of research personnel and the quality of research output: Hundreds of new journals are founded each year, more than 6,000 scientific papers are published every day, and research data doubles every 10 years at the current rate of activity (see chapter 3, Science and Physical Activity).

There is perhaps one key factor behind this lag. Many members of the profession do not fully appreciate the close link between research activity and the expansion of the knowledge base. They are unable or unwilling to understand the critical importance of generating new knowledge and refining existing knowledge. They have ignored the obvious fact that the production of valid and reliable research data generates the potential to engineer changes, to stimulate better adaptive responses to challenging issues or practical problems, and to question existing solutions and practices with a view to determining whether there are more valid or efficient ways of meeting consumer/client needs. In other words, research and scholarly inquiry are essential for the generation of knowledge, which in turn is the key to

innovative and creative policy and program development.

The physical activity sciences are no exception to this universal trend of close links among research, practice, and policy (see Figure 28.1). Both scientists and practitioners in the physical activity sciences have a vested interest in promoting the generation and dissemination of new knowledge, thus ensuring that the field advances and thrives into the next century. It is to be hoped that the current generation of students will enter the field with a clear understanding of the importance of generating, testing, and using scientific knowledge. More importantly, it is essential that some of them pursue research careers in this field. By the time that those who do so complete their PhD degrees, many of the contributors to this text will be retiring; ideally, we will be replaced by creative scholars with a strong commitment to scholarly inquiry.

Let us now turn to some of the critical issues that enthusiastic, creative, and innovative students should be thinking about. Many other issues that need to be addressed are beyond the scope of this book; perhaps they will be introduced in class discussion. Other issues will be raised and addressed in more advanced classes and texts, perhaps in the third or fourth year of undergraduate study. At that time, students interested in pursuing a research career should consult with the director of graduate studies and with active researchers in the field concerning how and where to become adequately prepared for a research career.

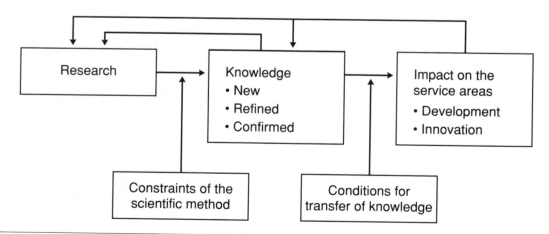

Figure 28.1 A paradigm for the role of research in the physical activity sciences. The service areas of the field can develop and expand with the increase in knowledge resulting from research activities in the various subfields. Progress in the service areas contributes to the research process by helping the scientists to formulate hypotheses and new questions.

Training for a Research Career

In the past, adequate training for a research career normally involved obtaining a doctoral degree in the physical activity sciences with a few basic courses in the parent discipline of the appropriate subfield. For instance, a researcher in biomechanics typically completed a PhD degree in kinesiology or physical education and some undergraduate and graduate courses in mathematics and physics. More recently, research-oriented doctoral graduates have completed a larger percentage of course work in the basic sciences and in the parent disciplines. As we enter the 1990s, a growing number of doctoral students, particularly in the biological sciences, consider postdoctoral research training to be essential.

In the next decade, the training of physical activity scientists probably will include a solid preparation in both the basic field and in the parent discipline(s) (physiology, biochemistry, mechanical engineering, sociology, psychology, etc.). In addition, 2 to 4 years of postdoctoral training may be necessary in a university or laboratory other than the one in which the PhD training was completed. The implication of this trend is enormous. Students contemplating a research career in the field must realize that it may take 10 to 12 years of study and training before they are fully prepared to conduct independent research and to contribute significantly to the knowledge base.

Support for Study and Research

A society that seeks to become a leader and a serious competitor in a world where information and technology are prime ingredients of success must allocate resources both to the training of future scholars and to the support of the research enterprise. Unfortunately, a look at Canada's current and expected levels of support for research in science in general and the physical activity sciences in particular is far from encouraging.

In many Western nations, public sector officials claim that research is an important priority and that their government grants a large amount of financial support to it. There is considerable variation among countries, however. Canada for example, spends about 1.3% of its Gross National Product on research and development (this is the lowest amount among Western nations) whereas the U.S.A. spends 2.7%. It has been estimated that in all fields, Canada has about 90 scientists per 100,000 inhabitants; the former West Germany has 150; and the U.S.A., 280. The general level of support for scientific activities in Canada is therefore quite low and inadequate for a nation that aspires to play a leading role in the new political, economic, and social order evolving in the 1990s.

In the physical activity sciences the funding picture is even worse. Direct research support for physical activity scientists in Canada is provided by three national granting agencies, as well as from some provincial organizations. For the 1988 calendar year, the National Science and Engineering Research Council had a total budget of about $320 million, the Medical Research Council about $170 million, and the Social Sciences and Humanities Research Council about $60 million. In contrast, for the same period, the National Institutes of Health in the U.S.A. had a budget equivalent to about $10 billion (Canadian). Moreover, for a variety of reasons, physical activity scientists generally have not fared well in competing for research grants from these agencies. The last 5 years, however, have seen a progressive increase in the number of physical activity scientists awarded research grants from one of the three major national granting agencies, as well as from the Canadian Heart Foundation, Canadian Diabetes Association, Health and Welfare Canada, and other organizations. In addition, Fitness Canada (through the Canadian Fitness and Lifestyle Research Institute) and Sport Canada spend about $1 million annually to support applied sport and fitness research. Further financial support is also available from various provincial bodies, from several foundations, and from the intramural research programs at each university.

The current level of financial support provided to Canadian scientists to help meet the considerable expenses associated with conducting research (for technical assistance, laboratory equipment, laboratory supplies, surveys, information retrieval, data processing, travel, and other expenditures) is generally below the level of support provided by other industrialized nations. Ultimately, in an environment where adequate funds are made available, the success of the scientists in securing financial support for research depends on the quality of the research training received and on demonstrated research productivity. Seen from that vantage point, the future looks more promising for a student considering a career as a physical activity scientist. Indeed, members of the next generation will be much better prepared to compete in the science game than physical activity scientists from preceding generations.

Conditions should gradually improve, however. Public opinion and university leaders are increasingly placing pressure on political leaders to augment the amount of financial support for science in Canada. An encouraging sign is the fact that several of the larger academic units in Canada and the U.S.A. that focus on physical activity research are currently receiving more than $1 million per year in competitive peer-reviewed research grants. These research environments thus constitute advantageous settings in which to complete doctoral and postdoctoral training.

The Future Research Environment

Future trends may well be specific to the various subfields; for example the trends may differ for the biochemistry of physical activity and the sociology of sport. Prospective candidates for a research career must consider all these changes, but some of these—the previously mentioned increase in academic requirements to become a scientist and the increasing cost of conducting research—will particularly affect the productivity and success of scholars in the field and the quality and quantity of new knowledge.

Another major influence on how scholarly work is conducted will be the growing need for collaboration by scholars, both within and between disciplines. First, there has been an increase in the amount of research initiated by groups of scholars working together within the same field or discipline. This cooperation allows scholars to address large questions by pooling their resources and merging the creativity of several minds.

Collaborative research also means increased sophistication and power of explanation, particularly when the scientists are from different fields or disciplines. Such interdisciplinary collaboration brings together individuals with different skills and approaches to solve a problem. This approach has become more accepted during the last few decades, and physical activity scientists will be increasingly involved in this trend. On the other hand, the increased popularity of interdisciplinary teams has also meant that some of the most creative and productive scientists have been recruited away from their basic disciplines by scholars in more prestigious and well-funded areas of study such

as cell biology, physiology, psychology, sociology, gerontology, and medicine.

A major change will be a shift in the purpose or level of the research conducted by the majority of physical activity scientists. In the past, and even during the last decade, many studies were descriptive; that is, they were designed to describe a phenomenon in terms of mean values, percentages of success or failure, individual differences, and other similar group data. Only a small proportion of the research was designed to answer mechanistic or process questions or to discover and explain the sources of variation in a given phenomenon. In the future, physical activity scientists will employ more powerful research designs to explain phenomena and to discover mechanisms that can be used to solve particular problems. As much as possible, investigators will conduct experiments wherein they have total control over the variables; at the least they will employ a quasiexperimental approach incorporating statistical controls over the contaminating variables.

As society increases its scrutiny of science, future physical activity scientists will live in an environment where they must meet ever higher standards of ethical conduct. Before initiating research, the scientist will be required to describe the intended treatment of experimental animals or human subjects and to ensure the confidentiality of privileged information.

Although the foregoing trends will likely evolve in all research, whether its focus is social science, biology, or physical science, there will be variations in the approaches and problems addressed by the various subdisciplines in the physical activity sciences field. Some of these concerns are addressed in the following sections.

The Future of Research in the Social Sciences

A growing interest in all forms of physical activity (e.g., triathlons, aerobic classes, fitness testing) will supplant the previously narrower focus on organized competitive sport. In the Canadian context, there will be more national studies, which will permit comparison across regions and provinces. From a more international perspective, cross-cultural comparative studies about patterns of physical activity, sport performance, and fitness, using both anthropological and sociological methods, will become more frequent. In addition, the various social science subfields will become more involved in policy-oriented and program evaluation research.

Another area of growing research interest concerns the needs of and the involvement and barriers to participation in sports and physical activity of special groups such as the elderly, the economically disadvantaged, and the disabled. Moreover, important historical events, technological developments, or changes in values that have a considerable impact on society will appear more often as the focus of studies in the social science subfields. These studies will examine the influence of these factors on mass sport participation; on professional and Olympic sport events; on the fitness, wellness, and active living movement; and on a score of other socially induced fitness issues. To illustrate, social scientists may study the impact of free trade between the U.S.A. and Canada on the future of professional sport in Canada or the impact of the sweeping political changes in Eastern Europe on the use of sport as an instrument of propaganda and political power.

The Future of Research in the Biological and Physical Sciences

Recent advances in technology, particularly in microelectronics and biotechnologies, make the future of research in the biological and physical subfields of the physical activity sciences quite exciting. Human movement will be studied more directly, and in real time, with the help of powerful high-speed recording devices and with analytical systems capable of handling vast amounts of data. Detailed segmental analysis of the human body in motion will be possible through a combination of new invasive and noninvasive techniques. Human performance will continue to be investigated not only in terms of the biological and physical characteristics of the human machine but also in terms of the motor task itself, central and peripheral neural determinants, attention, memory, parallel processing, imagery, and fatigue.

The biological subfields of the physical activity sciences will undoubtedly continue to explore the outcomes of physical activity in terms of the acute effects and the long-term adaptation of the various tissues, organs, and systems to exercise-induced stress; the present emphasis on tissue responses will continue unabated. As a result of new knowledge from the basic sciences, however, the physical activity scientist will increasingly employ the techniques of molecular and cellular biology to study the cellular, subcellular, and molecular responses of various tissues to exercise-related stresses. Scientists studying cell response and the molecular mechanisms involved when humans engage in exercise will use a variety of laboratory procedures, including tissue culture, monoclonal antibodies, recombinant DNA technologies, cloned genes, in vitro translation systems, and sophisticated protein separation techniques.

Summary

A research career is a very demanding profession with high academic requirements and standards, but also a very exciting and rewarding one that can provide a lifetime of intellectual stimulation. We hope the reader is aware by now that both physical activity scientists and practitioners have a responsibility to raise and to seek answers to scientific questions if the field is to advance and survive. The student who continues in this field will, over the next 3 or 4 years, learn more about the theories, scientific methods, and research processes unique to the field. An excellent way to facilitate development as a knowledgeable professional is to volunteer as a research assistant or research subject. Such activity provides an intimate exposure to the work and the joys and frustrations associated with the research process.

A knowledge of and appreciation for the research process is still essential for success in other occupations in the world of sport and fitness, too. Anyone involved in the field in whatever capacity must read the scientific journals and learn to interpret and adapt the results to his or her own setting or area of responsibility. Teaching, coaching, developing fitness programs, or establishing fitness or sport policies all require a working knowledge of the most recent and valid research. Only by knowing about and understanding current and valid research can anyone make the "correct" decisions or design the "appropriate" policy or program.

References and Further Readings

Brooks, G.A. (1981). *Perspectives on the academic discipline of physical education*. Champaign, IL: Human Kinetics.

Cavanagh, P.A. (1987). The cutting edge in biomechanics. In M.J. Safrit & H.M. Eckert (Eds.),

The cutting edge in physical education and exercise science research (pp. 115-119). Champaign, IL: Human Kinetics.

Kroll, W.P. (1982). *Graduate study and research in physical education.* Champaign, IL: Human Kinetics.

McPherson, B.D., & Taylor, A.W. (1980). Physical activity scientists. Their present and future role. In F.J. Hayden (Ed.), *Body and mind in the 90's./Le corps et l'esprit-prospective pour 1990* (pp. 165-191). Hamilton, ON: The Canadian Council of University Physical Education Administrators.

Park, R.J. (1987). Sport history in the 1990s: Prospects and problems. In M.J. Safrit & H.M. Eckert (Eds.), *The cutting edge in physical education and exercise science research* (pp. 96-108). Champaign, IL: Human Kinetics.

Stelmach, G.E. (1987). The cutting edge of research in physical education and exercise science: The search for understanding. In M.J. Safrit & H.M. Eckert (Eds.), *The cutting edge in physical education and exercise science research* (pp. 8-26). Champaign, IL: Human Kinetics.

Yuhasz, M.S., Taylor, A.W., & Haggerty, T.R. (Eds.) (1986). *Acadirectory: A Canadian sourcebook of physical education, kinesiology, and human kinetics.* London, ON: Sports Dynamics.

Chapter 29

The Future in Programs and Service Areas

Jacques Samson
Paul Godbout

Predicting what lies ahead is always a somewhat risky endeavor. Because this book describes the physical activity sciences as an emerging field of study and research, however, it is only natural that we should focus on the likely challenges of tomorrow, not only for those responsible for policy and program development but for all those working within this field.

It is difficult to predict the future when the past is characterized by such extraordinary developments that the present has, to many, become diffuse and cloudy. There can be no experts at predicting the future, for it is often extremely difficult to visualize the complexity of the present situation in sufficient detail to make accurate predictions. Such may indeed be the state of an emerging profession that has not yet come to grips with and reached a consensus about its own identity and role in society. Many writers have attempted to forecast the directions in which the physical activity sciences would go since Henry (1964) first raised the identity issue. Further complicating such prediction is the field's fast rate of growth. It may therefore be wise to ask ourselves first whether this evolution will continue, accelerate, decelerate, or stop.

Based on the evidence presented in previous chapters the following predictions appear reasonable.

- The physical activity sciences will continue to develop as a body of knowledge, both fundamental and applied.

- Physical activity as a method of achieving general well-being will continue to be regarded as a right of each individual citizen and more and more will be considered a social responsibility of public and private institutions and organizations.

- Physical activity will become more elective, voluntary, and discretionary. Future clients will be adults seeking individually structured self-developmental activities. As discussed in chapter 16, most of these new services will be rendered in nonschool organizations.

- Service areas will continue to develop and new ones may appear. Young professionals will likely face a turbulent marketplace with fewer permanent jobs available. However, the diversification of the professional practices will mean more opportunities for young, dynamic entrepreneurs. In the 1960s and 1970s, most students in physical education were preparing to teach children in schools. This is no longer the case. Clients now come from all ages, have very different needs, and expect to be treated accordingly. The schools are no longer the only employer of professionals in physical activity.

- Market opportunities or constraints will force most practitioners to redirect their professional practice one or more times during their careers. Regardless of the turbulence in job opportunities, the vast majority of the young professionals will provide activity service throughout their careers (Ellis, 1988).

- The organization of the profession is not likely to improve, and physical activity professionals will continue to be challenged by increased societal demands as well as by other professions trying to occupy these service areas.
- Both students and professionals will face the increasingly difficult challenge of choosing the information relevant to their own needs (see chapter 3, Science and Physical Activity).

These are but a few of the most significant trends that can be derived from a wide array of indicators that otherwise support or suggest contradictory directions of development. A student entering this challenging field would be well advised to consider them very carefully so as to recognize the short-lived fads that have been so frequent in the evolution of the profession. As Massengale (1987) warns, "people can establish some control over their professional destiny, although the extent of this control is most often associated with appropriate judgment, not necessarily with fact" (p. 2).

Yet, the professional's role in the evolution of the field should be not only reactive but also proactive. The future of the physical activity sciences rests within the hands of those professionals working either as practitioners or as researchers and very much in the hands of those now entering the profession. Hence, it is from this participatory viewpoint that we look at future directions in policies and programs that may affect this evolution.

Professional Preparation Programs

However reassuring it is to think that university programs are designed to prepare students for the future, these programs more often than not change very slowly, adapting retroactively and sometimes belatedly to the much faster changes in the career patterns, job opportunities, and even the role of physical activity in our society.

These programs have evolved over the last 30 years in response to a variety of internal and external pressures. One internal pressure has been to make the degrees represent a truly academic training, which is coupled with the related intensification of the search for the scientific foundations of physical activity. The diversification of professional practices and the ever-increasing involve-

ment of professionals from other academic backgrounds in physical-activity-related professional practices have added external pressures on physical activity programs to better prepare students for an increasingly competitive marketplace. To say that these are pressures is not to criticize them; on the contrary, they will contribute to the health of the field in the long run. We mention them only to help demonstrate the complex nature of the evolutionary forces that have affected and are likely to continue affecting university professional preparation programs.

There is, however, a growing conflict in Canadian universities between the need to provide undergraduate students with the most up-to-date scientific knowledge and the need to teach specific skills related to their future professional practice. Various academic pressures and promotion criteria have created an ever-widening chasm between science-oriented and professional-oriented faculty members and a progressive decrease in the interest of many faculty members for professional preparation activities in undergraduate programs. The propriety of task-related professional activities is frequently dismissed as being insufficiently academic, scientific, or content-oriented.

Thus, the various teaching activities within a program often become distributed among different faculty members who have less and less in common with one another. Twenty years ago, faculty members taught both theory courses such as physiology or pedagogy and activity courses. Today, there is an increasingly dangerous reliance for technical and practical skills to be taught by part-time personnel who lack the relevant scholarly abilities. Whether it is a direct consequence of this trend or a simple coincidence, an increasing number of professional organizations now offer various professional preparation courses and certification and accreditation programs.

However significant each of these factors may become, a likely corollary will be a renewed interest in the orientation and the content of university programs and a willingness to reassess them. More attention will thus be given to a fundamental distinction between the concepts of professional preparation and professional development. The former refers generally to the initial preparation of students entering the profession and is limited to those learning activities and experiences within the undergraduate programs. Professional development, on the other hand, is a much broader concept that includes any and all activities and experiences contributing to the improvement of the knowledge base as well as the quality of professional activity. Professional development is a life-long challenge facing all professionals and should begin immediately on receipt of the undergraduate degree.

The directions that university programs will take in the future depends largely on the proper and objective evaluation of current programs and a prospective assessment of foreseeable needs. Broader studies of these issues appear in *Body and Mind in the 90's* (Hayden, 1980) and in *Physical Education Professional Preparation: Insights and Foresights* (Hoffman & Rink, 1985). In forecasting likely solutions to these challenges, it is important to take into account the various pressures that are likely to have an impact on universities and the profession as a whole.

The Future Professional Environment

As we alluded to earlier, university programs are not always a true and current reflection of the environment in which today's students and tomorrow's professionals will work. Because a university degree is the key to entering the profession, however, it is of great importance to understand not only how to help improve university programs but also the major elements of the professional environment and the consequences these may have on career preparation.

First, the increased awareness of the benefits of physical activity in terms of general well-being and a clearer understanding that fitness and sports are important factors affecting personal development, self-realization, national culture, and international relations will produce various societal pressures. Society will require that young professionals entering the market be adequately prepared. Physical activity professionals will have to be aware of the benefits of physical activity in general and of the benefits or limits of the diverse activities offered as part of the physical activity services for clients of different ages and different needs.

These societal pressures may give rise to a reassessment of the university's role in society, or what L'Heureux (1980) called the "ivory tower–public utilities dilemma." Whether or not it takes place, the physical activity sciences professional must be prepared to deliver services to different clients whose needs may change rapidly, moving, for example, from youth-oriented sport activities to adult-oriented fitness activities. This will also require the ability to adapt quickly to a changing environment. Physical activity professionals are no longer preparing exclusively for teaching youth in well-structured school programs. More and more, young professionals are called to render services to a clientele of all ages in health, fitness, recreation and leisure, and sport occupations, often outside of the traditional educational institutions. As Sage (1987) points out: "The notion of a single, central mission for physical education—teacher preparation—has been abandoned" (p. 15).

Tomorrow's environment will also be dictated to a large extent by government policies. The future of many of the emerging new professional practices depends on the understanding that local, provincial, and national government policymakers have of the need to support physical activity participation, attainment and maintenance of fitness levels, and excellence in high-performance sports. For instance, any reduction in compulsory physical education classes in schools would have far-reaching and extremely negative consequences for the profession.

In Canada, government policies affecting physical activity may come from the federal, provincial, or local governments and from both education and municipal departments. However different these levels of government may appear to be in their policies and programs, they all have one thing in common: They must respond to the needs of their respective constituency.

Although they may appear to distance themselves from the exclusive responsibility for organization and funding of an increasingly wide variety of physical activities, government will continue to assume a leadership role. Thus, physical activity professionals must be prepared to play a major role in shaping future government policies. Early involvement in various sport and physical activity organizations may be the best way to influence government policies. Government will no longer be able to maintain the professional staffs necessary to develop and coordinate a host of programs; on the other hand, it will require the guidance and assistance of program-oriented organizations for policy development while maintaining minimum staff to coordinate and ensure the public accountability of financial assistance programs.

Tomorrow's challenge is not within government, however, but in nongovernmental organizations able to respond to the needs of society, possibly with some public financial assistance.

In addition, tomorrow's environment will be shaped by the private sector. Increased public demand and gradual government disengagement will give private sector organizations an increasing role in offering services and programs not only to their employees but also to the public in general.

The rules for private sector involvement are, however, very different from those of governments. Profitability and accountability often dictate very different approaches to the organization and administration of services. Opportunities and expertise often take a very real sense in this environment. A young professional must be prepared to adapt and to seize the opportunities, for someone else will be.

All in all, the outlook remains extremely encouraging. The environment is changing and so must the approach to professional preparation. In the context of diversified professional practices, there is a need for both a more general initial preparation at the undergraduate level to allow various points of entry into the profession and more opportunities for professional development on a continuing basis. The prudent individual will quickly learn to exploit fully the expertise available, using every opportunity to integrate the specific preparation (technical and practical) for diversified professional practices and the ever-expanding body of scientific knowledge on which these professional practices are based.

Major Challenges to Students

- Choosing an area of expertise
- Identifying the required body of knowledge
- Mastering the necessary abilities
- Developing alternative areas of professional practice
- Identifying the needs of prospective employers
- Acquiring the ability to adapt to changing needs of clients
- Identifying the means to maintain expertise
- Committing to a true professional attitude

Part III in this book describes the many areas of professional practice related to the physical activity sciences. Obviously, no 3- or 4-year program is sufficient for all of them. Choices must be made, but what to choose? Which area offers the best opportunities?

After reading chapters 16 through 27, it should be clear that the profession is exploding and that each and every one of these areas offers a variety of opportunities. But although the professional practices are expanding, so is the interest of profes-

sionals from other fields in getting a piece of the action, which creates a more competitive marketplace.

Probably the only area still restricted to the physical activity science graduate is teaching in the school. In spite of a declining birth rate, job opportunities should be on the rise in the 1990s because of an increase in retirements by those currently occupying these positions. Fitness and sport-related practices will continue to develop for the needs have not yet been fully met. The professionalization of coaches working at various levels of high-performance development will also offer many new opportunities. Other areas such as programs for the elderly and people with disabilities, outdoor programs, and workplace-based programs have only begun to develop and will continue to expand.

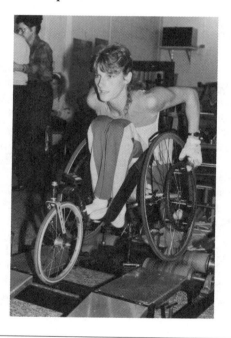

Research on the performance capacities of people with disabilities may lead to the creation of better physical activity programs.

Professional Leadership

Many professionals have long played a major role in the development of the field of study and research and of its many service areas through local, provincial, and national professional and scientific organizations. In recent years, however, this involvement has sagged from diminished commitment and leadership.

Many of the considerations previously discussed may have contributed to this withdrawal of many professionals, allowing outside pressures such as economic constraints, job insecurity, and the government's gradual disengagement from so-called noneconomically profitable interventions and its promotion of "privatization" as a deficit-reduction measure to exercise undue influence on the evolution of the profession.

Unfortunately, the university faculty members who could be producing social criticism and systems analysis of private and public policies and programs related to physical activity, fitness, and sports have been content to turn to other tasks instead. Many professionals have taken to watching the profession evolve, the older generation content to have a relatively secure position and satisfied that it should probably be someone else's turn, and the younger generation arguing that a profession that cannot guarantee a full-time job is not worth fighting for.

Fortunately, these same outside pressures appear to be awakening professionals, young and old. The last decade's ethos of self-promotion, justified by a so-called commitment to excellence and by various job-related pressures, has created a need for a renewed vision of the role of physical activity in our society and for a redefinition of who we are as a collective professional entity.

The body of knowledge concerning the effects of physical activity, the people who exercise, the reasons they do or don't, how they can be made to persevere, how they can be made to improve their performance, and the relationship between physical activity and well-being is increasing and will continue to increase rapidly. Similarly, the various service areas will continue to grow as a consequence of public demands for more opportunities to participate in all forms of physical activity. These trends will appear in fitness activity programs of all sorts in both the public and the private sector, in coaching at all levels (but particularly at the elite level), and in various forms of outdoor pursuits.

If this field is to fully emerge as a field of study and research, however, and avoid fragmentation into its many subfields, leadership attitudes and behaviors must change drastically. The increasing numbers of people now working in physical-activity-related professional practices who either come from other professions or have no professional background whatsoever render this need all the more acute. The diversification of professional practices and the ensuing specialization appear to be creating a centrifugal force on the profession;

many tend to lose sight of the fact that, whatever the orientation of their personal career, they all contribute in some way to a more physically active population. The field has gained academic credibility in spite of a tendency by many professionals to identify with a subfield of specialization rather than with the physical activity sciences as such, but this tendency poses a threat to the gains that have been made. Practitioners in all areas—teachers, coaches, fitness specialists, recreationists, and so on—must also identify themselves as physical activity professionals, particularly in areas where significant numbers of practitioners come from other fields and where outside agencies or organizations are developing certification programs, such as the fitness area and the coaching area.

Once again, universities and their faculties will likely play a crucial role. Faced with the prospect of fragmentation within the academic institution, new attempts at the structural reorganization of academic units built around the concept of physical activity sciences will take place. Strong academic units with a well-identified mandate are needed to contribute to the advancement of an equally well-defined body of knowledge. Universities must also prepare competent professionals who can service different clients and adapt to changing needs.

The Future Is Now

A student entering the profession full of enthusiasm and with a natural eagerness to become actively involved may find the picture we have painted to be somewhat troubling. That was not our intention, however. On the contrary, our purpose was simply to expose some of the complex evolutionary forces shaping the profession and thus modifying the traditional job opportunities. The outlook for young people seeking to become physical activity professionals is very positive and challenging, but the turbulence in the marketplace requires a certain aggressiveness toward the future, and in a sense, the future is now.

These evolutionary forces and major trends have numerous and far-reaching implications that are likely to affect anyone working in the field. The first of these implications, the explosion of job opportunities, is evident from the discussion in chapter 16. Whatever their motives, increasing numbers of people of all ages and from all walks of life are actively engaging in one form or another of physical activity. Perhaps as a result of the numerous campaigns designed to foster healthy behaviors, physical activity involvement is gradually developing into a popular lifestyle within the general well-being movement.

Not only are individuals demanding more opportunities and new forms of physical activity to suit their needs and interests, but governments, large corporations, small companies, and unions are beginning to recognize the value of physical activity for both the individual and for the organization. Thus many physical activity sciences graduates will find job opportunities in providing services to the public in general as well as to institutions willing to offer their employees physical activity services as part of an overall social benefit package.

The second implication has also already been mentioned, namely, that the central mission of physical activity practitioners has become service oriented. Furthermore, the notion of physical activity as an individual lifestyle will mean that the consumers themselves will often pay for the professional expertise needed to provide these services. Consequently, the practitioner will have to adapt constantly to the changing needs of the clients. Thus, as client interests change, so too will career patterns.

A third implication involves what could be called a professional commitment to excellence. The competition to attract and retain potential clients will increase. The fact that people need to be physically active will not ensure physical activity practitioners a job. They will have to sell their expertise and convince these potential clients that what they have to offer is worth paying for.

This is particularly important because an inevitable consequence of an individually oriented pattern of involvement in self-developmental activities is that people soon think they can do it themselves without all the inconvenience of group-structured constraints. Fitness equipment manufacturers have already begun to exploit this tendency and to market all sorts of do-it-yourself exercisers. From the point of view of the physical activity practitioner's career goals, this may become a dangerous trend.

Another implication for young physical activity professionals concerns the role of government in fostering the professionalization of different forms of services through various policies and programs. One such area is high-performance coaching. For many years, coaching has been viewed as a volunteer activity performed by parents and various people who had an interest in it, however tempo-

rary. With the advent of provincial and national elite development programs, however, more and more coaches are now employed on a full-time basis, from the national teams down to elite-oriented clubs.

A similar trend may be observed for all sorts of activities under the responsibility of local governments, school boards, and local clubs wishing to offer their clients a full complement of services. Thus, for example, many tennis clubs are now offering a complete spectrum of racquet sports as well as fitness activities and even aquatic activities. A direct consequence of this evolution in client-oriented services will be a need for a new generation of physical activity managers trained in program planning and management as well as in marketing and public relations.

Thus, the last implication of these evolutionary forces concerns the professional preparation and professional development of the new generation of physical activity practitioners. Because of the changing nature of the job opportunities, it is no longer possible or advisable for undergraduate programs to map out the career pattern of every student. On the contrary, these programs must offer a variety of opportunities from which the students can choose according to their personal interests and needs, which is why the future of professional preparation and professional development programs is so important. A beginning student is well advised not only to start planning a professional career pattern immediately on entering an undergraduate program but also to rely heavily on professional involvement and commitment to excellence. Personal expertise in one or several areas of professional practice will ensure job opportunities, but only professional involvement and an understanding of the evolutionary forces affecting the profession can provide guidance in this turbulent marketplace.

Summary

This book has presented many areas of expertise within the general domain of the physical activity sciences and its many service areas. In this last chapter, the most significant trends likely to influence the future of the profession are briefly discussed, particularly with respect to their impact on job opportunities.

Professional preparation within an undergraduate program is important but so is involvement in specific service areas. Such professional preparation involves not only acquiring a general body of knowledge but also mastering the specific abilities that constitute true professional expertise in a service-oriented profession.

References and Further Readings

Conant, J.B. (1973). *The education of American teachers.* New York: McGraw-Hill.

Ellis, M.J. (1988). Warning: The pendulum has swung far enough. *Journal of Health, Physical Education and Recreation,* **59**(3), 75-78.

Hayden, F.J. (Ed.) (1980). *Body and mind in the 90's/Le corps et l'esprit—prospective pour 1990.* Hamilton, ON: Canadian Council of University Physical Education Administrators.

Henry, F.M. (1964). Physical education: An academic discipline. *Journal of Health, Physical Education and Recreation,* **35**, 32-38.

Hoffman, H.A., & Rink, J.E. (Eds.) (1985). Physical education professional preparation: Insights and foresights. *Proceedings from the Second National Conference on Preparing the Physical Education Specialist for Children.* Reston, VA: American Alliance for Health, Physical Education, Recreation and Dance.

L'Heureux, W.J. (1980). University degree programs in the 90's: Ivory towers or public utilities? In F.J. Hayden (Ed.), *Body and mind in the 90's/Le corps et l'esprit—prospective pour 1990* (pp. 34-39). Hamilton, ON: Canadian Council of University Physical Education Administrators.

Massengale, J.D. (Ed.) (1987). *Trends toward the future in physical education.* Champaign, IL: Human Kinetics.

Sage, G.H. (1987). The future and the profession of physical education. In J.D. Massengale (Ed.), *Trends toward the future in physical education* (pp. 9-23). Champaign, IL: Human Kinetics.

Appendix A

Selected Canadian, North American, and International Scientific and Professional Organizations

Canadian Societies and Organizations

Canadian Academy of Sports Medicine (CASM)

Canadian Association for Health, Physical Education and Recreation (CAHPER)

Canadian Association of Sport Sciences (CASS)

Canadian Athletic Therapists Association (CATA)

Canadian Council of University Physical Education and Recreation Administrators (CCUPERA)

Canadian Federation of Sport Organizations for the Disabled (CFSOD)

Canadian Fitness and Lifestyle Research Institute (CFLRI)

Canadian Parks and Recreation Association (CPRA)

Canadian Physiotherapy Association: Sport Physiotherapy Division (SPD)

Canadian Public Health Association (CPHA)

Canadian Society of Biomechanics (CSB)

Canadian Society for Psychomotor Learning and Sport Psychology (CSPLSP)

Fitness Canada, Government of Canada

Sport Canada, Government of Canada

Sport Medicine Council of Canada (SMCC)

Other North American Organizations

American Alliance for Health, Physical Education, Recreation and Dance (AAHPERD)

American Academy of Physical Education (AAPE)

American College of Sports Medicine (ACSM)

Association for Fitness in Business

Association for the Anthropological Study of Play

National Recreation and Park Association (NRPA)

North American Society for Sport History (NASSH)

North American Society for the Psychology of Sport and Physical Activity (NASPSPA)

North American Society for the Sociology of Sport (NASSS)

International Organizations

International Council of Sport Science and Physical Education (ICSSPE)

Association Internationale des Ecoles Supérieures d'Education Physique (AIESEP)

Fédération Internationale de Médecine Sportive (FIMS)

International Association for Sports Information (IASI)

International Association for the History of Sport and Physical Education (HISPA)

International Association of Physical Education and Sport for Girls and Women (IAPESGW)

International Council on Health, Physical Education and Recreation (ICHPER)

International Recreation Association (IRA)

International Society of Biomechanics in Sports (ISBS)

International Society of Sports Psychology (ISSP)

International Sport Organization for the Disabled (ISOD)

Philosophic Society for the Study of Sport (PSSS)

Appendix B

Fitness and Amateur Sport Act

The formulation of "An Act to encourage fitness and amateur sport" in 1960 and 1961 (Bill C-131) was a powerful impetus for the growth of physical activity sciences. The statute has been updated as part of the revised statutes of Canada, 1989, project and is reprinted here for easy reference. Source: Department of Justice Canada; reproduced with the permission of the Minister of Supply and Services Canada, 1991.

CHAPTER F-25

An Act to encourage fitness and amateur sport.

Short Title

1. This Act may be cited as the Fitness and Amateur Sport Act. R.S., c. F-25, s. 1.

Interpretation

2. In this Act "agreement" means an agreement entered into under this Act;
"Council" means the National Advisory Council on Fitness and Amateur Sport established subsection 7(1);
"member" means a member of the Council;
"Minister" means the Minister of National Health and Welfare. R.S., c. F-25, s. 2; SI/80-68; SI/81-134; SI/82-206.

Objects and Powers

3. The objects of this Act are to encourage, promote and develop fitness and amateur sport in Canada, and, without limiting the generality of the foregoing, the Minister may, in furtherance of those objects,

(a) provide assistance for the promotion and development of Canadian participation in national and international amateur sport;
(b) provide for the training of coaches and such other personnel as may be required for the purposes of this Act;
(c) provide bursaries or fellowships to assist in the training of necessary personnel;
(d) undertake or assist in research or surveys in respect of fitness and amateur sport;
(e) arrange for national and regional conferences designed to promote and further the objects of this Act;
(f) provide for the recognition of achievement in respect of fitness and amateur sport by the grant or issue of certificates, citations or awards of merit;
(g) prepare and distribute information relating to fitness and amateur sport;
(h) assist, cooperate with and enlist the aid of any group interested in furthering the objects of this Act;

(i) coordinate federal activities related to the encouragement, promotion and development of fitness and amateur sport, in cooperation with any other departments or agencies of the Government of Canada carrying on those activities; and

(j) undertake such other projects or programs, including the provision of services and facilities or of assistance therefore, in respect of fitness and amateur sport as are designed to promote and further the objects of this Act. R.S., c. F-25, s. 3.

4. In furtherance of the objects of this Act, the Minister may with the approval of the Governor in Council make grants to any agency, organization, or institution that is carrying on activities in the field of fitness or amateur sport. R.S., c. F-25, s. 4.

Agreements Authorized

5. (1) The Minister may, with the approval of the Governor in Council, enter into an agreement with any province, for a period not exceeding six years, to provide for the payment by Canada to the province of contributions in respect of costs incurred by the province in undertaking programs designed to encourage, promote and develop fitness and amateur sport.

(2) In subsection (1) "costs" incurred by a province means the costs incurred by the province determined as prescribed in the agreement made under that subsection between the Minister and the province.

"Programs designed to encourage, promote and develop fitness and amateur sport" in respect of a province, means programs, as defined in the agreement made under that subsection between the Minister and the province, that are designed to further the objects of this Act. R.S., c. F-25, s. 5.

6. Any agreement made under this Act may be amended

(a) with respect to the provisions of the agreement in respect of which a method of amendment is set out in the agreement, by that method; or

(b) with respect to any other provision of the agreement, by the mutual consent of the parties thereto with the approval of the Governor in Council. R.S., c. F-25, s. 6.

Council Established ·

7. (1) There is hereby established Council, to be called the National Advisory Council on Fitness and Amateur Sport, consisting of not more than thirty members to be appointed by the Governor in Council.

(2) Each member shall be appointed to hold office for a term not exceeding three years.

(3) The Governor in Council shall designate one of the members to be chairman.

(4) Of the members of the Council, at least one shall be appointed from each province.

8. (1) A majority of the members constitutes a quorum of the Council.

(2) A vacancy in the membership of the Council does not impair the right of the remaining members to act.

(3) In the event of the absence or temporary incapacity of any member, the Governor in Council may appoint a person to act in place of that member during the absence or incapacity. R.S., c. F-25, s. 7.

9. The Council may make rules for regulating its proceedings and the performance of its functions and may provide therein for the delegation of any of its duties to any special or standing committee of its members. R.S., c. F-25, s. 7.

10. (1) The chairman of the Council shall be paid such remuneration as may be fixed by the Governor in Council.

(2) The members other than the chairman shall serve without remuneration, but each member is entitled to be paid reasonable travel and other expenses incurred by him in the performance of his duties. R.S., c. F-25, s. 8.

11. (1) The Minister may refer to the Council for its consideration and advice such questions relating to the operation of this Act as the Minister thinks fit.

(2) The Council shall give consideration to and advise the Minister on

(a) all matters referred to it pursuant to subsection (1), and
(b) such other matters relating to the operation of this Act as the Council sees fit. R.S., c. F-25, s. 9.

Administration of Act

12. Such officers, clerks and other employees as are necessary for the administration of this Act shall be appointed under the Public Service Employment Act. R.S., c. F-25, s. 11.

Regulations

13. The Governor in Council may make regulations

(a) defining for the purposes of this Act the expressions "fitness" and "amateur sport";
(b) respecting the provision of facilities in respect of fitness and amateur sport; and
(c) generally, for carrying into effect the purposes and provisions of this Act. R.S., c. F-25, s. 12.

Report to Parliament

14. The Minister shall, within three months after the end of each fiscal year, prepare an annual report on the work done, moneys expended and obligations contracted under this Act and cause the report to be laid before Parliament or, if Parliament is not then sitting, on any of the first fifteen days next thereafter that either House of Parliament is sitting. R.S, c. F-25, s. 13.

Credits for Figures and Tables

Table 2.1 From *Vice-Regal Patronage of Canadian Sport: 1867-1916* (p. 187) by M. McLaughlin, 1981, unpublished master's thesis, University of Alberta, Edmonton, AB. Reprinted by permission of the author.

Figure 9.1 From *Motor Control and Learning: A Behavioral Emphasis* (2nd ed., p. 65) by R.A. Schmidt, 1988, Champaign, IL: Human Kinetics. Copyright 1988 by Richard A. Schmidt. Adapted by permission.

Figure 10.1 From *Sport Competition Anxiety Test* (p. 33) by R. Martens, 1977, Champaign, IL: Human Kinetics. Copyright 1977 by Rainer Martens. Reprinted by permission.

Figure 10.2 From "The Development of an Instrument to Assess Cohesion in Sport Teams: The Group Environment Questionnaire" by A.V. Carron, W.N. Widmeyer, and L.R. Brawley, 1985, *Journal of Sport Psychology*, **7**(3), p. 248. Copyright 1985 by Human Kinetics Publishers, Inc. Reprinted by permission.

Table 12.1 From *Culture and Society* by G.P. Murdock, 1965, Pittsburgh: University of Pennsyl-vania Press. Reprinted by permission of Columbia University Press, New York.

Chapter 13 Highlight, page 110 From *To Know Ourselves: The Report of the Commission on Canadian Studies* (vols. 1 and 2), 1975, Ottawa, ON: Association of Universities and Colleges of Canada. Reprinted by permission of the Association of Universities and Colleges of Canada.

Figure 14.1 From "Methodological Trends in Laval University's Research on Teaching Physical Education" by M. Tousignant, J. Brunelle, and P. Godbout. In *Research Methodology in Teaching Physical Education and Sports* (p. 58) by C. Paré, M. Lirette, and M. Piéron, 1987, Trois Rivières: Département des Sciences de l'Activité Physique, Université du Québec à Trois-Rivières. Reprinted by permission of C. Paré, Université du Québec à Trois-Rivières.

Figures 23.3 and 23.4 From J.E. Himann, D.A. Cunningham, P.A. Rechnitzer, & D.H. Paterson, "Age-Related Changes in Speed of Walking," *Medicine and Science in Sports and Exercise*, **20**, p. 163, 1988, © by The American College of Sports Medicine.

Index

Page numbers in boldface type indicate figures or tables.

DATE DUE

MAR 22 1995			
MAR 13 1995			
NOV 17 1996			
DEC 16 1996			
NOV - 4 1999			
OCT 22 1999			
DEC 09 1999			
DEC 21 1999			
MAR 08 2000			
FEB 22 2000			
OCT 24 2000			
NOV 13 2000			
NOV 14 2000			
	261-2500		Printed in USA